A NEW PHILOSOPHY OF LITERATURE

The Fundamental Theme and Unity of World Literature

The Vision of the Infinite and the
Universalist Literary Tradition

First published by O-Books, 2012
O Books is an imprint of John Hunt Publishing Ltd., The Bothy, Deershot Lodge, Park Lane, Ropley,
Hants, SO24 0BE, UK
office1@o-books.net
www.o-books.com

For distributor details and how to order please visit the 'Ordering' section on our website.

ISBN: 978 1 84694 945 6

Design: Stuart Davies

Printed in the UK by CPI Antony Rowe
Printed in the USA by Offset Paperback Mfrs, Inc

A NEW PHILOSOPHY
OF LITERATURE

The Fundamental Theme and
Unity of World Literature

The Vision of the Infinite and the
Universalist Literary Tradition

Nicholas Hagger

BOOKS

Winchester, UK
Washington, USA

Books Published by Nicholas Hagger

The Fire and the Stones

Selected Poems

The Universe and the Light

A White Radiance

A Mystic Way

Awakening to the Light

A Spade Fresh with Mud

The Warlords

Overlord

A Smell of Leaves and Summer

The Tragedy of Prince Tudor

The One and the Many

Wheeling Bats and a Harvest Moon

The Warm Glow of the Monastery Courtyard

The Syndicate

The Secret History of the West

The Light of Civilization

Classical Odes

Overlord, one-volume edition

Collected Poems 1958 – 2005

Collected Verse Plays

Collected Stories

The Secret Founding of America

The Last Tourist in Iran

The Rise and Fall of Civilizations

The New Philosophy of Universalism

The Libyan Revolution

Armageddon

The World Government

The Secret American Dream

Acknowledgments

I acknowledge the memory of T.S. Eliot, whose thinking in his essays (such as 'Tradition and the Individual Talent') this work carries forward; and of the (to my young me) elderly Japanese poet Junzaburo Nishiwaki who, when I asked him for a distillation of the wisdom of the East in a *saké* – rice-wine – bar in Tokyo in 1965, wrote out for me on a business reply card to *Encounter* which happened to be before us, "+A + −A = 0, great nothing" (see p.346) and supplied me with the dialectical method I have used in all my historical, philosophical and literary Universalist work, in which metaphysical and secular contraries are reconciled in a synthesis.

Over the years I have benefited from many discussions with writers and poets now dead: E.W.F. Tomlin, Edmund Blunden, Frank Tuohy, Anthony Powell, Angus Wilson, Ezra Pound, John Heath-Stubbs, Kathleen Raine, David Gascoyne, and others, some of whose comments inform the text. I have benefited from discussions with Colin Wilson, whose Outsider was a quester, from 1961 to the mid-1990s. I acknowledge discussions spanning more than 50 years with the leading critic of our time, Christopher Ricks, who in spite of his Neoclassical principles was good enough to agree with my view of the reconciling power of Baroque poetry at an early stage and provided many stimulating thoughts. I appreciated a correspondence with Ted Hughes, who wrote to me in 1994, "I read your books with a sort of automatic assent."[1] He was extremely interested in literary Universalism and would have been very interested in this work.

I am grateful to Gillon Aitken for spurring me to distinguish two very different sensibilities, which focused my attention on the need for this book and precipitated its shape in my mind. Once again I acknowledge John Hunt, who immediately recognised the importance of stating the fundamental theme of world literature and of setting out the tradition of literary Universalism. And I am again grateful to my PA Ingrid who kept up with the brisk pace I set that, despite the enormous scope of 4,600 years of world literature, covered the ground from first research to completion in just over eight months (from 22 July 2010 to 31 March 2011).

"Come said the Muse,
Sing me a song no poet yet has chanted,
Sing me the universal."

Walt Whitman, 'Song of the Universal', in *Leaves of Grass*

"I must Create a System, or be enslav'd by another Man's."

Blake, 'Jerusalem', f.10, l.20

"You must teach the taste by which you wish to be relished."

Junzaburo Nishiwaki in conversation with
Nicholas Hagger on 21 December 1963

*

"In poets as true genius is but rare,
True taste as seldom is the critic's share,
Both must alike from Heaven derive their Light,
These born to judge, as well as those to write.
Let such teach others who themselves excel,
And censure freely who have written well.
Authors are partial to their wit,* 'tis true,
But are not critics to their judgment** too?...
A perfect judge will read each work of wit,
With the same spirit that its author writ:
Survey the WHOLE, nor seek slight faults to find
Where Nature moves, and rapture warms the mind."

Pope, 'An Essay on Criticism', lines 11–18, 233–6

*"Wit", "the unexpected, quick and humorous combining or contrasting of ideas or expressions" (*Concise Oxford Dictionary*); "a combination of dissimilar images, or discovery of occult resemblences in things apparently unlike...The most heterogeneous ideas are yoked by violence together" (Dr Johnson, *Lives of the English Poets*).
**"Judgment", "the critical faculty; discernment; an opinion or estimate; criticism" (*Concise Oxford Dictionary*).

"Pay no attention to the criticism of men who have never themselves written a notable work."

Ezra Pound, 'A Retrospect'

CONTENTS

The Light and the Shadow. Image symbolizing the synthesis of Universalism: the pediment at Copped Hall, Essex, showing two contraries, Light (*lumen*), right, and Shadow (*umbra*), left, either side of a sundial and above the Latin "*Me umbra regit vos lumen*". See pp.9, 294, 314, 346, 351. (Photo supplied by the Trustees of the Copped Hall Trust.)

Prologue

The Fundamental Theme of World Literature

This books presents the fundamental theme of world literature. It argues that its main thrust is the revelation that the universe is ordered and permeated by an infinite Reality which human beings can know. It shows that this traditional material has been restated in the literature of every culture and age, and that the quest for an ordering Reality that is behind and within everyday life was originally stronger than secular writing.

However, in many literary works, this level of Reality is missing. Especially today, writing is secular and there is only a personal and social reality. Consequently, many contemporary works are secular and materialist in presenting life in an accidental universe of purely physical processes that are devoid of purpose or meaning. This book argues that there needs to be a revolution in thought and culture to perpetuate the traditional material in a new literary movement so that once again it co-exists with secular writing. In other words, this book calls for a revolution in Western literature.

This call to revolution is in fact a call back to tradition, and I seek to carry forward the thinking in T.S. Eliot's essay, 'Tradition and the Individual Talent' (1919) in which Eliot urged poets to cultivate a historical sense and a feeling for "the whole of the literature of Europe from Homer", and to be aware of "the mind of Europe" as "no poet...has his complete meaning alone". In this work I evoke the literary tradition since Homer.

An investigation of the fundamental theme in world literature transports the reader into different cultures and civilizations, and focuses on all humankind. It therefore necessarily enters the uncharted territory of literary Universalism.

Universalism

Universalism's global perspective can be found in various disciplines outside literature. Historical Universalism sees the history of all humankind as a unity, as did Toynbee in his *Study of History*. Political

Universalism sees all humankind as one political entity, to be governed under a World State and a benevolent world government. Religious Universalism sees all religions as unified on the basis of a common experience known to all mystics in all ages and cultures: the experience of the Light, known to Christians as "the Divine Light" and to Catholics as "the Light of Glory" (*lumen gloriae*). Philosophical Universalism focuses on the universe as did the great philosophers of the past. Following a philosophically lean century dominated by logic and language, it sees a unified, orderly universe operating within "the infinite" as did the early Greek philosophers, and it too focuses on the unity of all humankind.

I have written extensive studies of historical Universalism (*The Fire and the Stones, The Rise and Fall of Civilizations*), religious Universalism (*The Fire and the Stones, The Light of Civilization*), political Universalism (*The World Government, The Secret American Dream*) and philosophical Universalism (*The Universe and the Light, The One and the Many, The New Philosophy of Universalism*).

In *The New Philosophy of Universalism* I set out a philosophy that focuses on the universe – indeed, an ordered cosmos – and challenged modern philosophy's focus on language and logic. I looked back to the Greek Presocratic philosophers who offered empirical explanations for the workings of the universe at the source of Western philosophy. I considered their metaphysical view of the universe. "Metaphysics", "*ta meta ta phusika*", were originally "the [works of Aristotle] *after* the Physics", but their study of first principles came to be misinterpreted as meaning "the science of things transcending what is physical or natural" (*Shorter Oxford English Dictionary*). "Metaphysics" therefore came to mean what is *beyond* physics, and as "*meta*" can be translated as "behind" as well as "after", "metaphysics" has also come to mean "what is *behind* physics": "the science of things behind, and therefore transcending, what is physical or natural". Metaphysics asks what had infinite being before the Big Bang that could account for how the finite, physical, natural universe came to emerge from its fiery birth, and what has continued to be behind, and order, the physical, natural universe ever since the Big Bang. Metaphysics have not been impressed by Materialist assertions that nothing pre-existed the Big Bang and that the universe is an accident ruled by random chance and without order.

2

In *The New Philosophy of Universalism* I blended a scientific, evidential view of the universe with a scheme for its metaphysical structure: out of the One (or Nothingness) manifested Non-Being, from which emerged Being and eventually Existence. I saw unified Being as behind and within the diversity of Existence, the world of appearance. Within a new centre of the self, the universal being, humans can look beyond Existence into Being, which they can receive as the metaphysical Light, and can grasp that the universe is layered, tiered, with the invisible energy of Being operating behind the surface Existence. (See diagram of Universalism's view of the structure of the universe, p.353.)

The faculty that perceives unity is what Coleridge called "the esemplastic power of the imagination",[1] "esemplastic" coming from Greek words *"eis en plattein"*, meaning "moulding or shaping into one". (Coleridge in *Biographia Literaria*, ch.X, wrote, "I constructed it myself from the Greek words *eis en plattein*, to shape into one," whereas the *Shorter Oxford English Dictionary* derives the word from *eis en plassein*, "moulding into unity, unifying".) All my studies of Universalism have been written from this faculty, which perceives similarities. It is very different from rational analysis, which perceives differences and makes distinctions.

Besides focusing on the universe and the universal order principle, Universalism focuses on humankind's place in the universe, and therefore on the oneness of humankind. Universalism also probes the natural world, the universal cosmic energies which stimulate the growth of organisms and plants, and the universal being within the self where these energies or rays are received by human beings.

The unity of humankind is a theme suited to times when there are attempts to govern the whole known world: the times of the Athenian Empire, Augustus's Roman Empire, the Crusades, the post-Renaissance European empires, and in our time the British Empire, the American Empire and globalization.

Literary Universalism
Literary Universalism reflects the Universalist approach in philosophy, history, religion and politics. In *The New Philosophy of Universalism* I devoted a few pages to the applications of Universalism, and spoke of

literary Universalism, which received a scanty two pages. I pointed out that literary Universalism sees all literature – the literature of all countries – "as one, an interconnected unity, one supra-national literature". This book extends Universalism to world literature.

I use "literature" in its primary meaning: "literary productions as a whole, the writings of a country or period or of the world in general" (*Shorter Oxford English Dictionary*). This definition is descriptive. It describes the process of literary production, publication and circulation, and includes any works written in the ancient cultures that have survived. To this definition has accrued a further definition first used during the Romantic Age, in 1812: "writings esteemed for beauty of form or emotional effect". This is a more evaluative definition, and suggests that some works are to be evaluated as literature while others do not qualify in terms of the Romantic criteria of beauty of form and emotional effect. Different movements, and ages have different criteria by which to evaluate what is and what is not literature, and a coming Universalist movement, and eventually Universalist Age, will have its own distinctive criteria.

Literary Universalism is concerned with the literary productions of the world as a whole, and focuses on works of art rather than printed matter which has no literary merit. Its criteria include whether a work of art reflects specific Universalist characteristics.

Twelve Universalist Characteristics
What are these characteristics? Within literature (and philosophy) the term "Universalism" incorporates "universe", "universal" and "universality". It focuses on the universe, on a universal principle of order and on humankind as a whole. It focuses on inner transformation to the universal being, the deeper self below the rational, social ego which is open to universal cosmic energies, the manifesting metaphysical Light. It focuses on universal human virtues, the standard from which writers have ridiculed the follies and vices of humankind.

In all times and ages, Universalist literature seeks confirmation that the universe is ordered by a Reality that surrounds it, which Greek Presocratic philosophers such as Anaximander of Miletus (who flourished c.570BC) described as the infinite, "boundless" (*to apeiron*). It holds that this Reality is perceived in many cultures as Light or Fire;

that all humankind is one; and that there are consequently similarities between cultures and civilizations. It holds that the universal being (or spirit) can know the Reality as the Light and (according to all cultures) achieve immortality; and that there is a universal virtue which measures human behaviour.

This book is a work of literary Universalism. It sets out the long tradition of Universalist literature that reflects this view and adheres to these criteria. In fact, in all ages each particular work of Universalist literature reflects the idea of Reality found in their culture and civilization, the metaphysical aspect of the fundamental theme; and until relatively recently the outlook of the traditional material could be located within the society and rituals that nourished it. In the interests of clarity it is worth setting out the twelve characteristics by which Universalism can be recognised. Universalism, and the metaphysical aspect of the fundamental theme, focuses on:

- the infinite (*to apeiron*) that surrounds the universe;
- the metaphysical Reality perceived in all cultures as Light (or Fire, which is a universal cosmic energy);
- the universal principle of order in the universe (universal in the sense that its effects are found in all aspects of Nature and its organisms);
- the oneness of known humankind behind its apparent diversity;
- the similarities in cultures and civilizations;
- the universal being (or self) that opens to the Light behind the rational, social ego;
- universal virtue, a standard by which to measure human follies, vices, blindness, corruption, hypocrisy, self-love and egotism, and on vices in relation to an implied universal virtue (when human interaction is considered from a secular perspective, as separated from its context of Reality);
- the promise of immortality of the universal being or spirit;
- an inner transformation or centre-shift from ego to universal being;
- the quest of the purified soul to confront death, in the ancient cultures by journeying to the Underworld, and to receive the secret Light of infinite Reality;

5

- a sensibility that approaches Reality through more than one discipline, the sensibility of a polymath; and
- a new perspective of unity in key disciplines: seeing world history as a whole; seeing the common essence (the inner experience of the Light) of all world religions; seeing the One that can be revealed by philosophy and science; seeing the World State that can unify international politics; and seeing the unity of world literature.

In the ancient world, in which religion was strong, these characteristics dominated society's rituals and were reflected in literature. Despite weakenings of this cultural activity which gave rise to periods of secularization in literature, this fundamental Universalist and literary perception of the universe can be found in all places and times. It is the archetypal literary theme that has been repeated in each generation. Each generation restates the traditional Universalist theme.

Outline of the Fundamental Theme
There are in fact two sides to the fundamental theme: the traditional metaphysical quest for Reality and, in periods of greater secularization, a more secular view of social reality that focuses on vices in relation to an implied virtue. In Part One of this book I trace the two aspects of the fundamental theme from their origins in the ancient world (ch.1) through the classical world (ch.2) to the medieval world (ch.3), the Renaissance (ch.4) and the Baroque (ch.5). I trace the conflict between the two aspects in the Neoclassical and Romantic traditions (chs.6 and 7) and their short-lived reunification in the Victorians (ch.8) and Modernists (ch.9). I examine the position in the later 20th century (ch.10) and conclude that the two aspects are still a force, despite widespread secularization.

In Part Two, drawing on the literary summaries at the end of each of the ten chapters in Part One, I outline how Universalism can reconcile and perpetuate the two aspects of the fundamental theme today (ch.1), and dwell on the reconciliation in poetry (ch.2). In the Epilogue I chart a new direction for world literature and consider the role of the Universalist tradition in the health of each civilization in which it flourishes.

The fundamental theme is the unifying principle of world literature, and through its lens world literature can be seen as a unity. I will inevitably be restricted in the number of poems, plays and novels I will be able to cite as complying with one or other of the two aspects of the fundamental theme, but the same principle (quest or vices) can be applied to texts that will not be mentioned in this work, with similar results. In this work I am concerned to establish the principle of the fundamental theme from a sample of highly respected texts rather than to analyze every existing text in world literature (an impossibly gargantuan task) to demonstrate the principle.

The title of this book, *A New Philosophy of Literature*, of course echoes *The New Philosophy of Universalism*, but it also states that this work introduces a philosophy of literature and falls under the category of philosophy of literature.

Philosophy of Literature

The philosophy of literature has been approached by analytic philosophers, who have related literary problems to aesthetics. The analytic perspective defines literature, distinguishing between oral and written literature, and discusses the identity of literary works. It addresses the nature of fiction and our emotional involvement with fictional characters. It discusses the concept of imagination and its role in the apprehension of literary works. It looks at theories of metaphor and postmodernist theory regarding the significance of authors' intentions and the interpretation of their work. And it examines the relevance of truth and morality to literary appreciation. These questions are raised in Christopher New's analytic *Philosophy of Literature*, and in an analytic anthology by Eileen John and Dominic McIver Lopes, also entitled *Philosophy of Literature*.

An analytic approach to the philosophy of literature sees a poem, a play, a novel, a short story as also being a work of literature, and the same applies to a work of oratory, an essay, philosophy or scripture. All these *genres* may also be literature. However, there is also popular or light literature, mass-market fiction written for escapist entertainment, which some would say is not good enough to warrant being called "literature". The analytic approach defines literature as "linguistic composition that has a certain property or properties of literariness".

"Literariness" involves "figures of language such as rhyme, metre (whether 'strict or free'), onomatopoeia, alliteration and eye rhymes".[2] It also deals with value theory, metaphysics (the definition of literature, theories of fiction and the ontology of literature) and the philosophies of language and mind (theories of fiction, emotional engagement, interpretation and metaphor).[3]

There is, however, an alternative approach to the philosophy of literature: the historical, traditional, Universalist approach. This is more pragmatic. Based on principles rather than theory, and perceiving through the creative "esemplastic" faculty that sees unity, it sees literature (to echo the definition on p.4) as all literary writings or works of art of the world as a whole that have ever been produced. Starting with the literature or written works produced in the ancient world, it considers the direction the fundamental tradition has taken, whether it has stuck to its course and the extent to which it has been challenged and superseded by a rival view of what literature is. This book pursues this tradition of the philosophy of literature.

Direction of the Fundamental Theme

The philosophy of history explores the direction of historical events and its interpretations of the rise and fall of civilizations, and seeks the pattern in and behind human events. Similarly the philosophy of literature explores the direction of literary events and its interpretations of movements and literary traditions, and seeks the pattern in and behind the themes of the works of the most significant authors of each age. It examines the fundamental theme of world literature in each age, and explores the direction it takes in the course of more than 4,600 years of recorded history. Literary events or works of course reflect, and often comment on, the historical events of their age.

This work falls under the category of "philosophy of literature" in the sense that it identifies the core literary theme of the last 4,600 years and explores the direction it has taken (while continuing to reflect the order within the universe and experience of the hidden Reality that traditionally bestows immortality). It traces the direction this fundamental literary theme has taken in recent years and draws conclusions regarding its weakening in the present time. We shall see that the quest for Reality in metaphysical periods encompasses and

8

incorporates the second aspect of the fundamental theme: the outlook in secular periods that human vices should be exposed. The fundamental theme consists of two opposites which alternate in their periods of dominance and which are reconciled from time to time.

Until now no attempt has been made to trace the direction of the universal fundamental literary theme. This book therefore breaks new ground. It attempts something that has not happened before. However, although the tracing of the traditional theme is "new" as a statement, the outlook of Universalism is as old as civilization. The Universalist tradition of literature has ancient roots and has always been with us. Detailing it may be new, but there have been many Universalist writers who have reflected the twelve characteristics and criteria of Universalism. Literature has always recorded intimations of Being and humankind's instinctive longings for order in the universe.

The quest for Reality as Light and its opposite motif within the fundamental theme, the exposure of vices, can be seen in terms of light and shadow. Light and shadow can best be approached through an image or symbol. At Copped Hall in Essex in the UK, an eighteenth-century ruin that is being restored, there is a remarkable 1890s sundial in the marble pediment above four Ionic columns. (See front cover and p.x.) Two male reapers recline on either side of the gnomon, back to back, holding scythes above reaped ears of corn. The one on the right is tousled-haired and bare-chested, and very much awake, having turned his head to look at us, gripping his scythe. The one on the left, also bare-chested, has wound his half-discarded cloak into a cowl-like hood round his head to shade him from the fierce sun and is at rest, with his eyes closed. He appears to be asleep as he his hands limply rest on his scythe, which is propped on one knee. Above them is an hourglass. The two figures could represent Work and Sleep, Day and Night. Underneath there is a Latin motto: *Me umbra regit vos lumen*. The sundial says, "Shadow rules me [i.e. the sundial], light rules you [i.e. all mortals who look at the sundial]".

I see the pediment as a symbol for the fundamental theme. One figure (*lumen*) represents the quest for a metaphysical Reality as Light. The other figure (*umbra*) represents the world, the shadows cast by the Light, the shadowy world of human vices which are measured in terms of its counterpart, virtue granted by the influx of the Light. From the secular perspective, light (in the sense of sunlight) rules us mortals as we depend on ripened grain.

We shall encounter the symbol again in Part Two. But it is now time to see how the two motifs of the fundamental theme, the metaphysical and the secular, are contrasted and conjoined within the literature of the last 4,600 years.

PART ONE

The Light and the Shadow:
The Fundamental Theme's
Metaphysical and Secular Traditions

"Whither, O splendid ship, thy white sails crowding,
Leaning across the bosom of the urgent West,
That fearest nor sea rising, nor sky clouding,
Whither away, fair rover, and what thy quest?"

Bridges, 'A Passer-By'

"Change in a trice
The lilies and languors of virtue
For the raptures and roses of vice."

Swinburne, 'Dolores', vii

1

The Early Literature of the Ancient World

Anyone preparing to set out the tradition of the metaphysical aspect of the fundamental theme of world literature, must first ask the question: what is world literature? The answer sharpens the definition of literature already offered (see pp.4 and 7-8).

World literature is essentially the writings of all civilizations and cultures in verse or prose. It includes all *genre*s: religious texts; mythology; philosophy; epic, lyric, elegiac, pastoral and didactic poetry; comedy; tragedy; history; satire; and oratory. Literature is supra-national. It transcends nation-states, and world literature is the aggregate of all the writings detailed above at all times. In the more sophisticated civilizations world literature conforms to artistic specifications which writers such as Aristotle and Horace have laid out.

In the early civilizations the writings that have survived mainly relate to the pastoral living, creation myths and religious rituals of early peoples. But there are still epic narratives, and an intent to follow artistic presentation. It is as though the early writers were imposing a structure of order on the apparently chaotic universe to reflect their sense of a fundamentally ordered universe which had a purpose and meaning.

In the early stages of all civilizations a religion forms round a metaphysical vision, and it is not surprising that writers living in an agricultural priest-dominated society reflected their conditions. In the very early civilizations the metaphysical aspect of our fundamental theme is strongly present.

The first civilization, the Indo-European Kurgans who came from the Caucasus and entered Central Europe from at least c.4500BC and buried their dead in long barrows with shafts, left no writings. Recorded history, and the first writing, began around 3000BC. The early works dating from this time convey the fundamental literary theme of an ordered cosmos ruled by Light, in which the spirit can be immortal.

As we look at the literature of the early civilizations, it will be helpful to keep an eye on the chart on pp.354-5.

Mesopotamia

The Sumerians came into Mesopotamia from shamanistic Central Asia and Siberia,[1] where priest-doctors known as shamans ministered to northern tribes. They brought with them the shamans' vision of the fundamental unity of an ordered universe of three worlds – Underworld, Earth and Sky, expressed in the poem 'Inanna's Descent to the Nether World'[2] – and the shamans' inner Light, which they passed on to their conquerors, the Akkadians and Assyrians.

Literature appeared in the Mesopotamian civilization by c.2600BC. Dating from c.2500BC, a Sumerian creation myth written on clay tablets discovered in Nippur, Mesopotamia is probably an epic on Kharsag, a town on the Lebanese-Syrian border. It features Anu, the chief Mesopotamian Sky God. His name meant "Sky" or "Shining", and he was head of the Sumerian pantheon by c.3000BC.[3] In the creation myth, the "Great Sons of Anu", the Anannage or Anunnaki, or "Great Shining Ones"[4] – who may have become the Sumerians (who were probably a mixture of Altaic and Indo-European stock) – come to Kharsag "where Heaven and Earth met".[5] There Enlil and his wife Ninlil set up a farm, and their primitive, grain-dominated life takes place in a universe dominated by Anu.

There are nine Kharsag epics, and the reference to Heaven and Earth meeting is in epic 2. In epic 1 Enlil's wife, "the lady of Kharsag" (Nin Kharsag), urges that a reservoir should be built so that food will be plentiful. "This perfect Eden is full of water". *Edin* in Sumerian means "plain", but the Eden of *Genesis* may have its origin in this paradisal Garden of Eden built at Kharsag. In epic 9 the reservoir bursts after a violent thunderstorm and:

"The House…was destroyed by the thunderstorm….
The Building of Knowledge was destroyed;…
The Settlement of Learning – the whole Settlement with
its food-storage building and its plantations, became marshland!
The Building of Learning…was crushed
by the thunderstorm; it was cut off and overthrown."[6]

The "House of Knowledge" may have anticipated the Tree of Knowledge. The flood may have influenced the story of Noah's Flood. After the flood the Anannage moved from Kharsag to Mesopotamia and founded city-states in what would become Sumeria. The building of the reservoir for the public good, the storm, the flood, the destruction of the farm and the settlement, all brought chaos but are described in an orderly epic as events in a universe presided over by Anu, the "Shining One".

Gilgamesh
The early Sumerian kings of c.3500BC were probably descended from a Kurgan dynasty, including Gilgamesh, the epic hero.[7] Around 2150BC there were three groups of stories written in Sumerian about kings of Uruk (or Erech), including a group about Gilgamesh.[8] The Sumerian *Gilgamesh and Agga of Kish* and the Akkadian *Epic of Gilgamesh* were first written c.1900BC.

The historical Gilgamesh ruled at Uruk, a city identified with modern Warka in central Iraq. He is in the list of Sumerian kings as the fifth ruler of the First Dynasty of Uruk[9], and is thought to have lived between c.2800 and 2500BC. Although Gilgamesh was a historical figure, much of the story of the *Epic of Gilgamesh* is fictitious, a mixture of mythology and a didactic religious text with a message: do the will of the gods, act as they have intended.[10] In the epic the gods and goddesses sometimes take part in the action but man's free will can choose his destiny and sometimes thwart the will of heaven.

There are different versions of the *Epic of Gilgamesh*. Texts in Akkadian appear in quantity from c.2300BC.[11] The main story is based on fragments of 12 clay cuneiform tablets dating from the 8th century BC, found at Nineveh in 1849 in the library of Ashurbanipal. These tablets in standard Babylonian, a dialect of Akkadian used only for literary purposes, incorporate Sumerian and Akkadian stories of c.2150BC. In one of the Sumerian stories the theme is Gilgamesh's quest for immortality, which is denied by the gods.

The main, standard Babylonian story is also about King Gilgamesh's search for immortality.

To curb Gilgamesh's harsh rule in demanding a "lord's right" over new brides, following entreaties from the young men of his kingdom, Anu causes Enkidu to be created, a wild man who lives among animals and eventually travels to Uruk, where there is a trial of strength between him and Gilgamesh. Gilgamesh is the victor and Enkidu becomes his friend and companion. Both men set out against Huwawa (or Humbaba), the guardian of a cedar forest. Gilgamesh returns to Uruk, rejects Ishtar's marriage proposal to him and kills the divine bull she sends to destroy him. The gods Anu, Ea and Shamash decide that Gilgamesh must die for killing the bull. Enkidu falls ill and dreams of a "house of dust" that awaits him. He dies and has a state funeral.

Distraught, Gilgamesh embarks on a quest for immortality. He attempts to learn the secret of eternal life. However, "when the gods created man they allotted for him death, but life they retained in their own keeping."[12]

The gods had tried to destroy humans by sending a flood. Gilgamesh journeys in search of Utnapishtim, the sage who survived the Babylonian flood that destroyed the city of Shuruppak by building a great ship (perhaps anticipating Noah's ark), to learn how one can escape death. Utnapishtim tells him about a plant that can renew youth. Gilgamesh obtains the plant but places it on the shore of a lake while he bathes, and it is stolen by a serpent. Gilgamesh weeps, having lost all chance of immortality. He unhappily returns to Uruk knowing that he will not become immortal, and the spirit of Enkidu visits him, with a grim report of the Underworld.

The metaphysical aspect of the fundamental theme is hinted at: the gods order the universe and control the Earth and the Underworld and decide what happens to humans. There is no escape from death. Nevertheless Gilgamesh pursues immortality and the infinite (eternal life). In table 10 of the Old Babylonian version, in which several tablets are damaged or missing, Shamash "spoke to Gilgamesh, 'Gilgamesh, where do you roam?/You will not find the eternal life you seek.'" Nevertheless, death is not the end, and the Underworld is within the gods' scheme. In the fragments of the tablets of the standard version that have survived Gilgamesh's soul does not blend with Shamash's Light. Perhaps the origins of the epic were too early for eternal life to be bestowed upon the King in c.2800-2500BC, or perhaps this

denouement of immortality has not survived. Tablet XII of the main
story is much shorter than tablet XI and is not part of the epic, but an
Akkadian translation of part of a Sumerian poem about the Nether
world.[13]

In a tablet reportedly from Sippar (18th or 17th century BC)
Gilgamesh does attempt to blend with Shamash's Light:

"Shamash grew worried, and bending down
    he spoke to Gilgamesh:
'O Gilgamesh, where are you wandering?
    The Life that you seek you never will find.'

Said Gilgamesh to him, to the hero Shamash:
...Let my eyes see the sun and be sated with light.
The darkness is hidden, how much light is there left?
    When may the dead see the rays of the sun?"[14]

Nevertheless Gilgamesh, who failed to achieve immortality and
become a god in his life, ironically became a god after his death and
judged the dead in the Nether world.[15]

In the various fragmented versions of tablets and lacunae, the *Epic
of Gilgamesh* reflects the 12 characteristics of the metaphysical aspect
of the fundamental theme of world literature and of Universalism.
Gilgamesh focuses on the Reality of the infinite gods, who order the
universe. He is on a quest to confront death, and he wants immortality
now. He wants to experience the Light of Shamash in his universal
being.

Dumuzi/Tammuz

The story of Dumuzi (the Sumerian form of Tammuz) is also set in an
ordered universe. In one early text, 'Inanna's Descent to the
Underworld', Dumuzi, a shepherd-god and vegetation-god, died and
was imprisoned in the Underworld and appealed to the Sumerian Utu,
who was now in charge of the universe. The best-preserved Sumerian
narrative poem, 'Enki and the World Order' says:

"Utu, the son born of Ningal,

Enki placed in charge of the entire universe."[16]

(Enki is addressed as the god who watches over the universe.) Utu evidently listened to Dumuzi's cry for help, for Dumuzi rose with the vegetation in the spring after Inanna, the queen of Heaven (and Dumuzi's wife or sister), descended to reclaim him.

About 2400BC Sumer was dominated by Akkad, its northern neighbour, and Utu became the Akkadian Shamash, the sun-god.[17] 'The Great Hymn to Shamash', the best of the Mesopotamian religious writings in cuneiform, addresses Shamash a god of divination: "You grant revelations, Shamash, to the families of men, your harsh face and fierce light you give to them....Which are the regions not warmed by the brightness of your light? Brightener of gloom, illuminator of darkness, dispeller of darkness, illuminator of the broad earth."[18] As giver of revelations, Shamash had become a god of mental light and those who opened to his divine influx became "Shining Ones" like the hero in this Sumerian text:

"He, whose body is shining splendour,
Who in the forest of fragrant cedars is cheered with joy,
Standing in the oracle-lace Apsu,
Purified with the sparkling lustration."[19]

By c.2200BC ziggurats, stepped pyramids surmounted by a temple, united Heaven and Earth and brought humankind closer to the Light of Utu-Shamash.

All the early works of Mesopotamian literature mirrored an ordered universe in which the infinite was metaphysical Light. The Sons of Anu, Gilgamesh, Dumuzi and the invokers of Shamash all frequented an ordered universe controlled by a god of Light. Death was not the end, for life of a different kind continued in the Underworld.

Egypt
The early Egyptian literature communicates the same view of the universe. It also had shamanistic roots and reflected a Sky World and Underworld, as well as Earth. The early Egyptian gods (Osiris, Isis and Horus) may have been Aryan-Sumerian gods. Ra, the sun-god, ruled

the Sky World. His solar bark sailed across the sky. By 2750BC it was believed that the Pharaoh (or King) was divine and that his soul blended with the sun-god. A passageway from the King's Chamber of the Great Pyramid, which was completed c.2560BC, seems to have been designed to allow the Pharaoh Khufu's spirit to escape to the firmament and take its place within the sun among the circumpolar stars.

The Egyptian Book of the Dead

In one passage the Egyptian *Book of the Dead* speaks in the voice of Ra: "I was Ra...when he began to rule what he had made....It means Ra...when he began to appear as king."[20] The Pharaoh *was* Ra, and on death he *was* Osiris.

The Egyptian cult of the sun-god did not only honour the exoteric sun. It also celebrated esoteric Light, for an experience of the Light in this life developed the *akh* or spiritual soul, which could then survive in the Judgement Hall. There are many references to the *akh* in *The Book of the Dead* and prayers for the deceased. Again and again we are told that the soul had to become an *akh* or "Shining One". A virtuous life meant becoming an *akh* seeing the Light.

The Pharaoh's body had a *ka* (or life force). It came to be believed that his dead physical body (*khat*) had to be mummified into a cocoon so that it would germinate or sprout a *sakhu* or spiritual body into which his *akh* ("glorious" or "shining one", or "spiritual soul") could pass. (Sir Wallis Budge wrongly translated the *akh* as *khu* in his 1899 edition of *The Book of the Dead*.) The *akh* in a *sakhu* dwelt in the Elysian Fields, the Egyptian Heaven after c.2000BC. (Pyramid texts from c.2000 to c.1800 refer to the region traversed by the deceased on their way to the Other World and to the Islands of the Blessed or the Elysian Fields.) Later, mummification ensured that the *ka* would be born again in a counterpart of Egypt, in which the Pharaoh would stand the best chance of reaching eternity.

The wording of the title, *"The Book of the Dead"*, was a mistranslation by Karl Richard Lepsius, the German philologist and translator, in the 19th century. The book's true title should be "Chapters of Coming Forth by Day" or "The Book of the Great Awakening". According to its rituals a deceased person spent his first night in the Underworld and emerged into Heaven at sunrise (*akhu*) the next day.[21]

Then his hymn to Ra celebrated the survival of his soul, his "coming forth by day", which the texts, spells and prayers worked to secure.[22]

Amon-Ra was the Light, and brought eternity *now*. The important thing was to become an *akh* or "Shining One" who was illumined. A virtuous life meant becoming an *akh*, seeing the Light. Chapter 64 of *The Book of the Dead* proclaims on an eleventh-dynasty coffin: "I am Yesterday and Today; and I have the power to be born a second time. I am the divine hidden Soul..., the Possessor of two Divine Faces wherein his beams are seen. I am the Lord of those who are raised up from the dead, the Lord who comes forth out of darkness....To the Mighty One has his Eye been given and his face emits light when he illumines the earth. I shall not become corrupt, I shall come into being in the form of the Lion-god; the blossoms of Shu shall be in me" (*im-i* as distinct from "upon me", *hr-i*). The blossoms of Shu are "the beams of the Sun-god", according to Budge's note; which will be "in me".

A vignette in 'The Chapter of Making the Transformation into a Lotus' (81A) shows the illumined soul like a lotus which grows from the neck and unfolds to the sun. The second version from the papyrus of Ani shows a blue lotus in full bloom, and the beautiful text can be translated in different ways. Either, "I am the pure lotus coming forth from the god of light (*akhu*), the guardian of the nostril of Ra, the guardian of the nose of Hathor. I make my journey, I run after him who is Horus. I am the pure one coming forth from the field." Or, "I am the pure lily coming forth from the Lily of Light (*akhu*). I am the source of illumination and the channel of the breath of immortal beauty. I bring the message, Horus accomplishes it." A more accurate translation of *akhu* is "Underworldly sunshine". The sense is: "I am pure and come from the Underworldly sunshine, the Light."

'The Chapter of Making the Transformation into a Living Soul' says: "I am the divine Soul of Ra proceeding from the god Nu; that divine Soul which is God....I am the lord of light." The speaker's soul is now immortal.

The Book of the Dead is full of the Universalist vision of the universal being as a Shining One" (*akh*) from the "Underworldly sunshine" (*akhu*): "Behold, I have come forth this day, and I have become an *akh* (or a shining being)" (65B); and "I am one of those *akh*s who dwell with the divine *Akh*, and I have made my form like his

19

divine Form, when he comes forth....I am a spiritual body (*akhu*) and possess my soul....I, even I, am the *akh* who dwells with the divine *Akh*" (78). The universal being is delighted to discover its immortality: I, even I,....

The Book of the Dead reflected old Egyptian ritual. The Great Pyramid was called "*akhty*": "horizon-dweller".[23] It shone like a Shining One for its polished limestone casing stones acted as mirrors and reflected the sun. Hence its name "pyramid" (from the Greek *pyramis*), a word that has associations with "fire" (Greek *pur*). Khufu, the Pharaoh who supervised the building of the Great Pyramid, would emerge into the pre-existent sunshine of the Heavenly horizon to "come forth by day". The *Old Kingdom Pyramid Texts* (c.2345-2150BC) suggest that in later times the *akh* flew to the circumpolar stars. Becoming an *akh* (spiritual soul) was a process within the order of the universe. Sun-rays were embodied in the architecture of Egypt: in the pyramid shape (rays of sloping sunbeams) and in the obelisk. Pyramids and obelisks also symbolized rays of Underworldly sunshine which illuminated the *akh*.

In the 14th century BC a heretical revolution swept Egypt. The worship of Amon-Ra was replaced by worship of the Aton as the sun's disk. Hands reached out from it, offering the hieroglyph of eternal life. Humans were shown reaching out to the hands and receiving a gift from the only god. The short-lived Aton was introduced by the Pharaoh Akhenaton in 1379BC and did not survive him in 1363BC. He was named after the Aton, his name being a combination of *akh* and Aton, "the shining spirit who serves the Aton". The Aton was clearly a principle of Light that ordered the universe and nourished all humankind. During Akhenaton's brief revolution against the priests of Amon-Ra, Egypt was at the centre of an ordered universe, and, as the 'Hymn to Aton' expressed, Aton was "sole god"[24] and could only be worshipped via Akhenaton: "There is none other that knows you, save your son Akhenaton, for you have made him skilled in your plans and your might. The earth came into being by your hand, just as you made them [i.e. mankind]".[25] To worship Aton the Egyptian people had to worship Akhenaton for only he and his family could worship Aton directly. The Egyptian people had been used to worshipping Amon-Ra directly, and their exclusion from direct worship of the Aton was as heretical as the dethroning of Amon-Ra.

After the death of Akhenaton the worship of Amon was restored and after the accession of his son Tut-ankh-amon ("Tut, the living image of Amon-Ra") the universe reflected in *The Book of the Dead* continued to operate. Beyond the world of the senses was the world of "the Shining Ones", whose *akh*s were filled with the "light of Ra".

Iran

The Indo-Europeans who settled in Europe after c.2350BC, possibly after being displaced from Akkad, also settled in Iran c.2250BC. They worshipped the "Wise Lord", Ahura Mazda, who represented the source of the Light.

Zoroaster, who is claimed to have lived at various times between c.6000BC and c.2000BC but is now thought to have lived between 660BC and 500BC, saw himself as a messenger of Ahura Mazda, the supreme god who created the twin spirits of light and dark (*Spenta Mainyu* and *Angra Mainyu*). Zoroaster seems to have had access to the religion of the earliest Indo-Iranians and of the Indo-Aryans who went on to India. This religion can be reconstructed from the Iranian and Indian sacred books, the *Avesta* and *Veda*s.

The Avesta

The *Avesta* that survives is only a fragment, the fourth part of the Sasanian *Avesta* (3rd-7th centuries AD). The *Gathas* ("songs" or "odes") are ascribed to Zoroaster himself (c.7th century BC). Zoroaster rejected the polytheism of the *Veda*s for the monotheism of Ahura Mazda. The universe has unity: "Grant me the power to control this mind, this Lower Mind of mine,...and put an end to all Duality, and gain the reign of One." (32.16.)

The *Gathas* are addressed to Ahura Mazda, for example: "Now will I speak to those who hear of the things which the initiate should remember; the praises and prayer of the Good Mind to the Lord and the joy which he shall see in the Light who has remembered them well." (*Yasna* 30.) A sacrificial hymn from an initiate says: "Glory to you, O Mazda! Lo, I turn from dazzling visions of your home of Light and find me weary in the strife again....Yet in the sacred Fire I pray you let my waking thoughts recall sights that can soothe and strengthen....I passed the Heavens Three…And soared to the place of Everlasting Light." (*Yasht* 22.)

Again: "And the wise walk on the side of Light, while the unwise follow the other until they grow wise….O Mighty Lord of Wisdom, Mazada! Supreme, Infinite, Universal Mind! Ahura! you that give Life to all! Grant me the power to control this mind, this Lower Mind of mine, this egoism, and put an end to all Duality, and gain the reign of One – as is desired." (*Gathas* 32.16.) And *Gatha* 33 speaks of "the man who is the best towards the righteous saint…having Light".

It is clear that Light in these passages was being seen in a vision of illumination, and that the metaphysical aspect of the fundamental theme of world literature was perpetuated in the early Iranian civilization. The universe of Light was kept functioning by fire-sacrifices in fire-temples such as the best-known at Naqsh-e-Rostam near Persepolis.

Mithras (Indian Mitra) was common to both the Iranian *Avesta* and the Indian *Veda*s, and possibly by 1700BC and certainly by 1380BC the gods of the Indo-Iranians were Mithras, Varuna and Indra, all of whom can be found in the Indian epic poem, *Rig Veda*. Zoroaster is strangely silent about Mithras. However, Mithraism continued into Hellenistic times.

In the myth, Mithras helped Ahura Mazda in his struggle against Darkness (which was ruled by Angra Mainyu or Ahriman). Mithras found the wild bull that was Ahura Mazda's first creation and killed it with a knife, and his supremacy was consequently acknowledged by the sun. As a result Mithras became the god of celestial Light and truth, and was *Sol Invictus* ("the invincible sun"), and equated with Shamash, Ra and Helios. In Roman times the emperor was *felix* because he was illumined by Mithras's Light and divine grace.

Mithraism arguably now became the Freemasonry of the ancient world. Initiates re-enacted the battle between light and darkness in a Mithraeum, a cavern or subterranean vault. (In the Attis mysteries an initiate was placed in a pit with a lattice across it, a bull was slaughtered on the lattice and blood gushed through onto the initiate.) Light fought darkness for the initiate's immortal soul in rituals such as this. This battle is reflected in a number of later Iranian texts.

India

The Indo-European Aryan-speakers who had settled all Europe and Iran arrived in the Ganges Valley c.1500BC after the decline of the Indus Valley culture (which had arisen c.2500BC).

The Rig Veda

Their descendants, the Indo-Aryans, produced the *Vedic* hymns. The *Rig Veda* was the oldest of the four *Veda*s, and the earliest sacred literature in India c.1500BC. The *Vedic* hymns were written to Indo-Aryan deities, especially to Agni, the Iranian fire-god.

In the *Rig Veda* the concept of order in the universe is expressed as *rta*: the harmony in Nature which, the early Indians believed, is a reflection of the divine harmony. *Rta* is cosmic order in Jeanine Miller's *The Vision of Cosmic Order in the Vedas*, and in such passages as: "The wise seers watch over their inspired intuition refulgent as heavenly light in the seat of *rta*", *Rig Veda* (X.177.2); and "By the song born of *rta* the sun shone forth" (X.138.2d).[26]

In the *Rig Veda*, a divine creative flame, the Light (*tapas*), is released from the darkness of the Absolute, and can be perceived in contemplation by *rsi*s, or inspired poets. It is personified in Agni, Varuna, Visvakarman and Prajapati. This "universal Light" (IX.48.4) or *tapas* is cosmic and has its source in the divine harmony outside Nature, which mirrors it. It shines in the heart of the inspired poet or *rsi* and is perceived as "an internal light" that is set within the heart (VI.9.6). It is the "hidden light" or *gulham jyotih* (VII.76.4cd) which is received by the poet as the archetypal vision granted to his ancestors who "found the light" (IV.1.14d). The poet grasps this vision anew as a revelation of truth that was known to his ancestors, and he frames it in song as did his Iranian ancestors.

In *The Vision of the Vedic Poets*, Professor Jan Gonda states that

"belief in a light which, being suprahuman in origin and penetrating into the heart of the inspired poets, illumined their mind, was the complement of the conviction that these poets owe their praeternormal knowledge and their religious and political inspiration to 'visions', that they 'saw' the truth about the deeds and power of the gods which they formulated in their hymns. These authors, indeed not rarely, alluded to an internal light which is in the heart of the poet or to which he gains access in his heart....This light is brought into connection with the sacral world of the inspired poet."[27]

The metaphysical aspect of the fundamental theme of the literature in the ancient world involves the revelation of the universal Light or *tapas*. It is the traditional and perennial task of the poet (*rsi*) in all cultures including our own to restate this contemplative vision of truth for his or her time. It is the task of all poets in all ages to rediscover the knowledge of the vision.

The *Rig Veda* speaks of Agni who brought down the Light as an intermediary between the *tapas* and *rsi*s and bestowed immortality:

"Agni, you are a sage, a priest, a king, protector, father of the sacrifice. Commissioned by us men, you ascend a messenger, conveying to the sky our hymns and offerings.....You are...giver of life and immortality....Purge us from taint of sin, and when we die, deal mercifully with us on the pyre, burning our bodies with their load of guilt, but bearing our eternal part on high to luminous abodes."[28]

Agni purged from sin and gave immortality on behalf of the gods in accordance with the metaphysical aspect of the fundamental theme of world literature. The *Rig Veda* makes it clear that Agni is a Shining One: "I call for you Agni, shining with beautiful shine....May he illuminate the nights that are longing for him." Agni illuminated the nights by shining into the soul.

In due course Agni ceased to be needed as an intermediary and was replaced by a sacrificial mysticism. In the *Brahmanas*, ritual commentaries on the four *Veda*s c.900-700BC, the fire surrounding objects sacrificed on fire-altars was identified with the fiery power of creation and the universe, *tapas*: "By sacrificing with this (fire)," the *Gandharva*s told the lonely King Pururavas,[29] "you will become one of us" (*Shatapatha Brahmana* XI.5).

Two epics with a more secular emphasis, the *Mahabharata*, which was on the *Iliad*-like war between the Kurus and Panchalas that took place between 1400 and 1000BC, and the *Ramayana* ("Epic of Rama"), which is on the *Odyssey*-like wanderings of Rama and his wife Sita among two races (the Kosalas and the Videhas) who lived between the 12th and 10th centuries BC, exist alongside the *Rig Veda*. They began a minority stream of secular Indian poetry and arguably marked the beginning of the secular aspect of the fundamental theme in world literature.

The Upanisads

By 600BC Vedism had grown into Brahmanism,[30] the work of Brahman as Supreme God, and the Atman (the divine within man, the universal being or Self) united with the eternal Brahman, the Light. The *Upanisads*, reputedly the work of Indian forest seers that can be dated to the 5th century BC, formed the final portion of the *Veda*s, known as the *Vedanta* ("end of *Veda*s"), and the earliest *Upanisad*, c.9th century BC, says: "By the Light of the Self man sits, moves about, does his work, and when his work is done, rests....The self-luminous being who dwells within the lotus of the heart, surrounded by the senses and sense organs, and who is the light of intellect, is that Self" (*Brihadaranyaka*). One must "unite the light within you with the light of Brahman" (*Svetasvatara*).

The metaphysical aspect of the fundamental theme of literature could not be more directly expressed:

"As sparks innumerable fly upward from a blazing fire, so from the depths of the Imperishable arise all things....Self-luminous is that Being, and formless. He dwells within all....He is the innermost Self of all....Self-luminous is Brahman, ever present in the hearts of all....In the effulgent (or shining) lotus of the heart dwells Brahman...the Light of Lights. Him the knowers of the Self attain....He is the one Light that gives Light to all. He shining, everything shines....Hail to the illumined souls!" (*Mundaka*.)

And:

"The truth is that you are always united with the Lord. But you must *know* this....To realize God, first control the outgoing senses and harness the mind. Then meditate upon the light in the heart of the fire....Thus the Self, the Inner Reality, may be seen behind physical appearance. Control your mind so that the Ultimate Reality, the self-luminous Lord, may be revealed....With the help of the mind and the intellect, keep the senses from attaching themselves to objects of pleasure. They will then be purified by the Light of the Inner Reality, and that Light will be revealed. Great is the glory of the self-luminous being, the Inner Reality....Follow only in the footsteps of the illumined ones, and by continuous meditation merge both mind and intellect in the internal Brahman. The glorious Lord will be revealed to you....Set fire to the Self within by the practice of meditation....Unite the Light within you with the Light of Brahman....as you practise meditation, you will see in vision forms resembling snow, crystals, smoke, fire, lightning, fireflies, the sun, the moon. These are signs that you are on your way to the revelation of Brahman....Said the great seer Svetasvatara: I have known, beyond all darkness, that great Person of golden effulgence. Only by knowing him does one conquer death....He is the great Light, shining forever. This great Being, assuming a form of the size of a thumb, forever dwells in the heart of all creatures as their innermost Self." (*Svetasvatara.*)

According to the *Upanisads* the consciousness of the Self is the fourth of four states of consciousness contained in the letters A, U, M and in the totality OM, the superconscious vision in which Atman and Brahman are one: "Beyond the senses, beyond the understanding, beyond all expression, is the Fourth. It is pure unitary consciousness, wherein awareness of the world and of multiplicity is completely obliterated. It is ineffable peace. It is the supreme good. It is One without a second. It is the Self." (*Mandukaya.*)

The Bhagavad-gita

The other main *Vedanta* work, the *Bhagavad-gita* ("Song of the Lord"), which is contained within the *Mahabharata*, has been dated to the 5th or 3rd centuries BC, or the 1st and 2nd centuries AD. Krishna, an incarnation of Visnu, visits Arjuna, who has refused to kill his kinsmen in the battle of Kurukshetra.

Arjuna asks, "How can one identify a man who is firmly established and absorbed in Brahman? In what manner does an illumined soul speak?"

Krishna replies: "He knows bliss in the Atman and wants nothing else. Cravings torment the heart: he renounces cravings. I call him illumined....This is the state of enlightenment in Brahman. A man...is alive in that enlightenment."

Arjuna has to understand that he must fight, and that he can still be illumined:

> "The illumined soul must not create confusion in the minds of the ignorant by refraining from work. The ignorant in their delusion...become tied to the senses and the action of the senses....Fix your mind on the Atman. Be free from the sense of ego. Dedicate all your actions to me. Then go forward and fight....The reward of all action is to be found in enlightenment....When you have reached enlightenment, ignorance will delude you no longer. In the light of that knowledge you will see the entire creation within your own Atman and in me."

Arjuna has to learn that the 'I' of the Atman of an enlightened person is quite different from the 'I' of the senses (the ego):

> "The illumined soul whose heart is Brahman's heart thinks always: 'I am doing nothing.' No matter what he sees, hears, touches, smells, eats....This he knows always: 'I am not seeing, I am not hearing: it is the senses that see and hear and touch the things of the senses.'...The Atman is the Light: the Light is covered by darkness: the darkness is delusion....When the Light of the Atman drives out our darkness that Light shines forth from us, a sun in splendour, the revealed Brahman."

Revealing himself to Arjuna in his divine form of Visnu, Krishna says: "Suppose a thousand suns should rise together into the sky: such is the glory of the Shape of Infinite God."

The Light of Atman passed into the growing worship of Visnu (and his ten incarnations, of which the main ones were Rama and Krishna), which began in the 7th century BC, and into the growing worship of Siva, who was first treated as Supreme God in the *Svetasvatara Upanisad*.

The *Yoga sutras* of Patanjali, who allegedly lived some time between 820 and 300 BC, were compiled between the 2nd century BC and the 5th century AD. To Patanjali, by means of intense concentration the concentrating mind (*citta*) vanishes, leaving the object concentrated on as the sole reality. *Samadhi* ("bliss" or "ecstasy") comes from eliminating the *citta* and concentrating on the "effulgent Light", which is "beyond all sorrow" (1.36).

Buddhist Scriptures
By 500BC there were many states in the Ganges Valley, and sects questioned orthodox Brahmanism. These included Buddhism. Siddhartha Gautama, who was born c.560BC into an area occupied by an Aryan tribe called the Sakyas, achieved his enlightenment (*bodhi*) at Bodh Gaya under a pipal or peepal tree (later called the Bo or Bodhi Tree) and became known as "the Buddha" (the "Enlightened One" or "awakened one"). In the Buddha's revolution against Vedism and Brahmanism, craving or desire, fire, must be extinguished.

In his revolutionary Fire Sermon (*Maha-Vagga* I.21) the Buddha declares that everything is on fire with craving:

"All things, O priests, are on fire....The eye O priests, is on fire; forms are on fire; eye-consciousness is on fire; impressions received by the eye are on fire...with the fire of passion, say I, with the fire of hatred, with the fire of infatuation....The ear is on fire; sounds are on fire; the nose is on fire; odours are on fire; the tongue is on fire; tastes are on fire; the body is on fire; things tangible are on fire; the mind is on fire; ideas are on fire; mind/consciousness is on fire; impressions received by the mind are on fire...with the fire of passion, say I, with the fire of hatred, the fire of infatuation....Perceiving this, O priests, the learned and noble disciple conceives an aversion for the eye, conceives an aversion from forms....And in conceiving this aversion he becomes divested of passion, and by the absence of passion he becomes free."[31]

When all craving and desire was extinguished one could achieve Enlightenment and Nirvana (a "blowing-out" of desire, leaving a state of bliss). The Buddhist Scriptures record the experience of Nirvana. In the second watch of the night of his enlightenment, the Buddha "acquired the supreme heavenly eye" and the world appeared "as though reflected in a spotless mirror".[32] The Buddha says of his Enlightenment: "When this knowledge, this insight had arisen within me, my heart was set free from intoxication of lusts,...becomings,...ignorance....Ignorance was beaten down, insight arose, darkness was destroyed, the Light came, inasmuch as I was there, strenuous, aglow, master of myself." (*Mahasaccaka Sutta.*)[33]

In his last sermon the Buddha advised: "Be ye lamps into yourselves, hold fast to the truth as a lamp."

Although he was "aglow" and a "lamp" as a result of his Enlightenment, the Buddha asserted that when desire is blown out there is "no self", meaning that there is no Atman. This doctrine, known as *anatta* (non-self), was taken up by Theravadic or *Hinayana* Buddhists. Even so, in the *Dhammapada* ("Way of Virtue") they assert the primacy of the Light: "The sun is bright by day...; but Buddha, the Awakened is bright with splendour day and night."[34] However, *Mahayana* Buddhists saw *anatta* as applying only to the personal ego and they continued to believe in an Atman-like universal self with which they were united during enlightenment. In the *Mahayana Surangama Sutra* (1st century AD, in Sanskrit) the Buddha distinguishes "the perception of our eyes and the intrinsic perception of Sight by our enlightened Mind that is conscious of the fallible perception of the eyes and receives "beams of Light".[35]

The metaphysical aspect of the fundamental theme of world literature is broadly maintained in Buddhist literature, for the concept of the Atman and Brahman is still fundamentally present in *Mahayana* literature, and *Theravadic* literature emphasizes the importance of the Light.

Jainism also questioned Brahmanism's orthodox tradition. Its religion was founded in the form we know by Vardhamana, who was born c.599BC, a contemporary of Buddha and Zoroaster. Jainism may be the original religion of the Hindu Brahmans,[36] which may have been merely reformed by Vardhamana, who was later called Mahavira ("great hero"). Mahavira spent twelve years as a wandering ascetic and achieved enlightenment at the age of forty-two.

Jainism's Sacred Book
The Sacred Book of Jainas (4.30) states the metaphysical aspect of the

fundamental theme of world literature: "One should ever make his own self radiant by the light of the three jewels."[37] The Light filled the Jain soul, which expanded to fill the whole body as the light of a lamp fills a large room as well as a small room. The passions had to be subdued so that the soul (like the Atman or universal being) could be purified and reach a state of bliss in which it could be filled with the Light.

China

The early literature of China is intertwined with legend. The *I Ching* ("Book of Changes") is a book of trigrams used in divination. The trigrams were reputedly discovered by the legendary Fu Hsi in the 24th, or even 29th, century BC on the back of a tortoise shortly after the Huang Ho or Yellow River culture began (c.3000-2500BC). Hexagrams were found and written down by Wen Wang in 1143/2BC[38] shortly before writing was officially discovered in China, and the Appendices were completed some 700 years later.

The *I Ching* was one of the five classics that Confucius (Kung Fu Tzu, 551-479BC) edited and preserved. In a troubled time Confucius looked back to the stability of earlier kings when the Supreme Ruler (known as Shang Ti or Ti) was an intermediary (like the Egyptian Akhenaton) between humankind and Heaven (*T'ien*). By the time of Confucius the enlightened man was the mediator between Heaven (*T'ien*) and Earth.

The *I Ching* is still consulted today. I recall sitting in the mid-1960s with an Executive Director of the Bank of Japan who startled me by suddenly producing sticks that resembled firework sparklers, which he shook up and laid out. He then told my fortune with reference to a battered Chinese copy of the *I Ching*. (He said that my fortune was one of the best *I-Ching* fortunes he had ever seen.)

The first anthology of Chinese poetry, the *Shih Ching* ("the Book of Songs", c.600BC), perhaps compiled by Confucius, consists of folk and festive songs, ballads and hymns that focus on love, courtship, farming, hunting, and going to war – more secular and slight topics than the quest of the fundamental theme.

The Tao Te Ching

The Shang dynasty (c.1766-1122BC) was the first archaeologically secure dynasty in China. It was followed by the Chou dynasty (c.1122-481BC), under which Confucius lived together with his contemporary Lao-Tze (who was born c.570BC). According to his biographer c.100BC, Lao-Tze, an archivist at the court, met Confucius and criticized his pride and ambition.

It has been questioned whether Lao-Tze in fact ever existed, and it has been suggested that his poems, the *Tao Te Ching* ("Book of the Way and the Power"), were a compilation made in the 3rd century BC. But although the doctrine of the *Tao* existed earlier than Lao-Tze, he has always traditionally been acknowledged as the founder of Taoism. "Lao-Tze" means "old master" or "old boy", his real name being Li-poh-yang.

The idea of the *Tao* (Way) has different levels. It can be seen as the way of one's life and of how a king should govern his country; or the way of the universe; or the way creation came out of the Void (poems 4, 11), which is similar to the Hindu Brahman: the One, the unity behind the multiplicity of the universe (poems 14, 42), the source of the impersonal, eternal energy (*ch'i*) behind the universe.

The Indo-European Iranian Light (or Fire) of Zoroaster seems to have spread through India and reached China. Iranian was the language in Chinese Turkestan in the 1st millennium BC. As a result there was an Indo-European influence on Taoism: the fire-sacrifice was internalized, and a subtle fire blended Heaven and Earth within the soul. The Light is crucial to Taoism.

According to the *Tao Te Ching*, the aim of life was to live in harmony with the *Tao*. The *Tao* is the basis for all things without having form itself (poems 14, 41). It is First Cause that existed "like a preface to God" or prior to God (poem 4). It is the "mother" and the "ancestor" of all things (poems 52, 4) that existed before Heaven and Earth (poem 25). It is "invisible", "vague and elusive" (poems 14, 35), "everlasting" and "unchangeable" (poems 7, 16, 25). It is "the great Form" (poem 35) and it cannot be described in known terms (poems 1, 32, 37, 41). It is Non-Being or *wu* (poems 1, 40), and "all things in the world come from Being and Being comes from Non-Being" (poem 40).[39]

This Universalist idea of the origin of all things is given even clearer expression by Chuang Tzu in the 3rd century BC: "There was Being. There was Non-Being before there was Being. There was

No-Non-Being before there was Non-Being. There was No-No-Non-Being before there was No-Non-Being."[40]

The *Tao* is also the Light which is neither perception nor yet non-perception: "We look at it and do not see it....Its name is The Subtle (formless)....Going up high, it is not bright, and coming down low, it is not dark. Infinite and boundless." (Poem 14.) In other words, we do not see the Light with our sense-perception, and it does not obey the laws of the sun, but is eternally present. The *Tao* "is indeed Subtle Light" (poem 36).

The aim of life is to return to the Light of *Tao*: "All things come into being, and I see thereby their return. All things flourish, but each one returns to its root. This return to its root means tranquillity. It is called returning to its destiny. To return to destiny is called the eternal (*Tao*). To know the eternal (i.e. *Tao*) is called enlightenment....Being in accord with *Tao*, he is everlasting." (Poem 16.)

The Taoist experiences in ecstasy a Reality that cannot be understood with the reason. He empties his mind and mirrors Heaven and Earth in an underlying Void (the Light), which inhabits his heart once it is cleansed (*hsin chai*). The macrocosm of the universe and the microcosm of man obey the same laws, and Taoism explains how the two should always exist in harmony.

The Zoroastrian dualism of light and darkness impacted on Taoism in its two forces, *Yin* and *Yang*. These two principles appear for the first time in the Third Appendix of the *I Ching* (1.32, 4th century BC.): "That which is unfathomable in (the movement of) the inactive and active operations is (the presence of a) spiritual (power)." The "unfathomable" is the formless Light, the inactive *Yin* and active *Yang* represent Zoroaster's twin spirits of darkness and light (*Angra Mainyu* and *Spenta Mainya*). *Yin* and *Yang* are also represented as Heaven (*Yang*) and Earth (*Yin*), with Man in between.

In Iran, India and China, Zoroaster, Buddha, Mahavira and Lao-Tze all lived at roughly the same time (the 6th century BC) and there is a homogeneity in their Universalist view of the universe. They perpetuated the metaphysical aspect of the fundamental theme of world literature which had begun in the Mesopotamian and Egyptian civilizations and had in the meantime passed to Israel.

Israel

The Anatolian, Syrian and Israelite civilizations adopted different forms of the Indo-European Sky Father. The Indo-European Hittites arrived in Anatolia c.2000BC, and expressed the ordered, unified universe through a Storm-and-Weather god during the Hittite Old Kingdom, which lasted from c.1700 to c.1500BC. The Hittites ruled Syria as a Hittite colony, and the Syrians expressed unity through their cloud-ruling Baal from c.1500BC.

The Indo-European fire-cults influenced the Semitic Hebrews who began on the banks of the Euphrates in Mesopotamia. The *Old Testament* tells of Abraham, who lived at Ur probably in the 19th or 18th-17th centuries BC, perhaps c.1750BC, as has been confirmed by a find of thousands of cuneiform tablets at Mari, a city on the Euphrates,[41] and migrated to Canaan in Palestine. He brought with him Ur's legal code, Hammurabi's "eye for an eye", to the Promised Land. As Hammurabi identified himself with the Mesopotamian god Shamash[42] Abraham must have brought a knowledge of Shamash. The Israelites went to Egypt and lived in bondage until their return to Canaan at the end of the 13th century BC under Moses, whose Ten Commandments founded Judaism as it has come down to us today.

The Old Testament

The *Old Testament* perpetuates the metaphysical aspect of the fundamental theme of world literature. It tells of YHWH, pronounced Yahweh (or less correctly, Jehovah), the Being who was First Cause. (YHWH may stand for *"Yahweh-Asher-Yahweh"*, which means "He Brings Into Existence Whatever Exists", i.e. he is Creator and First Cause.)[43] He evolved from a tribal "jealous" idol-god who "died" and rose for the spring Passover festival and manifested in sunlight and thunderstorm, and became a presence that could be known in the soul. He ruled the priest-kings in the kingdom David established c.1000BC and then the priests who controlled the country after the Exile of the 6th century BC. His exploits extend from the 20th to the 4th centuries BC and were written by many hands at different times.

We have seen that the metaphysical aspect of the fundamental theme of world literature focuses on the confronting of death and seeing of the Light of Being in the purified soul, and the *Old Testament* as a whole conveys this. Yahweh was at first seen in terms of light, fire and lightning like the Indo-European Sky-gods and storm-gods. Abraham sees Yahweh in the form of "a smoking furnace and a burning lamp" (*Genesis* 15.17) and Yahweh's first appearance to Moses was "in a flame of fire" (*Exodus* 3.2). Yahweh's appearance on Mount Sinai, when Moses was given the Ten Commandments, was after "thunders and lightnings" (*Exodus* 19.16) when "the Lord descended upon it in fire". Yahweh had led the exodus "by night in a pillar of fire, to give them light" (*Exodus* 13.21). Yahweh "shined forth from Mount Paran" (*Deuteronomy* 33.2), and in the 9th century BC Elijah, challenging Baal, invoked Yahweh, who sent down "fire" from heaven (*2 Kings* 1).

The *Psalms of David* see Yahweh as Light: "Out of Zion, the perfection of beauty, God hath shined" (*Psalm* 50.2); "the voice of thy thunder was in the heaven: the lightnings lightened the word" (*Psalm* 77.18) and "yea, the darkness hideth not from thee; but the night shineth as the day: the darkness and the light are both alike to thee" (*Psalm* 139.12) – clearly a reference to the Light.

Yahweh was increasingly seen as the Light: "The Lord shall be unto thee an everlasting light" (*Isaiah* 60.9). "For with thee is the fountain of life: in thy light shall we see light" (*Psalm* 36.9). Yahweh made "his face shine" upon humans he favoured, and lifted up "his countenance" upon them (*Numbers* 6.25). "The light shall shine upon thy ways" (*Job* 22.28). "The lord is my light and my salvation; whom shall I fear" (*Psalm* 27.1). "The Lord shall be a light unto me" (*Micah* 7.8)."Then shall thy light break forth as the morning" (*Isaiah* 58.8).

Yahweh descended as fire, spoke out of fire and had a countenance which shone as an everlasting Light. Although fire-sacrifices and burnt offerings were made to him at the ritualistic level in the Indo-European manner, he was also experienced in the soul as Light, an inner sun. Hence the ritual surrounding the tent of the Tabernacle, the mobile sanctuary which God revealed to Moses in a vision on Mount Sinai (*Exodus* 25), and its successors in the first and second Temple.

In the Tabernacle in the Temple of Solomon (10th century BC) and in the second Temple, there was a divine "Holy of Holies" within a Heavenly "Holy" and an earthly outer court. The gold Ark of the Covenant stood in the Holy of Holies, containing the "Testimony" which Yahweh gave the people of Israel. "And there I will meet with thee," Yahweh told Moses (*Exodus* 25.22), "and I will commune with thee from above the mercy seat, between the two cherubims which are upon the ark, of all things which I will give in commandment unto the children of Israel."

On the first day of the first month in the year following these words of Yahweh's, the Tabernacle was erected. "The cloud of the Lord was upon the tabernacle and fire was in it by night" (*Exodus* 40.34, 38). Yahweh came down and united with the world below and dwelt in the darkness of the Holy of Holies, from which the glorious Light of his indwelling radiated and his shining being, the bright radiance of his *Shekhinah* or Presence, revealed itself. According to the oral tradition of Talmudic and Rabbinical writings, the Tabernacle contained the Divine Light.[44]

In the 6th century BC the Judaistic Light was Iranised. The Jews in exile in Babylon from 587/6 to 538BC came into contact with the Iranian Light as Chaldean Babylon had been conquered by the Persian Cyrus the Great. The Jews of the southern kingdom of Judah, lamenting their exile "by the waters of Babylon", absorbed the Iranian monotheism of Ahura Mazda and a hierarchy of Babylonian angels.[45] (All the angels in the Biblical tradition with proper names derive from Babylon.) The Jews opened themselves to the Iranian dualism of Light and Darkness, to the Iranian Satan (Ahriman) and to guardian angels. As part of this process Yahweh blended with the Light of Ahura Mazda.

Whereas Taoism internalised the metaphysical aspect of the fundamental theme of world literature, the *Old Testament* externalized it. Yahweh is at first presented in terms of fire, lightning and storm. He then became a presence of Light, the *Shekhinah*, that dwelt in the mobile Tabernacle. He then became a Light shining in darkness that could be known by the soul. Yahweh took on some of the characteristics of Ahura Mazda.

Literary Summary

I can now summarise how the metaphysical aspect of the fundamental theme of world literature (see p.1) was presented in the early literature of the ancient world:

- The infinite that surrounds and orders the universe was present within: the Heaven/ Underworld of Dumuzi/Tammuz (Mesopotamia); the Elysian Fields/Underworld in the Egyptian *Book of the Dead* (Egypt); light and darkness, *Spenta Mainyu* and *Angra Mainyu* in the *Avesta* (Iran); the fire of Brahman "which created everything" in the *Svetasvatara Upanisad* (India); the *Tao* as the First Cause of all things, "infinite and boundless" (China); and Yahweh who "brings into existence whatever exists" (Israel).

- The metaphysical Reality seen as Light was embodied in gods: Utu-Shamash; Ra; Ahura Mazda; Agni/Brahman; *T'ien;* and Yahweh. It was also referred to as *tapas*, or universal Light (India).

- The order of the universe can be found in: Anu and Utu-Shamash, who ordered the universe (Mesopotamia); in Ra as the sun-god ruling the sky-world and Underworld, and in the Pharaoh as Ra in his life and continuing as Ra in death, who ordered the universe (Egypt); in Ahura Mazda, source of the Light, who ordered the universe (Iran); in *rta*, which ordered the universe (India); in the *Tao*, which ordered the universe (China); and in Yahweh, who ordered the universe (Israel).

- The oneness of known humankind is assumed by the writers of: the *Epic of Gilgamesh* (in which all humans are under the rule of the gods); the Egyptian *Book of the Dead*; the *Avesta*; the *Rig Veda* and *Upanisads*; the *Tao Te Ching*; and the *Old Testament*.

- The similarities in cultures and civilizations can be detected in: the Indo-European influence on the Mesopotamian, Iranian, Indian and Chinese civilizations; the Mesopotamian influence on the Egyptian and Israelite civilizations; and Zoroaster's influence on India and China.

- The concept of a universal being or self that opens to the Light behind the rational, social ego is in the Mesopotamian, Egyptian, Iranian, Indian, Chinese and Israelite civilizations and is named the *akh* (Egypt), Atman (India) and soul (Israel).

- Universal virtue is emphasized in: the stories of Gilgamesh, Dumuzi/Tammuz; the people in the Egyptian *Book of the Dead*; Mithras; Arjuna; Lao-Tze; and the *Old Testament* prophets.

- The promise of the immortality of the universal being is present in the rituals of: Dumuzi/Tammuz; the Egyptian *Book of the Dead* ("coming forth by day"); and Agni as "giver of life and immortality". It can be found in: Gilgamesh's confronting of death and thwarted search for immortality; the *Rig Veda*; *Avesta*; Brahmanism; Taoism; and the *Shekhinah*'s covenant with the Israelites.

- The inner transformation or centre-shift from ego to universal being is in: the myth of Tammuz's dying into the Underworld and rising in the spring (Mesopotamia); the bringing to birth of the *akh* in 'Making the Transformation into a Living Soul' (Egypt); the "control of this egoism" and "end to all Duality" in the *Avesta* (Iran); the seeking of the innermost Self in the *Upanisads* (India); the transformation from sense-perception (China); and the transformation from the ego to the soul in prayer (Israel).

- The quest of the purified soul seeking a life after death is in: Gilgamesh's quest for immortality (Mesopotamia); the rituals of the Egyptian *Book of the Dead* which proceed from ego to being (Egypt); the soaring "to the place of Everlasting Light" in the *Avesta* (Iran); the quest for the Light of the *rsi*s and Arjuna and in the wanderings which ended in the enlightenment of the Buddha and Mahavira (India); the quest for the eternal and enlightenment of the *Tao* (China); and the quest from darkness to the Light of Yahweh in the Tabernacle (Israel).

- The sensibility that approaches Reality through more than one discipline can be found in the ancient cultures' approach to the Light, which embraces early philosophy, religion, national history and literature. Details of individual authors have not come down to us, for many works have not survived and we often do not know the authors of those that have survived.

- The new perspective of unity in history, religion, philosophy and science, international politics and literature can be found in the early Mesopotamian creation myths and the ancient religions' approach to the Light in Egypt, Iran, India, China and Israel. Information is scanty in this early time, but the perspective of unity in disciplines is present.

Within the six civilizations whose early literature I have examined we have seen that there are variations on the metaphysical aspect of one fundamental theme of world literature. The classical world produced further variations.

2

The Literature of the Classical World

The metaphysical aspect of the fundamental theme of world literature – the quest of a purified soul to confront death and receive the secret Light of infinite Reality – was perpetuated in the Greek civilization and what was to become the classical, Graeco-Roman world.

Not every work of a writer writing in the classical period or in more recent times is about the metaphysical aspect of the fundamental theme. Many works are about the secular everyday world of Nature, love and social feelings. It is, however, true to say that for some the metaphysical aspect of the fundamental theme is the core of their work, that there are traces of it in their essential work. The totality of their work is a kind of chiaroscuro, a blend of light and darkness, in which their core is a quest for the metaphysical Light and the rest is more shadowy, more secular about the outside world. When we consider their work as a whole, we can see that the metaphysical and secular aspects of the fundamental theme form the essence of their work.

Greece

The Indo-Europeans settled in Greece in two waves. The first arrived c.3500BC and became the Pelasgians.[1] The second wave arrived c.2200BC, shortly after the Indo-Europeans settled Iran and India, and became the ancestors of the Mycenaeans. They called themselves Achaeans (*Achaioi*) and were possibly displaced from Akkad which was originally called Achaia.

The Mycenaean Mysteries and the Fundamental Theme

These bearded Achaean Greeks were the Danaoi of Homer. They brought with them their Indo-European Sky-god Dyaeus Pitar, who became Zeus, the Sky-god with his thunderbolt and storm-god, who resembled the Altaic Sky-god. They also brought Shamash, who developed into Hyperion-Apollo, the sun-god. He was "*Phoibos*" or "light-bearer", and Enlightener, the god of mental light. He prophesied through the Pythia, the priestess at the Delphic Oracle who sacrificed animals to the Sky-god (Zeus) and rose to the Sky World on the smoke, which resembled a World Tree.

The Mycenaean culture introduced three mystery religions. The mysteries at Eleusis go back to c.1800BC and worshipped Demeter, the Earth-Mother and Grain-Mother, along with her daughter Kore (Persephone), who was carried off into the Underworld by Pluto. An underground vault beneath the *telesterion*, the hall at Eleusis, served as a reconstructed Hades and elsewhere there was a reconstructed Elysium where the reuniting of Demeter and Kore was celebrated with torches. A papyrus fragment shows Herakles saying, "I have beheld the Fire....I have seen the Maid (i.e. Kore)."[2] The climax of the Mysteries, the *Philosophoumena*, presented a reaped ear of corn of brilliant gold.[3] It was presented in the *telesterion* in a brilliant light. The meaning of the Eleusinian mysteries was that the cycle of grain paralleled the cycle of man: grain sown in a field was like seed sown in man's universal being, "if it dies it bringeth forth much fruit" (*John* 12:24) – a new centre that reflects the Light.

The Greek Achaean Mycenaeans had brought with them the Sumerian Royal Sacred Marriage in which Tammuz's marriage to Inanna-Ishtar was celebrated at the Spring Festival at Isin, south of Babylon, at the end of the third millennium BC. This passed into the later Eleusinian Epoptic mysteries, in which Zeus married Demeter.

The Mycenaeans had also imported the Minoan bull-cult from Crete which had come from Anatolia. They invaded Crete, and the discovery of Linear B by Michael Ventris showed that Mycenaean Greek was spoken in both Mycenae and Minoan Knossos by the 15th century BC. A Cretan bull with a gold "rosette" on its forehead (c.1550-1500BC) was found in the fourth shaft grave at Mycenae.[4] The archaeologist Heinrich Schliemann, the discoverer of Troy, described the rosette as "a splendidly ornamented golden sun, of two and a fifth inches in diameter". It reflected a sun-cult connecting the bull with the sun, and therefore represented the Light.

The Dionysiac Bull mysteries originated in the Mycenaean Age and perpetuated the bull-cult. They showed how Dionysus-Zagreus was brought up by the Maenads, wild women who wandered through the mountains drinking wine and eating ivy berries which had a hallucinogenic effect. Dionysus had a Light like the "rosette" that could be acquired. This could be achieved by the physically intoxicated Maenads whose inner eye was stimulated into seeing the *theon eidos*, the "vision of the gods" or mysteries sent from Heaven, the coming of the Light, later mentioned in Euripides' *Bacchoi* or *Bacchae*.

The Orphic mysteries worshipped Orpheus, musician, author of sacred writings and priest of Dionysus, who was torn to pieces by the Maenads. Orpheus was a poet who could charm wild life into listening to his song, and after his death his head continued to sing. The Orphic Light was called Phanes, and was celebrated by fire-sacrifices. Orpheus taught that the soul could be reborn after death, and that after three pious lives in which the soul or universal being received the secret Light it could live in the eternal sunshine and bliss of the Isles of the Blessed.[5]

Many of the Greek myths go back to the Mycenaean time. Greek mythology contains many parables regarding the metaphysical aspect of the fundamental theme of world literature. Cosmology and cosmogony are reflected in the myths of Chaos, Elysium, Erebus, the Isles of the Blest, Lethe, Oceanus, the Styx, Pandora and Uranus. There are accounts of the major deities: Apollo, Ares, Artemis, Athena, Eros, the Graces, Hephaestus, Hera, Hermes, Persephone, Pluto, Poseidon, Selene, Uranus and Zeus. Their attributes and qualities are conveyed: they feed off ambrosia and nectar, wear the aegis and benefit from apotheosis. The heroes fight mythical creatures: the Chimera, Cyclops, Echidna, Gigantes, Gorgon and Hydra, and resist the wiles of Scylla and Charybdis and the Sirens. The questing heroes include Odysseus, Oedipus, Theseus, Jason and Orpheus. There are many Greek figures who fought in the Trojan War such as Achilles, Agamemnon, Odysseus and Ajax, and there are many Trojan heroes such as Hector, Paris and Priam.

Jason seeking the Golden Fleece, Orpheus seeking Eurydice in the Underworld, the attempt to retrieve Persephone from darkness and bring her back to light, Agamemnon's sacrifice of his daughter Iphigenia to gain a favourable wind from the gods that will take the fleet to Troy – all are parables of the quest of the hero which brings him to an encounter with death, the Underworld and infinite Reality. All the Greek poets and dramatists who referred to or related versions of these myths provided fragments of the metaphysical aspect of the fundamental theme.

The Mycenaean culture fell to the Dorians c.1100BC. The Mycenaeans handed on the secret of the Light as symbols within the Eleusinian, Minoan, Dionysiac and Orphic mysteries. The Indo-European fire-sacrifices to Zeus were thus handed on together with the symbols of bull's flesh, an ear of corn and fire.

Homer's Iliad

The universe of the Mycenaean mysteries was the universe of Homer's literature. Homer wrote in the 8th century BC, about the Trojan War, which Schliemann claimed from the evidence of his excavations at Hisarlik took place in the early 12th century BC. (Eratosthenes had given the date of the Trojan War as 1194-1184/3BC.)[6]

Troy was in Anatolia, which had been settled by Indo-Europeans known as Hittites from north of the Black Sea in 2000BC. Their descendants established the Hittite Old Kingdom (c.1700-1500BC), and according to cuneiform tablets discovered at Boğazköy, the Hittite ruler was the earthly deputy for a Storm-and-Weather god, embodying him in life and becoming him on death. After the decline of the Hittite Middle Kingdom (c.1500-1400BC), the Hittite New Kingdom restored the empire and conquered Syria (part of which was soon lost to the Assyrians). The Hittite Empire was invaded by the Phrygians, and then fell suddenly in 1225BC to "the Sea Peoples", probably the Bronze-Age Achaean Greeks or *Ahhiyawa*, according to Hittite tablets.[7] The Hittite collapse coincided with the destruction of Hisarlik, the city of King Priam, if the modern Hisarlik was indeed Troy, and it is possible that the Trojan War was a phase in the invasion of the Sea Peoples who brought the Hittite Empire to an end about the time Troy fell.[8] North Anatolia now became Aeolia, west and central Anatolia were occupied by the Phrygians and southern Anatolia became Ionia, into which Homer is thought to have been born: in the vicinity of modern Smyrna (Izmir).

To some the *Iliad* and *Odyssey* drew on a tradition of oral poetry, an inherited body of material repeatedly reworked and reperformed. To some, Homer is a name attached to the author of the core narrative of this tradition. To others he was a master poet who drew together a variety of legends and created one or two super-epics. To still others, the *Odyssey* was composed by a later hand, and countered the *Iliad* in being its thematic opposite: about peace instead of war, about survival rather than glorious death, about a father, husband and ruler rather than a heroic individual.

In Homer's two epics, the *Iliad* and the *Odyssey*, the Greek Zeus ordered the universe from his infinite world on Mount Olympus. The gods caused things to happen: an arrow to strike the best-protected part of a fighter's body, a bowstring to snap, armour to become unfastened, a stroke or heart attack, an epidemic, a storm at sea or the attention of marauders. The lives of mortals were lived in the knowledge that they would go to the Underworld on their death and (with luck) then to the Elysian Fields, the pre-Hellenic paradise the Greeks identified with the Isles of the Blessed. (In Homer the Elysian Plain was an island of perfect happiness at the end of the Earth, on the banks of the River Oceanus which surrounded the Earth.) Either way, there was the promise of immortality.

The action of the *Iliad* is overseen by the Olympian gods.

The opening lines of the poem declare, "And so the plan of Zeus was brought to fulfilment." The first event of the poem, Agamemnon's insult to the priest Chryses brings down divine wrath: Apollo's plague. Agamemnon arrogantly slights Achilles, who withdraws from the conflict and sulks, with disastrous consequences for the Greeks. (Achilles is only just mortal: his mother, the goddess Thetis, had attempted to bestow immortality on him by dipping him in an immortal pool, but the heel she held him by remained dry and therefore mortal.) The goddesses Hera and Athena are angry, and the war must continue so that they are appeased. The war progresses slowly because powerful gods support both sides, and Zeus is slow to support the Achaeans. After the appeals of the Greeks, Achilles, who is inspired by Athena, concedes that his friend Patroclus may take his place in battle, wearing Achilles' armour to disguise himself as Achilles and drive off the Trojans. Patroclus kills Sarpedon, a Trojan son of Zeus – who weeps tears of blood, not wanting him to die. Patroclus advances too far and is killed by the Trojan champion, Hector. Achilles' anger now turns against Hector. He kills him and mistreats his body. He is now consumed by both grief and wrath. Hector's father, King Priam, travels

43

to the Greek camp by night and begs Achilles to return his son's body. Achilles' anger gives way to pity, and the poem ends with Hector's burial. Troy will now be destroyed as Hector had foreseen: "There will come a day when holy Troy will be destroyed."

In the *Iliad*, Homer's perspective is not pro-Greek. He is even-handed between both sides, as one might expect of a poet who reputedly came from formerly-Anatolian Ionia (the vicinity of modern Izmir). To Homer, an enemy deserves compassion in a poem even though he does not receive it in real life.

But the gods are in charge. It is Apollo who smashes the Greek defensive wall in book 12.

Virtue was rewarded by the gods, who were anthropomorphic onlookers for much of the time, but could intervene when it suited their interests. Aphrodite caused the Trojan War by carrying Paris off to his chamber, enhancing his beauty and then fetching Helen. Zeus caused the Achaeans to fight by sending the likeness of Nestor in a dream to Agamemnon to say, "I am the messenger of Zeus....He has commanded you to arm the long-haired Achaeans with all speed for now you will take the wide-wayed city of the Trojans." Homer treats the gods humorously. There is a double stage of divine and human action. It is comic that Zeus, ruler of gods and men, is constantly bothered by his prying and nagging wife Hera, and that Hera distracts Zeus from the Trojan War into an amorous interlude in book 14. She seduces her husband on the top of Mount Ida, Crete, to give Poseidon more time to prevent Hector from annihilating the Achaean forces before Achilles can be persuaded to join them and effect an Achaean victory.

The philosopher Xenophanes of Colophon was critical of Homer's anthropomorphism: "But if cattle and horses or lions had hands, and could draw with their hands and make works of art like men, horses would draw the shapes of gods like horses and cattle like cattle, and they would make their bodies of the kind that each had themselves." And: "One god, greatest among gods and men, in no way like mortals in body or in thought."[9]

In spite of the anthropomorphism of the gods, the Indo-European and Dorian tier of the infinite was still unquestionably part of Homer's universe. Zeus stands outside time and presides over the universe, and

Apollo, as sun-god, controls the physical light of the sun and shines metaphysical Light into the soul. Universal being, so present in the mysteries, is missing from the two epic poems, which narrate action, but we know from the Mycenaean mysteries that it was widely known.

The *Iliad*, the oldest work in Western literature, focused on a single unified theme or action as no other literary work had previously done. It is a highly moral work on the wrath of Achilles and the fulfilment of the will of Zeus. Achilles breaks the Greek code of moral behaviour. In his quarrel with Agamemnon he is guilty of *hubris*, pride. In his refusal to accept Agamemnon's attempt to make amends he is guilty of *até*, the infatuation that leads to disaster. He also lacks *aidos* (respect for one's fellow men) by neglecting the gods. The disaster (*nemesis*) comes with the death of Patroclus, his punishment. His revenge on Hector shows a further loss of *aidos*. Homer's heroes perform the correct rituals to the gods, who live on nectar and ambrosia while humans suffer and make sacrifices.[10]

Homer's opinions of the gods are hidden within the anonymity of his epic medium, and the extent to which he departed from the traditional, oral tale is not known. It is likely that he was conveying the senselessness of war. In book 20 of the *Iliad* Zeus summons the gods and gives them liberty to assist either side. At the end of the poem Priam, King of Troy, has lost his son Hector, and Achilles, the main Greek hero and killer of Hector, has lost his friend Patroclus. But such things are the lot of mankind: "For this is the fate that gods have allotted to wretched mortals, to live in sorrow while they themselves are free from care." (*Iliad*, 24.525-6.)

Homer's Odyssey

The *Odyssey* is about the homecoming of Odysseus from Troy after ten years of wandering.

Odysseus encounters the Sirens, the bag of winds, the enchantress Circe who turns men into pigs, the Lotus-eaters and Polyphemus the Cyclops. In the course of his adventures Odysseus visits the Underworld and speaks to the ghosts of Agamemnon and Achilles, whose temper has led him to lose his life in battle. Odysseus never loses sight of his homecoming, of his home, family, friends and affection.

When he returns to Ithaca he adopts the dress of an old beggar and tests the loyalty of his swineherd, his servants, his son and his wife Penelope, who asks if he has any news of her husband. Homer gives us Odysseus's reaction: "Through guile he masked his distress." He kills the suitors. He finally loses his self-control and confirms his identity.

In the *Iliad*, Hector is killed, his wife foresees slavery for herself and death for her son, and things have fallen apart. In the *Odyssey*, Odysseus is reunited with Penelope, who has had parallel sufferings, and order is restored.

Both the *Iliad* and the *Odyssey* are about the breakdown of a moral order thought to be natural and divinely sanctioned, and about the restoration of that order.[11]

In the *Iliad* the moral order breaks down in Achilles' behaviour – his breach of *aidos* and his maltreatment of Hector's body – and is put right when he brings the Achaeans victory. Order is restored when the will of Zeus is fulfilled, and Troy falls to the Achaeans. But the restoration of order is fragile, and the breakdown actually continues into Agamemnon's homecoming, when he is stabbed by his wife's lover Aegisthus in his bath. In the *Odyssey*, Odysseus is seduced by the nymph Calypso on the way home and the suitors move in on Penelope and occupy Odysseus's house. Things are falling apart, but order is restored when Odysseus returns and kills the suitors – with the help of the gods.

Both the *Iliad* and the *Odyssey* evoke the metaphysical aspect of the fundamental theme in an infinite universe ruled by the gods and containing a moral order that leads to immortality in the Underworld or the Elysian Fields.

The Homeric Hymns

Most of the Homeric hymns are about the birth and childhood of gods, and the tone is often humorous and playful. The 'Hymn to Demeter' traces Demeter's wandering in search of Persephone and the founding of the sanctuary at Eleusis. The 'Hymn to Apollo' falls into two parts; the first part is to Apollo of Delos and celebrates Apollo's empire (the only Homeric hymn some assert was really written by Homer), and the second part traces Apollo's arrival at Delphi. The 'Hymn to Hermes' includes the exploits of the infant Apollo, including his discovery of a tortoise and his making of the first lyre. The 'Hymn to Aphrodite' is about her love affair with Anchises, the father of Aeneas.

The 33 Homeric hymns are dedicated to the following gods: Aphrodite, Apollo, Ares, Asclepius, Artemis, Athena, Cybele, Dionysus, Demeter, the Dioscuri, Castor and Polydeuces, Gaia, Helios, Hera, Heracles, Hermes, Hephaestus, Hestia, Pan, Poseidon, Pythian Apollo, Selene and Zeus. They convey the metaphysical aspect of the fundamental theme.

Hesiod

Hesiod was a little later than Homer, perhaps mid-7th century BC. His *Theogony* (or *Birth of the Gods*) set out the powers of the universe and the ruling gods in terms of their genealogy. There were four generations of gods, and Zeus dominated the third generation. Almost the whole of Greek mythology is covered in a genealogical index, anticipating Ovid's *Metamorphoses*. The whole poem is about the infinite's ordering of the universe.

The earlier *Works and Days* gives useful practical advice on how to work hard and do right. It includes vivid advice to farmers that anticipates Virgil's *Georgics* – within an ordered universe ruled by the gods.

Lyric Poets

A secular stream of lyric poetry about Nature, love poetry and drinking songs now appeared. In the 7th century lyric poetry flourished in both east and west through Archilochus of Paros (the first writer of Greek personal poetry), Callinus of Ephesus, Tyrtaeus, Simonides of Amorgos, Terpander of Lesbos, Stesichorus of Sicily and Mimnermus of Colophon. Early in the 6th century Sappho of Lesbos founded a school of lyric poetry with her love verses, and her contemporary Alcaeus of Lesbos told of his wanderings and longings for home.

The elegiac iambic and lyric poetry of the early Ionian Greeks in the 7th and 6th centuries BC was dominated by the gods, despite its secular subjects. For example Anacreon of Teos has a prayer to Artemis and an appeal to Dionysus. The paeans of the 6th/5th-century Pindar were in honour of Apollo or Artemis, and his dithyrambs were to Dionysus.

These Ionian poets reflected the religious culture of their time and with it the metaphysical aspect of the fundamental theme.

Pindar

The 6th/5th-century Pindar was the greatest of the nine lyric poets according to the Roman rhetorician Quintilian. Although much of his work serenaded athletes, victors in successive Games, his main theme was the Light. As C.M. Bowra put it, "Pindar's guiding and central theme is the part of experience in which human beings are exalted or illumined by a divine force, and this he commonly compares with light."[12] An example of this can be found in *Pythian 8*, which serenades the victory of a boy wrestler, Aristomenes of Aegina, in 446BC:

> "Creatures of a day! What is a man?
> What is he not? A dream of a shadow
> Is our mortal being. But when there comes to men
> A gleam of splendour given of heaven,
> Then rests on them a light of glory
> And blessed are their days."[13]

He also wrote of immortality and the transmigration of souls.

The Presocratic Philosophers of the 6th and 5th centuries BC

Homer and Hesiod perpetuated the context of the metaphysical aspect of the fundamental theme in world literature, and it was taken up by the Greek Presocratic philosophers of the sixth and fifth centuries BC. They attempted to explain the physical, natural world. They saw an ordered "cosmos". The Greek *kosmos* meant "the universe as a well-ordered whole" (*Concise Oxford Dictionary*), an ordered, harmonious system. The Ionian philosophers of Miletus and the Greek philosophers who moved to southern Italy were influenced by the monotheism of the Persian god Ahura Mazda, a strong presence in Ionia, which had been ruled by Persia since the 540BC.

Anaximander of Miletus, who flourished c.570BC, saw the world as emerging from the eternal, infinite, "boundless" (*to apeiron*). This was an eternally moving boundless Reality which threw up a finite germ (*gonimon*): the universe. The universe began from a finite germ within the infinite "boundless". (Compare the "infinite and boundless" in the *Tao Te Ching*.)

Xenophanes of Colophon in Ionia, who flourished c.530BC, saw "that which is" as motionless unity: "One god....Always he remains in the same place, moving not at all."[14] Some scholars claim that Xenophanes was an Ionian monist who asserted the unity of being, others that he was a pantheist asserting the unity of the material world of Nature. Theophrastus said: "Xenophanes...supposed that the all is one, or there is one principle, or that what exists is one and all....This 'one and all' is god."[15]

Heracleitus of Ephesus, who flourished c.500BC, held that Reality was fire which had always existed. He held that the world order was an "ever-living fire kindling in measure and being extinguished in measure"[16] that "ever was, and is, and shall be". The ever-living fire was the metaphysical Fire or Light that "ever was, and is, and shall be", and Heracleitus felt that the soul consists of eternal Fire.[17] He saw all opposites as being reconciled in an underlying unity so that although "everything is in a flux" (*panta rhei*)[18], "the way up and the way down are one and the same."[19]

Xenophanes' disciple Parmenides of Elea, who flourished c.450BC, saw the phenomenal world as an illusion, behind which was an immobile Being, the One. This was close to the singularity of modern physics. Space was a plenum: "Nor is it divided, since it all exists alike....It is all full of being."[20] Parmenides asserted the unity of Being as a monist. To him Reality conflicted with the world of appearances, and in his work the Way of Truth conflicts with the Way of Appearance.

Parmenides saw the One as infinite and a single "Whole",[21] according to one view. Melissus of Samos saw the Eleatic One as coming from infinity (*to apeiron*):[22] "It has no [spatial] beginning or end, but is infinite (or always was and always will be)."[23] Others claim that Parmenides saw the phenomenal world, the world of appearances, as finite, but the infinite One was still behind it.

There were, in fact, different views of the One. To Heracleitus, the One was in perpetual flux, and "god" was immanent in things or the sum total of things.[24] To Parmenides, the world of flux was an appearance, an illusion, and the One behind it was immobile.

The Tragic Dramatists of the 6th and 5th centuries BC: Aeschylus, Sophocles and Euripides

The focus of the philosophers on the infinite universe was reflected in the works of three great tragic dramatists of the 6th and 5th centuries, Aeschylus, Sophocles and Euripides.

The spirit of Greek tragedy is essentially religious in conveying a universe ruled by the gods. All three dramatists agreed with that, although there were minor differences of emphasis between them. Aeschylus did not question the existence of the gods or their justice, but saw the handiwork of the gods in everything. He focused on human beings, and considered Orestes' matricide as a moral issue and questioned whether Orestes was right to do what he did.

Aeschylus was the founder of Greek tragedy. He introduced a second actor when there had previously been only one actor and the chorus, and he subordinated the chorus to the dialogue. Of his 90 plays, only seven have survived.

In Aeschylus's *The Persians*, the Persians are guilty of *hubris*, pride, which is resented by the gods and is punished both nationally and, in the case of Xerxes and his mother Atossa, personally. Aeschylus fought against the Persians at Marathon and seems to have been an eyewitness at the sea battle of Salamis, which a messenger describes, and his sympathy with the Persian enemy in their tribulation enhances the play's tragic art. *Hubris* gets in the way of the questing soul's harmony with the infinite gods.

Sophocles accepted Orestes' rightness and concentrated on characterization. He was morally unconcerned, accepting traditional views without making an issue of his traditionalism. He did not think that divine rule required any explanation or defence.

In Sophocles' *Oedipus Tyrannos* ("Oedipus the King"), the gods have fore-ordained human events. At the birth of Oedipus, his parents, Laius, King of Thebes, and Jocasta, were warned by an oracle that their son would kill his father and marry his mother. They gave the baby to a herdsman with instructions to abandon him on a hillside so that they would avoid this fate. The herdsman gave Oedipus to a Corinthian, and he was brought up by Polybus, King of Corinth, believing himself to be Polybus's son. On reaching manhood he learned of the prophecy, and left Corinth to avoid the possibility that the oracle would be fulfilled. As he approached Thebes he was involved in a quarrel where three roads meet. He killed four of the five who were arguing with him, not knowing that their leader was his biological father, Laius. The survivor kept quiet out of fear. Thebes was focused on the Sphinx, who devoured anyone who failed to answer her riddle. The young Oedipus discovered the answer and rid Thebes of the monster. He was hailed as the new king, and married the widowed queen Jocasta, by whom he had four children, including Antigone.

Sixteen years later, at the beginning of the play, Oedipus is seen as a wise, just and happily married king. There has been a plague on Thebes, and it can only be lifted if the murderer of Laius is discovered. Oedipus launches a search for the murderer and vows to avenge Laius "as I would for my own father's sake". The seer Teiresias is asked to help. He knows that Oedipus was the killer and the truth is dragged out of him. But no one believes him. Jocasta had understood that Laius was killed by robbers, and tries to exonerate Oedipus. But she now has inklings of the truth and implores Oedipus to enquire no further. The herdsman arrives, and denies all knowledge of preserving the baby Oedipus out of fear of the consequences. Finally Oedipus realizes that the prophecies have already been fulfilled. He rushes out and stabs out his own eyes. Jocasta hangs herself. In contrast to the wise, just, happy king at the beginning of the play, Oedipus has blinded himself. He laments, "What need had I of seeing, to whose sight nothing was good?" (Line 1329.) He says that Apollo blinded him.

The message of the play is that in a universe ruled by the gods humans' free will is powerless to avert what the gods have decreed. Oedipus's anguished cry when he realizes that he has fulfilled the oracle, "*Io, io, io, io, io,*" "Alas, alas, alas, alas, alas," includes his awareness that the gods have brought his doom to pass. He has been blind in not realizing he had killed his father and married his mother, and the gods were responsible for his blindness, and now he is physically blind as a symbol of his mental ignorance and blindness.

Euripides was more of a modernist than the other two, and less conventional. His characters rebel against the injustice of the fate that is ahead of them. Medea does not accept her doom as Oedipus does, but plots the death of Jason's new bride and of her own children. The terrified chorus lament that man has forgotten the gods.

In Euripides' *Electra* and *Orestes*, Orestes kills his mother Clytemnestra, slayer of his father Agamemnon. It was Apollo who ordered the deed (lines 1244-6). Orestes is therefore destined to be acquitted by the court of the Areopagus, but he cannot escape the ensuing madness. It is made clear that Agamemnon would not have approved of the murder of his widow, and Euripides suggests that humans may be nobler than the gods they worship.

Sophocles said, "Aeschylus gave us men and women of colossal stature. Euripides depicted human nature as it is." He himself drew "men as they should be drawn in tragedy", fully characterized but sufficiently idealized to inspire an audience.[25] In the works of all three, the gods are mentioned at regular intervals, and there are frequent prayers and hymns to them. In Aeschylus's *Oresteia*, Sophocles' Oedipus cycle and Euripides' Trojan and Herakles cycles, the gods are in charge.

An era ended in 406/5BC when both Sophocles and Euripides died, 50 years after Aeschylus. Besides the progress in tragic drama, there had been an advance in the writing of history – Thucydides now stood alongside Herodotus for his reflective narrative on the Peloponnesian War – and also in the writing of comedy, in which Aristophanes had parodied Euripides. Although Athens fell in 404, closing the Peloponnesian War and ending the Athenian Empire, the city-state of Athens remained the literary centre of Greece and soon produced the historian Xenophon and the orator Demosthenes. However, Athens' main claim to distinction in the 4th century was in philosophy.

Plato
By the end of the 5th century BC Greek philosophy passed to the Sophists, who "made a living out of being inventive and clever" (*sophizesthai*), and eventually to Socrates. His dialogues are recorded by his pupil Plato, who wrote that "the Eleatic school, beginning with

Xenophanes and even earlier, starts from the principle of the unity of all things (or explains in its myths that what we call all things are actually one)".[26] One of his most metaphysical dialogues is the *Parmenides*, in which Parmenides, Zeno and Socrates discuss the Theory of Forms. (The *Theaetetus*, *Sophist* and *Politicus* complete a quartet of highly metaphysical dialogues.)

Plato visited Sicily c.388BC, and met Dion, the brother-in-law of the ruling tyrant Dionysus I, who said he would implement Plato's political ideas. In response Plato set out his political ideas in his *Republic*, which describes an ideal state run by philosophers. In this work he addressed the metaphysical aspect of the fundamental theme of world literature by declaring that, at the age of 50 "guardians of the state...must raise the eye of the soul to the universal Light which lightens all things, and behold the Absolute Good".[27]

Plato reflected Parmenides' view that reality differs from appearance in the *Republic* (book VII). There he argues that a fire (Reality) differs from the flickering shadows it throws on the wall of a cave.[28] In other words, the Light, the One, is Reality, and the shadows are appearances and illusory.

Plato is thought to have been an initiate in the Eleusinian mysteries, where he would have been taught to associate a ripe ear of corn with the Light (see p.40).[29] Socrates, too, may have been an Eleusinian initiate. Plato has Socrates say of initiation into the mysteries, "We were surrounded by rays of pure light, being pure ourselves and untainted by this object we call a 'body' and which we carry around with us now, imprisoned like shellfish" (*Phaedrus*, 250c).[30] The Greek language surrounding this passage is filled with the terminology of the Eleusinian mysteries, and has been taken as an admission by Socrates that he was an initiate at Eleusis.[31] (Plato's description in the *Republic*, book VII, of shadows thrown on the wall of a cave by a fire may have been inspired by the fire in the underground vault at Eleusis.)[32]

In *Phaedo* (69a) there is a passage that can be translated:

"There is but one true coin, and it is for this that we must go about exchanging all other things; this coin being the experience of a spiritual light. And perhaps, using its value as our base, and availing of it as our medium of exchange, we may buy and sell all such things as fortitude, temperance and justice; in a word, true virtue, through spiritual light."[33]

Other translators translate "spiritual light" as "wisdom".[34]

Plato is thought to have visited Egypt soon after 399BC, and he may have obtained his view of Reality, including Forms or Ideas (archetypes), from the Egyptian sense that Ra is everywhere. His belief in the immortality of the soul may also have come from his awareness of the Egyptian *akh*.

Plato thought deeply about immortality. In four dialogues he focused on eschatological myths, asserting that the soul is immortal and that the earthly life is one episode in a long journey. In *Gorgias* (523a-527a) he writes of the judgement of souls. In *Phaedo* (107c-115a) philosophers' souls get preferential treatment. In the *Republic* (X. 614b-621d) he writes of the Pamphylian Er's journey into the Other World. Er, a dead soldier, visits the Underworld but is allowed to return to Earth to report what he saw. In *Phaedrus* (253d-257a) he writes of the Winged Soul, comparing the soul's control of bodily passion and reason to a charioteer's control of a team of two horses.

In these myths Plato seeks to justify his theories of Forms and Recollection. He asserts the soul's immortality and the reincarnation or transmigration of souls (an Orphic idea).[35]

In *Laws* (c.360BC) Plato writes of the soul:

"Even in life, what makes each one of us to be what we are is only the soul; and when we are dead, the bodies of the dead are rightly said to be our shades or images; for the true and immortal being of each one of us, which is called the soul, goes on her way to other gods, that before them she may give an account."[36]

Plato reflected all the characteristics of the metaphysical aspect of the fundamental theme for literature: the infinite; Reality; order; the oneness of humankind; similarities in cultures; the being that opens to the Light; virtue; and focus on immortality.

Aristotle
Plato's pupil Aristotle took a different view. He was more of an empiricist and realist. Aristotle held that the world of sensible

phenomena and appearances was real and that "universals" (which Plato called "Ideas") are within the phenomena of Nature. In later summaries it was said that Plato advocated *"universalia ante rem"* ("universals before the thing") whereas Aristotle advocated *"universalia in re"* ("universals in the thing") or *"universalia in rebus"* ("universals in things").

Plato held that reality is Light, and that the phenomena of Nature have manifested from it as shadows. Aristotle held that the phenomena of Nature are, on the contrary, real and are observed by the senses in real sunlight. In other words, the shadows have their own reality, according to Aristotle.

Universalism reconciles the two contrary positions. An Aristotelian approach to contemporary science shows that we are living in an expanding universe, and that the universe can only be expanding into what the Presocratic Greeks called "the infinite" (*to apeiron*), beyond which is the metaphysical Reality from which the Big Bang emerged: the One, the primordial Fire of Heracleitus which is experienced as the Light. Universalism, which takes account of both hidden Reality and the scientific world of appearances, reconciles Plato and Aristotle by reconciling the Light and the so-called shadows it casts.

The views of Plato and Aristotle can be reconciled on this basis. A world in which sensible phenomena and appearances are real conceals a Reality that is hidden. The physical world, which is real, conceals a metaphysical infinite order which shapes it.

Universalist philosophers have a scientific approach to a metaphysical, orderly universe. The scientific approach to its appearances and laws is complemented by the revelation of the infinite law of order that is behind it.

In *The New Philosophy of Universalism* I showed that the universe is now thought to be expanding at an accelerating rate. I saw the expanding universe as the crest of a wave rolling forward, and imagined an astronaut surfer on the advancing expansion.

The expanding universe is space-time. What, then, is the surfer advancing into? What is the blackness around the edge of the expanding universe of space-time? It can only be the infinite, the boundless (*to apeiron*) which surrounds the universe and permeates it.

4th-Century Pastoral Poetry

After Aristotle there were a number of influential 4th-century Greek philosophers, dramatists and poets, notably Epicurus and his fellow student Menander, the dramatist.

Alexander the Great conquered the ancient world and transferred the centre of learning from Athens to Alexandria in Egypt. The Hellenistic poet Theocritus, who mainly lived in Sicily, invented pastoral poetry: idyllic poems about the lives, loves and singing-contests of simple shepherds and herdsmen in remote rural settings and rustic scenes. His bucolic poetry, and that of Callimachus of Cyrene, brought Nature, pictures of outdoor life and the rule of the gods to the townsfolk of Alexandria. All of them fell under the influence of Pan, the god of the countryside. In Menander's *Dyskolos* ("Difficult Man"), for example, Pan emerges from a cave of nymphs in the centre of the stage. The metaphysical aspect of the fundamental theme can still be found in the treatment of the universe in 4th-century pastoral poetry.

Rome

The Etruscans probably emigrated to Italy – Latium – from Anatolia. Their kings go back perhaps to c.1200BC,[37] and certainly to 800BC,[38] and lasted to 509BC. The legendary founding of Rome by the Trojan Aeneas in the 12th century BC, when he was said to have been welcomed by King Evandrus on the Palatine, may have been an early Etruscan contact, Trojans having left Troy and settled in Italy as Etruscans after the Trojan War. (Settlements around the ancient town of Tarquinia can be dated to the 12th century BC.) Rome was founded (or re-founded) by Romulus in c.754BC.

Soon after the Etruscans, c.475BC, the Latin League unified the Italians around Rome, and the Roman culture came to consist of a State religion, the Latin language, coinage, international legions, an urban network, the rule of law and civic institutions inherited through trade from Greece. These Roman cultural benefits were spread across the advanced Eastern provinces to the less-advanced Western provinces.

The Roman State religion was imported. The Etruscans may have accepted Greek influence near the end of their rule over Rome. They brought the prophetic Sibylline Books from the Greek colony at Cumae to Rome. When the Etruscan kings were expelled c.500BC Rome was faced with a shortage of grain and arranged for grain to be imported from Cumae. With it came a new round of Greek religion: the Olympian gods, including the Indo-European Sky-god Dyaeus Pitar, who became Jupiter (Ju-pitar), the Greek Zeus. With it came knowledge of the Sibyl of Cumae and Cumaean notions of the Underworld, including Pluto, god of the Underworld.[39]

Apollo arrived from the Greek colony at Cumae c.431BC. Two years before there had been a plague and according to Livy (4.25.3) on the recommendation of the Sibylline Books a Temple of Apollo Medicus was built to avert the plague.[40]

After the expulsion of the Etruscan kings, a Roman king of the sacred rites (*rex sacrorum*) embodied Jupiter.[41] He was similar to the Pharaoh who embodied Ra. The Roman State religion imported the Light among other foreign ideas. The shrine in the circular Temple of Vesta in the Forum at Rome contained the eternal fire, which had originated in Vedic India and was known to Indo-European Indians as *garhaptya* ("house-father's fire").[42] It was looked after by the Vestal Virgins. The Sky-god, solar god and 13 other solar deities were served by flamens (or more strictly, the Latin *flamines*), "those who blow (the sacred fire)" or "those who burn offerings". The chief flamen was the priest of Jupiter, *Flamen Dialis*.[43]

Roman religion provided order and structure, but was at first practical and organized, reflecting the character of the Roman people and their involvement in growing food on the land and their dependence on the powers of Nature.[44] No important Latin literature has survived from the first five centuries after the founding of Rome as shepherds and farmers tended their flocks and fields. Roman literature began after the First Punic War in the 3rd century BC. During the Punic Wars there was general anxiety, and all gods were appealed to. As a result, the Eastern cults of Astarte, Cybele and Mithras became established in Rome.[45]

Early Roman Poetry and Drama
Roman literature really began when Livius Andronicus, a prisoner-of-war, translated the *Odyssey* into Latin. Andronicus wrote Latin versions of Greek dramas and included the Greek approach to divinity in his works.

Naevius, the first Roman poet, wrote till after the end of the Second Punic War, translating or adapting from Greek originals the *Danaë* (i.e. "Trojans"), *Iphigenia* and *Andromache*, and at the end of his life wrote the first Roman epic, the *Bellum Punicum* about the First Punic War against Carthage. He established a precedent for a story connecting the First Punic War through Aeneas with Troy. Naevius laid the foundation of the Roman epic and Virgil was much in his debt.

Greek mythology had now been co-opted into the metaphysical aspect of the fundamental theme of world literature, and illustrations of the quest of Jason, Theseus, Orpheus and Odysseus contained aspects of the soul's quest for Reality. Roman poets and dramatists began to convey the metaphysical aspect of the fundamental theme through their focus on Greek myths.

Ennius, who was born 30 years after Naevius, wrote *Annales*, a historical epic on the history of the Roman state from the arrival of Aeneas to the events of his own time. The work became *the* Roman classic until Virgil's *Aeneid* dislodged it. He reflected State rituals: he gave an account of a State cult instituted by King Numa, and described a *lectisternium*, a ritual in which images of gods recline on couches at a banquet. Ennius translated two works from Greek with conflicting explanations for divinity. In *Epicharmus* the gods are natural physical presences, yet in *Euhemerus* the gods are former humans honoured for their good deeds.[46]

Plautus (who flourished between Naevius and Ennius) imitated Greek models. He wrote at least 21 comedies – two-thirds of the 130 attributed to him are spurious – and all owe their construction to the Greek originals of Philemon, Diphilus and Menander,[47] and draw on Greek mythology in which the Greek gods are in charge. His *Amphitryo* moves between the Greek god Hermes and his Latin counterpart Mercury, and revels in Rome's dual heritage with many puns, for example on words beginning "merc" (suggesting Mercury). His fellow dramatist Terence, a Berber born in Carthage who was brought to Rome as a slave, also based his plays on Greek originals by Menander or Apollodorus.

In these early works fragments of the metaphysical aspect of the fundamental theme of world literature were transmitted from the Greeks to the Romans through Greek mythology. Early Roman literature reflected this metaphysical aspect of the fundamental theme in their historical epic poems and comedies.

Early Roman Golden Age: Lucretius

The Golden Age in Roman literature began in the 1st century BC with Lucretius, whose didactic philosophical poem *De Rerum Natura* ("On the Nature of Things") is an imitation of the scientific works of the Greek philosopher Empedocles, a follower of Epicurus. It seems to be a materialistic work, referring to atoms long before they were discovered, and it seems to deny the metaphysical aspect of the fundamental theme, but its philosophy is close to the thinking of Gilgamesh: there is no eternal life, and men can free themselves from "anguish and distress of mind" and pursue pleasure (an Epicurean idea). The first line "*Aeneadum genetrix, hominum divumque voluptas*" ("Mother of the Aeneadae, pleasure of men and gods") addresses Venus as a figure of politics, myth and philosophy.[48] He invokes her as Muse, creator and guarantor of imperial peace. Lucretius contradicts the idea that in Epicureanism the gods do not intervene in mundane affairs.

Catullus

Catullus was influenced by the Greeks and Alexandrean poets such as Theocritus of Sicily (c.300-260BC) and Callimachus of Cyrene (c.305-240BC); hence his Alexandrine lines. He looked back to the brevity and direct style of Sappho, which he adapted to Latin in describing his affair in Verona with Lesbia, named after Sappho's Lesbos. She was later identified by Apuleius more than 150 years later as Clodia, sister of P. Clodius, Cicero's enemy, an immoral woman who turned Catullus's love into disgust and hatred.[49] Clodia was seven years older than Catullus, who was at first infatuated by her and soon came to loathe her because of her infidelities. He says she had 300 lovers, "bursting their groins" (11.15-24), and that she became a prostitute and went with anybody, including Egnatius (37). She was to be found plying her trade in alleyways (58).

Although regarded as a modernist, Catullus also wrote of archaic piety: "*Dianae sumus in fide*" (Poem 34 – "We are in trust of Diana"). In 'Peleus and Thetis', which reflects Greek mythology, he writes of the Golden Age: "In former times heaven-dwellers used to visit heroes' chaste homes in their full bodily presence and show themselves to mortal gathering when piety had not yet been spurned" (64.384-6). But, he says, after the age of sin began, the gods did not show themselves to humans. Human beings therefore no longer experienced the divine presence. Jupiter visited mortals during the Golden Age but now, Catullus says, humans and gods no longer eat together. In writing of gods visiting homes, Catullus may have been describing a *lectisternium* (images of gods at a banquet). In poem 68 Catullus shows a "shining goddess" ("*candida diva*"), who is actually his girlfriend arriving. She is seen in terms of an epiphany, or revelation, of a goddess.

Catullus writes of the fundamental theme of world literature in its absence, by saying it no longer happens. Jupiter does not visit homes and the only hint of a goddess is his girlfriend. In Catullus's work the Golden Age may be over and gods may not visit directly any more, but there is a strong sense of the soul seeking divine blessings among the explicit poems to Lesbia. In his envoy he prays that his addressee will receive divine blessings of the kind once bestowed by Thetis, and the world of the gods is never far away.

Prose: Cicero and Caesar

The 1st century BC was a stormy time. The Cataline conspiracy attempted to destroy the republic, and Julius Caesar fought a civil war with Pompey. It was a time when political eloquence flourished, and the key figure was Cicero, who modelled himself on the Greek Demosthenes and advanced Roman prose. He made four speeches as consul that saved Rome from the Cataline conspiracy – he talked of the gods' direct guidance and support against Cataline in a speech to the people – and 12 Philippic orations after the assassination of Julius Caesar. Cicero's philosophical dialogues, such as *De natura deorum* and *De divinatione* reflect his view that (despite his apparent secular worldly wisdom) the gods were behind everything. At home he entrusted the cult of the gods to his wife but always cultivated Minerva during political crises and spent months planning a shrine (*fanum*) for his dead daughter to achieve apotheosis. These works heralded in the Roman Golden Age of prose.

The role of the gods was emphasized in Varro's *Antiquitates rerum divinarum*, which amassed antiquarian material about Roman religion.

Julius Caesar's commentaries on the Gallic and civil wars were in the tradition of Thucydides, and his true beliefs about the gods can be gleaned from the fact that after ten volumes of silence about the gods in his *Commentarii* he cites a mass of omens and divine signs after his arrival in Asia:

> "It was established by counting back the total number of days that in the temple of Minerva at Elis, on the day that Caesar had fought his successful battle, a statue of Victory which had been placed in front of Minerva and had formerly faced the statue of Minerva had turned around towards the doors and threshold of the temple. On the same day, at Antioch in Syria, on two occasions there had been heard such a loud noise of an army shouting and trumpets sounding that the people put on armour and rushed to defend the walls. This same thing happened at Ptolemais. And in Pergama, in the hidden and secret temples, where it is forbidden for anyone but the priests to enter (the Greeks call them *adyta*), drums sounded. In Tralles, likewise, in the temple of Victory, where they had dedicated a statue of Caesar, they pointed out a palm tree which had sprung up in that period out of the pavement between the joints of the stones." (*De bello civili*, 3.1.5.3-6.)[50]

Caesar's travels were responsible for introducing the cult of Isis in the 1st century BC following his contact with Cleopatra, Queen of Egypt (who also had a love affair with Mark Antony and contact with Octavian).[51]

Virgil

The height of the Golden Age was the Augustan Age, which succeeded the Ciceronian Age. After the Battle of Philippi, armies were disbanded. Tired of wars, men delighted in living in tranquillity. Virgil's pastoral *Eclogues* imitated Theocritus. They told of cattle seeking the cool of the shade and the activities of shepherd boys (including one called Lycidas) and of the likes of the shepherdess Amaryllis.

However, Virgil introduced into his poetry an element of political allegory which had been largely absent in Theocritus. His vision of the Golden Age can be found in the fourth Eclogue, in which he intimated that a new Golden Age of peace and justice was about to return, which would perhaps counter Horace's pessimism in his sixteenth epode:

"*Ultima Cumaei venit iam carminis aetas;*
magnus ab integro saeclorum nascitur ordo:
iam redit et virgo, redeunt Saturnia regna;
iam nova progenies caelo demittitur alto."

"Now the last age of Cumae's prophecy has come;
The great succession of centuries is born afresh.
Now too returns the Virgin; Saturn's rule returns;
A new begetting now descends from heaven's height."[52]

This has been called the "Messianic Eclogue" as it seems to foretell, in 40BC, the birth of a child who would bring back the Golden Age. The child may be Octavian's or Antony's rather than Jesus, and the language is probably Sibylline rather than influenced by Hebrew.

His *Georgics* (published two years after the battle of Actium) were about the tillage of the land, his father's cornfields, coppices and hives. The work was influenced by Hesiod, Aratos and Lucretius, and its title (*georgica*, Greek for "books on farming") was taken from Nikandros.

The Aeneid

All epics have one of two plots: war and a quest or journey. The *Iliad* is about war, the *Odyssey* about a journey. The *Aeneid* combines the two: a journey in the first half and war in the second. (I combined the two in my epics: both Eisenhower and Bush are on a journey while they fight their wars in *Overlord* and *Armageddon*.)

The metaphysical aspect of the fundamental theme of world literature, the soul's quest for the infinite, is present within the *Aeneid*. Aeneas's quest for knowledge about Rome's coming greatness takes him to the Underworld and reunion with his father. He inhabits a universe in which the gods are in charge:

Juno, wife of Jupiter, is opposed to Aeneas in book 1. She persuades the wind-god Aeolus to scatter his fleet, which is blown towards Africa and Carthage. After Dido's suicide he returns to his kinsman Acestes in

Segesta, Sicily, where his father dies. In book 4, Juno, appearing in human form, persuades Trojan women to burn his ships. Four are destroyed. The shade of his father has asked him to descend to the Underworld to consult him, and he goes to the Sibyl at Cumae, who tells him he must find the golden bough to gain entry into the lower world. Eventually, in the Elysian Fields he meets the beatified spirit of his father and is shown a pageant of the souls of future Romans awaiting reincarnation, including Augustus. The cosmology adopted by Virgil suggests Pythagoreanism, with souls, polluted by experience on Earth having to be purified and cleansed in a kind of Purgatory before they can be born again. The beatified (the *pauci* or "few", 6.744) live permanently in Elysium. The metaphysical aspect of the fundamental theme of world literature, the purification of the soul to achieve union with the Light, is strongly present in Aeneas's visit to the Underworld.

The second half of the *Aeneid* is about Italy. In book 7 he meets Latinus, king of Latium, and his daughter Lavinia, whose suitor is Turnus, king of the Rutuli. Latinus wants Aeneas to marry Lavinia. Juno intrigues strife between Aeneas and Turnus. After a summary of Roman history in book 8, Aeneas visits Rome and in his absence Juno intrigues for Turnus to attack the Trojans' walled camp. In book 10, at a council of the gods and an angry debate between Juno and Venus, Jupiter declares that the outcome of the war must be left to Fate. Aeneas returns reinforced by Etruscans and there is an inconclusive battle, in the course of which his friend Pallas is killed. A truce is declared to bury the dead. Aeneas offers to settle the war in a single combat with Turnus. This takes place and Turnus is wounded and pleads for this life. Aeneas sees he is wearing Pallas's belt and kills him. During this narrative there are many references to traditional religious practices, which suggest Virgil's piety towards the gods.

Virgil's *Aeneid* looked back to Homer and a universe controlled by the gods. Virgil took over the Olympians from Homer, but the anthropomorphic gods are less satisfactory and more tedious as his tone is loftier than Homer's and the wrangling of the gods seems unworthy. The gods seem intruders. Nevertheless, they are present and order the universe as forces at work in human affairs, and mortals have epiphanies, moments of revelation, when gods appear to them. For example, in book 1 of the *Aeneid*, Aeneas is beautified by his mother Venus as he meets Dido. Aeneas " shone in the bright light, similar to a god in his face shoulders" (1.588-9). Where Catullus lamented that the gods were absent, Virgil celebrated their presence.

In Homer the Olympians are opposed by *"moira"* (or Moera, fate). In the *Aeneid*, the concept of Fate (*Fatum*) creates problems. Aeneas is a "chosen vessel" (*fato profugus*), and so the opposition of Juno is doomed to failure and seems foolish. Nevertheless, Aeneas's quest is on the metaphysical aspect of the fundamental theme.

Horace

Virgil's friend Horace – they journeyed to Brundisium in 37BC (Horace, *Satires*, 1.v) – lacked Virgil's depth of thought and breadth of reading. A soldier in Brutus's army who fought against Octavian/Augustus and was taken up by the patron Maecenas, who gave him his Sabine farm, he came to revere Augustus. He took his models from Greece: Archilochus of Paros, Alcaeus of Lesbos and Sappho. And he preached the Aristotelian doctrine of the Golden Mean (moderation in all things) in exquisitely crafted verse. Though a man of the world who enjoyed friends, books and wine, Horace's world was dominated by the gods.

The *Epodes* belong to the time after Philippi when he was poor and friendless. He had lost his father's small estate and become a Treasury scribe. Slight, immature works, the *Epodes* show the influence of Archilochus' iambics and are full of invective, love and wine. His *Satires* (c.35BC) or *sermones* (sermons), chatty essays, are full of self-revelation, and are based on the satires of Lucilius. He spent seven years writing his *Odes*, which are influenced by Archilochus and Pindar, and follow Catullus in bringing "Aeolian verse to Italian measures" (*Odes* 3.30.13). The first three books came out together in 23BC and include an ode to the ship carrying Virgil to Greece some time before Virgil's last voyage in 19BC.

In Horace's *Odes* the gods are present as is the metaphysical aspect – along with the secular aspect – of the fundamental theme. He praises Jupiter and other gods. He hymns Diana, Venus and Mercury, and blatantly imitates Pindar. Pindar in his second Olympian asks the Muse, "What god, what hero, what man shall we celebrate?" and answers:

64

Zeus, Heracles and Theron (the athlete he was serenading). Horace in his *Odes* (1.12) asks the Muse, "What man, hero or god shall we celebrate?" and after referring to Jupiter, Pallas and Liber (Dionysus), answers: Augustus, who is all three, following the establishing of the imperial cult.[53] Horace foretells his own immortality as a swan, Apollo's sacred bird.

Horace addresses gods as rustic images of piety (*Odes* 1.4; 3.8, 13, 18, 22-3). But in 3.22 he addresses Diana as he plants a pine by his villa and sacrifices a pig. This poem has been shown to have been written on 13 August, the birthday of Diana's temple on the Aventine Hill in Rome, and the day of Diana's festival in Italy. (It was the day Virgil's hero Aeneas spent in Evander's hut on the Palatine Hill where Augustus's palace would arise, along with temples to Diana and Apollo.) In other words, the private rites were linked with public rites, and Horace was writing within the context of the State religion.[54] In 3.23 Horace assures a rustic lady that her sacrifices have a role within Roman religion as they appease the Lares (household gods) and protect Italy from national disasters. Again the private rites of the *Odes* are linked to public rites.

Horace's late work made open reference to public rites, for Augustus commissioned him to write *Carmen saeculare* ("Song of the Age").[55] Horace undertook the work as an official duty in the same vein as a modern Poet Laureate. The *ludi saeculares* ("saecular games", ceremonial games held every *saeculum* or hundred years),[56] first staged in 249BC when the Sibylline oracle issued instructions, were revived by Augustus in 17BC, two years after the death of Virgil. The *Acta* of Augustus (discovered in 1890) record: "*Carmen composuit Q Horatius Flaccus*" ("the hymn was composed by Q Horatius Flaccus"),[57] and that a *carmen* was sung twice on the last of the three days of the *ludi* before Apollo Palatinus and then before Jupiter Optimus Maximus. On the first night, 31 May, Augustus sacrificed in the Campus Martius, Rome, wearing Greek dress. At night he sacrificed nine male lambs and nine female kids to the Moerae (Greek) or Parcae (Latin), the Fates, and a pregnant sow to Terra Mater (Mother Earth). Augustus and Agrippa each sacrificed a bull to Jupiter and a cow to Juno.[58]

In the *Carmen*, Greek and Roman rituals blended:

Horace begins by invoking Apollo and Diana. Stanza 2 is about Apollo's role as the new custodian of the Sibylline verses that controlled the *ludi*. Stanza 3 invokes Apollo as Sol, the sun, or Helios. There is an address to Ilithyia, goddess of childbirth. There are prayers to the Fates and the Earth.

Horace then returns to Apollo and Diana. The *Carmen* seems to turn to Jupiter and Juno, who must be addressed according to the *Acta*. However, they are not named. Virgil had suppressed the names of Apollo and Diana in his invocation in the *Georgics*, referring to them as "the extremely bright lights of the universe" (*clarissima mundi/lumina*, 1.5-6), and Horace now compensates for the suppressal of their names by invoking Apollo and his sister Diana as Phoebus, Sol, Lucina and Luna. Horace in turn suppresses Jupiter and Juno except for a brief mention of Jove (i.e. Jupiter) as Sky-god in line 32 and a mention of Jupiter's approval of the regime of Apollo and Diana in the last stanza. In other words, the Capitoline gods of the Republic have been replaced in the ritual by the Palatine gods of Augustus's Principate, and Horace's *Carmen* or song leaves Republican ritual behind to promote the new Augustan policy.

In the *Carmen* Horace presents Augustus's present actions as the fulfilment of the text of the *Aeneid*. Anchises, Aeneas's father, had prophesied that Augustus would achieve world dominance (*Aeneid* 6.792-800, lines that became a Sibylline oracle). Anchises says, in Sibylline language, "Remember, Roman,...to spare the conquered and battle down the proud" (*Aeneid* 6.851-3). In the *Carmen* Augustus is "superior to the one waging war, gentle to the prostrate enemy" (51-52), and his empire is world-wide (53-6). The *Carmen* tells us that Virgil's and Augustus's Sibylline oracles have come to pass.[59]

Officially the *Carmen* is a poem and not a rite, but by stating Augustus's new religious policy regarding Apollo and Diana so clearly, the *Carmen* has the force of a new rite.

Although Horace is more superficial than Virgil and his poems reflect a narrow range of subject, with limits of thought and feeling in accordance with the "golden mean", and would verge on the dull but for their minute elaboration and felicity, the metaphysical aspect of the fundamental theme of world literature can be found in his work as the soul opens to Apollo during private and public rites. Augustus is a god like the Egyptian Pharaoh under the developing imperial cult which came to see the Roman Emperor as a god during his lifetime. The cult socialised divinity. In *Odes* 3.25 Horace writes of "how to insert the eternal glory of Caesar among the stars and the council of Jupiter?" In *Epistles* 2.1.5-17 Horace says that Augustus is superior to the other demi-gods as he is honoured during his lifetime as a god rather than having to wait until after his death. Poets are the "temple-keepers" (*aeditui*) of the great (229-31). In Augustus's case the temple-keepers are Virgil, Horace and Varius (*Carmen*, 247).[60]

Elegists: Tibullus and Propertius

The metaphysical aspect of the fundamental theme also lurks within the works of the elegists Cornelius Gallus, Tibullus and Sextus Propertius.

Tibullus (who hated war and thought constantly of Delia, a plebeian named Plania) writes of rustic piety, following Callimachus. The first poem of his second book enacts a festival of purification, the Ambarvalia celebrated in late May for his local farm, a ritual that controlled the environment. It warded off disasters during ploughing and weaving, and being overrun by weeds and wolves.

Propertius, who was also influenced by Callimachus, writes of Cynthia (whose real name was Hostia, who died c.18BC). But he also writes about the cults of Bona Dea ("The good goddess") and Hercules at the Ara Maxima (4.9). He commemorated the *ludi quinquennales* for the festival of Apollo Palatine in 16BC. In poem 31 he tells Cynthia he is late because he has been looking at the new temple of Apollo Palatinus.[61] The elegists focused on everyday life within a universe whose natural rhythms were dominated by the gods.

Ovid

Ovid's debut was his love-elegies on Corinna (who may not have had a real-life inspirer like Lesbia, Delia or Cynthia). These elegies passed into *Amores*. The six books of the *Fasti* present a calendar for half the year, a record of festivals and anniversaries drawn from astronomy, history, legend, folk-lore and religion. Ovid's aim was to study ritual in the light of ancient records (*"annalibus eruta priscis"*, *Fasti,* 1.7-10).[62] They seem to be based on the *Aetia* of Callimachus. Book 6 includes a long section on Vesta's feast day on 9 June (249-348).

Ovid asks how Vesta could best be represented in art. He claims to be aware of a divine power communicating with him (251-6): "I was lost in prayer: I felt the influence of celestial divinity, and the glad earth gleamed with purple light. Not that I saw you, goddess – away with the lies of bards! – you were not one to be seen by a man. But the things I didn't know, concerning which I was held in error, were understood without anyone giving me information."

Metamorphoses

Though influenced by Virgil, Ovid produced a work that is not unified enough to be regarded as epic but is often (wrongly) regarded as epic: *Metamorphoses*. In 15 books based on Theocritus he adopted a systematic, encyclopaedic approach to mythography, focusing on bodies transformed into new shapes. Many of his chosen myths present gods. The metaphysical aspect of the fundamental theme of world literature, the quest for Reality, is in the transformations he recounts; for example, in his tales of Jason, Orpheus, Ulysses and Aeneas.

Ovid restates the metaphysical aspect of the fundamental theme in terms of mythology and transformation in 250 mythical tales which span from the creation of the world to the reign of Augustus. The underlying theme of the arrangement of the myths in *Metamorphoses* is of the transformation of chaos into an ordered universe.[63] The transformation of chaos is followed by a sweep through Greek mythology, which embodies and illustrates stages of the fundamental quest, beginning with Jupiter reporting to the gods on the transformation of man into beast and continuing with Apollo's slaying of the python and love for Daphne and with myths of quest: Jason, Theseus, Orpheus and Ulysses. Ovid progesses to the Trojan War.

The metaphysical aspect of the fundamental theme can be found in both Greek mythology and the Trojan War, as we have seen. Ovid presents the escape of Aeneas to Italy, the Roman kings, the transformation of Julius Caesar into a star – reminiscent of the Egyptian Pharaoh becoming the sun-god and dwelling among the circumpolar stars – which is to the glory of his adopted son Augustus. Book 15 asserts that it is the greatest glory of Julius Caesar to be "father" of Augustus.

But Ovid's flattery of Augustus did him no good. In AD8 he was banished by Augustus to Tomis on the Black Sea, his books were withdrawn from Roman libraries to counter his claim in the last lines of *Metamorphoses*, "If there be any truth in poets' prophecies, I shall live to all eternity, immortalized by fame." He himself said he committed "two crimes, a song and a blunder" ("*duo crimina carmen et error*", *Tristia*, 2.207). No doubt his *Ars Amatoria* ("The Art of Love"), which some felt was depraved, was the "*carmen*", for Augustus was trying to restore morality and marriage and would have felt undermined by Ovid, whose verses he may have held responsible for the adultery of his granddaughter, the younger Julia, with D. Silanus. But the work was ten years old when he was banished, and can only have been a pretext for the banishment. The "error" seems to have involved his accidental discovery of hidden information about the Julio-Claudian dynasty, which Augustus wanted to keep secret. It may have involved his daughter Julia. (I wrote a verse play, *Ovid Banished*, on the tyrannical persecution of the artist by the embodiment of the world government of the Roman time, and further details are discussed in the Preface to that work.)

Ovid's artifice made some of his earlier work seem artificial. His elegiac last works from exile, the autobiographical *Tristia* and *Epistolae ex Ponto*, reveal a wretched soul who longs for Rome and pleads unsuccessfully to be allowed back.

In the poems of Catullus, Virgil's *Eclogues* and *Georgics*, Horace's *Odes*, Ovid's *Amores* and in the elegies of Tibullus and Propertius a secular stream of verse exists alongside the metaphysical aspect of the fundamental theme.

Seneca and Lucan

The Golden Age included the history of Livy but was already in decline when Seneca wrote, "They have forgotten to speak the Latin tongue at Rome." He expounded Stoic philosophy in 12 Dialogues and wrote his tragedies, which worked out the Stoic doctrine of practical necessity in action. These plays would influence Corneille and Racine, and the Elizabethan dramatists including Shakespeare. Seneca's nephew Lucan wrote an epic poem, *Pharsalia* (on the civil war between Pompey and Caesar), which breaks off in the tenth book of a 12-book scheme. It is a vision of the dying Republic as the Roman people suffer from a fratricidal civil war and are subjected to slavery under Caesar's tyranny. The work is an anti-*Aeneid* in the sense that it despises rather than glorifies Augustus's forebear, Julius Caesar.

The Silver Age

The Silver Age of Roman literature accommodated Statius, the Elder Pliny, Martial, Quintilian, Tacitus, Juvenal (who satirized vices), the Younger Pliny, Suetonius, Apuleius, the *Pervigilium Veneris* ("The Night Watch of Venus"), Tertullian and other Latin-Christian patristic writers. The metaphysical aspect of the fundamental theme of world literature can be found in a number of their works, and in the works of Lesser Augustans and other Roman authors too numerous to consider here. In this work I am stating the two aspects of the fundamental theme of world literature in terms of the line of the Universalist tradition, and it is important to preserve the clarity of the line by concentrating on the main reflecters of the metaphysical and secular aspects of the fundamental theme in each age, and not to clutter it with too many minor writers.

The Christian Classical World

The end of the classical period in the Imperial Roman world was marked by the steady rise of Christianity.

The New Testament

The *New Testament* reflects the metaphysical aspect of the fundamental theme of world literature.

The three synoptic Gospels (*Mark, Matthew* and *Luke*, ADc.65-83) describe Jesus's transfiguration by the Light on Mount Tabor in ADc.28, and his Gilgamesh-like quest for eternal life in Heaven. Jesus was a preacher of the Light, and many of the parables were about the Light.[64] He came into conflict with the Sadducean Jewish hierarchy and the Roman Governor and was crucified.

St John's Gospel of Light (ADc.100) presents a different view of Jesus, emphasizing a number of "I am" pronouncements, most notably "I am the light of the world" (8.12). John moved away from the historical Jesus of the three synoptic Gospels. He was defending

Christianity against Gnosticisn and associated Jesus with the Light of *gnosis* to attract Gnostics to Christianity. He also identified Jesus as the Lamb of God.

St Paul experienced the Light on the road to Damascus in ADc.35, and an account of his experience appears in the *Acts* (ADc.85). He told the Jews of Antioch in ADc.46 that the Lord had told him, "I have set thee to be a light of the Gentiles" (*Acts* 13.47). Paul Gentilized the Light in the course of his travels and letter-writing. The metaphysical aspect of the fundamental theme lurks behind Paul's account of his travels: his quest for eternal life which ended in his being martyred (probably beheaded) in Rome in AD68.

The Dead Sea Scrolls

The literature of the *New Testament* was written alongside a stream of unofficial gospels preserved at Qumran as the Dead Sea Scrolls, most notably the Essene gospels in the buried Essene library. Gospels such as the Essene *Book of Jesus* portray Jesus as an Essene Master preaching to "Children of Light". Again, the metaphysical aspect of the fundamental theme is behind these Essene scriptures: Jesus teaches the Light as he progresses towards eternal life.

Gnostic Gospels

Gnostic gospels emerged in Syria and then Egypt in the 1st and 2nd centuries AD. They rivalled Christianity before 150, putting forward a syncretistic universalist religion. They blended Iranian dualism; the thought of Mesopotamia, India and Greece; and Judaism and Christianity. Their texts presented the metaphysical aspect of the fundamental theme: they hold that man's spirit (*pneuma* or "spark") is enclosed in his soul (*psyche*), and when the *pneuma* is lit a man is illumined and knows the Light. His resulting *gnosis* or knowledge releases him from his imprisoning body to return to the divine realm after death.

The texts of Basilides and Valentinus (who may have been the author of the Valentinian *Gospel of Truth* c.150), the *Gospel of Marcion of Sinope*, the *Apocryphon of John* ("Secret Work of John"), the Naasene *Gospel of Thomas* and the texts of the Mandaeans or Sabaeans of Syria/Palestine – all told the story of the metaphysical aspect of the fundamental theme with their own variations.[65]

Hermetic and Neoplatonist Texts

Related Gnostic texts emerged in Alexandria. The Hermetic pagan *Corpus Hermeticum* (middle of 1st century-end of 3rd century) consisted of 18 discourses, of which *Poimandres* is the first. It begins with a vision in which the Light is described as the *Nous* (Mind), which is seen by human *nous* (mind). The Hermetic *nous* replaced the Gnostic *pneuma*, and the metaphysical aspect of the fundamental theme lurks behind the Hermetic view of the universe.

The Hermetic, Gnostic mysteries influenced Neoplatonism, a syncretistic Alexandrian philosophy which sought to return to the Light of the One. Its founder, Plotinus (3rd century BC) drew on Plato's *Dialogues* and his Ideas or Forms. Plotinus proclaimed One Reality and a hierarchy of Forms in the divine mind. An ascetic human soul could ascend to the One through *Nous* back to the One: "We may believe that we have really seen, when a sudden light illumines the soul: for this light comes from the One and is the One." (*Enneads*, VI, 9,9.) The soul makes the "flight of the alone to the Alone" into union with the One. In the *Enneads*, Plotinus restated the metaphysical aspect of the fundamental theme.

Manichaean Texts

The Manichaean Iranian texts, the system of Mani (3rd century) set out in *Kephalaia*, were also in keeping with the metaphysical aspect of the fundamental theme. Mani's *gnosis* was expressed in the form of a creation myth. Light and Darkness were infinite and always existed. Darkness aggressed against the Light and produced Adam and Eve, the first humans. Light sent the luminous Jesus to Adam and made him eat of the Tree of Knowledge. Humans were thus creatures of Darkness with a modicum of Light within them.

Mani was an "Apostle of the Light" ("messenger of the Light") and claimed to be superior to Jesus, to be the "supreme Illuminator". Like Jesus he suffered. His passion at the hands of the Zoroastrian Magi lasted 26 days, and he was executed in chains. The metaphysical aspect of the fundamental theme lurks behind the *Kephalaia* and in Mani's life, for the soul is on a quest to escape bodily imprisonment and return to the Light.

Clement of Alexandria's Miscellanies

The Gnostic Light dimmed in the 3rd century. Christian theologians defended Christianity and largely obliterated Gnostic writings. Irenaeus, Bishop of Lyons, had defined mainstream Christianity, and Tertullian, another anti-Gnostic Father, reinforced this hostility to Gnosticism in his writings. The main attack on Gnosticism came from the Alexandrian School. Alexandria had produced the pagan Light of Hermetic thought, Alchemy and Neoplatonism, and in the 2nd century it produced Clement of Alexandria.

A Universalist, Clement reconciled the opposite creeds of his day. He distinguished Christian Gnostics who lived according to the Gospels and the Light, and orthodox Christians who lived according to the Law. His Alexandrian School defeated Gnosticism by re-Christianising the Gnostic Light. Clement blended Greek Platonism, the Judaic Mosaic tradition and Christianity.

Clement's *gnosis* was knowledge of God: becoming a part of the Being of God, an experience which anticipated the experience of immortality. In *Miscellanies* (7.10.57) he writes: "And so knowledge easily translates the soul to the Divine and Holy which is akin to it, and by its own light conveys a man through the stages of mystery until it restores him at last through the supernal place of rest, teaching the man who is pure of heart to gaze on God, face to face, with perfect silence and understanding." Clement restated the metaphysical aspect of the fundamental theme.

The Golden Ass

The Roman Empire Romanized the local gods throughout the Empire and identified them with the gods of Roman State religion. Jupiter was adopted in place of Zeus, Taran, Baal and Sol, and the Germanic Wotan/Odin became Mercury. The syncretizing process gathered force from the Christian movement towards monotheism, and Jupiter-Sol became the chief Roman god in the 3rd century. The Isis mysteries involved the Light.

In *The Golden Ass* by Apuleius,[66] Lucius is initiated into the Isis mysteries in Corinth. The priest's head was shaved, and a metal receptacle for alcohol was placed on it. The alcohol was set alight in a dark room, and it shone for some seconds. Lucius reports that there "came from Isis a Light and other unutterable things conducive to salvation....I will record as much as I may lawfully record for the uninitiated....At midnight I saw the sun shining as if it were noon." The metaphysical aspect of the fundamental theme lurks behind this description: the soul turns away from the senses and, following the example of the light in a darkened room caused by blazing alcohol on the priest's head, experiences the metaphysical Light.

Sayings of the Desert Fathers

The Desert Fathers now restated the metaphysical aspect of the fundamental theme. Constantine founded Constantinople and made it the Roman capital in 330. There was now an alliance between the Church and the Roman State, and many contemplatives chose to leave for the deserts of Egypt, Syria and Palestine in the 4th century. They joined ascetics driven into the desert by the Roman persecutions of Decius. (In 250 all Roman citizens were ordered to sacrifice to the Roman State gods in the presence of commissioners, and many Christians defied this edict.)

Many had been influenced by Manichaean asceticism and by Clement's Christian Gnosticism. In the clean desert air many lived to great ages. Anthony the Hermit, who lived to be 105, Pachomius, Gregory of Nyssa and St Ephraem Syrus in the 360s, and John the Dwarf all reflected the metaphysical aspect of the fundamental theme in sayings that passed into print:[67] their souls withdrew from the life of the senses and were (in the words of Gregory of Nyssa) "made bright and luminous...in communion with the real Light". Christ acted on their souls as fire that burns away the impurity of iron (as John of Lycopolis said). John Cassian of Marseilles was trained as a hermit in the Egyptian desert, where he spent seven years. He described how the soul is caught up in an ecstasy he called the "prayer of fire".

The Eastern desert mystics prepared the way for Eastern Orthodox Christianity, which emphasized the Divine Light of the Transfiguration.

Augustine and Gregory

In the West, Christianity absorbed the challenges from Manichaeism and Neoplatonism through St Augustine, who was a Manichaean from 371 to 382 and then a Neoplatonist until his conversion in 386. His

Christian Neoplatonism was a Christian adaptation of pagan Neoplatonism.

The metaphysical aspect of the fundamental theme of world literature was perpetuated by Augustine in his *Confessions* (c.400), which are about his quest for a Reality he perceived as Light:

"I entered (within myself). I saw with the eye of my soul, above (or beyond) my mind, the Light unchangeable. It was not the common light of day that is seen by the eye of every living thing of flesh and blood....What I saw was something quite, quite different from any light we know on Earth. It shone above my mind....It was above me (or higher), because it was itself the Light that made me, and I was below (or lower) because I was made by it. All who know the truth know this Light, and all who know this Light know eternity." (7.10.)

In his *De Civitate Dei* ("City of God") Augustine praises the Platonists for saying that: "the light of our minds for learning all things is the same God Himself by Whom all things were made" (8.7), and he sees humankind as One in the "City of God": all humankind are citizens of God. He seeks to understand the experience:

"This power of reason...withdrew my thoughts from their normal course and drew back from the confusion of (sensuous) images which pressed upon it, so that it might discover what light it was that had been shed upon it....And so, in an instant of awe, my mind attained to the sight (vision) of the God who IS. Then, at last I caught sight of your invisible nature." (7.17.)

Both these works show the infinite Reality as Light, the order of the universe, which can be known behind the normal mind. In its Oneness immortality and eternity can be found.

The metaphysical aspect of the fundamental theme can be found in the works of Augustine's contemporary, Prudentius, whose allegorical *Psychomachia* ("The Contest of the Soul") and poems on Christian doctrine used the symbolism of light and darkness.

The second school of Benedictine practical contemplative prayer derived from the desert mystics, especially John Cassian. St Benedict's

Dialogues speak of "a light shed from above" that "dissipated all the darkness of the night" (*Dialogues* 2.35). The writings of Pope Gregory the Great, who reluctantly became pope in 590, were in the Benedictine contemplative tradition. In *Homilies on Ezekiel* he introduces the metaphysical aspect of the fundamental theme (2.2.12-14): "There is in contemplation a great effort of the mind when it raises itself up to heavenly things....And sometimes indeed it prevails and soars above the resisting darkness of its blindness, so that it attains to somewhat of the unencompassed (or boundless) Light (*lumen incircumscriptum*)." He writes of "the light of interior quiet".[68] Pope Gregory's Light inspired and Christianized the Dark Ages.

In absorbing the Manichaean and Neoplatonist Lights Augustine let into Christianity the Manichaean view that sexual desire belonged to Darkness and the Devil (the Iranian Ahriman), and set the pattern for the Middle Ages.

Literary Summary

The main references to the metaphysical aspect of the fundamental theme of world literature in the classical world are as follows:

- The infinite that surrounds the universe is in: Homer; Anaximander's *to apeiron*; Plato; Virgil's infinite universe that, like Homer's, includes the Underworld; the *New Testament*; and the Essene Dead Sea Scrolls.
- The metaphysical Reality seen as Light is in: Pindar's Light; Parmenides' One; Xenophanes' "one god"; Plato's guardians raising "the eye of the soul to the universal Light"; Socrates' experience of the Eleusinian "rays of pure light"; the *New Testament*; the Essene Dead Sea Scrolls; Gnostic, Manichaean and Neoplatonist texts; *The Golden Ass*; St Augustine's *Confessions*; and Pope Gregory the Great.
- The order of the universe can be found in: Zeus and Jupiter; the *rex sacrorum*'s embodiment of Jupiter; Homer's fulfilment of the will of Zeus; Greek myths in which order is destroyed and restored, for example Sophocles' *Oedipus*; Plato; Virgil's Fate (which coincides with the will of Jupiter who wants the founding of Rome); Caesar's omens; Horace's championing of Apollo and

Diana and invocation to Vesta; Ovid's *Metamorphoses*; the *New Testament*; the Essene Dead Sea Scrolls; and Gnostic texts.

- The oneness of known humankind was assumed by: the Athenian Empire; Plato; the Roman Empire; and the *New Testament*.
- The similarities in cultures and civilizations can be detected in the Greek and Roman civilizations, which became one Graeco-Roman or Hellenistic culture.
- The universal being (or self) that opens to the Light behind the rational, social ego is in: Plato's soul as charioteer; Virgil's Aeneas who "shone in the bright light"; the *New Testament*; and the Gnostic texts.
- Universal virtue is exercised in: Homer's criticism of Achilles; the Greek plays of Aeschylus, Sophocles, Euripides and Menander; Plato; and the Roman plays of Plautus, Terence and Seneca; also Horace's support for public religious rites; and the *New Testament*.
- The promise of the immortality of the universal being is present in: Homer's Underworld and Elysian Fields; Pindar's and Plato's many references to immortality; Virgil's Elysium; and the *New Testament*.
- The inner transformation or centre-shift from ego to universal being is found in: the Mycenaean mysteries, for example those at Eleusis; Plato; the Roman rites of Vesta; Ovid's *Metamorphoses*; the *New Testament*; St Augustine; and Pope Gregory the Great.
- The quest of the purified soul is in: the Greek mysteries; Odysseus's visit to the Underworld; Plato's assertion that earthly life is one episode of a long journey;[69] Aeneas's visit to the Underworld; the public rites of Roman religion; and the *New Testament*.
- The sensibility that approaches Reality through more than one discipline can be found in: Homer (poetry, epic); Xenophanes of Colophon (poetry, philosophy); Parmenides of Elea (poetry, philosophy); Plato (philosophy, teaching in Academy, statecraft in letters to Dionysus I and in *Republic*); Aristotle (philosophy, logic, sciences, *Poetics*); Demosthenes (political orations, statesman); Julius Caesar (history, military leader, ruler and dictator, statecraft); Cicero (political oratory, philosophy and

law); Virgil (poetry, epic); Horace (poetry and criticism in *Ars Poetica*); and Ovid (poetry, *Ars amatoria*, *Metamorphoses*, poetic letters from Black Sea).

- The new perspective of unity in history, religion, philosophy and science, international politics and literature can be found in: Graeco-Roman creation myths (unified history and religion); Plato (unification of philosophy); Aristotle (unification of science); Livy (unification of history of Rome in 142 books, of which books 11-20 and 46-142 have been lost); and Clement of Alexandria (unification of Greek Platonism, the Jewish Mosaic tradition, Christianity and Gnosticism).

The metaphysical aspect of the fundamental theme, which was present in both the West Roman and East Roman Empires during the spreading of Christianity at the end of the classical world, now passed into the Christian early Middle Ages.

3

The Literature of the Middle Ages

The Middle Ages was a period of European history that has been dated to c.395-1500: from the collapse of the Roman Empire to the beginning of the Modern Age. The death of Theodosius precipitated the division of the Roman Empire between East and West, and this was followed soon after by the sack of Rome and fall of the Roman Empire in 410. After that Latin ceased to be the official language of the Western world and Roman culture and the gods of Greek mythology ceased to be predominant. The Middle Ages had begun in earnest with the fall of the Western Roman Empire in 476, and the beginning of their end was signalled by the fall of Constantinople in 1453, which contributed to the beginning of the Florentine Renaissance.

The term "Middle Ages" (*medium aevum*) was coined in the 16th century.[1] Another term for much of the same period but focusing on the disruption of invasions, the "Dark Ages" (*saeculum obscurum*), was first recorded in 1602.[2] In fact the concept of a Dark Age originated with the Italian scholar Petrarch, who in the 1330s criticized late Latin literature as "dark" in comparison with the light of classical antiquity.[3]

In actuality Europe was still unified by Rome's Christian Church, which preserved the learning and language of the Roman world, and Latin was preserved as the universal language of churches. The *Bible* was translated into Latin: the Vulgate version (in the language of the common people) was made by St Jerome. This period was one of learning and growth as groups of fighting peoples who had broken away from Roman ideas and language became unified nations, and languages emerged such as English, French, German, Norwegian, Italian and Spanish, and were used to create a new national literature.

The Fundamental Theme in Europe

The breakaway from Roman ideas was accelerated by the growing influence of barbarians. Constantine had founded a "New Rome" on the site of Byzantium in 324. The Roman capital was moved there in 330 and named Constantinople ("the city of Constantine"). The Roman Empire admitted Goths and Franks in 379. Visigoths, Ostrogoths and Gauls all invaded Italy between 402 and 407. In 410 Alaric, leader of the Visigoths, returned to Ravenna, the seat of the Emperor Honorius, and demanded land and money. He pillaged Rome for three days. The barbarians were on the move and throughout the 5th century they created kingdoms: the Vandal kingdom in Africa, the Visigothic kingdom in Spain and Gaul, and the kingdom of the Salian Franks and Alamanni in the north.

By the 6th century Ireland and Britain had become the centre of learning and they preserved Latin culture lost to the rest of Europe. The monastic schools of Ireland and Britain had already been established, and Ireland had a Latin church literature by the time of St Patrick's arrival in 432. Bede's *The Ecclesiastical History of Britain* is full of information about the church in Britain in the early Saxon period.

The Anglo-Saxon poetry in Old English from 650 to 1000 reflects the insecurity of the age of national migrations: external threats, the bleak solitude of wanderers and seafarers and longing for lords at home. The *Anglo-Saxon Chronicle* recorded events prior to the 9th century and continued until 1154, and provided an objective, secular view of the invasions of Britain during the Dark Ages.

There is also a strong Christian theme of the soul seeking immortality which touches on the metaphysical aspect of the fundamental theme in poems such as 'The Dream of the Rood', in which the cross tells of the crucifixion and resurrection, and sufferings of spirits in Hell and the joys of saints and angels in Heaven; and 'Genesis B' (the translation of a lost German poem), which anticipates *Paradise Lost* in describing the temptation of Eve. In both poems, as in the Middle-English 'Pearl', in which the poet has a vision of his daughter who died in infancy and is instructed in submission to God's will, the soul's journey to immortality in Heaven is a strong theme.

Anglo-Saxon Beowulf

The Old English Poem *Beowulf*, c.700, which refers to historical events that can be dated to the early 6th century,[4] may have been written in England, not far from the ship-burial at Sutton Hoo.[5] It was ostensibly about the Danish royal family and the quest of a hero from the Geats of

South Sweden to kill a monster, Grendel, that had for twelve years terrorised Heorot, the hall in which the Danes slept.

> Beowulf kills Grendel by tearing off his arm, and Heorot is then terrorized by Grendel's mother. After a fight in a cave under water, Beowulf kills Grendel's mother. He is rewarded with treasures and returns to Sweden, where he becomes king and rules for 50 years. In his old age his land is terrorised by a dragon, and in the course of killing it he is mortally wounded. His pre-Christian funeral rites are described. There are in the poem two cremations and a royal ship-funeral: Beowulf is cremated on a pyre on his barrow.

Beowulf touches on the metaphysical aspect of the fundamental theme for Beowulf himself can be seen as a Christian champion of forces of goodness and light against forces of evil and darkness. The monsters are shown as enemies of God and human acts of violence, disloyalty and ambition are shown to bring retribution as did Agamemnon's *hubris* in the *Iliad*. Like the Greeks, Beowulf faces fate (*wyrd*) that comes to all men. His quest is rewarded with Germanic immortality: we are to suppose from his pre-Christian cremation that Beowulf goes to Valhalla, the residence of Odin where dead heroes go in Scandinavian mythology.

Icelandic Elder Edda

In the early Middle Ages wandering minstrels travelled round Europe chanting long epic poems containing news of battles, kings and crusades. In Iceland sagas were recited: family or heroic narrative poems that were not written down until later, by which time Iceland had been colonised by Vikings who brought with them their language of Old Norse.

The *Elder Edda*, an Icelandic collection of poems in Old Norse c.800-1100, begins with the Völuspá ("Sibyl's Prophecy"), which tells of creation and the birth of the world, the history of the gods, the origin of evil, and prophesies the death of the gods and the world's destruction. The second part recounts the youth of the hero Sigurd (Siegfried), his marriage and death. Taken as a whole, the *Elder Edda* employs Germanic mythology to convey the metaphysical aspect of the fundamental theme. (Snorri Sturluson's early-13th-century *Prose Edda* was a manual to instruct poets in Icelandic metres and mythology.)

The orally transmitted Finnish epic, *Kalevala* ("Land of Heroes") also recounts the beginning of the world and the battle of a Finnish hero, Väinämöinen, to recover a mill that produces salt, meal and gold and symbolizes happiness and prosperity. The metaphysical aspect of the fundamental theme lurks behind this poem.

German Nibelungenlied

A Middle High German epic, *Nibelungenlied*, written c.1200, continues the focus of the *Elder Edda*. It recounts the struggle between the gods and the giants and again focuses on Siegfried.

> The Rhinegold has been taken from the river and is put in a cave guarded by a dragon which is killed by the hero Siegfried, prince of the Rhine. He is led to where the goddess Brunhild sleeps, surrounded by a ring of fire, waiting for a hero to wake her. The twilight of the gods is told and the return of the gold to the Rhine maidens, a story later taken up by Wagner in *Der Ring des Nibelungen*. Siegfried can be seen as a latter-day Gilgamesh; he is killed and has a ceremonial funeral.

Siegfried's quest and death echo elements of the metaphysical aspect of the fundamental theme.

Earlier, the Old High German *Hildebrandslied* ("Song of Hildebrand", c.800) was a secular, heroic and grim account of a duel between father and son. The *Life of St Servatius* by Hendrik van Veldeke (known in German as Heinrich von Veldeke), a mid-12th-century rendering of a saint's life in the medieval Dutch Limburg dialect, also touched on the metaphysical aspect of the fundamental theme.

French Chanson de Roland

Heroic French *chansons de geste* ("songs of deeds") were composed by poets in northern France. Many dealt with legends connected with Charlemagne. The *Chanson de Roland*, c.1100, tells of how a part of Charlemagne's army, retreating from Spain, was killed in battle by the Spanish at Roncevaux. Roland is presented as fighting Saracens rather than Basques. Elements of the metaphysical aspect of the fundamental theme are present although there is a secular love interest. The anti-Saracen theme was reflected in the mid-12th-century Spanish *Poema* (or *Cantar*) *de mío Cid*, which tells of the fall from favour and restoration of Rodrigo Díaz de Vivar, a Castilian noble known by the Arabic title *sidi*, "lord", who led the Spanish struggle against the Moors.

The *chansons* formed what has been called the "Matter of France" – as distinct from the "Matter of Rome" (retelling old Greek and Roman stories) and the "Matter of Britain",[6] which retells legends surrounding Arthur.

St Symeon

In the early 11th century St Symeon, the New Theologian quested for Reality and saw the Light as God: "The Light already shines in the darkness, in the night and in the day, in our hearts and minds....God is Light....those who have not seen this light, have not seen God: for God is Light" (*Homily* LXXIX.2)

St Bernard and Hildegard

The Benedictine St Bernard of Clairvaux spread the Cistercian movement which had been founded in 1098, and promoted the Second Crusade. In his 86 *Sermons on the Canticle of Solomon* the Light is expressed as human love: the soul is seen as a Bride, being ravished by a Bridegroom. In many passages Bernard described the contemplation of the intellect, "when the Lord comes as a consuming Fire and His Presence is understood in the power by which the soul is changed" (*Sermons on the Canticle of Solomon*, 75.7-8). The "light illuminating the intellect" comes through "narrow apertures" (*Sermons on the Canticle of Solomon*, 41.3). The metaphysical aspect of the fundamental theme is reflected in St Bernard's account of the soul perceiving the infinite metaphysical Reality of the Light.

The Benedictine nun Hildegard of Bingen wrote:

"I have always seen this light, in my spirit and not with external eyes....The light which I see is not located, but yet is more brilliant than the sun....I name it 'the cloud of the living light'....But sometimes I behold within this light another light which I name 'the living light itself'. And when I look upon it, every sadness and pain vanishes from my memory, so that I am again as a simple maid and not as an old women."[7]

Hildegard knew of the Light and reflects the metaphysical aspect of the fundamental theme.

Abelard and Heloise

The Letters of Abelard and Heloise in the second decade of the 12th century restate the metaphysical aspect of the fundamental theme. Peter Abelard was a French scholastic philosopher and the greatest logician of the 12th century. He taught mainly in Paris and Heloise was his pupil. After the end of their love affair and marriage she became a nun and he became a monk in the Abbey of St Denis. She wrote him three long letters and he wrote three letters back, including his advice as to how she should adapt the rule of Benedict for women. His lengthy account of his misfortunes, *Historica calamitatum*, quotes from St Jerome: "The senses are like windows through which the vices gain entry into the soul."[8]

Abelard came into conflict with St Bernard and was condemned by the Church. He died in a Cluniac priory. The metaphysical aspect of the fundamental theme lurks behind the story of the two lovers as they chose to live in their souls rather than their senses and sought eternal life through religious orders.

French Grail legends

By the 12th century long epic poems and sagas had been followed by romances, or *romans*. These dealt with heroic deeds and battles. The first medieval verse romances were based on the "Matter of Britain", legends associated with King Arthur that particularly focused on the Grail. The first Grail romance was told by Chrétien de Troyes, who lived in the court of Marie de Champagne, daughter of Eleanor of Aquitaine. Eleanor was the queen consort of both Louis VII of France, whom she accompanied on the Second Crusade, and Henry II of England, and she was the mother of Richard I and King John, and the most powerful woman of the age.

Marie de Champagne encouraged courtly romance at her court in

Poitiers. The story of the Grail, the Cup of the Last Supper, may have been brought back from Jerusalem, perhaps by Count Derrick of Alsace, whose 12th-century countship chapel at Brugge (the French Bruges) contains floor-set tombstones showing Grail cups. Chrétien dedicated his *Perceval* or *Le Conte du Graal*, c.1180-90, an unfinished work, to Count Derrick's son, Philippe d'Alsace, Count of Flanders, who tried to marry Marie Countess of Champagne in 1182.

In Chrétien's *Perceval*, a simpleton brought up by his mother after his father and elder brothers had been killed seeks knighthood and has a series of adventures, and encounters the *graal*, a dish of plenty covered in precious stones, when offered shelter in the castle of a fisherman (the Fisher King). A procession brings in the *graal* behind a bleeding lance. The *graal* gives off great light – which represents the Light – and Perceval later learns that the cup contained the Host (Christ's body). He has been instructed by Gornemant de Gohort to ask the meaning of the procession, but forgets to do so. As a result there will be a disaster for the surrounding lands. The metaphysical aspect of the fundamental theme is adhered to, for Perceval is now on a quest to find his way back to the castle of the *graal*, which symbolizes the Light, while Gawain seeks the bleeding lance (the spear that pierced Christ's side).

Later treatments of the Grail were told in French by Robert de Boron, a Burgundian knight (c.1200-1210), which fixed the fictional history of the Holy Grail in the reign of King Arthur, and in German by Wolfram von Eschenbach (1207), and eventually of course in English by Thomas Malory in *Morte D'Arthur* (1485). These works also contain elements of a quest for truth.

But it is the Old French *Queste du Saint Graal* (c.1220), part of the prose *Lancelot* or *Vulgate cycle*, that is particularly interesting. The Grail appears at Arthur's court at Pentecost, during the evening meal when all the knights are seated in silence, at the beginning of this work:

"There entered the Holy Grail covered with a white cloth; but no one was able to see who was carrying it. It entered by the great door of the hall....As it passed before the tables, they were straightway filled at each place with viands as the occupant desired. When all were served, the Holy Grail departed at once so that they knew not what had become of it."

The entry of the Grail is accompanied by a bright light that "made the palace sevenfold brighter than it was before". Only Galahad could look at the Grail.

> After this episode the knights set out to search for the Holy Grail, and the story follows Gawain (Arthur's nephew), Lancelot, Galahad, Perceval and Bors. Eventually Galahad, Perceval and Bors come to the castle of Corbenic at Sarras, and "a man came down from heaven, garbed in a bishop's robes, and with a crozier in his hand and a mitre on his head". This is Josephus, son of Joseph of Arimathaea, and his head is inscribed, "The first Christian bishop, the same who was consecrated by our Lord in Sarras." He shows the three men the Grail, the Holy Vessel, from which a man bleeding from his hands, feet and side appears and speaks. Galahad asks to pass from earthly life to "life eternal", and he falls on the flagged floor and is borne to Heaven.

The metaphysical aspect of the fundamental theme is present in this story as a knight is on a quest for the Grail, which symbolizes the Light, and ends in requesting eternal life – which unlike Gilgamesh at first (but like Gilgamesh eventually) he receives.

The distance between West and East had been bridged by the Crusades, but it widened following the West's military action against the East, after the Latin Venetians and Crusaders took Constantinople in 1204.

Norman Lais

Anglo-Norman literature (literature in the French dialect of medieval England, also known as Norman French) was full of legends of saints and religious allegory. Marie de France, who wrote Anglo-Norman Breton *lais*, short narrative poems not unlike romances, is thought to have lived at the court of Eleanor of Aquitaine in the late 12th century. As nothing is known of her except that her name was Marie and she lived in France, it is not impossible that she was in fact Marie de Champagne writing under a pseudonym. She contributed to a secular stream of poetry along with the *trouvères*, the early French lyric poets, and the *jongleurs* (*joglars* in Provençal) of the 12th and 13th centuries who wrote Provençal love songs.

The conflict between the metaphysical aspect of the fundamental theme and a growing secular approach is caught in the late-12th-century poem in French metre, 'The Owl and the Nightingale', in which the two birds debate witchcraft, the Church and marriage and express two entirely different attitudes to life, one metaphysical (the owl) and the other secular (the nightingale).

French Roman de la Rose

The French *Roman de la Rose* ("Romance of the Rose") is in two sections. The first (written by Guillaume de Lorris, c.1240), based on Ovid's *Ars amatoria* ("Art of Love", c.1BC), is an allegorical love poem in which a lover obtains a rosebud, symbol for courtly love, thanks to the intervention of Venus. The Lord of the garden comes into the allegory along with *Amor* (Love) and the French names for other abstractions (aloofness, calumny, shame or modesty, pleasure and indolence). Around 1280 Jean de Meun added to the story so it dealt with religion and morality. The Virgin Mary lurked behind stories of courtly love despite their secular associations, and the metaphysical aspect of the fundamental theme of a quest for meaning is behind this romance.

Franciscan Verse

A Franciscan tradition formed after St Francis of Assisi (who died in 1226), a member of the Umbrian school of verse-writers. His *Canticas* expressed his quest for religious truth and Light. He describes the Beatific Vision in *The Little Flowers of St Francis* as "a rapture and uplifting of the mind intoxicated in the contemplation of the unspeakable savour of the Divine sweetness...and a burning sense within of that celestial glory unspeakable", i.e. the Light.

Dante's Divine Comedy

The metaphysical aspect of the fundamental theme was perpetuated by the Franciscan Dante. A member of the White Guelf party in Florence, as one of the six priors of the city he was involved in the banishing of

Cavalcanti from Florence in 1300, one of the poets he described as of the *dolce stil nuovo* ("sweet new style", *Purgatorio* xxiv, 55) and his "first friend". (In exile Cavalcanti caught malaria and though he was permitted to return to Florence, died soon afterwards, having influenced Dante's style with his love poems.)

Dante was exiled when the Black Guelfs came to power in 1302 and became a wanderer, sheltered by Italian princes in various cities, notably Verona and eventually Ravenna, and never saw Florence again. In his work courtly and Christian love were united as his ideal lady, Beatrice Portinari, who he first saw when he was nine and who died sixteen years later in 1290, guided his Christian devotion. He celebrated his love for Beatrice in *La vita nuova*, and the metaphysical aspect of the fundamental theme can be found in his *La divina commedia* ("The Divine Comedy", c.1308-21), which describes his journey from being lost in a dark wood, through Hell where his guide is Virgil, then through Purgatory and finally to Paradise, where his guide is Beatrice. Dante quests for metaphysical truth and the Light and finds it in Paradise.

The fundamental truth is in the *Commedia* as a wanderer visits the Underworld after death like Homer's Odysseus and Virgil's Aeneas, and describes the people he finds there and what they have done to deserve their punishments or rewards.

In *Paradiso* (c.1318-21) he has a vision of the Divine Light.

Gazing into the eyes of Beatrice, now an angel, he sees the Infinitesimal Point: "One point I saw, so radiantly bright, so searing to the eyes it strikes upon, they needs must close before such piercing light." After he and Beatrice enter the Empyrean, "now a living light encompassed me; in veil so luminous I was enwrapped that naught swathed in such glory, could I see....Light I beheld which as a river flowed." He sees a circle of yellow light at the centre of the Celestial or Sempiternal Rose, the light of God's glory, the *lumen gloriae*, which had become a dogma in 1312. This is the Beatific Vision of the "Light Supreme" (*somma luce*), "the eternal light", "one simple light" (*un semplice lume*).

In *Paradiso*, cantos xxviii and xxxiii, Dante gives an "eye-witness" account of his experience of the Light (which begins with his description of the Infinitesimal Point, here presented in a different translation):

"I saw a point that sent forth so acute a light, that anyone who faced the force with which it blazed would have to shut his eyes, and any star that, seen from earth, would seem to be the smallest, set beside that point....Around that point a ring of fire wheeled....O Highest Light (or Light Supreme)....I presumed to set my eyes on the Eternal Light so long that I spent all my sight on it!...Whoever sees that Light is soon made such that it would be impossible for him to set that Light aside for other sight; because the good, the object of the will, is fully gathered in that Light; outside that Light, what there is perfect is defective....The Living Light at which I gazed – for It is always what It was before....Eternal Light, You only dwell within Yourself, and only You know You; Self-knowing, Self-known, You love and smile upon Yourself!"

In the course of describing the inhabitants of his *Inferno*, Dante gives examples of all kinds of sinful behaviour, follies, vices, blindness, corruption, hypocrisy, self-love and egotism. Correspondingly in *Paradiso* he gives examples of all kinds of virtuous behaviour and offers a standard of universal virtue by which all sins and vices can be measured. Dante reflects the metaphysical aspect of the fundamental theme in the whole *Commedia* by setting out the imperfections of the ego and the virtues of the transformed self.

Dante considered the governance of all humankind in his prose work *De Monarchia* (*On Monarchy*, sometimes translated *On World Government*, 1317-18), in which he longed for a universal Emperor, probably hoping he would be the ruler of Verona, his friend Can Grande della Scala.

Everyman

In the 14th century strolling players presented miracle, morality and mystery plays in market-places, castles or outside Abbey gates. The cycles of Chester, York and Wakefield appeared after c.1300. The earliest of these plays to have survived can be dated to the late 1320s and 1330s.[9]

Everyman, an English morality play of Dutch origin (its Dutch title being *Elckerlijk*), conveys the metaphysical aspect of the fundamental theme of world literature for Death summons Everyman, and of his friends only Good-Deeds is willing to accompany him. The other characters include God, Messenger, Knowledge, Beauty, Strength and other abstractions, and it treats the fate of man's soul allegorically. Everyman is in the position of Odysseus or Aeneas, entering the domain of Death. Good-Deeds, weakened by Everyman's neglect but strengthened by Knowledge, makes possible the immortality of the soul that Gilgamesh sought, and in his last speech Everyman says, "Into thy hands, Lord, my soul I commend."

14th-century Mystics

The 14th-century mystics wrote of the metaphysical aspect of the fundamental theme. Their contemplative life can be traced back to the 12th-century *Ancrene Wisse* or *Ancrene Riwle* ("Guide of Anchoresses"), parts of which are entitled 'The Custody of the Senses' and 'Regulation of the Inward Feelings'. It sets out the contemplative life in which the soul disciplines the sensual mind and quests for the Light, or "Greek fire". Richard Rolle (who died in 1349) in *The Fire of Love*, the 14th-century anonymous *Cloud of Unknowing*, Walter Hilton (who died in 1396) in *The Ladder (or Scale) of Perfection* and the nun Julian of Norwich in her *Revelations of Divine Love*, which describes the 16 visions she had on 8 May 1373 – all convey the metaphysical aspect of the fundamental theme of world literature.[10]

The Italian St Catherine of Siena, who founded the *Ordo Sanctissimi Salvatoris*, worked tirelessly to bring Pope Gregory XI back to Rome and to initiate a new crusade. She died exhausted at the age of thirty-three in 1380, having written her *Dialogo* in 1378-9. She had had a vision of Christ crucified in a blaze of light, and rays streaming from his wounds pierced her body and left her with stigmata in five places, which were extremely painful. She heard the words (ch.85): "I, Fire, the Acceptor of sacrifices, ravishing away from them their darkness, give the Light." She wrote to Brother William of England: "I...write to you...with desire to see you in true light. For without light we shall not be able to walk in the way of truth....The soul...ought to go on with all zeal to the perfect light."

Catherine died very young, her body racked with pain and worn out from her work for the Pope, and her preserved head – diminutive and wimpled, eyes closed – and one finger can be seen behind glass in the church of San Dominico in Siena. Catherine's work conveys the metaphysical aspect of the fundamental theme.

English Piers Plowman
The English allegory *Piers Plowman* by William Langland (B-Text, 1377-9) is about a dream.

> Langland falls asleep among hills and has a vision of the world: a tower of truth is separated from a dungeon of wrong by a valley, in which all people are living. A thousand set off to seek St Truth. The way is difficult to find, and Piers the ploughman offers to guide the pilgrims if they will help him plough his half-acre. At the end a great Light appears before the gates of Hell, the *lumen Christi*, and demands entry so that "Christ, the son of the King of Heaven, may enter". Christ has now blended with Piers Plowman. The gates of Hell burst open and "our Lord caught up into his Light all those that loved him".

Again, the metaphysical aspect of the fundamental theme can be found: in his dream Langland is seeking truth through the world as a pilgrim and is filled with the Light.

English Sir Gawayne and the Grene Knight
In an English poetic romance of about this time, *Sir Gawayne and the Grene Knight* (c.1380, probably based on a Germanic horror story), Sir Gawain encounters a strange knight at Arthur's court.

> They exchanges promises: Gawain will have a chance to cut off the knight's head but a year later must give him the opportunity of cutting off Gawain's head. Gawain duly beheads the knight, who picks up his head and rides away. Gawain is later hosted by a strange man who makes only one demand of him: he must tell him truly what he has done each day. After a year Gawain goes in search of the Green Knight and submits to beheading, but only receives a tap on his neck. He discovers that the Green Knight is his host, and that if he has told the truth the Green Knight's sword will not harm him. The tap was for being less

than truthful about an event concerning the Green Knight's wife.

Again, the metaphysical aspect of the fundamental theme lurks behind the story. A knight goes in quest of a man who will cause his death, but is reprieved for being virtuous and telling the truth. His courage, good faith, courtesy and chastity are all celebrated as he faces the ordeal of the beheading challenge within an infinite, ordered universe.

Petrarch and Boccaccio

The 14th-century Petrarch was pre-Renaissance in looking to classical authors and Church Fathers and rejecting medieval scholasticism in his poetic *Rime*, or *Canzoniere*, a collection of sonnets, songs, six-line verses, ballads and madrigals which tell of his love for Laura. His epic poem on the Second Punic War, *Africa*, was unfinished when he died.

His strict forms and discipline influenced his successors, including Boccaccio, author of the mid-14th-century *Decameron*, a prose collection of 100 secular stories divided into ten days in which a group of ladies and gentlemen escaped a plague ravaging Florence and in a suburban villa told each other stories condemning vices to pass the time. He treated his contemporary urban society with humour and an awareness of inherent tragedy, for the plague threatened his characters with early death.

Boccaccio looked back to Dante, on the first 17 cantos of whose *Inferno* he wrote a commentary. An early Humanist, he also looked forward to the Renaissance and influenced Chaucer.

In both Petrarch and Boccaccio metaphysical and secular aspects of the fundamental theme can be found.

Chaucer's The Canterbury Tales

Chaucer, writing in Middle English, drew on all the themes of his day, including the "Matter of Rome". In his *Troilus and Criseyde*, based on Boccaccio, he deals with an episode in the Trojan War which Homer mentions. He wrote his own version of *Roman de la rose* and an allegory, *The Parliament of Fowls*.

In the *Canterbury Tales* (1385-1499) he tells of a group of pilgrims progressing from Southwark to the shrine of St Thomas à Becket. The pilgrims journey to a shrine which was believed to have healing powers, and their lay foibles are presented within a religious framework that Chaucer accepts. Each one of them tells a story to pass the time (an idea Chaucer took from Boccaccio's *Decameron* (1348-53), and the *Prologue* vividly presents their characters, covering a cross-section of medieval society. Although much of the material is secular, the metaphysical aspect of the fundamental theme lurks behind the scheme.

Chaucer's 24 (out of a planned 31) Canterbury tales, of which Chaucer personally tells two, assume a standard of universal virtue by which to measure and condemn human follies, vices, blindness, corruption, hypocrisy, self-love and egotism, the impediments in the social, immediately pre-Renaissance, world that block the contemplative quest for truth and Reality known in the medieval monasteries. Many of the tales have their origin in Boccaccio, and it is worth listing the tales and the follies they highlight and vices they condemn.

1. *The Knight's Tale* condemns destructive rivalry in love. Palamon and Arcite compete for Emelye (Emilia), sister-in-law of King Theseus of Athens, in a tournament. Arcite wins but Venus arranges for him to be thrown from his horse, and he dies. After prolonged mourning Palamon and Emelye are united.

2. *The Miller's Tale* is a ribald story condemning the deception of a husband (a carpenter, which the reeve had once been) and of a lover.

3. *The Reeve's Tale* condemns robbery and revenge. It is an indecent story of two clerks who are robbed by a miller of part of their meal and revenge themselves on the miller's wife and daughter.

4. *The Cook's Tale* condemns drinking. It breaks off after 58 lines when Perkyn, who likes to drink, moves in with a friend who also likes to drink and whose wife is a prostitute.

5. *The Man of Law's Tale* condemns jealousy. Constance, the daughter of a Christian emperor of Rome, marries the Sultan of Syria on condition that he becomes a Christian. Through the plotting of the Sultan's jealous mother she is cast adrift in a boat.

6. *The Wife of Bath's Tale* condemns celibacy. It contains a prologue in which the wife describes her five deceased husbands. The tale is about an Arthurian knight who has to answer the question, "What do women most desire?" He is told the correct answer, "sovereignty", by a hideous witch on condition that he marries her. When he does so, she is restored to youth and beauty.

7. *The Friar's Tale* condemns extortion. A summoner meets the Devil dressed as a yeoman and they agree to share what they are given. They meet a carter who curses his horse, commending it to the Devil, but the Devil will not take it as the commendation does not come from the heart. Later they come across an old woman and the summoner tries to extort twelve pence from her. She commends him to the Devil, who carries him off to Hell because her curse came from her heart.

8. *The Summoner's Tale* condemns greed. It tells of a greedy friar who undertakes to divide a deathbed legacy amongst his community. The legacy is breaking of wind, and he has to devise a plan to divide it justly.

9. *The Clerk's Tale* condemns importunity. It is about the trials of a relentless husband. The humble Griselda deals with the trials of the Marquis Walter with virtuous patience.

10. *The Merchant's Tale* condemns infidelity. An old man marries a young wife and goes blind. She makes love to her suitor in a pear-tree, at which point Pluto restores the husband's sight. Proserpine inspires the wife to explain that his sight was restored by her activities in the pear-tree, which is why she was there.

11. *The Squire's Tale* condemns desertion. An envoy from the king of Arabia brings magic gifts to the king of Tartary, including a ring for the king's daughter Canace. This enables her to understand the language of birds. A female falcon tells her the story of her own desertion by a tercel (male hawk, i.e. falcon).

12. *The Franklin's Tale* condemns persistence in love. A woman, Dorigen, is pressed by her lover, the squire Aurelius, and imposes an

impossible condition, that all the rocks on the coast of Brittany should be removed. A magician achieves this, but the lover releases her from her promise out of remorse.

13. *The Physician's Tale* condemns corruption. Virginia is killed by her father at her own request to escape the attentions of a corrupt judge, Apius.

14. *The Pardoner's Tale* condemns covetousness and other sins: drunkenness, gluttony, gambling and swearing. During a plague three revellers set out to find Death, who has killed one of their companions. An old man tells them they will find him under a particular tree, but when they arrive they find a heap of gold. Each plots to obtain sole possession of the gold and they end up killing each other.

15. *The Shipman's Tale* condemns stinginess. The wife of a stingy, niggardly merchant asks a priest to lend her a hundred francs to buy fine clothes. The priest borrows a hundred francs from the merchant. He hands it to the wife, who in gratitude grants him favours. The priest later tells the merchant that he has repaid the hundred francs to the wife, who cannot deny receiving it.

16. *The Prioress's Tale* condemns religious intolerance. A widow's child is murdered by Jews because he sings a Latin hymn about Mary as he walks through a ghetto at Lincoln on his way to school. He continues to sing the hymn after death, and as a result his body is discovered.

17. Chaucer's *The Tale of Sir Thopas* condemns hero-worship. It is a parody of knightly romance. Chaucer ridicules such tales, and the host interrupts him, to say that the story is boring.

18. Chaucer's *The Tale of Melibeus* condemns injury at the hands of enemies. After Melibeus's wife Dame Prudence is beaten by three enemies and their daughter is left for dead, husband and wife debate the redress available to them.

19. The Monk's Tale condemns worldliness. Probably based on Boccaccio' *Concerning the Falls of Illustrious Men*, it is about the tragic endings of 17 historical figures who have fallen from high positions.

20. The Nun's Priest's Tale condemns deception. A fox deceives a cock about his intentions by praising his father's singing, and is in turn deceived by pausing to boast of his victory, allowing the cock to escape.

21. The Second Nun's Tale praises virtue. It describes the miracles and martyrdom of the Roman Cecilia and her husband Valerian.

22. The Canon's Yeoman's Tale condemns roguery. It tells how an alchemical canon tricks a priest out of £40 by pretending to teach him the art of making precious metals.

23. The Manciple's Tale condemns infidelity. Phebus has a crow that is white and can imitate any person's speech. It reveals his wife's infidelity to him. In a fury Phebus kills his wife and then, in remorse, plucks out the crow's white feathers, removes its power of speech and throws it "unto the devil", which is why crows are now black.

24. The Parson's Tale condemns the Seven Deadly Sins. It is in prose – probably Chaucer's notes for a poetic tale that was never written – and details the character of each of the Seven Deadly Sins (pride, envy, anger, sloth, covetousness, gluttony and lust) and the penance due for each, urging penitence.

To sum up, the vices in Chaucer's tales are: rivalry in love, deception, robbery, revenge, drinking, jealousy, extortion, greed, importunity, infidelity, desertion, persistence in love, corruption, stinginess, intolerance, hero-worship, injury, worldliness, roguery, pride, envy, anger, sloth, covetousness, gluttony and lust.

Chaucer's Canterbury tales, then, all focus on aspects of virtue and vice. For all their worldliness and occasional ribaldry, they deal with a quest for truth and the exposure of falsehood and the Seven Deadly Sins.

At the very end of the *Canterbury Tales* Chaucer makes retractions

("The Maker of this Book here takes his Leave"), distancing the author from the non-spiritual elements in his work as was customary in the Middle Ages. He asks[11] Christ to "have mercy on me and forgive me my sins: and especially for my translations and enditings (i.e. inditings, literary compositions) of worldly vanities, which I revoke in my retractions: as are...*The Tales of Canterbury*, those that tend towards sin...; so that I may be one of those that at the Day of Judgement shall be saved." Chaucer's retractions are a personal statement of his compliance with the metaphysical aspect of the fundamental theme. (For further details of Chaucer's underlying religious view, see Appendix, pp.359-62.)

Chaucer's work contains both the metaphysical and secular aspects of the fundamental theme. It is about the metaphysical quest and also the secular vices which are condemned in relation to implied virtue.

The Scottish ballads of the 14th and 15th centuries and the works of Henryson and Dunbar, and the pre-Renaissance English poems of Gower and Skelton reflected a new interest in courtly love. By the time of Chaucer and his immediate successors the medieval world was already dying and there were signs of early Humanism. The first inklings of the Renaissance can be found in Chaucer's work and gather pace from now on.

The Fundamental Theme in the East

The metaphysical aspect of the fundamental theme in the East is found in early Islamic literature.

Islam: the Koran

The *Koran* was revealed to Mohammed, a camel-driver, in a cave of Hira, near Mecca, in c.610, when Mohammed saw the opening passage written in letters of fire on cloth. The Will of Allah (*Al-Ilah*, "the Strong One", or *ta'hala*, "the most high or Supreme One") was made known in the *Koran* in terms of the Light:

> "Allah is the Light of the heavens and the earth. His light may be compared to a niche that enshrines (or wherein is) a lamp, the lamp within a crystal (or glass) of star-like brilliance (or as a pearly star). It is lit from a blessed olive tree neither eastern nor western (or neither of

the East nor of the West)....Allah guides to His Light whom he will."
(Ch.24.)

Allah says in the *Koran* (ch.50), "We created man....We know the
promptings of his soul (or what his soul whispers within him), and are
closer to him than the vein of his neck (or the jugular vein)".[12] These
statements of the relationship between the soul and the Light are in
accord with the metaphysical aspect of the fundamental theme.

Sufi Writings

Sufism originated with the Zoroastrian Magi and absorbed Hermeticism
and Neoplatonism. The Sufi saw the universe as a reflection (or
shadow) of the Light of Allah, which he also reflected.

In the 9th century Abu Yazid al-Bistami, or Bayazid, described
losing his earthly self and body consciousness within the Light of
Allah, and the achieving of eternal life. Al-Hallaj was crucified for
blasphemously identifying himself with Allah in Baghdad: *"Ana
l'Haqq."* ("I am God.") His servant records his words on the cross,
which make it clear that he was identifying himself with the Light.

Al-Nuri was also executed for heresy. He said, "Once I beheld the
Light, and I fixed my gaze upon it until I became the Light." The
Persian Ibn Sina, or Avicenna, wrote in his 11th-century *Stages of the
Mystical Life*: "The soul then has reached the light of the Sun and is able
to receive the Divine Illumination when it wills, free from all worldly
distractions."[13] Al-Ghazali wrote in the *Revival of the Religious
Sciences* (ch.4) that the third stage of belief in the unity of God "is to
perceive by the inward light of the heart".

The Persian Seljuq-Turk Omar Khayyam reflected the metaphysical
aspect of the fundamental theme in his independent four-line poems,
which were translated by Edward Fitzgerald as one poem in 1859
(rearranged in 1868). Using Sufi imagery, he wrote of being in divine
contemplation in terms of being intoxicated with wine, and the reader is
invited to journey towards "Thou" (Mohammed, and also Allah).

Suhrawardi led the illuminative school of philosophy, which united
philosophy and mysticism. He described the journey of the mystic
before he reached *ma'rifah* (the *gnosis* of illumination). Ibn al-Arabi
taught the Unity of Being (and therefore the unity of all existence) in

the early 13th century.

All these Sufis reflected the metaphysical aspect of the fundamental theme in which the soul withdraws from the bodily senses and knows the infinite metaphysical Reality of the Light. The Persian poets Attar, Rumi, Hafez, and Jami all echoed the metaphysical aspect of the fundamental theme.[14]

A secular stream can be found in two works of Persian origin: *The Thousand and One Nights*, first mentioned in the 10th century, and Firdawsi's *Shahnameh*, an epic on the deeds of Persian heroes and kings.

India: Buddhist and Hindu Texts

The Indian literature of the late classical period was dominated by *Mahayana* Buddhism, which spread into South-East Asia, Tibet, China and Japan. Indian monks travelled along the silk route to China and in Japan *Mahayana* became the State religion in the 8th century.

The main *Mahayana* text, *Maha-prajna-paramita-sastra* ("Great Perfection of Wisdom Treatise") sees Reality as "the Void" (*sunyata*), an emptiness that is also a fullness, the Light.

In the 5th century the Indian Yogacara school taught "Mind-Essence", the "storage of Universal Mind", the Light. It spread to China as Fa-hsiang and to Japan as Hosso (where it centred on the oldest temple in Japan, Horyu-ji).

The Indian Avatamsaka School spread to China as Hua-yen and, in the 8th century, to Japan as Kegon. Its main text the *Avatamsaka-sutra*, told of Vairocana (Sanskrit for "the Illuminator"), the supreme Buddha, and his Enlightenment (which is represented in the Dai-butsu, the colossal bronze Buddha at Nara, in Japan). It taught the "totality" of the universe, and the Oneness behind multiplicity, an idea reflected in the Stone Garden in the Ryoan-ji temple in Kyoto. This shows shingle that is raked in different patterns to represent a sea of Becoming, and interspersed rocks that represent Being. The shingle and rocks represent the unity of creation. They may be seen as sea and rocks, earth and mountains or clouds and mountains, and suggest that the universe is composed of one stuff, the Light of the "Illuminator".

The Indian Saddharmapundarika School spread to China as T'ien-t'ai and, in the 9th century, Japan as Tendai. Its main text, the *Lotus*

Sutra held that the aim of all is to be a Buddha and achieve Enlightenment. The Buddha is represented as an eternal being surrounded by a thousand *arhat*s and bodhisattvas, like the thousand *Kannon*s at the Tendai Sanjusangendo temple in Kyoto, Japan. The text teaches that all things are of the Void and temporary and are one in their Voidness.

The Indian Pure Land School spread to China as Ching-t'u and to Japan as Jodo. It was brought to Japan by the Tendai School but by the 13th century the Jodo sect had separated from Tendai. Its main text, the Pure Land Sutra, taught about Dharmakara, a monk who was known as the Buddha of Unlimited Light (Japanese *Amida*, "endless light").

Indian Tantric Buddhism (2nd century) spread to Sri Lanka (Ceylon) and elsewhere as Vajrayana, which sought to recapture the experience that made Gautama "the Enlightened One". Its main text Bhagavata-Purana held that man has a diamond-like nature, the diamond representing the Light.

A late Tantric form for *Mahayana* Buddhism, Mantrayana, spread to China as Chen-yen and, in the 9th century, to Japan as Shingon. Its main text, the *Dainichi-kyo* saw the universe as being within Maha-Vairocana, "the Great Illuminator", the Light.[15]

All these Schools taught the metaphysical aspect of the fundamental theme: the soul's quest for contact with metaphysical Reality perceived as Light.

The Indian Hindu texts reflect the metaphysical aspect of the fundamental theme. Siva was first treated as the supreme God in the *Svetasvatara Upanisad*. Saivism (the worship of Siva) developed during the Gupta Empire c.320 and spread to South-East Asia and the Mediterranean, where it may have influenced Plotinus and Clement of Alexandria. The main text of Tantric Hinduism, the *Six Teachings* or *Six Doctrines*, awakens Kundalini, the energy coiled at the base of the spine like a serpent, which rises to the subtle centre or *chakra* in the crown of the head, uniting Siva and his consort Sakti, and giving enlightenment, *samadhi*.

Vaisnavism worshipped Visnu, and was a rival to Saivism. Its main exponent was the monist Sankara, who wrote of the awakening of the self in terms of the Light:

"The Self alone lights up the mind and powers, as a flame lights up a jar....A light does not need another light; it shines of itself....Here, verily in the substantial Self, in the hidden place of the soul, this steady shining begins to shine like the dawn; then the shining shines forth as the noonday sun, making all this world to shine by its inherent light."

All these Hindu texts reflect the metaphysical aspect of the fundamental theme.

Tibet: Tantric Buddhist Texts

Indian Tantrism reached Tibet between the 6th and 11th centuries. The Tibetan Tantric Buddhism was a synthesis of *Mahayana* and Vajrayana (Tantric Buddhism). Its main text, the *Six Teachings* or *Six Doctrines*[16] presents the way to the Clear Light as a negative way: "Imagine not, think not, analyze not, meditate not, reflect not, keep in the Natural State." The art of dying is to die seeing the Clear Light, so that the Clear Light is recognised after death. In the case of a lama the prayer is: "Reverend Sir, now you are experiencing the Fundamental Clear Light, try to abide in that state which now you are experiencing." For all others the prayer is: "O nobly born, listen. Now you are experiencing the Radiance of the Clear Light of Pure Reality. Recognise it....Your own consciousness, shining, void and inseparable from the Great Body of Radiance, has no birth, nor death, and is the Immutable Light." The conscious recognition of the Clear Light induces *samadhi*, an ecstatic consciousness "such as saints and mystics of the West have called Illumination".

The Tibetan *Book of the Dead* describes the Light, which can be experienced by the living as well as the dying. Like the Egyptian *Book of the Dead* it was a guidebook to illumination. Both these Tibetan Tantric Buddhist texts reflect the metaphysical aspect of the fundamental theme for the soul quests to see metaphysical Reality as Light, which gives immortality.[17]

China: The Secret of the Golden Flower

Buddhist and Hindu monks had travelled down the silk route to China. Chinese Neo-Taoism began in the 3rd and 4th centuries with Tantric alchemical techniques in search of immortality. In the 8th-century religion of the Golden Elixir of Life (which was influenced by Manichaeism and Gnosticism) the Chinese form of Kundalini was an inner fire which circulated round the subtle body and was known as a dragon (the Chinese version of the Indian serpent). *Ching* (sexual energy), *ch'i* (vitality which attains to *Tao*) and *shen*, the luminous personal spirit illumined by the Light, all circulated in meditation, and when the *shen* was transformed into the golden elixir or liquefied gold a special saliva formed in the mouth which congealed into the Seed of Immortality. *The Secret of the Golden Flower* describes how to circulate the Light, which is known as "the Golden Flower": "The Golden Flower is the light....The Golden Flower is the elixir of Life."

The Secret of the Golden Flower reflects the metaphysical aspect of the fundamental theme because the soul in meditation receives the circulating Light and achieves the immortality for which Gilgamesh sought.[18]

A secular stream can be found in the lyrical poetry of the Tang dynasty and the *shih* poems of Lu Yu in the Sung dynasty. This stream persisted throughout the medieval period.

Japan: Zen Kadensho

The Indian 4th-century *Dhyana* School was spread along the silk route to China as *Ch'an*, an amalgamation of *Mahayana* Buddhism and Taoism, by the Indian monk Bodhidharma in the 6th century. Its main text, *Lankavatara Sutra* held that all possess Buddha-nature. *Ch'an* held that meditation was the way to experience enlightenment, gradually (according to its Northern School), suddenly (according to its Southern School). The Southern School of Southern Enlightenment held that the body is a "lamp" for the "Light". In the *Sutra of Wei Lang* Hui-Neng wrote: "Within the domain of our mind there is *Tathagata* of Enlightenment who sends forth a powerful light which illumines externally the six gates (of sensation) and purifies them." The Southern School spread to Japan as Zen between the 7th and 12th centuries.

Japan was then dominated by Shinto, the pre-Buddhist religion of Japan which was the product of an Indian *Mahayana* influence on Taoism. It was shamanistic and dealt with spirits, *kami*, particularly the *kami* of ancestors who I saw living in nesting-boxes on trees in one of the palace gardens when I was in Japan. The One *Kami* of the universe could be known as inner sun.

I was given an urn with a golden chrysanthemum on it (the Shinto equivalent of the Golden Flower) by a member of the Japanese imperial family. This was to be used as a receptacle for my ashes and denoted that Shinto immortality had been conferred on me by the Emperor as a special mark of respect.

Zen *satori* was an awakening to the experience of enlightenment that Gautama the Buddha had under the Bo tree. Zen gave rise to Nō drama in the 14th century. Zeami's (or Seami's) *Kadensho* (or *Kwadensho*), the "Book of the Flowery Tradition", dwells on the untranslatable *yugen*, which is often described as "true beauty and gentleness" or "mystery and depth". "If one aims at the beautiful, 'the flower' is sure to appear." The *yugen* was a Zen concept, and came from China: the Golden Flower. The "inner beauty and gentleness" of the *yugen* was the inner beauty and gentleness of the Light "beneath the surface". The Zen texts reflect the metaphysical aspect of the fundamental theme and the soul's quest for metaphysical Reality as Light.[19]

A secular stream connected with courtly love can be found in the 8th-century *Manyo-shu* ("Collection of Ten Thousand Leaves"); in the 11th-century *Tale of Genji* by Murasaki Shikibu, which describes the loves of Prince Genji and the women in his life and whose dark tone reflects a Buddhist sense of the vanity of this world; and in the 12th-century *Heike monogatari* ("The Tale of the Heike"), which is about *samurai* warriors.

The Eastern literature of the Middle Ages reinforces the "wisdom of the East" of antiquity and reflects the metaphysical aspect of the fundamental theme. As in the medieval West, where mainstream Christianity dominated the emerging secular tradition, in the East the metaphysical aspect of the fundamental theme is by far and away the mainstream tradition, with secular love poems emerging alongside it but not obliterating it.

In both Western and Eastern medieval literature there is a minority secular tradition. The French romances such as the *Roman de la Rose*, the Sufi worldly view of wine in Omar Khayyam's verses, the Indian, Chinese and Japanese focus on courtly love may all be regarded as descriptions of the external world, although many poems may also at the same time conceal symbols of the metaphysical aspect of the fundamental theme.

Literary Summary
The main references to the metaphysical aspect of the fundamental theme in world literature during the increasingly secular Middle Ages are as follows:

- The infinite that surrounds the universe is in: the Grail legends; Dante; and the *Koran*.
- The metaphysical Reality seen as Light is in: Chrétien's *Perceval*; Dante; *Piers Plowman*; the *Koran*; Sufi texts; Buddhist and Hindu texts; Tibetan texts; the Neo-Taoist Clear Light; and Japanese Zen.
- The order of the universe can be found in: the *Elder Edda*; the *Kalevala*; the *Nibelungenlied*; Dante; and Buddhist, Hindu and Neo-Taoist texts.
- The oneness of known humankind can be found in: Augustine's *De Civitate Dei*; and Dante's *De Monarchia*.
- The similarities in cultures and civilizations were emphasized in: the Roman Empire; the Roman Church's alliance with Charlemagne's empire and the Habsburg territories; Buddhist and Hindu texts. The similarities were not emphasized in the West during the age of national migrations.
- The universal being (or self) that opens to the Light behind the rational, social ego is in: Dante; St Catherine of Siena; and the Neo-Taoist *The Secret of the Golden Flower*.
- Universal virtue is in: Dante; *Everyman*; and *Sir Gawayne and the Grene Knight*.
- The promise of the immortality of the universal being is present in: Beowulf's journey to Valhalla; 'The Dream of the Rood'; Dante; Everyman's quest in response to death; and Buddhist, Hindu and Neo-Taoist texts.
- The inner transformation or centre-shift from ego to universal being is found in: Dante; and St. Catherine of Siena.
- The quest of the purified soul is in: *Beowulf*; Sir Galahad's quest for the Grail in *Le Conte du Graal*; Dante; and Zen.
- The sensibility that approaches Reality through more than one

104

discipline can be found in: Omar Khayyam (astronomy, algebra, philosophy, jurisprudence, history, medicine, alchemy and poetry); Dante (poetry, philosophy, statecraft in *De Monarchia* and diplomacy); Petrarch (poetry, epic poetry, essays, letters, ambassador); and Chaucer (poetry, romance/*Troilus and Criseyde*, translation).

- The new perspective of unity in history, religion, philosophy and science, international politics and literature can be found in Dante (unification of international politics in *De Monarchia*).

The increasing secularization found alongside the metaphysical aspect of the fundamental theme in the Middle Ages was intensified as a result of the Humanist Renaissance, after which the metaphysical tradition co-exists with the secular tradition within the fundamental theme.

4

The Literature of the Renaissance

The Fundamental Theme and History

The metaphysical and secular streams in literature are related to stages in history. In my work on the philosophy of history[1] I showed that 25 civilizations each go through 61 stages in their rise-and-fall cycle and then pass into another civilization, and that their motive force was an early vision of the metaphysical Light, round which a religion formed. When this vision ceases to be transmitted and weakens, its civilization displays the symptoms of secularization and begins to decline. Historical civilizations pass through stages in which the vision of the Light is strong and stages in which secularization becomes prominent.

In history, as civilizations progress there is a constant conflict between the vision of the metaphysical Reality and a more secular outlook. It is therefore completely understandable that within the fundamental theme of literature a vision of metaphysical Light should be in conflict with a more secular outlook. In each living civilization – the North-American, European, Indian, Chinese, Tibetan and Japanese civilizations – the metaphysical aspect of the fundamental theme in literature is strong during the first half of its rise-and-fall parabola and has periods (like the present period within the contemporary European civilization) when it weakens in the face of a more secular outlook in literature, which begins to predominate. The strength or weakness of the metaphysical aspect of the fundamental theme is a reflection of the dynamic and prevailing *zeitgeist* of its civilization: the strength or weakness of the vision of metaphysical Light.

From now on my setting-out of the fundamental theme, which was universal at the beginning of the world's civilizations in the 3rd and 2nd millennia BC, conveys a story in which both metaphysical and secular aspects of the fundamental theme co-exist: the quest for Reality, strong when a commitment to virtue and the vision of the Light is widespread; and a more secular outlook when focus on everyday life, on the falling-short of virtue and on vices, is more prevalent, filling the void left by the absence of the metaphysical quest. It is as if the shining of the sun casts shadows, and shadow becomes more interesting than the sun. In short, in secularized times writers move away from the metaphysical aspect of the fundamental theme to its secular aspect: exposing imperfections and vices, flaws of human character that are destructive to the social order.

It would be possible to lay out the rise-and-fall pattern of 25 civilizations, showing progression from a strong metaphysical vision to increasingly strong secularization, and to superimpose on it all the literary works that we have been considering and will consider. It would then be seen that there is a correspondence between the metaphysical vision within the civilization and the metaphysical aspect of the fundamental theme in literature, and a correspondence between periods in which the metaphysical vision is almost absent and is replaced by a more secular outlook in literature that focuses on the flaws of human nature which in the Church-dominated Middle Ages were regarded as "sins".

The Fundamental Theme and the European Renaissance

The Renaissance began a period of increased secularization in Europe. It was a "rebirth" of the spirit of ancient Greece and Rome, a revival of a new spirit of learning and of intellectual and artistic enquiry. Classical scholars known as Humanists led a revival of the arts and literature following a number of inventions and discoveries and following the fall in 1453 of Constantinople to the Turks, which drove Greek scholars to Italy. They brought with them Greek literature which had been virtually unknown in Western Europe, and the new texts were spread by the new technique of printing. The Renaissance began in Italy because it was near to Greece and welcomed refugee Greek scholars bringing Greek manuscripts, and because it had inherited the ancient Roman classics.

Soon afterwards, in 1492, Columbus's voyage to America opened European minds to a New World hitherto unknown and led to the development of overseas empires and increased knowledge about the world. In the same year the Spanish *reconquista* of Isabella and Ferdinand expelled the Moors from Spain. The Protestant Reformation led by Martin Luther introduced a new form of Christianity based on the individual. All these events awakened the minds of Italians, Greeks, Moors (who taught the Italians how to make paper), Germans and English.

The Italian Renaissance

Earlier than that, in May 1439, Gemistos Plethon had visited Florence with the Byzantine Emperor's delegation to bring the Byzantine and Catholic faiths together.

Ficino

Plethon had been received by Cosimo de' Medici, and had told him that all the works of Plato should be translated, an idea Cosimo put to Marsilio Ficino in 1462. Ficino revived Plato's Academy at the Medici's summer palace, the Villa Medici at Careggi just outside Florence.

Ficino translated the works of Plato and of the Neoplatonist Plotinus from Greek into Latin, and he reflected Plato's use of the metaphysical aspect of the fundamental theme. In *Theologica Platonica* he gave the human soul a central place in the universe and urged that the soul links the highest and lowest beings through its universal, infinite aspirations. In the course of its inner ascent through higher and higher degrees of knowledge and love the soul would be able to contemplate God after death. He argued for the immortality of the soul and held that love and friendship is a communion based on the soul's love for God. This was the basis of spiritual or "Platonic" love, which passed into literature in the 16th century.

In his twelve books of letters Ficino writes of the Light. In *Liber* I, letter 4, "a theological dialogue between God and the soul", God says, "You have the soul, an incorporeal light....It alone gives life to the incorporeal."[2] And in letter 39,

> "Whenever the actions of eating, accumulating, feeling or imagining either entirely cease or are greatly reduced, then the vision of the mind will be correspondingly sharp, so that whatever is observed by the mind is observed more clearly under the power of light. Then indeed the soul will observe through itself, and it will see that light of the intellect more clearly than it now sees the light of the senses through the glass

windows of this bodily prison. Entirely at peace, it will perceive through its own perfect transparency the highest impressions in the light of the divine sun. So bright is that light, that the light of this sun becomes a shadow in comparison, and because it is so clear it is hidden from impure eyes but fully manifest to those that are pure."[3]

In *Liber* VI, letter 20, Ficino tells us "God is light,"[4] and in *Liber* VIII, letter 56, God "is the light".[5]

In his commentary on book 7 of Plato's *Republic* Ficino writes: "Light is threefold: divine, intellectual, and visible. The divine light is called the Sun of the other two Suns; the intellectual light is called the angelic Sun...; the visible light is the Sun in the heavens and its effulgence....The light within the angelic mind is the activity and image of the divine light."[6]

I have all seven volumes of Ficino's letters translated to date, and on every page there is a reference (sometimes through Plato) to the metaphysical aspect of the fundamental theme: the soul's relationship to God perceived as Light.

Machiavelli

Humanism revalued man. It opposed the medieval view that an individual had little value, and saw man as the centre of the universe, linking the earthly and spiritual lives through the power of his soul. Humanism nevertheless remained faithful to Christian beliefs.

In *Il principe* ("The Prince", 1513) Niccolò Machiavelli, secretary to two governing bodies of the Florentine Republic after the Medici were expelled and an envoy to Italian provinces and to the French court of Louis XII, held up Cesare Borgia as the self-interested model for rulers to follow. The book was dedicated to Lorenzo de' Medici, Cosimo's grandson, and explains to him the best ways to acquire, hold and protect a state. A virtuous, stable state sometimes requires unvirtuous, even cruel behaviour to maintain it, Machiavelli maintains, and admirers of the book have included Frederick the Great, Napoleon, Mussolini, Stalin and the Mafia. Machiavel (i.e. Machiavelli) is a character in Marlowe's *The Jew of* Malta, and lurks behind Iago's duplicity in *Othello*. Machiavelli called for a united Italy under a monarch (Lorenzo) who would rule by expedience. He lost his position when the Medici returned in 1512. In this work he saw politics as a science divorced from ethics.

Machiavelli himself aspired to Christian values. He derived his self-interested principles from the history of the Roman Empire in *Discorsi sopra la prima deca di Tito Livio* ("Discourses on the First Ten Books of Tito Livy", 1513), in which he argued that in times of danger the State may have to put aside high morality. However, he insisted that civic virtue is liberty's best defence. He had been sent to Rome to observe the election of Pope Julius II in 1503, having a few months earlier observed the decline of Cesare Borgia and having celebrated his imprisonment in Spain in 1504 (which he thought Cesare deserved as a rebel against Christ).

It has been suggested that *The Prince* was a satire, ridiculing the duplicitous behaviour of politicians and of tyrannical rule,[7] or that it was designed to undo Lorenzo,[8] but it can be best understood as guidelines for protecting a virtuous state. Rousseau wrote:

"Machiavelli was a proper man and a good citizen; but, being attached to the court of the Medici, he could not help veiling his love of liberty in the midst of his country's oppression. The choice of his detestable hero, Cesare Borgia, clearly enough shows his hidden aim; and the contradiction between the teaching of *The Prince* and that of the *Discourses on the First Ten Books of Tito Livy* and the *History of Florence* shows that this profound political thinker has so far been studied only by superficial or corrupt readers."[9]

Machiavelli had deep feelings for religion and a hidden deep morality which came out in *La mandragola* ("The Mandrake", 1518).

Machiavelli's work touches on the metaphysical aspect of the fundamental theme, for his soul quested into ruthless, expedient politics which he actually despised and ended up on the side of virtue – he writes of his despair of seeing virtue triumph – and of the Light, and his religious nature is apparent on every page.

His contemporary Castiglione's *Il cortegiano* ("The Courtier", written 1513-18) presents the perfect courtier and his ideal relationship with the prince. The perfect courtier embodies the highest moral aspirations of the Renaissance, and the work touches on the metaphysical aspect of the fundamental theme by extolling virtue.

Ariosto and Tasso

In the 16th century two poetic epics with crusading contents touched on the metaphysical aspect of the fundamental theme. Ariosto's *Orlando furioso* was on the struggle between Charlemagne and the Moors, drew on the French Roland: loves within a crusading context and the defence of the Christian religion. Tasso's *Gerusalemme liberate* ("Jerusalem Delivered", 1575) was on the Christians' struggle with the Saracens. In the first scene the angel Gabriel comes to Godfrey de Bouillon and tells him that he has been chosen by Heaven to lead a crusading army and besiege Jerusalem. Devils in conclave in Hell endeavour to thwart him. (The similar involvements of Christ and Satan in battles in my *Overlord* and *Armageddon* can be seen as the continuation of a long tradition that began with Homer and includes Dante and Tasso.) In the poem's successor, *Gerusalemme conquistata* ("Jerusalem vanquished", 1593), Godfrey, leader of the Christians, wrests Jerusalem from the infidels, but the ideals of the Catholic Counter-Reformation elevate the moralistic above artistic considerations, and the poem is flawed.

About the same time the Portuguese Luis de Camões' epic poem *Os Lusiades* wrote of the history of Portugal through the descendants of Lusus, the legendary founder of Lusitania, the early name for Portugal, and of the voyages of the Portuguese navigator Vasco da Gama. This work touches on the quest for truth but as in much Renaissance literature conveys this through the social world.

The French and Dutch Renaissance

The Renaissance spread from Italy to France as soldiers invading Italy with Charles VIII in 1494, Louis XII in 1500 and Francis I in 1515 brought back to France news of the new painting, architecture and literature flourishing in Italy.

Rabelais

After many years of being dominated by monasteries, French writers were now outspoken, particularly François Rabelais, a Benedictine monk and later priest who mocked the Scholastic church hierarchy, schools and universities, theologians, lawyers and philosophers while describing the fantastical adventures in prose of two eponymous giants in *Pantagruel* and its successor *Gargantua*.

However, Rabelais remained a disciple of Erasmus (see below) and Humanist Christianity, and in his "Prologue of the Author" at the beginning of *Pantagruel* he wrote: "There is one irrefutable answer: it is the will of the mighty and beneficent God, on whom I rely, whom I obey, whose most holy message of good news I revere." In *Pantagruel* he is serious about the divine gift of fertile matrimony, and in *Gargantua* he is emphatic that a Christian prince is God's agent. His work touches on the metaphysical aspect of the fundamental theme as it is a quest for truth within the *débris* of Scholasticism, and an affirmation of God within the new Humanism.

Ronsard

The poet Pierre de Ronsard, one of the group of five poets of *La Pléiade* to which Rabelais also belonged, set out to create a French Renaissance literature that would rival the Italian Renaissance literature. His Horatian odes, Italianate sonnets (*Les Amours*), elegies, philosophical and reflective poems (*Les Hymnes*) and the first four books of a French national epic, *La Franciade*, were written between 1540 and 1580. His lyric poetry expressed a love of Nature, a hatred of death and a sadness that all things must die, an echo of Gilgamesh's outlook on the universe that touches on the metaphysical aspect of the fundamental theme.

Montaigne

Montaigne's *Essais* ("Essays", written between 1571 and 1580) reflected his problems: ambition, pain and death. He wrote that we must prepare for death as "the goal of our career..., the necessary object of our aim," and "learn to meet it steadfastly and to combat it".[10] In his 'Apology for Raymond Sebond' he writes of man's ignorance of God and attacks the vanity of reason. The existence of God and the immortality of the soul, he claims, are incapable of rational proof but must be accepted on faith. His later essays dwell on the pain caused by his kidney stone, and he praises the effortless virtue of Socrates. His essays touch on the metaphysical aspect of the fundamental theme as they are a quest for truth, certain of what the self can know, and urge a virtuous life during the soul's progress along the way to God.

Erasmus

The Dutch Desiderius Erasmus became an Augustinian canon and was sent to study at the University of Paris in 1495. He took against Scholastic theology and came into contact with Humanist groups in England (around Sir Thomas More, John Fisher and John Colet) and in Italy. In *Encomium Moriae* ("Praise of Folly", 1511), which Erasmus claimed was written in a week to amuse his friend Sir Thomas More, a work in the Lucianic style, Erasmus wrote:

"Although this perfect happiness can only be experienced when the soul has recovered its former body and been granted immortality, since the life of the pious is no more than a contemplation and foreshadowing of that other life, at times they are able to feel some foretaste and savour of the reward to come. It is only the tiniest drop in comparison with the fount of eternal bliss."[11]

He sees the contemplative life as anticipating the life of the soul after death. His evangelical humanism drew on the Platonist tradition of Ficino via Pico della Mirandola and Colet: man's moral achievement and perfection were outside theology.

In 1516 Erasmus published a translation into Latin of the *New Testament* based on the Greek text, and arguably did more to challenge the Catholic Church before 1517 than Luther, who followed his example by translating the *Bible* into German in 1522.

Erasmus lived as a scholar, but his work reflects the metaphysical aspect of the fundamental theme for in *Praise of Folly* the soul quests for truth, recognises folly along the way and knows that it has been granted immortality.

The English Renaissance

The first glimmerings of the English Renaissance took place in the 1520s.

More

Erasmus's friend Sir Thomas More read the classical authors, including Plato, and the Church Fathers. He campaigned for Erasmus's religious and cultural program and his *Utopia* was published in Latin at Louvain under Erasmus's supervision in 1516 (and in English in 1551). It was inspired by the narrative of the voyages of Amerigo Vespucci, and presented an ideal state, More's version of Plato's ideal republic, to cloak a satirical exposure of the social and political evils of his day, to expose the origin of social imperfections and convey opinions conflicting with those accepted by Henry VIII's court.[12] (William Penn followed and implemented its scheme when he founded Philadelphia.) In the 1520s More attacked Luther's dogmas – Erasmus looked on Luther as an upstart – and was eventually beheaded for refusing to recognise Henry VIII as head of the English Church.

More's life and work reflect the metaphysical aspect of the fundamental theme as he quested for truth, offered Utopian improvements to the human working life and espoused virtue, choosing to be beheaded rather than accept the Reformation and renounce his beliefs regarding God's Church. After his death the Reformation took hold in England with the appearance of William Tyndale's *Bible* in 1539, Cranmer's *Book of Common Prayer* in 1549 and Foxe's *Book of Martyrs* in 1563.

Silver Poets: Wyatt and Surrey

The Silver Poets of the 16th century were minor poets who at first sight do not appear to relate to the metaphysical aspect of the fundamental theme but rather to its secular aspect as they devote themselves to transmitting secular love poems in Italianate forms. They seem as much interested in technique as in content.

Sir Thomas Wyatt (or Wyat), a courtier and diplomat, introduced the Petrarchian sonnet from Italy. He is thought to have been a lover of Anne Boleyn before her marriage to Henry VIII, and he was imprisoned in the Tower following the alleged discovery of her infidelities. At first sight he seems to be a wholly secular influence, but two spells of imprisonment – the second for being an ally of Thomas Cromwell – took him to his *Penitential Psalms*, and his quest for truth through love and his disillusion and psalms touch on the metaphysical aspect of the fundamental theme.

The Earl of Surrey, a nobleman, studied Petrarch, and his translation of the early books of the *Aeneid* presented the first use of blank verse in English literature. He served in the army in France and was beheaded when barely 30 in 1546 a few days before the death of Henry VIII. His crime was ostensibly quartering the royal arms and advising his sister to become the King's mistress, but he was in reality being accused of plotting to set aside the succession of the young Edward VI and to assume the throne. His quest for love likewise reflects virtue and truth, as when in his poem 'In praise of Wyatt's Psalms' he writes:

> "Where he doth paint the lively faith and pure,
> The steadfast hope, the sweet return to grace,
> Of just David, by perfect penitence;
> Where rulers may see, in a mirror clear,
> The bitter fruit of force concupiscence."

He identifies with Wyatt's exposure of the vices of rulers. Like Sir Thomas More, Wyatt and Surrey were both alert to the virtue of the state.

Thomas Sackville's 'Induction' to *A Myrrour for Magistrates* goes back to the medieval tradition. The poet reflects on the miserable end of great ones and visits the realm of the dead to hear their complaints. After crossing the Acheron he enters the kingdom of Pluto and hears the complaint of the Duke of Buckingham. This work touches on the metaphysical aspect of the fundamental theme as the poet's quest for truth takes him, like Odysseus, Aeneas and Dante, into the Underworld, where he confronts immortality in the form of the spirits who have survived death.

John Lyly's prose *Euphues* was an attack on irreligion. A young Athenian (a disguise for an Oxford student) succumbs to the vices of Naples (London) and loses his virtue and loyalty in friendship. He is disillusioned when his fickle mistress takes up with an unworthy suitor, and he returns to Athens (Oxford) and now preaches caution. The book touches on the metaphysical aspect of the fundamental theme as there is a quest for truth through vice which ends in the affirmation of virtue. (The book's sequel, *Euphues and his England*, displays the virtue and constancy to be found in London, and throughout England, an idealised picture.)

Sidney

Sir Philip Sidney, a nobleman from Wilton, politician and diplomat who dreamt of grouping Protestant nations against the Pope and the King of Spain in support of Sir Francis Drake, worshipped the Queen and wrote Italianate sonnets to an unattainable lady. His *Astrophel and Stella* is thought to be addressed to Penelope Devereux, the daughter of the 1st Earl of Essex who was married against her will to Lord Rich. She was in love with Charles Blount, the Earl of Devonshire, and married him after her divorce. "Astrophel" suggests "Astra", "star", the meaning of "Stella", and "phel" puns on "phil", "lover", but is also short for Philip. Thus "Astrophel" is "the lover of the star, i.e. Sir Philip Sidney".

Sidney's *The Old Arcadia*, which drew on *Orlando furioso* and was probably written to please his sister, the Countess of Pembroke, is set in Arcadia, where King Basilius has retired and brings up his daughters as shepherdesses. Two strange princes, one disguised as a peasant, the other as a woman, introduce passion and end up marrying two of the daughters. The work has insights into the moral confusion of the two princes.

Sidney married the daughter of Sir Francis Walsingham, who was in charge of the Queen's intelligence service; and became governor of Flushing. The flower of England's youth, he died young, aged 31, in a minor battle against the Spanish at Zutphen. He was wounded three fingers above his knee and took twenty-two days to die, during which he prayed much and read the *Bible*.

Sidney had lived his life on a notion of human perfection, personal virtue and wisdom. He wrote in *An Apologie for Poetrie* or *The Defence of Poesie*, that poetry makes truth shine through the fog of sense. His work touches on the metaphysical aspect of the fundamental theme as it is a quest for perfection and virtue, and also for truth.

Spenser

Sidney's death left Spenser as the main Elizabethan poet. *The Fairie Queene*, an Italianate romance he worked on for 20 years and left unfinished when he died, came out in two chunks. The first chunk came out with the help of Sir Walter Raleigh (or Ralegh) who owned lands to the east of Spenser's estate in Cork, Ireland, where Spenser was secretary to the new lord deputy of Ireland, Lord Grey of Wilton (a friend of the Sidney family). As his introductory letter to Raleigh of 1589 indicates, it is an allegory based on King Arthur, a knight "perfected in the twelve private morall vertues, as Aristotle hath devised".

Arthur has a vision of the Fairie Queene and seeks her out. The poem itself is about the adventures of Arthur's 12 knights, all of whom exemplify a particular virtue (for example, holiness, temperance, chastity, friendship, justice and courtesy). Only six out of the planned 12 books were completed, and the twelfth book, which Spenser told Raleigh would account for the origins of the adventures and be "the beginning therefore of my history", was never written.

The scheme was to some extent modelled on Ariosto's *Orlando furioso* and Tasso's *Gerusalemme liberata*. It celebrates the Tudor dynasty, with the Fairie Queene, Gloriana, representing Elizabeth I (who is also the virgin Belphoebe and Lucifera, "the maiden queen"). Arthur, who is in love with the Fairie Queene, may embody Leicester (Elizabeth's favourite).

But despite the topical allusions, the scheme is similar to the Grail legend. Arthur symbolizes divine grace, and the Redcrosse Knight represents the Christian soul in quest of truth who is confronted by the alternatives of Protestantism and Catholicism, and the lapse of faith in the 16th century.[13] Spenser reflects the metaphysical aspect of the fundamental theme as he narrates a scorned lover's quest for truth and a metaphysical Fairie Queene (if we disregard the Tudor associations), and extolls all the virtues.

Raleigh

Sir Walter Raleigh, besides being an English adventurer, favourite of Elizabeth I, colonizer of America and author of *The History of the World* (which was written in the Tower), was a minor poet sometimes grouped with the Metaphysicals. His verses in 'The Ocean's Love to Cynthia' (or 'The Ocean, to Cynthia') are addressed to Cynthia (Elizabeth I) and suggest his disillusion with the court. At the end of the poem he writes: "My mind's affection and my soul's sole love,.../To God I leave it." In 'The Lie' he rails against the court: "Goe soule the bodies guest." Raleigh's poetic output was slight, but in these passages he touches on the metaphysical aspect of the fundamental theme for his soul turns away from the life of the body and seeks for God.

'The passionate mans Pilgrimage' used to be attributed to Raleigh and was thought to have been written while he was under sentence of death in the Tower from 17 November to 6 December 1603. The poet expects to die the next day: "Seeing my flesh must die so soone,/And want a head to dine next moone,.../Set on my soule an everlasting head." However, it has been questioned whether this poem was in fact written by Raleigh, and his authorship is now so doubtful that the author is regarded as anonymous. Whether or not the author was Raleigh, the poem reflects the metaphysical aspect of the fundamental theme for it begins with a reference to the scallop shell pilgrims brought back from Santiago de Compostela in North Spain: "Give me my Scallop shell of quiet,/My staffe of Faith to walk upon,/My scrip of Joy, Immortall diet,/My bottle of salvation." The poem refers to immortality: "And when our bottles and all we,/Are filled with immortalitie...."

In this work Raleigh – or "Anonymous" – reflects the metaphysical aspect of the fundamental theme for his soul, confronting death like Gilgamesh, is on a pilgrimage to immortality.

1590s English Poetry of Infatuation

The 1590s saw a renewed interest in mythological poetry and love sonnets, including Spenser's *Amoretti*. Three mythological tales about infatuation (a new, daring Renaissance theme imported from Italy), derived from Ovid's *Metamorphoses* and *Heroides*.

In Marlowe's unfinished *Hero and Leander* (c.1592), which was based on a 5th-century work by an Alexandrian, Musaeus, Leander, a youth at Abydos, regularly swims across the Hellespont to see Hero, a priestess of Aphrodite at Sestos. One night Leander is drowned in a storm, and Hero throws herself into the sea in despair.

In Shakespeare's *Venus and Adonis* (1593), Venus is in love with Adonis and prevents him from hunting so that she can woo him. The next day she finds him dead, killed by a boar.

Shakespeare's *The Rape of Lucrece* (1594) is about love of a darker kind. Lucrece, the Roman wife of Tarquinius Collatinus, is raped, her beauty having inflamed the passion of Sextus, the son of the Etruscan Tarquin, king of Rome. Unavenged, she takes her life, and the Tarquins (Etruscans) are expelled from Rome and replaced by a republican government.

In these three mythological poems the infatuation of Leander, Venus and Sextus destroys the lovers. Infatuation is an impediment to the quest for truth and Reality that results in immortality, a secular rather than a metaphysical expression of the fundamental theme. Marlowe and Shakespeare are showing an alternative way to the cloistered contemplation of the Middle Ages – an alternative Marlowe as an atheist seems to have sided with emotionally – and although fashionable it is destructive and is not a way that achieves inner truth.

Most of Shakespeare's 154 sonnets probably date from the 1590s. They take up the theme of infatuation.

The sonnets tell a story of a friend of the poet's who steals his mistress, a dark lady the poet is infatuated with, and of a rival poet. Sonnets 1-17 urge the friend, who has rank and beauty, to marry. Sonnets 18-126 form a sequence of 108 sonnets, the same number as in Sidney's *Astrophel and Stella*. They are addressed to "Mr W.H.", who could be William, Lord Herbert, later the Earl of Pembroke whose seat was Wilton, as was Sidney's and whose 1630 statue stands in the Bodleian Library's Schools Quadrangle. Those who argue that W.H. stands for Henry Wriothesley, the Earl of Southampton, have to explain why the W.H. has been reversed, and those who believe it is a printer's erroneous dedication to Mr W.Sh (William Shakespeare) have to explain why the S was omitted.

Within the social situation of the infatuation and triangle there are reflections on truth, beauty, death and immortality – in the sense of posthumous fame – through verse (a Renaissance treatment of immortality after death), which touch on the metaphysical aspect of the fundamental theme. Shakespeare's sonnet 55 follows Spenser's *Amoretti*, sonnet 75 in championing the perpetuation of one's name.

English Drama

The 1590s saw a revival of English drama which implemented the secular aspect of the fundamental theme: condemnation of vices in relation to an implied virtue.

An early drama had appeared in 1561, *Gorboduc* by Sackville and Norton, a Senecan tragedy based on Geoffrey of Monmouth.

> Gorboduc condemns greed and destructive revenge. The play is about a king of England whose sons quarrel over the division of the kingdom. One kills the other and is then murdered by his mother in revenge.

The revival of English drama began with the opening of the first London theatre, called The Theatre, in the suburb of Shoreditch in 1576. Translated material on which dramatists could base plays appeared by 1578. Holinshed's *Chronicles*, which narrated the history of England, Scotland and Ireland, appeared in 1577 and the following year North's version of Plutarch's *Parallel Lives* came out, with anecdotes illustrating the moral character of his subjects. There were travel narratives such as Hakluyt's *Principall Navigations, Voiages, and Discoveries of the English Nation*, which appeared in 1589.

In the 1580s "University wits" appeared, Oxford graduates who wrote plays to be performed at court: a romantic story with a compliment to Elizabeth I, who was represented as Cynthia, or the moon. Such wits included John Lyly, author of *Endimion*, and George Peele, whose *The Araygnement of Paris* drew on Paris's handing the apple to Venus, Diana now presenting it to the Queen; and whose *David and Fair Bethsabe* narrated a *Bible* story like the mystery plays. Robert Greene, another University wit, wrote a historical play, *James IV*, and Thomas Lodge wrote a pastoral romance called *Rosalinde* (1590), from which Shakespeare took the story of *As You Like It*.

The "tragedy of revenge", in which an egocentric drive for revenge brings about the hero's destruction as surely as infatuation, began with Thomas Kyd's play *The Spanish Tragedie* (c.1590, published anonymously in 1592).

> In *The Spanish Tragedie*, the vice was revenge. The play condemns the destructive revenge of an old man, Hieronimo against those who were

responsible for his son's death. Hieronimo carries out his revenge in a play within a play, in which the two murderers Lorenzo and Balthazar, are killed. Hieronimo bites out his tongue and then runs offstage to kill himself, having been destroyed by his desire for revenge.

Besides the play within a play, there is a fencing-match which turns into a duel, and both ideas were taken up by Shakespeare in *Hamlet*. In fact, Kyd is thought to be the author of a lost play called *Hamlet* from which Shakespeare took his story.

Marlowe

Christopher Marlowe, who in his short life was a government intelligence agent before he was stabbed to death in a pub in Deptford, wrote seven plays in blank verse (counting the two parts of *Tamburlaine the Great* as two plays). The fundamental unity of Marlowe's work is in his theme of a Machiavellian lust for power, which was both fascinating and reprehensible to Elizabethan audiences and which in the Renaissance time was an impediment to the quest for truth. This lust for power was the vice in relation to the implied virtue of the secular aspect of the fundamental theme:

1. *Dido, Queen of Carthage* (c.1586) condemns seeking power through sexual exploitation. Dido is fanatically infatuated by Aeneas (a state induced by Cupid). Based on Virgil's *Aeneid*, bks 1, 2 and 4, the play is about Dido's failure to persuade Aeneas to stay with her in Carthage and her subsequent suicide.

2-3. *Tamburlaine the Great*, Parts 1 and 2 (c.1587), condemns seeking power through conquest. Part 1 is about an over-reacher's rise to power which challenges the medieval concept of knowing, and remaining in, one's fixed place. It relates the rise of the Scythian shepherd-robber, Tamburlaine, to the throne. He allies himself with Cosroe, the King of Persia's brother, who leads a rebellion against the crown. Tamburlaine then challenges Cosroe for the throne and defeats him. He conquers the Turkish emperor and falls in love with the daughter of the Soldan (Sultan) of Egypt. In Part 2 he conquers Babylon, drawn in a chariot by four vanquished kings, and eventually dies.

4. The Jew of Malta (performed c.1591) condemns seeking power through money. It is based on Marlowe's work as an intelligence agent. The Grand Seignior of Turkey has demanded a tribute from Malta, which is to be paid by Jews. Barabas, a rich Jew, has his wealth confiscated and his house turned into a nunnery, and in revenge intrigues the death of his daughter's lover and then of his daughter. He betrays the fortress of Malta to the besieging Turks, who make him their governor as a reward. He plots to destroy the Turkish commander and his force by inviting them to a banquet at which the floor collapses, hurling them all into a cauldron. He is betrayed and is himself hurled into the cauldron and dies.

5. Edward II (performed c.1592) condemns seeking power through great beauty, through acting unconventionally in having a personal favourite. It tells of Edward's favourite, Piers Gaveston, who is executed following the revolt of the barons, and then of his favourite, Spenser (Hugh le Despenser); and of his estrangement from Queen Isabella. Supported by her lover Mortimer, she rebels against the king, who abdicates and is murdered in Berkeley Castle.

6. Dr Faustus (c.1592) condemns seeking power through knowledge. The play is about Faustus's ambition to win power and honour. He turns from the sciences to magic, conjures up Mephistophilis and makes a pact with him that he will surrender his soul to the Devil in return for 24 years of influence, prosperity and fame in the course of which Mephistophilis will give him everything he demands. He receives all he asks for including the calling-up of Helen of Troy, but after 24 years Mephistophilis returns to take his soul and, anguished, Faustus is carried off to Hell. The fundamental theme is strongly present in reverse: a quest for truth not through virtue and contact with the infinite Reality as Light but through vice, darkness, and contact with Lucifer in Hell.

7. The Massacre at Paris (c.1592) condemns seeking power through sectarian exploitation. The Machiavellian Duke of Guise kills a Hugenot Admiral and triggers the Catholic St Bartholomew's Day massacre in Paris of 1572, in which Hugenots were murdered.

Marlowe presented a world in which the exercise of power dominated and made impossible the contemplative tradition of the metaphysical aspect of the fundamental theme. His plays were morality plays about heroes who aspired to fanatical love, unlimited dominion, unlimited wealth, ideal beauty, forbidden knowledge, unlimited sectarian influence, and overreached themselves and were destroyed by their overreaching.

The Fundamental Unity of Shakespeare's Plays

Shakespeare took up the Elizabethan drama which Marlowe and his contemporaries developed, and gave the public what it wanted. He took his plots from history, *Plutarch's Parallel Lives* and Italian sources. He seldom invented a story, preferring Aristotelian imitation of previous works, and experimented with different styles adopted by his models.

Shakespeare's first period, when he was learning how to handle character and blank verse and under the tutelage of other playwrights, ended with *Romeo and Juliet* and *A Midsummer Night's Dream* in 1591. His second period began after the theatres were closed due to the plague, and lasted from 1595 to 1601. During this time he wrote most of his plays about English history, following the fashion Marlowe set with *Edward II*; the mature works; and most of the sonnets. His third period began in 1601 and lasted until 1609, during which he wrote his tragedies and seemed to be in a time of mental anguish and despair. His fourth period shows a ripening, a coming to terms with life in which he created tragi-comedies, ending with *The Tempest*.

Shakespeare wrote 39 plays if *Henry VIII, The Two Noble Kinsmen* and the lost *Cardenio* are included and the doubtful *Edmund Ironside* and *Sir Thomas More* are excluded. (An incomplete transcript has survived for *Sir Thomas More* with revisions in five hands, one of which – Hand D – is thought, with strong support, to be Shakespeare's: three pages of More as sheriff of London pacifying a May-Day rebellion against foreigners, perhaps the only lines he contributed to this play.) The tally of 39 allows for the fact that in some plays he collaborated and only wrote part. All touch on the metaphysical aspect of the fundamental theme, but in a negative way: condemning vices in relation to an implied virtue.

In each of the plays the main character has a flaw, a defect in virtue

– virtue being an important characteristic of the metaphysical aspect of the fundamental theme – which indicates an egotistical self. This flaw drives his characters to commit egocentric acts such as usurping the throne, which shake the order of the Great Chain of Being. Shakespeare has a standard of universal virtue by which to measure, and condemn, human follies, vices, blindness, corruption, hypocrisy, self-love and egotism (see p.4).

In the comedies the flaw is recognised, and the flawed character realizes the error of his ways and begins a process of transformation. In the histories the flaw is an act such as a usurpation which has consequences which are often not felt for a generation or two. In the tragedies it is a fatal flaw which destroys the flawed character.

All the flaws in the 39 plays have to be addressed before the quest of the purified soul for truth and Reality can begin. In other words, Shakespeare's plays are about imperfect people whose imperfections are addressed, bringing them to the point where they can embark on the metaphysical aspect of the fundamental theme – which they touch on in the course of their inner development or purification.

We will take a look at the flaw in each of the plays, proceeding in accordance with the groups in the *First Folio*: comedies, histories and tragedies. The comedies and the tragedies are presented in alphabetical order, the historical plays in chronological order of the kings. The probable chronological order in which the plays were performed is listed at the back.[14]

The comedies vary from sunny, witty works full of banter to complicated and frankly unbelievable farces, to darker plays such as *The Tempest*. In all his plays Shakespeare drew on previous, generally Italian plays, and in several plays made much of confusion caused by identical twins, cross-dressing, mistaken identity, "bed tricks" (in which a woman disguises herself as another to be with the man she loves) and shipwrecks, devices often implausible and sometimes tiresome. Nevertheless, he gets to the heart of egotistical human nature and presents flawed and therefore, to many, real human beings. I state the flaw within the theme of each play as briefly as possible:

1. All's Well That Ends Well. The flaw is snobbishness. A nobleman, Bertram, is to wed an orphaned commoner, Helena, on the orders of the

King of France, and is offended by the inequality of their backgrounds and sets off to war. Helena follows him to Florence and after her "bed trick" (in which, disguised, she takes the place of another lady) he realizes the error of his ways, is transformed and accepts her as his wife.

2. *As You Like It.* The flaw is Duke Frederick's usurpation. Duke Frederick has usurped the lands of his brother, and when his daughter Rosalind falls in love with Orlando, he banishes Rosalind, who flees to the forest of Arden disguised as a man. Eventually she marries Orlando in front of her father. Duke Frederick sets out to destroy his brother and his followers but is converted by "an old religious man", sees the error of his ways, is transformed and restores the dukedom to his brother.

3. *The Comedy of Errors.* The flaw is the Duke of Ephesus's strictness in his enforcement of justice. Any Syracusan found in Ephesus is to be executed unless he can pay a ransom of a thousand marks. Aegeon, a Syracusan merchant, is arrested while searching for his twin sons in Ephesus, who are both (improbably) named Antipholus. They appear just as he is about to be executed. (To confuse things, they have twin slaves who are both named Dromio.) The ransom is offered, but the Duke of Ephesus relents, sees the error of his ways and frees Aegeon, who is reunited with his family. All blindness and confusion of identities are no more.

4. *Cymbeline.* The flaw is Cymbeline's tyrannical disposition. Cymbeline banishes the husband his daughter Imogen has secretly married, and she sets out to find him in the forest. Cymbeline's two long-lost sons (stolen in their infancy) save their sister, Imogen, from her enemies and save Cymbeline in battle against the Romans, who have invaded Britain. Imogen, a page to a Roman general, is captured and reveals herself to Cymbeline, who is reconciled to her and overjoyed to be reunited with his two sons. He had just sentenced one of them to be executed, and now spares all prisoners. He sees the error of his ways.

5. *Love's Labour's Lost.* The flaw is King Ferdinand of Navarre's

unrealistic pretension and self-deceit. He makes three of his lords sign a declaration vowing that they will study with him for three years and not see a woman in that time. They fail to keep their oaths when a diplomatic mission consisting of the Princess of France and her ladies arrive. They soon forget their vows. Their wooing is interrupted by the death of the Princess's father, and the ladies impose an ordeal on their lovers, banishing them to a hermitage for a year. King Ferdinand sees the error of his ways.

6. *Measure for Measure.* The flaw is Angelo's hypocrisy. The Duke of Vienna asks his deputy, Angelo, to rule while, disguised as a friar, he investigates the moral decay of his dukedom. His deputy condemns fornicators to death, including Claudio, but blackmails his sister, a nun: her virtue or Claudio's life. The Duke overhears and in a "bed trick" Mariana, who was once betrothed to Angelo, takes Isabella's place. The Duke marries Isabella. Inflicting just punishment ("measure for measure") should be tempered by mercy, and Angelo, who has tried to commit the very act for which he condemned Claudio, sees the error of his ways and all are united in marriage.

7. *The Merchant of Venice.* The flaw is Shylock's greed. Shylock lends money to Antonio, who lends it to his friend Bassanio, who uses it to woo Portia. When Antonio is unable to pay it back Shylock insists on his bond, a pound of flesh, from which Portia (in disguise) saves Antonio by pointing out that no blood must be spilt. Shylock's daughter elopes with an anti-Semite and, angry and filled with grief, he now sees the error of his ways and Antonio's wealth is restored.

8. *The Merry Wives of Windsor.* The flaw is Sir John Falstaff's insincerity towards women. Falstaff, impoverished, woos two wives who rule their husband's purses, insincerely pretending to be lovestruck when he is only interested in money. They make a fool of him, as do the jealous husbands. Falstaff sees the error of his ways.

9. *A Midsummer Night's Dream.* The flaw is Egeus's tyrannical behaviour towards his daughter. Egeus orders his daughter Hermia to marry Demetrius. Both love another and she refuses. Theseus, Duke of

Athens, who is about to marry Hippolyta, gives Hermia four days to obey her father, or else be executed or enter a nunnery. Hermia flees to a wood outside Athenian jurisdiction and under the control of fairies, whose love potions confuse. Egeus and Theseus see the error of their ways, that justice should not be inflicted without mercy, forgive the runaways and all ends well.

10. Much Ado About Nothing. The flaw is Benedick's disdainful self-love. Benedick scorns romantic love and being married, and Beatrice scorns men not up to her wit. They have met when the Prince of Aragon, with Benedick in his suite, visits Messina. Both are tricked into believing that the other secretly loves them. This love is tested when Benedick's friend Claudio is told that Beatrice's friend Hero is unchaste and Claudio spurns her at the altar. The misunderstanding is sorted out and Benedick sees the error of his ways and becomes a married man.

11. Pericles. The flaw is Pericles' excessive mourning. Pericles, Prince of Tyre, forced to flee King Antiochus for discovering his incestuous affair with his daughter, is shipwrecked at Pentapolis and marries Thaisa, who bears a daughter on the return journey to Tyre. She appears to have died in childbirth and is laid to rest in a chest at sea and carried to Ephesus alive. Pericles is melancholic and in distemper. He leaves his child, Marina, with the governor of Tharsus, whose wife wickedly plans to murder her, for she has grown into a talented and charming young woman, overshadowing her daughter's chances. The murder is interrupted by pirates, who carry Marina off and sell her into a brothel. Pericles is distraught at what he understands to be Marina's death and swears to mourn the loss of his wife and daughter for the rest of his life. Marina's purity, piety and virtue win the admiration of Lysimachus, the governor of Mitylene, where Pericles encounters her. She tries to cure his distemper and he recognises her resemblance to his wife. He finds Thaisa in a temple at Ephesus, and husband, wife and daughter are reunited. Pericles sees the error of his ways, and the gods have made "my past miseries sports".

12. The Taming of the Shrew. The flaw is Katherina's shrewish temper. Katherina has a bad temper and is wooed for her dowry by Petruchio, who pretends to find her courteous and gentle despite her rude rebuffs. He keeps her waiting on her wedding day, appears in old clothes, refuses to attend the bridal feast, and hustles his wife off home. There he deprives her of food and sleep, saying the food and bed are not up to her standard, and he takes her back to her father's house tamed. She is the most submissive of three wives at another wedding feast and sees the error of her ways and is transformed. (One can imagine Shakespeare's actors exaggerating Katherina's rudeness and Petruchio's politeness, and the audience's guffaws.)

13. The Tempest. The flaw is usurpation. The King of Naples ousts and exiles Prospero, the Duke of Milan, with the help of Prospero's usurping brother. Prospero's magic brings the King of Naples, his son and the usurping brother to his island, and arranges for his daughter to fall in love with the King of Naples' son. This reconciles the enmity between Milan and Naples and restores Prospero's dukedom. All return to Naples. The King of Naples and Prospero's brother have seen the error of their usurping ways.

14. Troilus and Cressida. The flaw is Troilus's infatuation with a flirtatious girl. Troilus, a Trojan, falls in love with Cressida, a flirtatious, thoughtless, ready-jilting Greek captive, Pandarus's niece. Pandarus sets up an assignation between Troilus and Cressida. They pledge constancy. An exchange of prisoners has been agreed, and Cressida must return to the Greek camp. Diomedes arrives in Troy to fetch Cressida. Troilus is distraught and breaks the news to Cressida. They exchange tokens, a glove and a sleeve. After Cressida leaves, Ulysses says she is a slut. Troilus fears she will fall in love with a Greek when she returns. He asks Ulysses to take him to her father's tent where, hidden, they watch Cressida flirt with an insistent Diomedes, to whom she gives the sleeve Troilus gave her. After Diomedes leaves she speaks of her own inconstancy. Troilus is furious and vows to kill Diomedes in the battle next day. Cressida sends him a love letter, which he tears up. Troilus sees the error of his ways and is no longer love-sick for a flirtatious girl. (The editors of the *First Folio* could not decide whether this play was a comedy or a tragedy, but Troilus is not destroyed by his flaw and the play is therefore clearly a comedy.)

15. Twelfth Night. The flaw is self-love. Olivia, blinded by self-love, is egotistically absorbed in grieving for seven years for her brother. She spurns her suitors, including Orsino, who pines for her and is also blinded by self-love. She falls in love with a messenger, a shipwrecked twin who dresses as a man, Viola, who calls herself Cesario. She was sent to Olivia by Orsino, with whom she is secretly in love. Olivia and Orsino, who thought they were in love with others, end up with the twins, and in a sub-plot Malvolio is tricked by Olivia's uncle, Sir Toby Belch. In the end Olivia sees the error of her ways and calls Malvolio "sick of self-love" (her own complaint) and all are united in love except for Malvolio.

16. The Two Gentlemen of Verona. The flaw is Proteus's ruthless inconstancy. Proteus is betrothed to Julia in Verona. He leaves her and travels to Milan and falls in love with his friend's girlfriend Silvia, betraying his friend and Julia. He reveals to the Duke of Milan his friend Valentine's intention to abduct Silvia, who is the Duke of Milan's daughter. Valentine is banished and leaves a group of robbers, and Proteus continues to woo Silvia, having taken on a page, who is Julia disguised as a boy. Valentine returns to find Proteus with Silvia. Proteus is filled with remorse, and Valentine offers Silvia to him, to the dismay of Julia. He swoons and is recognised by Proteus, who now sees the error of his ways and he marries Julia while Valentine marries Silvia.

17. The Two Noble Kinsmen. The flaw is egocentric interference in love. In Thebes two cousins, Palamon and Arcite are in prison following a battle. Palamon sees Emelia, Duke Theseus's sister-in-law. Arcite also falls in love with her, betraying his cousin, and the two cousins quarrel. Arcite defeats Palamon in a duel, following which the loser is to be executed. But Arcite dies under his horse and bequeaths Emelia to Palamon. Arcite has seen the error of his ways and acts nobly.

18. The Winter's Tale. The flaw is Leontes' suspicious jealousy. Leontes is suspicious and jealous and believes his wife Hermione is having an affair with his friend Polixenes, King of Bohemia. He imprisons Hermione, who gives birth to a girl, and Leontes sends the child to Bohemia, to be placed on a desert shore to perish. His wife and son are reported to have died, his son of grief. Sixteen years later Leontes is reunited with his daughter, Perdita, and his wife. The son of Polixenes, Florizel, falls in love with Perdita. Leontes realizes the error of his ways and is transformed, and the children are reunited.

19. Cardenio. The flaw seems to be destructive infatuation. The story is unknown, but in *The Ingenious Gentleman Don Quixote of La Mancha*, the lover of Lucinda is driven mad by the loss of her and is finally reunited with her. It is likely that Shakespeare's lost play is on the same theme. The play was performed in 1613, and a manuscript of the play was owned by the 18th-century editor of Shakespeare's plays, Bishop Warburton, whose cook Betsy was reported to have used it to light his fire, presumably beneath her cooking-pot.

To sum up, the flaws in the comedies are thus: snobbishness, usurpation, strictness, tyrannical behaviour, pretension, self-deceit, hypocrisy, greed, insincerity, self-love, excessive mourning, shrewishness, infatuation, inconstancy, interference in love and jealousy. It is interesting to compare this list of Shakespeare's flaws with the list of Chaucer's vices on p.96.

Shakespeare's histories comprise two tetralogies, one on the War of the Roses, the other on the causes of these wars. These tetralogies are preceded by *King John* and succeeded by *Henry VIII*.

20. King John. The flaw is King John's self-interested involvement in the killing of Arthur. King John has no heir and is implicated in killing the alternative ruler Arthur just as Elizabeth I was implicated in killing Mary, Queen of Scots, in 1587. The killing of Arthur stores up trouble and John dies unhappily at Swinstead Abbey.

21. Richard II. The flaw is Richard's tyrannical behaviour. Richard, a rightful king, acts as a tyrant by breaking his own laws. He arbitrarily exiles Henry Bolingbroke, murders his uncle and robs another uncle, John of Gaunt, of his property on his death to pay for his Irish wars. He loses his crown to Gaunt's son Bolingbroke, the Earl of Lancaster, who returns from exile to retrieve what Richard seized but usurps the throne. After the murder of Richard he becomes a tyrant. He is a better king than Richard but lacks title to the throne.

22. Henry IV, Part 1. The flaw is Henry's egocentric usurpation of the crown. Henry IV usurps the crown from Richard II and he is now under pressure from the rebellion of the Percys – by Hotspur in Wales and by his father, the Earl of Northumberland, in York – and wants to lead a crusade as penance. Henry's son, Harry or Hal, who has preferred the taverns and the company of Sir John Falstaff, kills Hotspur. Henry's usurpation of the crown shakes the order of the Great Chain of Being and is responsible for the unrest which will lead to the Wars of the Roses.

23. Henry IV, Part 2. The flaw is still Henry's usurpation of the crown. After the rebellion of Archbishop Scroop, Mowbray and Hastings, Henry IV reflects on the betrayal of the nobles who once helped him and, having collapsed in the Jerusalem Chamber, dies. Hal becomes Henry V and realizes he must transform himself. He banishes Falstaff, who is put in prison, to make a break from his life in taverns.

24. Henry V. The flaw is Henry's warmongering, which will cause trouble in future. Encouraged by the Church (which wants to escape taxes), Henry insists that his ancestral claim to the French throne is just and scorns the hand of the French king's daughter which has been offered to buy him off. He arrests Scroop, Grey and Cambridge for treason and invades France with an army including knaves, captures Harfleur and wins the Battle of Agincourt. He accepts the hand of Katherine of Valois, the king's daughter, which was on offer before the war, now presenting it as a great triumph; thus uniting England and France. He will produce a son who will again face war in France, and the Chorus points out that Henry VI will lose France.

25. Henry VI, Part 1. The flaw is Henry IV's usurpation and Henry V's warmongering, which now affect a new generation. As a result of Henry V's legacy of aggression, the infant Henry VI cannot control his nobles, whose quarrels bring disasters to the maintenance of his title to the French crown against the forces led by Joan of Arc, who seeks to restore the Dauphin, the French king's heir deposed after Agincourt.

The title is doubtful because of Henry IV's usurpation. The Yorkist claim to the throne counters Henry's title through the Lancastrian line, a conflict symbolized by the roses picked in Temple Garden.

26. Henry VI, Part 2. The flaw is still Henry IV's usurpation, which gives Henry VI insufficient title to the crown and causes the War of the Roses. The Earl of York's followers, most notably Richard, Duke of York, battle with Henry's Lancastrians, causing father to kill son and vice versa. Henry marries Margaret of Anjou to cement his title. Henry has to cope with Jack Cade's rebellion.

27. Henry VI, Part 3. The flaw is the usurpation of the crown by Richard, Duke of Gloucester, from his brother, which will store up further trouble. The crown is usurped by the House of York when the Yorkists defeat Henry's Lancastrians and Henry, held in the Tower, is murdered by Richard, Duke of Gloucester, the younger brother of the Yorkist claimant who takes the throne as Edward IV. More conflict is set up.

28. Richard III. The flaw Is Richard, Duke of Gloucester's usurpation of the crown. Richard, Duke of Gloucester, usurps the crown by murdering his brother Clarence, and wooing Anne, the widow of Edward, Prince of Wales. After the death of Edward IV, Richard pretends to be innocent and pure but his machinations to usurp the crown include: executing Hastings, Rivers and Grey; murdering the princes in the Tower (Clarence's sons); marrying his niece Elizabeth of York; and executing Buckingham. Finally he is defeated by Richmond, the last heir to the Lancastrian line to the crown, at Bosworth. There is a general reconciliation under Richmond, who rules as Henry VII and marries the Yorkist heir Elizabeth of York so that their children will unite both lines of succession.

29. Henry VIII. The flaw is Henry's ruthlessness in creating Protestantism, which will store up problems until the invasion of the Spanish Armada. Henry VIII is wilful and self-interested, and executes his adviser the Duke of Buckingham; divorces Queen Katherine of Aragon; intrigues the fall of Wolsey; and marries Anne Bullen (Boleyn), who is crowned queen and produces Elizabeth. (A cannon fired at the end of Act 1 burnt down The Globe in 1613.)

To sum up, the flaws in the histories are: self-interestedness, usurpation, tyrannical ruthlessness and warmongering.

In Shakespeare's tragedies, his heroes have a fatal flaw, or defect of virtue, a negative characteristic of the ego which destroys them. The elimination of this flaw or negative characteristic would transform the heroes and remove an obstacle, indeed obstruction, that blocks their quest for truth and opening to a Reality beyond the social world.

30. Antony and Cleopatra. The flaw is Antony's infatuation for Cleopatra. He is enthralled by her beauty. He tears himself away from Cleopatra and returns to Rome on the death of his wife Fulvia and ends his estrangement from Octavius Caesar by marrying his sister Octavia, which makes Cleopatra jealous. He leaves Octavia and returns to Egypt, earning the enmity of Octavius. He loses the battle of Actium against Octavius, who pursues him to Alexandria where Antony dies, destroyed by his infatuation by Cleopatra.

31. Coriolanus. The flaw is Coriolanus's arrogance and revenge. He wins his name after capturing the town of Corioli from the Volscians. The triumphant Roman general returns to Rome and it is proposed that he should be consul but he is arrogant and contemptuous of the Roman rabble and becomes unpopular. The tribunes secure his banishment. He joins the Volscians and leads them against Rome out of revenge. His mother, wife and son come out and beg him to spare the city. He makes a treaty favourable to the Volscians and leaves. The Volscian general Aufidius accuses him of betraying Volscian interests and his faction murder Coriolanus in Antium, a Volscian town.

32. Hamlet. The flaw is Hamlet's indecisive revenge for Claudius's usurpation. Claudius has murdered his brother, the King of Denmark, Hamlet's father, and has seduced the king's wife, Hamlet's mother, Gertrude. He has usurped the throne from Hamlet and married his mother. Hamlet's father's ghost (an encounter with the infinite) urges revenge. Hamlet feigns madness to escape suspicion that he is plotting to kill King Claudius. He tests the ghost's story by enacting a play for the king, reproducing the events of the murder. He kills Polonius, believing the king was listening behind the arras. The king sends Hamlet to England, planning to have him killed there. Pirates return him to Denmark where Polonius's son kills him in a fencing duel with a poisoned sword. Hamlet stabs Claudius, whose usurpation has destroyed him. Hamlet's mother has drunk a poisoned cup intended for Hamlet, whose indecisive revenge has destroyed her. He could have killed Claudius when the king was at his prayers, but dithered. During the play Hamlet has been on a quest for truth and exposure of falsity and has been thinking about infinite Reality: "I could be bounded in a nutshell and count myself a king of infinite space" (II.ii.264). Hamlet's thought processes touch on the metaphysical aspect of the fundamental theme.

33. Julius Caesar. The flaw is Brutus's usurpation. Brutus believes that Julius Caesar is betraying the Republic by turning his rule into dictatorship, and he reluctantly joins the conspirators who are Roman lovers of freedom. But following Antony's speech at Caesar's funeral, he cannot convince the Roman people that his cause is just. Antony, Octavius and Lepidus oppose Brutus and Cassius and defeat them at the battle of Philippi, where the two conspirators kill themselves. Brutus has acted for noble, virtuous reasons but the murder of Caesar was a usurpation that has destroyed him.

34. King Lear. The flaw is Lear's self-love and love test: his attachment to power as he divides his kingdom, his desire for flattery, his petulance and blindness. Lear resolves to renounce power and abdicate by dividing his kingdom among his daughters in accordance with their affection for him. Whereas Goneril and Regan express extreme affection and receive a third of the kingdom each, Cordelia is too truthful to take part in hollow flattery and says she loves him according to her duty. Infuriated, Lear divides her share between the other two daughters, and requests that he should retain a hundred knights and stay with each daughter in turn and be maintained by them. Goneril and Regan turn him out in a storm, and, out of his wits he is eventually received by Cordelia, and undergoes an inner transformation, a shift from his ego to his deeper self. They are caught up in a battle between English and French forces and are both imprisoned. Cordelia is hanged and Lear dies from grief, realizing that she loved him truly and that the flattery of the other two daughters was meaningless. Lear has been destroyed by his wilful love test.

35. *Macbeth*. The flaw is Macbeth's ambition to usurp the crown. Macbeth and Banquo, generals of Duncan, king of Scotland, encounter three witches on a heath who prophesy that Macbeth will be thane of Cawdor, and then king. Immediately afterwards he learns that he has been made thane of Cawdor. His ambition to be king whetted and urged on by Lady Macbeth, Macbeth murders Duncan during a visit Duncan makes to his castle. Macbeth usurps the crown. The witches had forecast that another general, Banquo would have a line of kings and that Macbeth would have no line. He arranges the murder of Banquo but Banquo's son escapes. He sees Banquo's ghost (another encounter with the infinite). He returns to the witches and is told to beware of Macduff, the thane of Fife, who has joined Duncan's eldest son. Macbeth's troops attack Macduff's castle and kill his wife and children. Guilt-stricken, Lady Macbeth loses her reason and dies. The army of Macduff and Duncan's son kill Macbeth, who has been destroyed by his ambition to usurp the crown.

36. *Othello*. The flaw is Othello's jealousy. Othello, a Moor and general serving the Venetian state, has secretly married Desdemona, the daughter of a Venetian senator. He takes Desdemona to Cyprus to lead the Venetian forces against the Turks, who are attacking the island. He promotes a soldier, Cassio, to the rank of lieutenant, offending an older soldier, Iago, who had expected to be promoted and plots his revenge. Iago discredits Cassio as a soldier, and Cassio is stripped of his new rank. He plants suspicions of Desdemona's fidelity in Othello's mind, associating her with Cassio, and arranges for a handkerchief given by Othello to Desdemona to be found on Cassio. Othello murders Desdemona in a fit of jealousy. Then letters are found revealing Iago's guilt and Cassio's innocence. Horrified that he has killed Desdemona without cause, Othello kills himself out of remorse. His potential for jealousy has destroyed him.

37. Romeo and Juliet. The flaw is enmity. The Montagues and the Capulets, the two main families of Verona, are enemies. Romeo, son of Montague, falls in love with Juliet, daughter of Capulet, at a feast, and they are married. A friend of Romeo meets Tybalt of the Capulet family, who is infuriated that Romeo was at the feast, and in the ensuing quarrel Romeo kills Tybalt. He is banished and leaves for Mantua. Juliet's father proposes to marry her to Count Paris. A friar advises her to drink a potion the night before her wedding that will render her apparently lifeless for 40 hours. He will alert Romeo. The message goes astray, and Romeo hears that Juliet is dead. He goes to where Juliet is lying and poisons himself. Juliet wakes and, seeing Romeo dead by her side, stabs herself and dies. The Montagues and Capulets are now reconciled. Their feud and enmity has destroyed both Romeo and Juliet.

38. Timon of Athens. The flaw is Timon's hatred of mankind. Timon, wanting to impress, has given generously to friends, flatterers and parasites, but he has borrowed the money. Asking them for assistance, he is deserted by them. He holds one last banquet and serves his guests dishes filled with warm water, which he throws in their faces. He leaves the city and lives alone in a cave and becomes a misanthrope. While digging for roots he finds a horde of gold, but remains embittered. He dies, and on his tomb by the sea is an epitaph expressing his hatred of mankind, which has destroyed him.

39. Titus Andronicus. The flaw is Titus Andronicus's revenge. Queen Tamora of the Goths has her sons rape and mutilate Titus Andronicus's daughter Lavinia over her lover's corpse and frames Titus's sons. Lavinia tells Titus what happened. Out of revenge Titus, a Roman general, takes Tamora captive, kills her two sons and bakes them in a pie, which he sets before Tamora, who eats morsels of her sons. He kills Lavinia so that her shame will die with her, and then stabs Queen Tamora and is then killed. His drive for revenge has destroyed him.

To sum up, the flaws in the tragedies are: infatuation, arrogance, revenge, indecision, usurpation, self-love, attachment to power, ambition, jealousy, enmity and hatred of mankind. Bradley wrote of the nobility of Shakespeare's tragic heroes, and Orwell countered by citing

Lear's ignoble failure to renounce power. We can now see that all Shakespeare's tragedies – and comedies and histories – are about flaws which are vices, or, at any rate, defects of virtue.

Within these plots about flaws or defects of virtue Shakespeare touches on the metaphysical aspect of the fundamental theme in many places. Shakespeare writes of "the lark at heaven's gate" in *Cymbeline*, Act 2, sc.3. The quest for truth, transformation, purification of the soul, confronting death (for example, in *Measure for Measure* the Duke's, under the circumstances cruel, advice to Claudio, "Be absolute for death"), musing on the infinite, on immortality (as in *Hamlet*'s "To be or not to be") and virtue appear in most of the plays. Shakespeare approaches Reality from the impediments in the social world of the Renaissance as distinct from the contemplative life of the cloister experienced by many of the medieval questers for truth.

Jacobean Drama

Ben Jonson, Shakespeare's rival and friend, condemned the fairy-tale plots of romantic Elizabethan comedy (such as *A Midsummer Night's Dream* and *The Tempest*) and wrote sardonic comedies which exposed and corrected the vices of his time. They ridicule gulls. In his world cheats dupe gulls, who are hypocrites, misers and boasters. According to Jonson everyone has a "humour", a ruling trait or passion which determines a person's characteristics.

1. In his *Every Man In his Humour* (performed 1598), the irrational jealousy of the merchant Kitely, husband of a pretty young wife living in a house of gallants, brings out the humours of each character (excessive concern for morals, boastfulness, deception).

2. In *Every Man Out of his Humour* (performed 1599), several characters are dominated by different humours (discontent, cynicism, eagerness to marry, being domineering, devotion to fashion, miserliness, ambition, social climbing, envy) and are driven out of them.

3. *Cynthia's Revels* (1601) satirizes court vices: wealth, prodigality, impudence, voluptuousness, folly, frivolity, self-love, and obesity. The characters all drink of "the fountain of self-love" (the subtitle of the play).

In his later plays the main humour is greed.

4. In *Eastward Hoe* (1605), a satire on the first voyage to the New World in 1602 of Bartholomew Gosnold, *alias* Captain Seagull, Sir Petronel Flash filches a dowry and sets off for Virginia with Quicksilver, who has robbed his master. They are wrecked on the Isle of Dogs and brought before the deputy-alderman and then go to prison.

5. In *Volpone* (performed 1605-6), the eponymous hero feigns that he is dying and his accomplice Mosca extracts gifts from his would-be heirs.

6. In *The Alchemist* (performed 1610), Lovewit's greedy servant Face and his associates use his house to cheat gullible people by promising them the philosopher's stone.

7. In *Bartholomew Fayre* (performed 1614), Bartholomew Cokes is robbed of his purses, his cloak and sword, and his future wife, and his servant is robbed of their marriage licence. In a general ridiculing, three characters are put in the stocks.

Each humour in Jonson's plays is a vice. The names of the characters suggest their humours: Sir Politick Would-Be, Lovewit, Dame Pliant, Waspe, Zeal-of-the-land Busy. In *Volpone*, the main characters are named after creatures: Volpone (fox), Mosca (fly), Voltore (vulture), Corbaccio (crow), Corvino (raven). Their unbelievable names suggest that they are walking ideas who have little human life. As in the case of Chaucer and Shakespeare, the vices Jonson satirizes are egocentric impediments to a soul embarking on the quest for truth of the medieval contemplative cloister, and therefore touch on the metaphysical aspect of the fundamental theme while focusing on its secular aspect.

Jacobean revenge tragedy explored the humanist attitude to death in contrast to the medieval attitude in which there was a desire for immortality. After many crimes, the dying Jacobean tragic heroes found no immortality. The died in defiant doubt or Stoic acceptance, defined by their vices of lust, infatuation and revenge which signified a backsliding from virtue.

Lust is the theme of Cyril Tourneur's *The Revenger's Tragedy* (printed 1607).

In *The Revenger's Tragedy*, Vendici's mistress has been poisoned by a lecherous duke. Vendici eventually murders him by tricking him into kissing the poisoned skull of his mistress. By the end most of the characters have killed each other. Vendici survives but confesses to the murder of the duke, and is led off to be executed. Lust has triggered revenge and destroyed everyone.

John Webster's revenge plays are condemnations of lust that destroys and ends in despair:

The White Devil (*The White Divel*, 1609-12) condemns lust which breeds violence: "violent lust leaves none." Duke Brachiano lives in Italy, presumably in the castle at Bracciano outside Rome, which I have visited and which can still be visited today.[15] He seduces Vittoria, wife of Camillo, and arranges for his wife, the sister of the Duke of Florence, to be poisoned. His accomplice, Vittoria's brother, contrives the death of Camillo. Vittoria is tried for adultery and murder and sentenced to confinement. She is carried off by Brachiano. The play ends with the revenge of the Duke of Florence, who poisons Brachiano, and the deaths of Vittoria and her brother. The word "lust" has echoed through the play, but the main characters blame the court and great men.

The Duchess of Malfi (*The Dutchesse of Malfy*, 1612-13), a play set in the court of Italy's Amalfi, also condemns lust. The duchess, a widow, lusts for Antonio, her steward, and secretly marries him despite a warning by her brothers, the Cardinal and Ferdinand, Duke of Calabria, that she must not remarry. They set Bosola to spy on her, and she flees with Antonio. Ferdinand and Bosola capture her, torture her and strangle two of her children. Bosola kills Antonio and the Cardinal, and is then killed by Ferdinand, who has gone mad. Lust has triggered the revenge and is responsible for widespread destruction. Bosola has said, "We are merely the stars' tennis-balls, struck and bandied/Which way please them."

Thomas Middleton and William Rowley's dark tragedy, *The Changeling* (performed 1622), also condemns lust.

In *The Changeling*, Beatrice-Joanna employs the pustulous, repellent De Flores to murder the man her father (governor of Alicant) wants her to marry, so she can marry Alsemero. To her horror, De Flores, having spoken in innuendos of "blood", "service" and "honour", words which to him convey a sexual connotation but which to Beatrice are straight, exacts his reward while Beatrice's maid takes her place in Alsemero's bed in a "bed trick". The lust and infatuation which drove her to murder finally destroys her as De Flores kills her and then himself.

It should be pointed out that infatuation is also the theme of some of the semi-romantic comedies written in the Elizabethan time.

In Thomas Dekker's *The Shoemaker's Holiday*, a suitor to the Lord Mayor of London's daughter, sent to France to prevent the match, disguises himself as a Dutch shoemaker who supplies the Lord Mayor's family with shoes and succeeds in his suit and becomes Lord Mayor of London himself.

In Thomas Heywood's *A Woman Killed with Kindness*, a perfect wife takes up with a guest welcomed by her husband. It ends with her dying alone full of remorse.

A rich period in drama included the works of John Marston, Francis Beaumont and John Fletcher, Philip Massinger, John Ford and James Shirley, some of whom collaborated with others and with Shakespeare.

During the Renaissance the metaphysical aspect of the fundamental theme weakened as literature became more secular, reflecting the secular themes of classical writers the Renaissance imitated such as Virgil, Horace and Ovid. Renaissance verse and drama were dominated by lust, infatuation and revenge, themes developed in Italy which obstruct the quest for truth that leads to immortality. The English Renaissance plays focus on the corrupt world and vices that need to be transformed into contemplative calm and virtue for the metaphysical aspect of the fundamental theme to be explored. The literature of the Renaissance is therefore a social prelude to the metaphysical aspect of the fundamental theme: either a satirical condemnation of vices and a ridiculing of obstacles to the quest for truth; or a surrender to chaotic living in which the contemplative quest for truth cannot begin.

Bacon

Francis Bacon, the founder of Freemasonry on his youth and of other secret groups, including, perhaps, Rosicrucianism, wrote philosophical and literary works in prose, notably *Essays*. His *New Atlantis* (left unfinished at his death in 1626) is an account of a visit to the island of Bensalem in the Pacific, an island in the tradition of More's Utopia, and of its social conditions. Bacon describes Solomon's House, a college of natural philosophy "dedicated to the study of the works and creatures of God".

Bacon's life's work was on the metaphysical aspect of the fundamental theme, the quest for truth which leads to Reality and the prospect of immortality. A large part of his energy was put into shaping the secret doctrines of hidden Freemasonic groups, but he was essentially a man of the Renaissance who took up Montaigne's question, "What do I know?" His *Advancement of Learning*, considered methods of advancing knowledge and defects in the advancement of knowledge in his day. He analyzed the divisions of knowledge – history, poetry and philosophy – and set the tone for the Metaphysical 17th century when there was a return from secular focusing on vices to the metaphysical aspect of the fundamental theme itself.

Literary Summary

The main references to the metaphysical aspect of the fundamental theme in world literature during the secularized Renaissance are as follows:

- The infinite that surrounds the universe is in: Ficino's letters and works on Plato; and Marlowe's *Dr Faustus*.
- The metaphysical Reality seen as Light is in: Ficino's letters and works on Plato; and Luther.

- The order of the universe can be found in: Ficino's letters; and Shakespeare's use of the Great Chain of Being.
- The oneness of known humankind can be found in: More's *Utopia*; and Marlowe's *Tamburlaine*.
- The similarities in cultures and civilizations are emphasized in: More's *Utopia*; Marlowe's *Tamburlaine*; and Bacon's *New Atlantis*.
- The universal being (or self) that opens to the Light behind the rational, social ego is in: Ficino; and Erasmus.
- Universal virtue is in: Ficino; More; Erasmus; Machiavelli; Montaigne; Sidney; and Spenser's *The Fairie Queene*; and the loss of virtue is lamented in Lyly; Marlowe's and Shakespeare's poems and plays; Jonson; and Jacobean revenge tragedy.
- The promise of the immortality of the universal being is present in: Ficino's letters and works on Plato; More; Erasmus; and 'The passionate mans Pilgrimage' (once attributed to Raleigh).
- The inner transformation or centre-shift from ego to universal being is found in: Ficino; and Erasmus.
- The quest of the purified soul is in: Ficino; More; and Spenser's *The Fairie Queene*.
- The sensibility that approaches Reality through more than one discipline can be found in: Leonardo (painting, sculpture, architecture, musician, science, mathematics, engineering, inventions, anatomy, geology, cartography, botany and writing); Michelangelo (painting, sculpture, architecture, poetry, letters and engineering); Ficino (Platonic scholarship, philosophy and letters); Sir Thomas More (writing of *Utopia*, statecraft and diplomacy); Erasmus (writing of *Praise of Folly*, Biblical scholarship, theology, languages and diplomacy); Sidney (poetry, novel/*Arcadia*, *An Apologie for Poetrie*, letters); Shakespeare (plays, poems, sonnets); Marlowe, (plays, poetry, translation); and Bacon (essays, satire, Freemasonry, Rosicrucianism).
- The new perspective of unity in history, religion, philosophy and science, international politics and literature can be found in: Ficino (oneness in philosophy); and Raleigh (unification of history in *The History of the World*, 1614).

The retreat of the Renaissance from the inner to the outer, social world is reflected in the coming Baroque literature, which retrieved the metaphysical aspect of the fundamental theme from the growing secular outlook that spread from Italy.

5

The Literature of the Baroque

The Renaissance, having turned away from the metaphysical aspect of the fundamental theme, its quest for metaphysical Reality, to its contrapuntal secular aspect, its focus on the vices of society, had produced new thinking about the human condition and about the basis of knowledge, and this was reflected in advances in science and philosophy in Bacon, Descartes, Pascal and Hobbes. During this time the Protestant Reformation was resisted by the Catholic Counter-Reformation, and there was civil war in England, France and Germany, and a war of liberation against the Spanish in the Netherlands. The civil, political and religious conflicts threw up the Baroque style in European art and literature, a Universalism which was designed to reconcile all divisions.

The Baroque style was worked out in Italy – in Rome and Bologna – around 1600. Having renounced the Renaissance popes' dreams of temporal hegemony, the new popes sought to proclaim a spiritual empire through a grandeur and universality based on contemporary Rome that would revive the grandiose style of ancient Rome. The Baroque combined the temporal and the spiritual, the vanity of earthly pomp and the supremacy of the divine: sense and spirit. It contrasted illusion with Reality, showed that "all the world's a stage" in the social domain, and appealed to a boundless imagination that reached far beyond the playhouse and made epic poetry possible.

Rome-based Baroque was soon internationalised and its characteristics swept through Europe: a new dynamic style of painting, sculpture, architecture and music which emphasized movement and apparent freedom, dynamic flow rather than static order. The High-Renaissance classicism and universal perfection of Leonardo da Vinci blended with the mannerism and contortions of restless Michelangelo, and both the perfect body and the restless soul were present in the Baroque. The Baroque showed human beings as feeling creatures and dwelt on their emotional responses. It was felt that a composition should express a universal emotion. This approach passed into European literature.

The Baroque, combining sense and spirit, filled churches with sunbursts, symbols for the metaphysical Light. It took European literature back to the metaphysical aspect of the fundamental theme: a turning away from theatrical illusion to Reality as Light and to the immortal spirit. The term "baroque" came from the Portuguese *barroco* (Spanish *barrueco*), a term from gemmology meaning an "irregular pearl", a rough or imperfect pearl that had its own distinctive individuality in relation to other pearls. A work of art was seen as a work of misshapen individuality rather than of classical perfection. It should be ornamented and grandiloquent, and should convey the metaphysical scheme.

Within the Baroque there were a number of styles, one of which was the Metaphysical. In English literature the followers of this style combined intellectual speculation with conversational immediacy and focused on subjects that were both sensuous and metaphysically spiritual. They used imagery that is organic rather than illustrative, and fused thought and feeling. They made extensive use of wit, which Dr Johnson defined in his 'Life of Cowley' as when "the most heterogeneous ideas are yoked by violence together".[1] Their interplay of opposed ideas and emotions made for a poetry of great complexity, but this was eased by their colloquial language and ready reference to their experience.

English Metaphysical Poets

The term "Metaphysical poets" was coined by Johnson in his 'Life of Cowley': "About the beginning of the 17th century appeared a race of writers that may be termed the *Metaphysical Poets*."[2]

The English Metaphysical poets began with John Donne. Dryden had written of Donne in 1693: "He affects the metaphysics, not only in his satires, but in his amorous verses, where nature only should reign; and perplexes the minds of the fair sex with nice speculations of philosophy, when he should engage their hearts, and entertain them with the softnesses of love."[3] Earlier still Drummond of Hawthornden had spoken of poets who made use of "Metaphysical Ideas and Scholastical Quiddities".[4] The Metaphysical poetry of the 17th century is concentrated and adorned with conceits that are "hammered out" with argument and persuasion reminiscent of Scholasticism and very much concerned with the relationship between soul and body. Whereas during the Renaissance the metaphysical aspect of the fundamental theme of a virtuous quest had been left to one side as writers explored the secular vices in society in their poems and plays, now the Metaphysical poets returned to the metaphysical aspect of the fundamental theme, sometimes blending it with poems on infatuation and lust, topics that fascinated the Renaissance writers.

Donne

The English Metaphysical poets[5] were mainly Church-of-England priests, vicars and thinkers. Before he became a priest in 1615 and then Dean of St Paul's in 1621, John Donne wrote love poems as a man about town. He was secretary to Sir Thomas Egerton, keeper of the great seal, but secretly married his wife's niece, Ann More in 1601, the year he was elected MP, and was dismissed and briefly imprisoned. He wrote of his disgrace, "John Donne, Ann Donne, undone." In the course of these poems he reveals his learning in anatomy ('A Valediction: of my name, in the window'), in chemistry ('Loves Growth'), in science, medicine and alchemy ('A nocturnall upon S. Lucies day') in astronomy, gold-beating and navigation ('A Valediction: forbidding mourning'), and in optics ('The Extasie').

Some of the early poems in his *Songs and Sonets*, written in the 1590s, touch on the metaphysical aspect of the fundamental theme. 'Aire and Angels' is about the body and soul, as is 'A Valediction: forbidding mourning', in which Donne, leaving his wife for a visit to France in 1611, argues that absence cannot unjoin their "two soules...which are one". In 'The Extasie' he writes of lovers' souls meeting outside their bodies. 'The Dreame' is about the metaphysical Light: "As lightning, or a Tapers light,/Thine eyes, and thine noise wak'd mee..../Perchance as torches which must ready bee,/Men light and put out, so thou deal'st with mee,/Thou cam'st to kindle." The Light that "cam'st to kindle" was at first mistaken for "an Angell". The "shapeless flame" and "lovely glorious nothing" at the beginning of 'Aire and Angels' refer to the Light: "Twice or thrice had I loved thee (i.e. the Light),/Before I knew thy face or name;/So in a voice, so in a shapeless flame,/Angells affect us oft and worship'd bee;/Still when, to where thou wert, I came,/Some lovely glorious nothing (i.e. the Light) I did see."

Donne wrote an unfinished satirical epic, *Metempsychosis, The Progresse of the Soule*, which bears the date 1601. The idea behind it was that souls could transmigrate and be reincarnated, an idea he later rejected. In his satire, the soul of the forbidden apple eaten by Eve in the Garden of Eden passes through a succession of fallen humans. Had the poem been finished this contaminated soul may have ended up reincarnating as the soul of Robert Cecil, the Earl of Essex's enemy.

The idea of the progress of the soul touches on the metaphysical aspect of the fundamental theme, and it is a measure of Donne's interest in this theme that he returned to the title, interpreting it within a more orthodox Christian context rather than in terms of reincarnation, in his poem 'The Second Anniversarie, Of the Progresse of the Soule' (1612), which advocates, "Forget this rotten world..../Look upward." Donne contemplates what it is like "in our death-bed": "Thinke thy selfe labouring now with broken breath." He advocates that legacies should be made, the vices that fascinated the Renaissance: "Give one thy Pride, to'another give thy Lust." He addresses the soul, "Thinke further on thy selfe, my soule..../Thinke in how poore a prison thou didst lie." The soul is imprisoned in the body at birth, and achieves liberty on death: "But thinke that Death hath now enfranchis'd thee,/Thou hast thy'expansion now, and libertie..../Thinke thy shell broke, thinke thy soule hatch'd but now." Donne's thinking is on the metaphysical aspect of the fundamental theme: on the soul achieving immortality.

Donne's Divine Poems – the sequence of 'La Corona' and the 'Holy Sonnets' – are similarly on the soul and the metaphysical aspect of the fundamental theme. 'Good Friday, 1613. Riding Westward' laments: "I am carryed towards the West/This day when my Soules forme bends toward the East./There I should see a Sunne, by rising set,/And by that setting endlesse day beget." He is riding in the wrong direction, towards worldly darkness rather than towards the divine Light and "endlesse day".

'Satyre III' advocates, "Seeke true religion. O where?" His answer contains an unforgettable statement of the quest for truth: "On a huge hill/Cragged, and steep, Truth stands, and hee that will/Reach her, about must, and about must goe;.../Yet strive so, that before age, deaths twilight,/Thy soule rest..../...and mysteries/Are like the Sunne, dazling, yet plaine to all eyes." Truth stands like a castle on a hill and the path that leads to it is an upward spiral, and at the top is the dazzling Light.

Donne's *Sermons* are full of the metaphysical Reality seen as the Light. Writing of reason's destructive impact on the Light, he says:

> "They had a precious composition for lamps, amongst the ancients, reserved especially for Tombes, which kept light for many of hundred of yeares; we have had in our age experience, in some casuall openings of ancient vaults, of finding such lights, as were kindled (as appeared by their inscriptions) fifteen or sixteen hundred years before; but, as soon as that light comes to our light, it vanishes. So this eternall, and this supernaturall light, Christ and faith, enlightens, warmes, purges, and does all the profitable offices of fire, and light, if we keep it...in the proper place,...but when wee bring this light to the common light of reason...it may...vanish."[6]

Elsewhere in the Sermons, Donne writes of the metaphysical Light "as a flower at Sun-rising", "as the Sun at noon". He "cannot so much as wish, that that Sunne would shine upon him, he doth not so much as know that there is such a Sunne." At death, "behold then a new Light." At death "I shall see the Sonne of God, the Sunne of glory, and shine myself, as that sunne shines". To Donne, the light that dwells in us is like a coal: "God, who, as he is immortal himself, had put a coal, a beam of immortality into us, which we might have blown into a flame, but blew it out by our first sin" (*Devotions upon Emergent Occasions, Meditation 1*).[7]

In *Devotions upon Emergent Occasions*[8] Donne writes of the oneness of humankind:

> "No man is an Iland, intire of it selfe; every man is a peece of the Continent, a part of the maine; if a Clod bee washed away by the Sea, Europe is the lesse, as well as if a Promontorie were, as well as if a Mannor of thy friends or of thine owne were; any mans death diminishes me, because I am involved in Mankinde; And therefore never send to know for whom the bell tolls; It tolls for thee."

Herbert

A vicar, George Herbert looked back to the way lust shut out the quest for Reality during the Renaissance in 'Sighs and Grones': "My lust/Hath sow'd fig-leaves to exclude thy light." In 'Heaven' the echo of "delight" is "Light". *The Temple,* which is subtitled 'Sacred Poems and Private Ejaculations', is full of Christian themes and references to church ritual. His more secular elder brother, Lord Herbert of Cherbury, the father of Deism, wrote in 'Elegy over a Tomb': "Doth the Sun now his light with yours renew?" The Sun is the Deist Light.

Vaughan

Henry Vaughan, known as "The Silurist" because his family came from Brecknockshire, where the Silures once lived, wrote two volumes of religious poetry, *Silex Scintillans* ("The Glittering Flint", suggesting sparks from a flint-stone). He wrote from "Th'Inlightned spirit" ('The Retreat'). In 'The Morning-watch' he says: "The Pious soul by night/Is like a clouded starre, whose beams though said/To shed their light/Under some Cloud/Yet are above,/And shine." The Light is not revealing itself, and Vaughan retreats "twelve hundred houres" "Unto that hour/Which shew'd thee last, but did defeat/Thy light", and searches and racks his soul "to see/Those beams again". The "Morning" of the title suggests the break of day on the outer world, but within the poem becomes the breaking of the Light on the inner world. 'The Dawning' asks: "Will thy all-surprizing light/Break at midnight?"

'The World' is Vaughan's best-known mystical poem. The soul must aim to be the Light's bride: "I saw Eternity the other night/Like a great Ring of pure and endless light,/All calm, as it was bright." Fools "prefer dark night/Before true light." In 'They are all gone into the world of light!', the dead "are all gone into the world of light". In 'Cock-crowing' God is "Father of lights" and "immortall light and heat." In 'The Night' Vaughan states: "There is in God (some say)/A deep, but dazling darkness."

Vaughan carried forward George Herbert's tradition, as did Richard Crashaw, whose *Steps to the Temple* echo Herbert's *The Temple*. In this, he wrote a poem, 'Hymn to Sainte Teresa', describing St Teresa's girdle as "Sparkling with the sacred flames,/Of thousand soules" who were led "to kisse the light/That kindled them". He probably took orders and frequently visited the community at Little Gidding in the early 1640s.

Quarles and Traherne

Francis Quarles, an Essex Anglican who had eighteen children, wrote about the absence of Light in 'Wherefore hidest thou thy face, and holdest me for thy enemie?" (*Job* 13.24): "The Sun-shine of thy soule-enliv'ning eye."

Thomas Traherne, who was ordained in 1660, presented the Light in 'On News' as "the Gem,/The Diadem,/The Ring Enclosing all", "the Heavenly Eye/Much Wider than the Skie". His *Centuries of Meditation* refers to the beatific vision in which we see God and his creatures "in a Divine and Eternal Light" (3.60). The world would be "a region of Light and Peace, did not men disquiet it" (1.31). Elsewhere he writes: "Those pure and virgin apprehensions I had from the womb, and that Divine Light wherewith I was born are the best unto this day, wherein I can see the Universe."

Marvell

Andrew Marvell began as a Royalist but his sympathies switched to Cromwell when he tutored Lord Fairfax's daughter at Nun Appleton, Yorkshire, c.1651/2. He wrote much of his lyric poetry, including 'The Garden', about this time. 'On a Drop of Dew' is about the Light in the soul, for the soul, "that Drop, that Ray/Of the clear Fountain of Eternal Day", remembers its former height and "recollecting its own Light,/Does, in its pure and circling thoughts, express/The greater Heaven in an Heaven less".

The metaphysical aspect of the fundamental theme can be found in his best-known poem, 'The Garden', which is set in the garden of Fairfax's Nun Appleton House, where the soul glides into the boughs like a bird and "whets, and combs its silver Wings" and "Waves in its Plumes the various Light." It is clear from the previous stanza, in which "the Mind" withdraws into itself, that the contemplative soul is central to the poem. In 'A Dialogue between the Soul and Body', the soul complains that the body is a "Dungeon" to which it is inslav'd": "A Soul hung up, as 'twere, in Chains/Of Nerves, and Arteries, and Veins." Marvell was a deeply metaphysical poet, and the metaphysical aspect of the fundamental theme is never far away in such poems as 'A Dialogue,

Between the Resolved Soul, and Created Pleasure', 'The Coronet', 'To his Coy Mistress' and 'The Definition of Love'.

It is interesting to note that Marvell wrote in obscurity and though MP for Hull from 1659 died unknown as a poet. Meanwhile Abraham Cowley was hailed as the great poet of his time, and having been overrated was later derided. We now think of Marvell as a great poet and of Cowley as a minor poet.

Cavalier Poets

A group of English Metaphysical poets had been influenced by Ben Jonson's satirical, epigrammatic and sometimes complimentary verses: Thomas Campion, Robert Herrick, Thomas Carew, Sir John Suckling and Richard Lovelace. The last three of these were known as Cavalier Poets, along with Lord Herbert, Aurelian Townsend, William Cartwright, Thomas Randolph, William Habington, Sir Richard Fanshawe, Edmund Waller and the Marquis of Montrose. They were Cavalier poets both in being Royalist and in mistrusting over-earnest, intense, Puritan attitudes. They treated life in a cavalier, *blasé* manner, writing poems between intervals of living and accepting the ideal of the Renaissance gentleman who was a soldier, lover, wit, man of affairs, musician, and poet, all in one. Their poems touch on the fundamental theme.

European Baroque Style

The Baroque was present in the European poetry of the 17th century, in the 33 French, German, Dutch, Spanish and Italian poets anthologised in Frank J. Warnke's *European Metaphysical Poetry*, poets such as Marino (Italian), D'Aubigné (French), Gryphius (German), Vondel and Huygens (Dutch), and San Juan de la Cruz (*alias* St John of the Cross, Spanish). Warnke regards the Baroque style, and its Metaphysical variation, as international phenomena, manifestations of the unity of European culture. In a view shared by Odette de Mourgues in *Metaphysical, Baroque and Précieux Poetry*,[9] he sees the literary Baroque style as parallel to but distinct from the Metaphysical style, although many of the 17th-century European poets are both Baroque and Metaphysical: Baroque in being characterized by extravagance of language and a concern with appearance and reality, and in their religious impulse and reference to the new science; and Metaphysical in being concerned with a protagonist who, with wit and wordplay, confronts the perplexities of experience, and in the longing of the soul to be liberated from the body.

Cervantes

The Spanish Miguel de Cervantes' *Don Quixote de la Mancha* (1605, 1615) satirizes the chivalrous romance (of the kind written by Amadis of Gaul and Palmerian of England) just as Chaucer does in the first of his own two tales in *Canterbury Tales*.

> Don Quixote, a poor gentleman from La Mancha, is out of his wits as a result of his love for tales of chivalry, and imagines he has been called to travel in search of adventures on an old horse, accompanied by a squire. He devotes himself to a village-girl who is unaware of his affection, and in his disordered imagination he believes that when he tilts at windmills he is tilting at giants. One of his friends disguises himself as a knight and forces him to return home, where he dies.

Don Quixote sees poetic truth whereas his squire sees historic truth. The work deepens from satire into a philosophical commentary on life: how the imagination can distort outer reality and open up another level of reality. In this work the quest of the metaphysical aspect of the fundamental theme is blended with the deception of poetic truth, which gives a false impression of the world and becomes a metaphor for the metaphysical view of Reality.

The Fundamental Theme in Milton

The Baroque style, as distinct from the Metaphysical style, can be found in the poetry of John Milton, Cromwell's Latin secretary who went blind and was succeeded by Marvell. At the Restoration Marvell, now MP for Hull, used his influence to secure Milton's release from prison. Milton's most Baroque work was *Paradise Lost*.

Milton's grand style in *Paradise Lost* embodies the Baroque grandiloquence and urge to probe behind appearance to Reality, and it conveys a religious impulse – the story of the Fall – in imagery that frequently expresses the new scientific thinking. Milton conceived the idea of writing a great epic poem in 1639, and it was not begun in earnest until 1658 and not finished until 1663 – some 25 years from the outset. Each of the poem's twelve books complies with the metaphysical aspect of the fundamental theme: a quest for truth in which Metaphysical Reality is experienced as Light, in the course of which death is confronted and immortality assured. We can see this by taking a look at the 12 books and relating them to the metaphysical aspect of the fundamental theme:

Book I. Milton invokes the "Heav'nly Muse" and states his theme of the Fall of Man through disobedience. His aim is to "justifie the wayes of God to men". Satan summons a council.

Book II. The infinite universe is presented as Satan passes through the realm of Chaos to visit Earth.

Book III. Milton invokes celestial Light and says that "God is Light". God emphasizes that man will fall through free will.

Book IV. Satan is expelled from the Garden of Eden, where he has squatted like a toad.

Book V. God sends Raphael to warn Adam to be obedient.

Book VI. Raphael describes how Satan is forced to leap through Chaos into the deep along with his followers.

Book VII. Raphael describes the six days of creation that end with the creation of man, and warns Adam that the punishment for eating the fruit of the Tree of Knowledge is death.

Book VIII. Adam asks about the motions of heavenly bodies. Milton could not decide between the Ptolemaic and Copernican systems, and Adam is answered: "doubtfully". Adam relates his own creation and his need for rational fellowship, his companion Eve.

Book IX. Eve is persuaded to eat an apple from the Tree of Knowledge.

Adam, recognising that she is doomed, also eats so that he will die with her. They cover their nakedness and are filled with negative emotions and accuse each other.

Book X. God's son judges Adam and Eve and pronounces sentence of death. Adam and Eve resolve to seek mercy.

Book XI. God decrees that Adam and Eve must leave Paradise. Eve laments, Adam pleads.

Book XII. Adam learns of the consolation for his sin. He and Eve will have "a paradise within". They are led out of the Garden.

In the course of *Paradise Lost* Adam has discovered truth and Reality, and that he can connect with God as Light within. He has known the eternal world but must submit to death, as must Eve. The promise of immortality for their souls is real.

Paradise Lost is full of the Light of God, the object of the quest of the metaphysical aspect of the fundamental theme. The rebellious angels are, like the heroes of Renaissance tragic drama, "far remov'd from God and light of Heav'n" and "the happy Realms of Light", "that celestial light". God is the "Fountain of Light", "glorious brightness" with the "full blaze" of his beams. Milton invokes the Light at the beginning of book III: "Hail, holy Light.../God is Light,/And never but in unapproached Light/Dwelt from eternitie..../So much the rather thou Celestial Light/Shine inward, and the mind through all her powers/Irradiate." The fundamental theme is central to *Paradise Lost*. Milton asserts in *Paradise Regained*: "He who receives/Light from above, from the Fountain of Light,/No other doctrine needs."

Milton was blind, and contrasts the outer darkness of his blindness with the inner Light. His sonnet 'When I consider how my light is spent' (i.e. extinguished), written in 1652 as an early reaction to his blindness, asks, "'Doth God exact day-labour, light deny'd?'" In 'Samson Agonistes' he is "shut up from outward light", but "though blind of sight,.../With inward eyes illuminated,/His fierie vertue rouz'd." Outward blindness brought with it the compensation of inner illumination and virtue, the most sought-after goals of the quest for truth of the metaphysical aspect of the fundamental theme.

Bunyan

The Puritan John Bunyan's *Pilgrim's Progress* (1678, 1684) is on the metaphysical aspect of the fundamental theme. The author dreams of Christian fleeing from the City of Destruction without his wife and children, and his pilgrimage through an allegorically-named landscape that includes the Slough of Despond and the Shadow of Death, to the Celestial City, which is seen in terms of the Light ("Yonder shining light"). Like Everyman he encounters figures named after their traits: Mr Worldly Wiseman, Faithful, Hopeful and The Giant Despair. (Jonson had also named his characters after their traits.) Part 2 is about his wife's and children's pilgrimage through the same terrain. Bunyan's text is about the quest for Reality which brings immortality.

French Influence

Meanwhile the Baroque Age was producing Baroque poetic tragedies[10] in France.

Corneille and Racine

The finest of these were written by Pierre Corneille between 1635 and 1674 and Jean Racine between 1664 and 1691. These tragedies were more classical than the plays of the English, French and Spanish Renaissance. They depended more on Graeco-Roman literature and mythology, and reflected classical stoicism: the virtues of self-mastery and control of the passions which lead to invulnerability and the tranquillity of the soul. Violations of this ideal produced follies and vices which, as in the case of the Renaissance writers of tragedy, the Baroque tragic poets focused on. They exposed the vices of selfishness, self-love and falsity.

Corneille founded French classical tragedy on the essentials of Graeco-Roman tragedy in *Medée, Cinna, Horace and Polyeucte*. He dwelt on man's limitations with a simplicity and directness that were Roman. Racine's tragedies were similarly drawn from Graeco-Roman themes: *Andromaque, Iphigenie, Phèdre, Britannicus, Bénice* and *Mithridate*. He wrote of the folly of human passion and the tension between passion and duty with a complexity that was Greek. Baroque art conveys the protean theme of metamorphosis, of getting behind masks and disguises, and while exposing flaws and social vices both dramatists touch on the fundamental theme of ideal virtue through which the soul comes to know Reality.

Molière and English Restoration Drama

The greatest French writer of the 17th century emerged before Racine: Molière (the name assumed by Jean-Baptiste Poquelin), the creator of French classical comedy in prose. In *Le Tartuffe* and *Le Misanthrope* he exposes the falsity of bores, fops and hypocrites, and holds up for admiration the virtue of generosity.

The Restoration English plays of Dryden, Wycherley, Congreve, Otway, Vanbrugh, Farquhar and Etherege all came from the French influence of Molière. It must be grasped that during the Puritan rule of Cromwell in England the court of Charles-II-to-be was in exile in France, and many Royalists were influenced by the French dramatic scene. Molière's rising popularity in Paris coincided with the Restoration, and the French attitudes were introduced to England when the Royalists returned. The English theatres had been closed for nearly twenty years at Cromwell's instigation, and the tradition of Elizabethan acting had been lost. There was no memory of it in London, and so there was no continuity between the Elizabethan plays and Restoration drama, which ridiculed affectations and false attitudes in love and marriage in the French manner of Molière.

Dryden

Milton had reflected the French interest in Graeco-Roman literature in *Samson Agonistes*, a poetic tragedy that assimilated the Greek tragedies of Aeschylus, Sophocles and Euripides. But the foremost English echoer of Corneille and Racine was John Dryden, who scratched a meagre living by writing 29 plays. Dryden was shallower than Corneille and Racine, but his play *All for Love*, on Antony and Cleopatra, reflects French Baroque tragedy, an influence that explains Dryden's relative avoidance of the metaphysical aspect of the fundamental theme in his plays.

John Dryden was the most influential poet, verse dramatist and prose writer from 1660 to the end of the 17th century. He clearly thought of poetry as a medium for the metaphysical aspect of the fundamental theme. He wrote in the Preface to *Tyrannick Love*:

> "By the harmony of words we elevate the mind to a sense of devotion, as our solemn music, which is inarticulate poesy, does in churches; and by the lively images of piety, adorned by action, allure the soul: which while it is charmed in a silent joy of what it sees and hears, is struck at the same time with a secret veneration of things celestial, and is wound up insensibly to the practice of what it admires."

But though his aim was to take the soul to "things celestial", he was very involved in the outer world and was scorned for chopping and changing in his views. He wrote an elegy on the death of Cromwell, then changed to the Royalist side. Later he turned from Anglicanism to Roman Catholicism. He was greatly troubled by the constitutional crises of the late 1670s, and broke new ground by mocking identifiable characters in his satirical, political mock-heroic poems, 'Absalom and Achitophel' and 'Mac Flecknoe'.

In 'Absalom and Achitophel' Dryden reverted to the Renaissance theme of examining vices. As he said in his introductory note "To the Reader", "The true end of satire is the amendment of vices by correction."[11]

The poem is an allegory on Lord Shaftesbury's (Achitophel's) party's attempt to exclude the Duke of York from the succession and set the Duke of Monmouth (Absalom) in his place. Dryden attempted to influence the outcome by showing the true character of the tempting Shaftesbury. He shows Charles II's (David's) transformation from the playboy of the opening lines to the "godlike" monarch at the end. Charles is a symbol of order in Dryden's first Royalist poem, '*Astraea Redux*'.

The opening of '*Religio Laici*', a defence of Protestantism, is on the metaphysical aspect of the fundamental theme: "Dim as the borrow'd beams of Moon and Stars/To lonely, weary, wondering Travellers/Is Reason to the Soul..../And as those nightly Tapers disappear/When Day's bright Lord ascends our Hemisphere;/So pale grows Reason at

Religions sight;/So dyes, and so dissolves in Supernatural Light."
Dryden is saying that just as the stars grow dim at the break of day, so
reason grows dim and "dissolves" in the Light, which is "supernatural".
Dryden had written at the age of nineteen, in 1650, of "sparks divine"
and "Celestial fire". Eleven years after 'Religio Laici' (1682) he wrote
in 'Veni, Creato Spiritus'[12] that God is a "Source of uncreated Light",
"thrice Holy Fire".

At the end of his life Dryden cut a rather sad figure. He was devoted
to literature and a quiet life in which he could write, but felt he could
have succeeded more in other professions. He asked in his 'Dedication
of Examen Poeticum' (published in 1693),[13]

> "For what other reason have I spent my life in so unprofitable a study?
> Why am I grown old in seeking so barren a reward as fame? The same
> parts and application, which have made me a poet, might have raised me
> to any honours of the gown, which are given to men of as little learning
> and less honesty than myself."

His life's poetic work had brought him little financial reward and his
quest for fame had been "barren". He may have felt deep down that he
had only partly fulfilled the poet's prime task, of perpetuating the
quest for Reality and immortality that is the metaphysical aspect of the
fundamental theme.

Although there are glimpses of the metaphysical aspect of the
fundamental theme in Dryden's work, he wrote objective poetry
enmeshed in the outer world and T.S. Eliot remarked with some justice
that he ignored the soul (displayed "a dazzling disregard of the soul").[14]
There is much in his work that does not reflect a quest for truth that
leads to knowledge of Reality and immortality. He seems to have been
more interested in writing about Shaftesbury and Monmouth, and the
conflicting claims of the Anglican and Catholic faiths, than in revealing
the hidden Reality behind all things – which he clearly knew about,
judging from the opening lines of 'Religio Laici'. Dryden kept the
metaphysical aspect of the fundamental theme alive at the end of the
Metaphysical 17th century, but only just.

Baroque's Social Perspective

The Baroque movement in literature spread to Germany, Holland, Italy, Spain and Portugal. The French and English tragedies and comedies of the second half of the 17th century ridiculed follies and exposed flaws and vices, but, presenting characters in their social roles, stopped short of the individual, private quest for Reality and immortality. They had an entirely different approach from the probings of Reality of the English Metaphysical poets who had restored the metaphysical aspect of the fundamental theme, and from Blaise Pascal's apology for the Christian religion in his fragmentary *Pensées* ("Thoughts"). They nevertheless laid the foundations for 18th-century classicism or, as it is frequently called as it revived the outlook of Graeco-Roman literature, Neoclassicism.

Literary Summary

The main references to the metaphysical aspect of the fundamental theme in world literature during the Baroque Age are as follows:

- The infinite that surrounds the universe is in: Donne; Milton's *Paradise Lost*; Bunyan's *Pilgrim's Progress*; and Dryden.
- The metaphysical Reality seen as Light is in: Donne's poems and *Sermons*; Cervantes' *Don Quixote*; Milton's *Paradise Lost*; Vaughan; Traherne; and Bunyan's *Pilgrim's Progress*.
- The order of the universe can be found in: Donne; Milton's *Paradise Lost*; Bunyan; and Dryden.
- The oneness of known humankind can be found in: Donne's "no man is an island"; and Bunyan.
- The similarities in cultures and civilizations are emphasized in: Milton's *Paradise Lost*; and Dryden.
- The universal being (or self) that opens to the Light behind the rational, social ego is in Marvell's "drop of dew" and his poems on "soul and body".
- Universal virtue is in: Donne; Milton; Corneille; Racine; Molière; and Restoration comedy.
- The promise of the immortality of the universal being is present in: Donne's *Sermons*; and Milton's *Paradise Lost*.
- The inner transformation or centre-shift from ego to universal

being is found in Marvell.

- The quest of the purified soul is in: Donne; Milton; and Dryden.
- The sensibility that approaches Reality through more than one discipline can be found in: Donne (poetry, sermons and work as Dean of St Paul's); Milton (poetry, polemical writing and work as Cromwell's Latin secretary); Marvell (poetry, work as MP); and Dryden (poetry, plays, criticism, translation).
- The new perspective of unity in history, religion, philosophy and science, international politics and literature can be found in: the thinking of Milton; and Bossuet (unification of history in *Discours sur l'histoire*, 1681, which attributed the rise and fall of empires to Providence).

The Baroque now passed into Neoclassicism, which focused more on sense than on a mixture of sense and spirit, and followed the secular aspect of the fundamental theme: condemnation of vices in relation to implied virtue.

6

Neoclassical Literature

Neoclassicism is a term that describes the habit of deliberately imitating the works of antiquity, most notably the great authors of the Graeco-Roman period, especially its poets and dramatists. It distinguishes modern classicism from Graeco-Roman classicism. Neoclassical authors followed Graeco-Roman aesthetic principles and critical precepts as laid down in Aristotle's *Poetics*, Horace's *Art of Poetry* and Longinus's *On the Sublime*. They reproduced Graeco-Roman forms: the epic, eclogue, elegy, ode, satire, tragedy and comedy. They set out rules that would help writers be true to Nature, in the sense of writing what is generally true and plausible. As Pope wrote in 'An Essay on Criticism' (1.88-9): "Those rules of old discover'd, not devised,/Are Nature still, but Nature methodised." The first imitators wrote in Latin, and their successors wrote in their own European languages.

During the 18th century the style of Neoclassicism reacted against the Baroque by emphasizing harmony and grandeur, focusing on human limitations with balance, restraint and clarity. The formal restrictions of Neoclassicism allowed for concentration and intensity.

Classical Reason and Rationalism
Neoclassicism came to be associated with rationalism: the view that the thinking reason, not the soul, can approach Reality as Descartes had taught through his "I think, therefore I am" ("*Cogito ergo sum*"). The reason pursued order, symmetry and scientific knowledge.

Neoclassicism, then, was partly a theory of imitation and partly a faith in the powers of reason, the thinking "I" of the social ego which operates in many to the exclusion of the deeper universal being. The Neoclassical rationalist ideal was strengthened by the philosopher John Locke's *Essay Concerning Human Understanding*, which focused on human nature and shunned purely abstract thinking while introducing concrete instances; by George Berkeley's *Principles of Human*

Knowledge; and by David Hume's work on the theories of knowledge in *An Enquiry concerning Human Understanding*.

Classicism was not affected by Plato's, and Neoplatonists', sense that there is an invisible world that is infinite behind the existing world. In short, the new Classical Man turned his back on the metaphysical aspect of the fundamental theme, suspecting that there is no quest for a hidden Reality and immortality. Like the Renaissance dramatists, 18th-century Classical Man focused on his social role and the ideal of virtue, and satirized all falling-short of this ideal.

Ficino and Erasmus, and their findings from their scholarly labours, were now cast aside, and their quest for immortality and virtue became a principle of social rectitude. The Neoclassical mind, like Descartes', aimed at universality and to establish the primacy of reason over imagination, and expressed itself in satire, argument and wit. Works of art should now contain a simple moral truth that condemned falsehood, shallow opinions, imagination, and the follies and vices of fellow human beings. They castigated a vice rather than a particular individual. Whereas the Metaphysical poets had followed the vision of the Light at the metaphysical end of the spectrum of the fundamental theme, Neoclassical writers operated at the other end of the spectrum in the shadows thrown by the Light, the vices of the fallen world rather than individual virtue.

Nevertheless, there was passion in the 18th century, in response to philanthropy, religious fervour and sentiment in personal relationships. This side of Classical Man led to the psychological novels of Fielding, Defoe, Smollett, Richardson and Sterne, and to the sublime Nature poems of James Thomson.

There was feeling in 18th-century literature, but thinking had primacy. This split between thinking and feeling T.S. Eliot called "a dissociation of sensibility",[1] which he attributed to the Civil War. (I shall take issue with this view, see pp.238, 326-7, 343.) Before then, for example in the poems of Donne, he argued, thinking and feeling were fused. Dryden had shown signs of classicism in the second half of the 17th century. He had revealed a love of order, and he loved the ancients – he was also the translator of Virgil, Juvenal, Persius, Horace, Ovid and Theocritus, representatives of the Graeco-Roman tradition – and he had written in balanced statements that are full of rationalising and owe little to confessional experience. He had a knowledge of the rules of the French writers, and his style was realistic and eloquent. His verse contains moral commonplaces and is full of didacticism.

The English Augustan Age

The Augustan Age in English literature was named after the period of literary distinction under Augustus, who ruled the Roman Empire from 27BC to AD14 when Virgil, Horace and Ovid wrote their great works. The term "Augustan Age" was used by George I of himself, for he saw himself as an Augustus. It was also applied in France to the age of Corneille, Racine and Molière.

The English "Augustan" poets of the early and mid-18th century looked back to their Roman counterparts, the Roman Augustan poets, and aspired to emulate, and equal, their epistles, elegies and satires. Pope wrote Horatian letters in deliberate imitation of Horace. Goldsmith in his periodical *The Bee*[2] printed a retrospective 'Account of the Augustan Age in England' (1759) in which the English Augustan Age was identified with the reign of Queen Anne (1702-1714) and the era of Congreve, Prior and Bolingbroke.

Pope

Alexander Pope's growth had been stunted by a severe illness when he was twelve. His early 'An Essay on Criticism' came to the attention of Addison and Steele, who between them produced *The Spectator*, and the next year, in 1712, Pope's mock-heroic *The Rape of the Lock* appeared. It condemned a quarrel between two families following Lord Petre's cutting off of a lock of Miss Arabella Fermor's hair. A year later he began a friendship with Jonathan Swift. His *Imitations of Horace* appeared from 1733, and his mock-heroic *The Dunciad* ridiculed his fellow poets. In his letter to Dr Arbuthnot of 2 August 1734 he spoke of his "abhorrence of vice". He translated Homer's *Iliad* and *Odyssey*. His devotion to the Augustan time and to Rome led to the Grand Tour as mid-18th-century tourists made their way to Rome and Naples to marvel at the buildings of the Roman Empire.

Pope knew about the fundamental theme's metaphysical quest for Reality that confers immortality. In his early 'The Dying Christian to his Soul' (1708) he writes: "Vital spark of heavenly flame!/Quit, oh quit this mortal frame!" In 'An Essay on Criticism' he writes that poets and critics "both must alike from Heav'n derive their light", (I.13) and Nature is "one clear, unchang'd and universal light". (I.71) In 'Eloisa to Abelard' Eloisa knew "eternal sunshine on the spotless mind". In 'An Essay on Man' Pope writes of "the soul's calm sun-shine".

Pope's 'Essay on Man' attempts to "justifie the wayes of God to men" (Milton's aim in *Paradise Lost*) and prove that the scheme of the universe is the best of all possible schemes even though it appears to contain evil and imperfection. He writes of the oneness of humankind (I.267): "All are but parts of one stupendous whole,/Whose body Nature is, and God the soul." This poem shows great awareness of the metaphysical aspect of the fundamental theme.

However, as a Neoclassical poet consciously imitating Horace, Pope gives the impression of preferring to satirize the superficiality and triviality of society – the outrage at a mere cutting of a lock of hair and the dunces who masquerade as poets – than to reveal the infinite Reality that lurks behind the visible world.

Defoe

Daniel Defoe laid the foundations for the novel in his documentary narratives which are based on travels. His picaresque *Robinson Crusoe* (1719) and *Moll Flanders* (1722) both use a real travel background. The story of Crusoe was based on the experience of Alexander Selkirk on one of the inhabited islands of the Juan Fernandez group in the South Pacific. In *Moll Flanders* the travel is to the New World. Moll, like her mother, was transported to Virginia for theft – Defoe condemns the social conditions in London that made survival difficult – and there, with one of her former husbands, a highwayman, she inherits a plantation and lives in prosperity.

Defoe was a journalist of the outer world who wrote of low-life adventures in realistic detail. His many documentary works do not convey the metaphysical aspect of the fundamental theme, but he influenced Swift, some of whose works did.

Swift

Jonathan Swift, the greatest writer of the Classical Age, was told by his cousin Dryden, according to Dr Johnson,[3] "Cousin Swift, you will never be a poet." Nevertheless, along with Prior and Gay he wrote light, mocking verse, very often on a trifle, making light of his own death in 'Verses on the Death of Dr Swift': "The Time is not remote, when I/Must by the Course of Nature dye." He was a member of the Scriblerus Club along with Pope, Arbuthnot, Gay and others.

He had been ordained in 1694 and wrote an ironical *Argument against Abolishing Christianity*. He left the Whigs and joined the Tories in 1710. He published *Gulliver's Travels* in 1726, the only one of his works for which he was paid (£200), the rest of his works being published anonymously. 'A Modest Proposal', an ironical proposal that the Irish problem should be solved by killing the poor, starving children of Ireland and serving them to the landlords as food to be eaten, came out three years later. When he died he was buried by Stella, to whom he had written letters (*Journal to Stella*, 1710-13), and the epitaph on his tomb refers to his "savage indignation": "*Ubi saeva indignatio ulterius cor lacerare nequit.*" ("Where fierce indignation can no longer tear his heart.")

His "savage indignation" is apparent in his satirical *Gulliver's Travels*, which ridicules the follies and vices of England. Each book ridicules vices:

Book 1. The vices are self-importance, vanity and pride. Gulliver, a surgeon, is shipwrecked on the island of Lilliput where the inhabitants are six inches high and everything is in proportion on this diminutive scale. The Emperor's pomp and vanity, the civil feuds of the people and the war with their neighbours across the channel are made to look ridiculous by the smallness of the scale. English political parties and religious disagreements come down to wearers of high heels or low heels and whether eggs are eaten at the big end or little end.

Book 2. The vices are again self-importance, vanity and pride, but perceived from a different perspective. Gulliver, in Brobdingnag where the inhabitants are as tall as steeples and buildings are in proportion, explains European manners, government and learning to the king. The king says: "I cannot but conclude the bulk of your natives to be the most pernicious race of little odious vermin that nature ever suffered to crawl upon the surface of the earth."

Book 3. The vices are superiority, pride and foolish speculation. Gulliver, in Laputa, a flying island, finds the philosophers, men of science and historians utterly impractical. In the Academy of Projectors professors attempt to extract sunshine from cucumbers. The people of a race who are immortal, the Struldbrugs, are miserable.

Book 4. The vices are superiority, pride and misanthropy. Gulliver, in the land of Houyhnhnms, horses who have reason, contrasts their rational, clean society with the Yahoos, who are filthy and brutal. Convinced of the sordidness of existence, Gulliver recoils from his family in disgust when he returns home.

The clue to Swift's attitude is in his letter to Pope of 29 September 1725: "When you think of the world give it one lash the more at my request. I have ever hated all nations, professions, and communities, and all my love is towards individuals: for instance, I hate the tribe of lawyers, but I love Councellor Such-a-one, and Judge Such-a-one....But principally I hate and detest that animal called man, although I heartily love John, Peter, Thomas, and so forth. This is the system upon which I have governed myself many years (but do not tell). Upon this great foundation of Misanthropy (though not [in] Timons manner) the whole building of my Travells is erected."

Swift is on the side of individuals, and when Gulliver sides with the Houyhnhnms' reason against the Yahoos, Swift is siding against the generic rather than the particular. When he sides with their reason against the individual members of his family, he has fallen into misanthropy. Swift is condemning how the Houyhnhnms' reason has driven Gulliver to loathe individuals and be misanthropic. Their reason represents the Age of Reason, and Swift is therefore confronting the Age of Reason, which can drive one mad through misanthropy.[4] (See Appendix 2 for a more detailed account of Swift's view of the Age of Reason in *Gulliver's Travels*; pp.431-2, 433-4, 438-46 for Swift's handling of virtue and vice in this work; and p.438 for a further discussion of Gulliver's misanthropy.)

Swift is on the side of order, and in *The Tale of a Tub* (1696), a prose satire based on the practice of seamen who when they encounter a whale throw a tub into the sea to divert it from attacking their ship, he defends religion and government from the attack of Hobbes' *Leviathan* and all who would undermine religion. However, he is more interested in satirizing the institutions of the English political system and the new philosophers and scientists, and in advancing an ideal of virtue that is independent of the Age of Reason, than in the quest for infinite Reality, to which, as an ordained priest, he presumably assents. He does not reflect the metaphysical aspect of the fundamental theme directly, but rather, like the Renaissance tragic dramatists, shows the vices of humankind in relation to ideal virtue, the Age of Reason's standard which he undermines in his onslaught on the perversity of the Age of Reason's philosophical and scientific thinkers, and which, he demonstrates, leads to loathing of individuals and misanthropy.

Like Pope, Swift attacks human flaws and the political and social system rather than describing the quest for Reality and immortality. As he himself said in a letter to Pope,[5] he wrote "to vex the world rather than divert it".

Johnson

Samuel Johnson's writings ensured the survival of Neoclassicism. He was many-sided, writing essays in the *Rambler* and the *Idler*, writing his *Lives of the English Poets* and the first *Dictionary of the English Language*, and being a brilliant conversationalist and the subject of James Boswell's *The Life of Samuel Johnson*. He also wrote poems, most notably two satirical poems, and a short novel, *Rasselas*.

The first of his satirical poems, 'London', is a reflection on London's vices and on the oppression of the poor. Better known is his imitation of the tenth satire of Juvenal, 'The Vanity of Human Wishes', which comments on the vanity of ambition: ambition for power, learning, military glory and beauty. Johnson describes the ambitious: "Unnumber'd Suppliants Croud Preferment's Gate,/Athirst for Wealth, and burning to be great." In the end his religious faith triumphs: "Still raise for Good the supplicating Voice,/But leave to Heav'n the Measure and the Choice."

The History of Rasselas, Prince of Abyssinia, a didactic romance that came out a few weeks after Voltaire's *Candide*, was written in a week during the evenings to pay for his mother's funeral and settle her debts.

Rasselas, weary of pleasure in the "happy valley", travels to Egypt to study and concludes that happiness is unobtainable. The philosopher advising him declares (in ch.X) that the "business of a poet" is to "examine not the individual, but the species" and to write "as the interpreter of nature, and the legislator of mankind...presiding over the thoughts and manners of future generations". Johnson's phrase "the legislator of mankind" was taken up by Shelley in *A Defence of Poetry*: "Poets are the unacknowledged legislators of the world."

Rasselas is on a quest for truth and life choice, and the philosopher, Imlac, gives him a lecture "on the nature of the soul" (ch.XLVIII). It is agreed that "the Being which made the soul, can destroy it" and that "the choice of life is become less important" than "the choice of eternity". *Rasselas* is on the metaphysical aspect of the fundamental theme.

Johnson balanced his focus on vices such as ambition with the quest for Reality and immortality.

Sentiment and Realism in English Literature

The metaphysical aspect of the fundamental theme can be found in the later poets of the Neoclassical Age. These Nature poets wrote a poetry of sentiment and anticipated the Romantic Age.

Poetry of Sentiment

James Thomson's 'Seasons' provides new images of external Nature in artificial diction. Thomas Gray's 'Elegy Written in a Country Churchyard' presents dusk, wildlife, the tombs of former villagers "to Fame and Fortune unknown" and the peace of souls at one with God. William Collins' 'Ode to Evening' echoes Gray's dusk.

William Cowper's 'The Task' is about the countryside. His despairing poem 'The Cast-Away', written shortly before his death, is about man's isolation and helplessness. A man overboard, alone at night in a dark sea, deliberately drowns himself: "he drank/The stifling wave, and then he sank." There is no "light propitious" that could save him. (Cowper was convinced of his own sin and unworthiness.) Cowper's 'Light Shining out of Darkness', better known as the hymn 'God moves in a mysterious way', is about illumination. ("Behind a frowning

Providence/he hides a Smiling face".)

George Crabbe's realistic 'The Village' and 'The Borough' (which is based on Aldeburgh) describe country life. Oliver Goldsmith's 'The Deserted Village' was also about village life and has an elegiac tone similar to Gray's.

All these poets focus on the world of Nature rather than on an infinite Reality hidden behind it that bestows immortality. Nevertheless all these poets share the Neoclassical love of order and sense that the soul is linked to God.

Novels of Sentiment

The novel of sentiment (based on emotion rather than reason) began with Samuel Richardson's epistolary *Pamela* (1740-1) and *Clarissa* (1748-9), letters written with immediacy and subjective, psychological analysis. An austere Puritan who was opposed to the display of self, Richardson was writing love letters on behalf of girls when only thirteen, and he was concerned with right and wrong in the choices of virtuous middle-class young ladies, issues which appealed to their sentiment; an extension of the Renaissance focus on social vices to an edifying concern with the ethical dilemmas of the virtuous.

Oliver Goldsmith's *The Vicar of Wakefield* (which was sold by Dr Johnson for £60 to prevent Goldsmith from being arrested for debt, 1766) continued the novel of sentiment by telling of the adventures and tribulations, which sometimes seem picaresque, of the vicar and his six children after the vicar has lost all his money. The sentiment arising from threats to the family and home is addressed to the heart, and readers identified with the family's predicament.

Laurence Sterne's *Tristram Shandy* (1759-67) further developed the sentimental novel. The book's narrative in stream-of-consciousness is constantly interrupted by digressions for humorous effect. Set in the Shandys' parlour and garden, it is about Sterne's personality and ego: it begins with Tristram's conception and he is not born until the third book, and the account of his life is unfinished.

Sterne's appeal to the senses and to sentiment continued in *A Sentimental Journey through France and Italy* (1768), in which episodes of travel are imbued with emotion.

These novels of sentiment were not quests for a Reality behind the visible world and the possibility of immortality. They were about adventures in the social world and their effects on the emotions. In a famous image in *Phaedrus* (246, 253d) Plato compared the intellect, the part of the soul that must guide the rest of the soul to truth and enlightenment, to a charioteer whose vehicle is drawn by two horses, one white and one black. The white horse is disciplined and obedient, and represents rational, moral will and the positive passions of the higher levels such as righteous indignation. The black horse is powerful and unruly, and represents emotion and desire, the bodily appetites, passions and instincts. The charioteer directs the chariot or soul to prevent the two horses from galloping in different directions.

In the novel of sentiment the soul is not in control of unruly emotion. Plato would have disapproved of the novel of sentiment, believing that sentiment should be controlled. The quest for Reality is beyond the senses, into the infinite and awareness of an ideal virtue, whereas the novelists of sentiment focused on the senses and the emotions that arise from reacting to follies and vices described by the Renaissance writers.

Realistic Novels

Alongside the novel of sentiment was the realistic novel. This began with Henry Fielding, who satirized *Pamela* with *Shamela* (1741) and then wrote the episodic, almost picaresque *Joseph Andrews* (1742), beginning a *genre* of "comic romance" that broke away from Richardson's epistolary form and would eventually lead to Dickens and Thackeray.

In his Preface to *Joseph Andrews* Fielding said his object was to defend what is good by displaying "the Ridiculous", which he claimed arises from affectations, and ultimately from vanity and hypocrisy. Joseph progresses from stable-boy to footman and is involved in travels and adventures on the road before marrying a milkmaid.

Fielding's *Tom Jones* (1749) is about a foundling who also has adventures on the road before marrying the squire's daughter. In his Dedication Fielding writes "that to recommend goodness and innocence hath been my sincere endeavour in this history". He offers a picture of society in the outer world.

In his Preface to his episodic picaresque *Roderick Random* (1748) Tobias Smollett says he wishes to arouse "generous indignation...against the vicious disposition of the world". His theme is indignation at vice. Penniless, Roderick is pressed into becoming a sailor and is present at the siege of Cartegena, Spain. He becomes a footman and eventually marries his love.

Smollett's epistolary *Humphrey Clinker* (1771) is about the interplay of characters on a trip from Wales to London and thence to Scotland.

The realistic novelists aspire to display virtue among the vices, and like the Renaissance dramatists do not follow the metaphysical aspect of the fundamental theme of the quest for Reality. Their reality is purely social, but they convey a universal virtue in practical situations.

Jane Austen's realistic, anti-sentimental novels, though published in the second decade of the 19th century, are Neoclassical in spirit. In *Pride and Prejudice, Sense and Sensibility, Mansfield Park, Emma, Persuasion* and *Northanger Abbey* the heroines live limited, narrow lives in the countryside. They are 18th-century figures, ruled by reason and common sense, scornful of "sensibility" (or being susceptible to emotional impressions) and of excess, characteristics associated with the Romantic movement.

In each of her novels she exposes, satirizes and ridicules vices: pride and prejudice (Elizabeth, Darcy in *Pride and Prejudice*), excessive susceptibility and openness to emotional impressions and lack of principle (Marianne and Willoughby in *Sense and Sensibility*), lack of principle (the Crawfords in *Mansfield Park*), patronising help (Emma in *Emma*), duplicity (William in *Persuasion*) and snobbish estimation of wealth and romance-induced suspicion (General Tilney and Catherine in *Northanger Abbey*). The heroines are all relatively self-controlled: Elizabeth, Eleanor, Fanny, Emma, Anne and Catherine.

In all these six novels vices are satirized in relation to an ideal standard of virtue, and there is no quest for a Reality behind the social world.

Realistic Plays

Just as the realistic novels reacted against the sentimental novels, so realistic plays reacted against the sentimental comedies of the 18th century, which were first introduced by Sir Richard Steele in 1701.

Oliver Goldsmith's *She Stoops to Conquer* (1773) satirized the family emotions of sentimental comedy in farce, in which a private residence is mistaken for an inn. Young Marlow, visiting his bride-to-be for the first time, asks to be directed to an inn and is directed to her house. He pursues her, believing she is a servant. She is later bashful in her true role, but by then the misunderstanding has punctured the sentiment normally associated between future bride and groom.

Richard Sheridan carried on the reaction.

In *The Rivals* (1775), sentiment is ridiculed when Captain Absolute, who is in love with Lydia, to press his suit claims to be Ensign Beverley, which will make him more likely to be accepted. His father arrives to propose a match between him and Lydia. In the confusion of identities, the usual sentiment between betrothed is punctured.

In *The School for Scandal* (1777), there is a similar confusion of identities as the extravagant Charles, who is in love with Marie, is tested by his uncle from India whom he has never met, who professes to be a money-lender.

In this play some of the characters have Jonsonian names such as Lady Sneerwell and Mrs. Candour. We are back in Shakespeare's confusion of identities and the ridiculing of follies and vices in, it must be said, pretty unbelievable farce. The metaphysical aspect of the fundamental theme is largely ignored.

Gibbon

The history of Edward Gibbon's *History of the Decline and Fall of the Roman Empire* (three volumes, 1776, 1781, 1788) blamed the fall of the Roman Empire on religion and barbarians.

It shows the Western Roman Empire as being subverted by barbarians, and the East Roman Empire – he means the Byzantine Empire – as challenged by the Holy Roman Empire under Charlemagne and then by the Ottoman Turks, who perpetrated the fall of Constantinople in 1453. He describes the link between the ancient and modern worlds from the establishment of Christianity to the conquests of the Muslims and the crusades. Both Christians and Muslims are questers for an infinite Reality and for immortality, and though ostensibly Gibbon is writing of secular historical events, his work reflects the metaphysical aspect of the fundamental theme.

French Neoclassical Literature

In French literature the Neoclassical Age took over from the Baroque Age about 1685, when Molière, Corneille, Racine and La Rochefoucauld were of the past. François Fénelon's *Télémaque*, a didactic romance, focused on Telemachus's voyage to Nestor's Pylos to search for his missing father in *The Odyssey* and taught the virtue of the enlightened monarch. Relativism came in, the view that good and bad are relative concepts, that what is good for one society may be bad for another. French dramatists included Voltaire (a pen-name adopted by François-Marie Arouet). Beaumarchais' *Le Barbier de Séville* and *Le Marriage de Figaro* boldly criticize the nobility and paved the way for the 1789 French Revolution which closed the French Neoclassical Age.

The Enlightenment in France, America and Germany

The Enlightenment (a term taken from the German *Aufklärung*) is a term that describes the rational, philosophical, scientific *Zeitgeist* which rejected superstition, was sceptical and practised religious tolerance. The divine gift of reason enabled men to understand the universe, science was slowly and quietly replacing religion. Descartes,

Locke, Newton and Voltaire were the main writers associated with the Enlightenment.

These ideas had already reached France in the philosophy of Gottfried Wilhelm Leibniz. Voltaire, a novelist, satirist, historian, poet, dramatist, polemicist, moralist, critic and letter-writer, was the universal genius of the Enlightenment, best known for his philosophical satires about the evils of life from which the reason should give protection, such as *Zadig* (1747) and *Candide* (1759). In his *Lettres sur les Anglais* (1734) he criticized the nobility, again anticipating, or at least pointing forward to, the French Revolution.

Denis Diderot and Jean d'Alembert brought out the *Encyclopédie*, which advanced the idea of progress and strengthened Utopianism. (The pre-Romantic Jean-Jacques Rousseau, author of *Confessions*, 1781-8, seems to have descended from the Enlightenment's theory of progress, arguing that man is naturally good and that society exerts a corrupting influence which does not make for progress.)

Pope's 'Essay on Man' (1733-4) was printed in French more than sixty times before 1789, and its message of order, harmony and optimism contributed to the Enlightenment.

All these Neoclassical writers concentrated on vices and ignored the metaphysical aspect of the fundamental theme.

The American literature of the 18th century, the century of American independence, was overtly political as the writings of William Bird, Benjamin Franklin, Thomas Paine and Thomas Jefferson were all under the shadow of the creation of the United States. Franklin, Paine and Jefferson were deeply influenced by the French Enlightenment. However all three were Freemasons and had links with the 1776 Bavarian Illuminati, groups that quested for the infinite Reality behind the visible world, venerated virtue and sought immortality, and as in the case of Bacon, their works touch on the metaphysical aspect of the fundamental theme which through the secret Freemasonic society dominated their waking lives.

The German Enlightenment built on the foundations of rationalism laid by Leibniz. Germans read the 18th-century writers in translation and there was a reaction against rationalism. Milton's *Paradise Lost* made some Germans insist that the imagination should not be dominated by reason. Gotthold Ephraim Lessing produced "tragedies of common life", plays on domestic tragedies.

Goethe

Wolfgang von Goethe lived in a time of overlap between Neoclassicism and Romanticism. The value of feeling was being discovered, and reason now seemed to have limitations. Man was seen to be linked to Nature by instinct, impulse, emotion and intuition. The ideal of the Neoclassical Age was *Humanität* "(Humanness"), a term used by Johann Gottfried von Herder, in which intellect and feeling should be balanced.

The *Sturm und Drang* ("Storm and Stress") movement sought to overthrow rationalism. The term *Sturm und Drang* was taken from Klinger's Romantic play on the American War of Independence, which appeared in 1775. Goethe belonged to the movement. Rousseau's revolt against literary convention, including the unities in drama, inspired the new movement. The cult of Nature replaced Christian religion, and individual conscience was valued. Egotism crept into literature in contexts of strain and stress, protest and revolt, yearning and disillusion. Friedrich Schiller's *Die Räuber* ("The Robbers", 1781) brought *Sturm und Drang* to a new level. In this play Karl takes to the woods to address the evils perpetrated by his father's court.

Sturm und Drang lacked self-discipline, and a new moral idealism appeared in the philosophy of Kant and in the poetry of Goethe and Schiller. There was a new stability in form and ideas. Goethe wrote *Die Leiden des jungen Werthers* (*The Sorrows of Young Werther*, 1774), a semi-autobiographical epistolary novel in which Werther falls in love with Lotte and eventually kills himself; and *Wilhelm Meisters Lehrjahre* (*Wilhelm Meister's Apprenticeship*, 1777-1829), a questing *Bildungsroman* or educational novel on the conduct of life.

The period from 1794 to 1805 when Goethe and Schiller were in close friendship in Jena and Weimar marked the culmination of Neoclassicism. Schiller provided theory, Goethe practice, including a new way of producing drama.

Goethe's *Faust*, Parts 1 and 2 (1808, 1832), embody Neoclassicism's highest peak. Goethe had had links with the 1776 Illuminati – for a while his codename in Adam Weishaupt's movement, which quested for Reality and immortality, was Abaris[6] –

and the story of Faust is on the metaphysical aspect of the fundamental theme:

> Part 1 begins with a Prologue in Heaven. Mephistopheles is given permission to destroy Faust's virtuous soul, and the Lord believes he will fail. Mephistopheles visits Faust, who enters into a compact to be his servant if he can be made to say *"Verweile doch! Du bist so schön!"* (*"Stay, you are so beautiful!"*) Mephistopheles attempts to delight Faust, intriguing his seduction of Gretchen, who kills herself. Faust's better self is full of remorse.

> In Part 2 Faust pursues Helen of Troy, recalling her from Hades. She is taken from him, and their son Euphorion, who is based on Byron and personifies poetry and the union of the classical and the Romantic, vanishes in flame. Faust, wanting to serve his fellow human beings, reclaims submerged land from the sea, but is blinded by Care. Satisfied in his conscience at his own good works, for he has fulfilled himself by his striving and selfless actions, Faust cries out to the moment, "Stay, you are so beautiful!" and falls dead. Hell tries to seize his soul, but unlike the ending of Marlowe's *Dr Faustus*, angels bear him away.

Faust, like Goethe, knows the quest for a Reality beyond the visible world, and the possibility of immortality. In *Part One* (1808) he asks: *"Bin ich ein Gott? Mir wird so licht!/Ich schau' in diesen reinen Zügen/Die wirkende Natur vor meiner Seele liegen."* ("Am I a god? Light fills my mind. I see in these pure features the way Nature works within my soul.")

It seems that he has seen the Light. Faust's salvation by striving also touches on the metaphysical aspect of the fundamental theme. "Angels, hovering in the higher atmosphere, bearing all that is immortal of Faust, say (V, 11936–7), *"Wer immer strebend sich bemüht, den können wir erlösen."* ("He who strives without ceasing/We can redeem.") Faust's soul strives towards Reality and he fulfils himself, retaining by his selfless deeds the ideal of virtue (except perhaps during his mistreatment of Gretchen).

Faust's quest for Reality beyond the visible, his striving and selfless actions, took him beyond the Neoclassical view of the human condition.

Literary Summary

The main references to the metaphysical aspect of the fundamental theme in world literature during the Neoclassical period are as follows:

- The infinite that surrounds the universe is in: Pope; Johnson; and Goethe.
- The metaphysical Reality seen as Light is in: Pope; and Goethe.
- The order of the universe can be found in: Pope; and Goethe.
- The oneness of known humankind can be found in Pope's "stupendous whole".
- The similarities in cultures and civilizations are emphasized in: Swift's *Gulliver's Travels*; Gibbon; and Goethe.
- The universal being (or self) that opens to the Light behind the rational, social ego is in: Pope; Johnson; and Goethe.
- Universal virtue is in: Pope; Swift; Johnson; the realistic novels of Jane Austen; and Goethe.
- The promise of the immortality of the universal being is present in: Johnson; and Goethe.
- The inner transformation or centre-shift from ego to universal being is found in Pope's 'Eloisa to Abelard'.
- The quest of the purified soul is in Goethe.
- The sensibility that approaches Reality through more than one discipline can be found in: Pope (poetry, unfinished epic *Brutus*, prose 'Epilogue to the Satires', translation); Swift (poetry, novels, polemical essays); Johnson (poetry, literary criticism, lexicography in compiling the first dictionary and novel, *Rasselas*); Voltaire (novel/philosophical satire, history, epic poetry, drama, criticism, letters); and Goethe (poetry, drama, literature, theology, philosophy and science).
- The new perspective of unity in history, religion, philosophy and science, international politics and literature can be found in: Gibbon (unification of European history to 1453 in *The History of the Decline and Fall of the Roman Empire*, 1776-88); and Goethe (unification of organic science).

Neoclassicism had now been overtaken by the Romantic movement, which returned to the metaphysical aspect of the fundamental theme as comprehensively as did the Metaphysicals.

7

Romantic Literature

The metaphysical aspect of the fundamental theme's quest for Reality was immensely strong during the Romantic Age.

The Romantic Revolution
The Romantic Revolution began in Germany. It evolved from the *Sturm und Drang* movement of the early 1770s and the view of Goethe and Schiller that art is the spontaneous expression of the personal experience of the individual artist's creative genius. The German Romantics of 1797 were based in Jena. The group, which included Novalis, the philosopher Schelling and Hölderlin, revolved round the brothers Friedrich and August Schlegel, and it was Friedrich Schlegel who first used the word "Romantic" in a literary context.

The English Romantic movement of 1798 had its origins in Blake's 1789 *Songs of Innocence*. Wordsworth and Coleridge brought out *The Lyrical Ballads* on 4 October 1798. By then they were making a long visit to Germany to make contact with the German Romantic movement, having left England on 16 September and remaining in Wordsworth's case until April, and in Coleridge's case until July, 1799. Coleridge studied physiology and *Bible* criticism, and steeped himself in German metaphysics, at the University of Göttingen while Wordsworth lived in Goslar (at 86 Breitestrasse). There is no record of their meeting Goethe, but they both met Klopstock in September.

The English movement was relatively undoctrinaire: the word "Romantic" does not appear in Wordsworth's *Preface to the Lyrical Ballads*, Coleridge's *Biographia Literaria* or Shelley's *Defence of Poetry*. There was therefore no great breach in the continuity between English Neoclassical and Romantic literature, which had evolved from Gray and Cowper, as W. Jackson Bate first pointed out in *From Classic to Romantic*.

French Romanticism was arrested by the French Revolution, for Neoclassicism was restored and from 1790 to 1820 it was dangerous to question the official line in literature, especially under Napoleon's Imperial rule. Lamartine introduced Romanticism into French poetry in 1820, and Hugo introduced it into French drama in 1830.

Romanticism was thus a German-English, or Anglo-Saxon, movement. It surfaced after a wave of Evangelical Protestantism, a "religion of the heart" that swept through both countries. It contained both Realist and Idealist strands. Wordsworth's poems about solitaries (for example 'Michael' and 'The Solitary Reaper') are realistic whereas his sense in the *The Prelude* of "unknown modes of being" suggests an Idealist outlook. Idealism holds that Reality is approached through the mind. The Idealist strand was the stronger as the best English Romantics saw behind the Neoclassical "inanimate, cold world" (Coleridge's 'Dejection: An Ode') to the infinite, eternal Reality beyond it. The Greek "*meta*" can mean "behind" as we saw on p.2, and so the Romantics' metaphysical Reality was the Reality *behind* the physical world.

The English Romantic Imagination
The English Romantic poets believed that they were linked to this infinite Reality through their imagination.

Whereas the Neoclassical poets had written in general terms of common experience, dwelling on familiar appearance as interpreters, and had regarded the imagination as "fancy" (visual impressions and metaphors) that should be controlled by their rational "judgement", the English Romantic poets saw themselves as creators rather than interpreters, and they believed that they created from the active imagination which reflected God's shaping of the universe, not from the passive part of the mind which recorded impressions, as Locke, described and was "a lazy looker-on on an external world" (Coleridge)[1]. They mistrusted all views of the mind and the universe that were based on Locke's mechanistic approach, as Coleridge made clear: "If the mind be not passive, if it be indeed made in God's image,…there is ground for suspicion that any system built on the passiveness of the mind must be false as a system."[2]

To the Romantics the imagination was the most vital of the mind's activities, and it was the source of spiritual energy. It connected the mind to the infinite, and its inspiration was God operating in the human soul, whose immortality it guaranteed, as Blake wrote:

"This world of Imagination is the world of Eternity; it is the divine bosom into which we shall all go after the death of the Vegetated body. This World of Imagination is Infinite and Eternal, whereas the world of Generation or Vegetation is Finite and Temporal. There Exist in that Eternal World the Permanent Realities of Every Thing which we see reflected in this Vegetable Glass of Nature. All Things are comprehended in their Eternal Forms in the divine body of the Saviour, the True Vine of Eternity, The Human Imagination."[3]

Coleridge took this up and claimed that the imagination reflected the workings of the creative activity of God:

"The primary Imagination I hold to be the living Power and prime Agent of all human Perception, and as a repetition in the finite mind of the eternal act of creation in the infinite I AM."[4]

This view was also held by Wordsworth, Shelley and Keats. Shakespeare had also been aware of it for in *A Midsummer Night's Dream* Theseus suggests that the imagination bears no relation to external reality: "The poets' eye in a fine frenzy rolling,/Doth glance from heaven to earth, from earth to heaven;/And, as imagination bodies forth/The forms of things unknown, the poet's pen/Turns them to shapes, and gives to airy nothing/a local habitation and a name." Hippolyta contradicts him, saying that the imagination's images are not "airy nothing" but represent reality: "But all the story of the night told over,/And all their minds transfigur'd so together,/More witnesseth than fancy's images,/And grows to something of great constancy,/But, howsoever, strange and admirable."[5]

To the English Romantic poets, the imagination is a form of insight that reveals truth as Light which the ordinary rational mind cannot see. Blake explained: "Mental things are alone Real; what is call'd Corporeal, Nobody Knows of its Dwelling Place: it is in Fallacy, and its Existence an Imposture. Where is the Existence Out of Mind or Thought? Where is it but in the Mind of a Fool?"[6] According to a 'Fragment' in Blake the materialist scientific theories of Democritus and Newton could not deny the divine Light: "The Atoms of Democritus/And Newton's Particles of Light/Are sands upon the Red sea shore,/Where Israel's tents do shine so bright." Blake is referring to the tent of the tabernacle in which the divine Light shone. The tents are an image to present the Romantic imagination as the Light.

The Romantics' quest for Reality as Light through the imagination expressed the metaphysical aspect of the fundamental theme. It was a search for an unseen world that inspired their minds from beyond, appealing not to their logical mind but to their complete self, and turned them into poets. Blake rejected the Neoclassical generalising of Johnson:

"To Generalize is to be an Idiot. To Particularize is the Alone Distinction of Merit. General Knowledges are those Knowledges that Idiots possess....What is General Nature? is there Such a Thing? what is General Knowledge? is there such a Thing? Strictly Speaking All Knowledge is Particular."[7]

Contact with the unseen world fused the poet's soul with the divine, an experience Coleridge sought to capture in 'Kubla Khan': "And all should cry, Beware! Beware!/His flashing eyes, his floating hair!/Weave a circle round him thrice,/And close your eyes with holy dread,/For he on honey-dew hath fed,/And drunk the milk of Paradise."

To Blake, Wordsworth, Shelley and Keats the visible world mirrored eternity. They wrote of the search for an ulterior Reality and saw the imagination as a divine power, the power of the Light, from which everything real derives. This Reality manifests into, and is masked by, visible things. As Blake wrote: "One Power alone makes a Poet: Imagination, The Divine Vision."[8] In 'Auguries of Innocence' he describes this masked Reality: "To see a World in a Grain of Sand/And a Heaven in a Wild Flower,/Hold infinity in the palm of your hand/And Eternity in an hour."

To the English Romantic poets, the visible world mirrored, and was a tangible symbol of, the invisible world, and so a spiritual Reality was at work in all living things. It poured into the soul. The ultimate Reality expressed itself in the imagination, the power which creates and reveals. The senses' appreciation of beauty revealed absolute Reality which the visible world masked. Beauty therefore revealed truth: the ultimately real that is permanent and universal. For Wordsworth, the imagination links to the One and is known by children. It is still known by mature poets, who have retained the childhood power in later life: "For feeling has to him imparted power/That through the growing faculties of sense/Doth like an agent of the one great Mind/Create, creator and receiver both,/Working but in alliance with the works/Which it beholds."[9]

Wordsworth saw the imagination as Reason, saying it "Is but another name for absolute power/And clearest insight, amplitude of mind,/And Reason in her most exalted mood."[10] Most of the other English Romantic poets, however, saw the imagination as superior to Reason, dethroning the supreme position Reason held under Neoclassicism. Shelley wrote of poetic images as "nurslings of immortality" in *Prometheus Unbound*, in which a Spirit describes the poet: "He will watch from dawn to gloom/The lake-reflected sun illume/The yellow bees in the ivy-bloom/Nor heed nor see, what things they be;/But from these create he can/Forms more real than living man,/Nurslings of immortality!" The implication is that humans are being nursed by Nature towards immortality.

To the English Romantic poets, imagination was a unifying faculty. Coleridge asserted "the esemplastic power of imagination".[11] "Esemplastic" comes from the Greek "*eis en plattein*" (Coleridge; *plassein* in *Shorter English Dictionary*, see p.3), "to mould into One". To Coleridge, the imagination makes bits into a whole in a process that is the opposite of the reason's analysis, which makes distinctions and reduces into bits. Shelley followed him in seeing the imagination as a unifier. Poetry to him was "the expression of the Imagination" because it brought diverse things together in harmony instead of separating them through analysis. In *A Defence of Poetry* he wrote that the poet "not only beholds intensely the present as it is, and discovers those laws according to which present things ought to be ordered, but he beholds the future in the present, and his thoughts are the germs of the flower and the fruit of latest time". He adds, "A poet participates in the eternal, the infinite, and the one."

Reality is a timeless, unchanging, complete order, and the visible world is a broken reflection of it. The poet uncovers the invisible absolute real that is behind visible phenomena. He presents the whole in its unity and shows that the phenomenal depends on the real unity behind it, the many on the One.

Through the imagination the English Romantic poets found an unseen transcendental order which explains the world of appearances. The Romantic movement was an attempt by the solitary soul to discover the world of spirit. It is an expedition into the unknown, the quest for Reality of the metaphysical aspect of the fundamental theme given fresh expression. Through their poetry poets were able to penetrate into a world denied to most of their fellow human beings who saw only the visible world, and their creations were embodiments of eternal things perceived by the imagination. The English Romantic poets saw the visible world as within the infinite Reality of the metaphysical aspect of the fundamental theme, which made humans "nurslings of immortality".

A great influence on Romanticism, and on the development of its view of the imagination, was Thomas Taylor, the Platonist, who revived an anti-Christian Neoplatonism. Romanticism therefore lay outside the mainstream Christian tradition. He inspired the first generation of English Romantic poets.

Blake

The metaphysical aspect of the fundamental theme returns with the mystic William Blake, a printer, engraver and artist as well as poet who illustrated and published his own work. Blake's *Songs of Innocence* and *Songs of Experience* contain complementary poems with opposite perspectives, that suggest "the two contrary states in the human soul" and his doctrine of contraries.

Songs of Innocence contains poems of childhood simplicity that convey a world that is good. *Songs of Experience* presents a world contaminated by unnatural restraint, frustration and evil. The two "contraries" are reconciled in *The Marriage of Heaven and Hell*, in which soul and body are no longer identified with reason and evil: "Man has no Body distinct from his Soul….Energy is the only life, and is from the Body….Energy is Eternal Delight."

Blake reconciled Taylor's pagan Neoplatonism with Swedenborg's spiritual Light, which Swedenborg believed is inwardly within the natural light of the sun. There was therefore a Neoplatonist dimension of four ascending (or here descending) worlds behind the "fourfold vision" Blake referred to in verses within his letter to Butts of 22 November 1802. He writes that these "were composed about a twelve month ago, while walking from Felpham to Lavant to meet my Sister": "Now I a fourfold vision see,/And a fourfold vision is given to me;/'Tis fourfold in my supreme delight/And threefold in soft Beulah's night/And twofold Always. May God us keep/From Single vision & Newton's sleep!" The fourfold vision is of the Light, as the first two lines of the poem make clear: "To my Friend Butts I write/My first Vision of Light."

Blake's universe is controlled by the Light, making infinity and eternity possible. In his 'Auguries of Innocence' (c.1803) Blake evokes infinity and eternity in the important lines I quoted on p.182: "To see a World in a Grain of Sand/And a Heaven in a Wild Flower/Hold Infinity in the palm of your hand/And Eternity in an hour." In his long poems he journeys from the ego to the universal being which can see the Light. He calls the ego "the Spectre": "Each man is in his Spectre's power/Until the arrival of that hour,/When his Humanity awake/And cast his Spectre into the Lake." The ego is also "Urizen" ("Your reason"). The Light is called "Los" ("Sol" in reverse, the Light being within natural sunlight according to Swedenborg).

Blake had personal experience of the Light. He wrote in his letter to Hayley of 23 October 1804[12] that he had seen the Light after twenty years of darkness:

"Suddenly, on the way after visiting the Truchsessian Gallery of pictures, I was again enlightened with the light I enjoyed in my youth, and which has for exactly twenty years been closed from me as by a door and by window-shutters....Dear Sir, excuse my enthusiasm or rather madness, for I am really drunk with intellectual vision whenever I take a pencil or graver into my hand, even as I used to be in my youth, and as I have not been for twenty dark, but very profitable, years. I thank God that I courageously pursued my course through darkness."

Twenty years from 1804 takes us back to 1784, five years before the appearance of *Songs of Innocence* and eleven years before the *Songs of*

Experience.

Blake's entire poetic and artistic work was a quest for the infinite, eternal world behind the natural world. This infinite, eternal world is in contact with the imagination, which it inspires. He referred to the oneness of humankind when he wrote, "All Religions are One." His entire *oeuvre* is on the metaphysical aspect of the fundamental theme.

Coleridge

Coleridge, a Unitarian, incorporated Neoplatonism as is revealed in 'Religious Musings' (1794) in which the "Passions" are "enrobed with Light" from "one Mind", "omnipresent love,/Whose day-spring rises glorious in my soul/As the great sun".

Neoplatonism is in 'Kubla Khan' (1798), in which the "sunless sea" recalls Plotinus's sea or "lake" of material existence. It is in 'Dejection: an Ode' (1802): "from the soul itself must issue forth/A light, a glory, a fair luminous cloud" of joy.

This joy is Coleridge's "shaping spirit of imagination", and as he has said that the joy is also the "light", he is saying that the imagination is the Light. In *Biographia Literaria* he quotes Plotinus on the need to watch for intuitive knowledge "till it suddenly shines upon us; preparing ourselves for the blessed spectacle as the eye waits patiently for the rising sun". The imagination shapes into one and seeks to return to the One Light from which it came.

Coleridge ranked the inner life of creative imagination above the outer life of Nature. In 'Dejection: an Ode' he wrote: "I may not hope from outward forms to win/The passion and the life, whose fountains are within." In ranking the "within" above the "outward" he is very close to Blake, who wrote, "Nature has no outline, but imagination has." Blake's Los and Coleridge's shaping light are also close, but Coleridge did not meet Blake until c.1818 (according to Crabb Robinson's diary), too late for there to be a direct influence.

'The Ancient Mariner' is on the metaphysical aspect of the fundamental theme. It is about the quest of the soul:

The mariner kills an albatross for no apparent reason and has thus sinned against the brotherhood of living things (a Neoplatonist idea). His guilty soul is punished by being isolated on a windless sea, and it is finally redeemed. The turning point is when he blesses the water-snakes, and begins to love Nature rather than seek to destroy its creatures. Celestial spirits take over the dead bodies of the crew.

Coleridge presents the Oneness of Nature and its eternal, absolute values in temporal, phenomenal shapes, which are symbols. Symbols present the eternal world in temporal form. Coleridge shapes or moulds his symbols into a myth about a crisis in the human soul.

Coleridge's work embodies the metaphysical aspect of the fundamental theme as it is about the quest for Reality as Light and imagination.

Wordsworth

Wordsworth's work also embodies the metaphysical aspect of the fundamental theme. He met Coleridge in 1795, and the two men were linked through their joint publication of the *Lyrical Ballads* and their love for the Hutchinson sisters. They read their early work to each other, and Wordsworth developed his view that "poetry is the spontaneous overflow of powerful feelings". However Wordsworth saw the One as "from without in" rather than "from within out", contrary to how Coleridge saw it.

In *The Prelude* he identified the One as the "Wisdom and Spirit of the universe" (1.401), the "one great Mind" (2.257) which flows into the hearts of humankind and all forms of Nature. The mind opens to "influxes" of the One Mind (a Swedenborgian idea), and an "auxiliar light" comes from the mind (2.368) and glorifies what it sees in Nature. This is like Coleridge's "luminous cloud" and it is the result of a flowing-in of Nature. The title of the poem 'Influence of Natural Objects' means "The flowing-in of the Wisdom and Spirit of Nature into the heart".

In 'Tintern Abbey' (1798) Wordsworth describes how his soul opens to the One: "Almost suspended, we are laid asleep/In body, and become a living soul..../And I have felt/...a sense sublime/Of something.../Whose dwelling is the light of setting suns,/A motion and a spirit, that impels/All thinking things, all objects of all thought,/And rolls through all things." The dead pass into the One Spirit to be "rolled round in earth's diurnal course,/With rocks and stones and trees"

('Poems on Lucy', 1799).

However, in 'Ode, Intimations of Immortality from Recollections of Early Childhood' (written between 1802 and 1806) Wordsworth writes on the soul and laments that he has lost the vision. He no longer sees Nature "Apparelled in celestial light", "the visionary gleam" he knew as a boy. Boys are close to their souls' origin in immortality and a boy "beholds the light and whence it flows". As he grows he "perceives it die away/And fade into the light of common day".

The first four stanzas describe how, like Coleridge in 'Dejection: An Ode', he has lost the "celestial light": he knows "that there hath past away a glory from the earth." In the middle stanzas he explains this glory in terms of a far memory of pre-natal existence, which a child can recall. The last three stanzas show that life still has a meaning despite the loss of his vision, and are an answer to Coleridge's 'Dejection: An Ode': "Our souls have sight of that immortal sea/Which brought us hither."

The "inward eye" is connected with perceiving meaning. In his 'I wandered lonely as a cloud' (1804) he writes of the "inward eye" on which the daffodils "flash".

Wordsworth's work is on the metaphysical aspect of the fundamental theme as his soul quested for the Reality of the One, the Light, which flows into human minds and the phenomena of Nature. The One Light was Neoplatonist and linked to the One Mind, a Swedenborgian idea.

Shelley

The Neoplatonist One Light can be found in Shelley's poetry after 1815: in 'Alastor', in which Alastor is "obedient to the light/That shone within his soul"; in 'Hymn to Intellectual Beauty' in which an "unseen Power" visits "each human heart", the "Spirit of Beauty" whose "light alone" gives "truth to life's unquiet dream"; and in 'Mont Blanc', in which the "everlasting universe of things...flows through the mind".

In 'Adonais' (1821) Keats passes into the One Neoplatonist Spirit of Light on his death. We are told: "The One remains, the many change and pass;/Heaven's light forever shines, Earth's shadows fly;/Life, like a dome of many-coloured glass,/Stains the white radiance of Eternity,/Until Death tramples it to fragments" (LII).

Shelley continues: "That Light, whose smile kindles the

Universe,/That Beauty in which all things work and move/…now beams on me." It is clear that Shelley's Intellectual Beauty is the Light.

Shelley's work is on the metaphysical aspect of the fundamental theme as in his core poems he presents a soul questing for Reality as Light, which he called Intellectual Beauty.

Keats

Keats took up the idea of beauty from Shelley. He wrote to his brother George on 29 October 1818 of "the mighty abstract Idea I have of Beauty in all things". He had read Thomas Taylor the Platonist at his friend Benjamin Bailey's, and his Neoplatonist Idea of Beauty suggested that a spiritual Reality lurked behind natural phenomena.

In his 'Ode on a Grecian Urn' (May 1819) the message of the urn, according to inverted commas placed round the words in the volume Keats published in June 1820, is "Beauty is truth, truth beauty". Keats used "truth" to mean "Reality", and so the urn's message is: "Only the beautiful is real, and only the real is beautiful."

This message can be linked to his early letters: "I am certain of nothing but of the holiness of the Heart's affections and the truth of Imagination – What the Imagination seizes as Beauty must be truth – whether it existed before or not" (letter to Benjamin Bailey, 22 November 1817); "The excellence of every art is its intensity, capable of making all disagreeables evaporate, from their being in close relationship with Beauty and Truth" (letter to George and Thomas Keats, 21 December 1817); and "I never can feel certain of any truth but from a clear perception of its Beauty" (letter to George and Georgiana Keats, 18 December 1818).

Much of Keats' work is about the world of the senses, a "vale of Soul-making". His Odes focus on the transience of life and of his own fleeting existence as "One Whose Name was writ in Water". He found his images of timelessness, permanence and eternity in an urn and the song of the nightingale, not in the Light.

Keats' work is on the metaphysical aspect of the fundamental theme in so far as he presents the soul questing for Reality, or Beauty and Truth, but he does not concentrate on the metaphysical aspect of the fundamental theme as much as Blake, Coleridge, Wordsworth and Shelley. In much of his work he is Keats "the poppy-drowsy", drunk with the joys of Nature and its many visual, tactile images on which his senses feasted.

The Romantics and Metaphysics

The English Romantics depended on inspiration, which sometimes deserted them, as Coleridge lamented in 'Dejection: An Ode' and Wordsworth complained in 'Ode, Intimations of Immortality'. Their presentation of the beyond was through experience. Blake and Keats rebelled most against the concept of Reason. Blake wrote: "The Emmet's Inch and Eagle's Mile/Make Lame Philosophy to smile." Keats asked, "Do not all charms fly/At the mere touch of cold philosophy?" The Romantics' metaphysics was to some extent an Idealism, in which the mind creates Reality; but it was also a non-Idealistic bold reflection of the One from which everything emerged. The Romantics rejected abstraction and so could not produce works like Dante's *La divina commedia*, which included the philosophy and political thought of the Middle Ages, and Milton's *Paradise Lost*, which reflects man's history and place in the universe.

The Romantics perceived the visible world with great vividness and conveyed a vision of the One from which it came: a vision of the Light. They caught the moment and glimpsed the eternal world beyond it. They moved from the temporal to the timeless.

The End of English Romanticism

The main impetus of the Romantic period in English poetry ended with the death of Keats and Shelley. Its five main poets – Blake, Coleridge, Wordsworth, Shelley and Keats – were in agreement that the creative imagination gave an insight into an unseen order behind the visible, phenomenal world.

Byron

Lord Byron denied the importance of the imagination and did not believe in a transcendental order, and in this he was a Neoclassical Augustan: an egotistical poser who wrote about his ego and what he wanted the world to think of him.

Byron did not see a Reality behind the social world, and did not write of a quest for the infinite even though *Childe Harold's Pilgrimage* is about the travels of a pilgrim that resemble his own travels. Like the Renaissance dramatists he exposes follies and vices and by implication stands for virtue and truth as do the Neoclassical poets.

In *Childe Harold's Pilgrimage* the vice is lust, which Childe Harold turns from to journey to foreign lands. The fundamental theme of a quest is reflected in this pilgrimage. A "childe" was a young person training to become a knight, and the title suggests initiation. The poem was originally called "Childe Biroun's" (a variant of "Byron's") "Pilgrimage", reflecting Byron's autobiographical spiritual initiation into Reality and his attempts to cope with it.

In the comic, ironic and satirical *Don Juan*, the vice is lust, as a result of which the unprincipled Don Juan is sent to travel abroad.

Byron was brought up in Scotland among Calvinists, and though at Cambridge he became a Voltairean deist and then a cynic he secretly remained a Calvinist, and beneath the outer conniving laughter inwardly condemned Childe Harold and Don Juan for their reprobate lifestyle.[13] The theme of *Don Juan* is a worldly pilgrimage through society's ills: war, religion, tyranny, restraints on personal liberty, injustice and hypocrisy. It is a Neoclassical version of the metaphysical aspect of the fundamental theme as Byron's quest or journey to Reality is to a social reality, not a metaphysical one. (Byron's flaw, like Pope's, was: "He never looked beyond this world. He never aspired to the heights of metaphysics or mysticism. His poetry was devoid of spirituality.") [14]

Byron sent out signals that he was more of an Augustan than a Romantic poet early on. His first long work praised Pope, and in *Don Juan* he wrote: "Thou shalt believe in Milton, Dryden, Pope;/Thou shalt not set up Wordsworth, Coleridge, Southey." The Romantic poets, apart from Shelley, detested him. Wordsworth called him a "monster", Coleridge called his poems "Satanic" and Keats called *Don Juan* "flash".[15] He admired formal and restrained classical poetry, but wrote formless poetry with a love for the limitless and excess. He did not go along with the Romantic view of the imagination, but his attitudes of rebelliousness and escape make *Don Juan* a Romantic work, even though it is realistic and satirizes hypocrisy, social and sexual conventions and sentimentality.

Carlyle

The prose works of the Victorian Age touch on the metaphysical aspect of the fundamental theme. Carlyle's *Heroes and Hero Worship* presented a view that humankind progresses though its great men who see into the heart of things, a quality developed by the quest for Reality, and that the masses follow them. In *Sartor Resartus*, he wrote that man needs the soul, not the trappings of society: government, education and success, which are as inessential as clothes. In *Sartor* (book 2, ch.7) he described his experience of the Light in 1821, when he was 26. After a period of great wretchedness, following his abandonment of teaching in 1819, "There rushed like a stream of fire over my whole soul; and I shook base Fear away from me for ever. I was strong, of unknown strength; a spirit, almost a god." He now believed that the universe was an expression of one great indivisible Force, and his *Sartor* aimed to embody "the Divine Spirit of religion in a new Mythus...and vesture".

After the 1830s

In the 1830s, Romanticism in English poetry dwindled. Clare wrote of the death of rural life from the perspective of a hedge-setter and day labourer, but spent the last years of his life in asylums for the insane. His work belongs to the Romantic Age but is not on the metaphysical aspect of the fundamental theme. The pre-Romantic Crabbe, Scott, Campbell, Moore and Southey also contributed to the Romantic movement. There were traces of Romanticism in Tennyson's mysticism and Arnold's 'The Scholar-Gipsy', and Romanticism eventually paled into the works of William Morris, Pater and Ruskin.

European Romantics

European Romanticism had the Romantic yearning but none of the Romantic vision of a superior order of Being. The French Chateaubriand wrote of René's longings for the infinite in his short novella *René* (1802), but dwelt on his imagination and his melancholy.

In Benjamin Constant's confessional novel, *Adolphe* (1807, published 1816), suggested by his long liaison with Mme de Staël,

Constant's Romantic individualism is full of self-knowledge and psychological analysis which condemn vices in relation to implied virtue:

> In Constant's *Adolphe*, the vice is the hero's mistreatment of the possessive older woman he has made his mistress as a sentimental experiment. He uses her cynically without an appropriate emotional response, as a result of which she dies.

The central figure of the French Romantic movement was Victor Hugo, whose *Les Contemplations* were meditations on his daughter's death and again touch on the metaphysical aspect of the fundamental theme. Gérard de Nerval was another member of the Romantic group of 1830, and his imagery in poems written between times of mental breakdown and madness was later influential.

The German Hölderlin had absorbed Plato's view of the poet as a seer, and in 1800 wrote in 'Home' (*'Die Heimat'*), "For they who lend us the heavenly fire, the gods, give us sacred sorrow too." In 1826 in 'Conviction' (*'Überzeugung'*) he wrote of the Light: "As day surrounds men with bright radiance, and with that Light which has its origin on high unites all the dim objects of perception, such is knowledge deeply attained by the human intellect." His work touches on the metaphysical aspect of the fundamental theme.

Heine deflated his emotion with ironic self-criticism, calling himself "the last Romantic". There is little trace of the vision of the English Romantic poets in Hugo, Heine, Lamartine or Lermontov.

European Romantics did not see the visible world as a shadow of eternity, the Light, and so they did not reflect the metaphysical aspect of the fundamental theme but, like Constant, focused on vices in relation to virtue.

Romanticism was a revolt against tradition and authority, reason and classical science. It emphasized individualism, or individual consciousness, and the organic vitality of Nature, and reacted against the Neoclassical treatment of Nature as a dead ornament. It opposed the authority of the relatively tyrannical political order; the rationalism of Descartes and the Enlightenment; and the mechanistic science of Newton and the Empiricism of Locke. Its Victorian successors came to terms with the new science.

Literary Summary

The main references to the metaphysical aspect of the fundamental theme in world literature during the Romantic Age are as follows:

- The infinite that surrounds the universe is in: Blake's infinite; Coleridge's primary imagination; Wordsworth's One; and Shelley's One.
- The metaphysical Reality seen as Light is in the concepts of the imagination, Beauty and the One in: Blake; Coleridge; Wordsworth; Shelley; and to a lesser extent Keats.
- The order of the universe can be found in the One of: Blake; Coleridge; Wordsworth; and Shelley; and in the Truth of Keats.
- The oneness of known humankind can be found in Blake's 'A Song of Liberty' ("Empire is no more!" and "Everything that lives is Holy") and his "All Religions are One".
- The similarities in cultures and civilizations are emphasized in: Blake's "All Religions are One"; and Byron's *Don Juan*.
- The universal being (or self) that opens to the Light behind the rational, social ego is in: Blake's universal being that perceives Los behind the Spectre/Urizen; Coleridge's 'Dejection: An Ode'; and Wordsworth's 'Ode on Intimations of Immortality' – and in all poets who assert the imagination.
- Universal virtue is in: Blake; Shelley's *Prometheus Unbound*; and Byron's *Don Juan*.
- The promise of the immortality of the universal being is present in: Blake; Coleridge's spirit in 'The Ancient Mariner'; Wordsworth's 'Ode on Intimations of Immortality'; and Shelley's "Spirit of Light" in 'Alastor' and his 'Adonais'.
- The inner transformation or centre-shift from ego to universal being is found in: Blake's transformation from the Spectre/Urizen to the universal being that perceives Los; Coleridge's Ancient Mariner's transformation from sin to redemption; and Wordsworth's *The Prelude*.
- The quest of the purified soul is in: Blake; Coleridge's 'The Ancient Mariner'; Wordsworth's *The Prelude*; and Shelley's

'Alastor'.

- The sensibility that approaches Reality through more than one discipline can be found in: Blake (printing, engraving, art, poetry); Coleridge (poetry, literary criticism and philosophy); Wordsworth (poetry, letters, prefaces); and Shelley (poetry, verse drama, *A Defence of Poetry*, letters).
- The new perspective of unity in history, religion, philosophy and science, international politics and literature can be found in Blake (oneness in religion).

The Victorian writers were more realistic and looked to blend Romanticism with Neoclassicism.

8

Victorian Literature

English Poetry

The Romantic impulse subsided. The English Victorians stood back from the Romantic Age and, reacting conservatively against the French Revolution, discovered a social conscience as a result of the Industrial Revolution. Wishing to reduce injustice and inequality following the 1832 Reform Bill, they combined the Romantic love of Nature with the Neoclassical view of society, exercising self-restraint and control over emotion. They followed the scientific advances and the evolutionary theory of Darwin's *Origin of the Species* (1859), and lived in an age of increasing doubt. They were high-minded and morally serious, and perpetuated the two aspects of the fundamental theme.

Tennyson

Tennyson represented the Age as he expressed its assumptions and underlying misgivings. The third son of the Church-of-England rector of Somersby, Lincolnshire, he became acquainted with Arthur Hallam in Cambridge and travelled with him on the Continent. Hallam became engaged to Tennyson's sister Emily, but died in Vienna in 1833.

Tennyson expressed his grief in *In Memoriam* (1833-1850), 131 elegiac poems that presented the progression of his feelings regarding Hallam's death (despair, numbness, disintegration, struggling with his emotions, eventually hope and triumphant calm remembrance), and also his own anxieties about change, evolution and the insignificance of man in an apparently indifferent universe. He tried to reconcile death and his grief with a belief in providence, and willed himself to progress from despair to hope despite his intense doubt. He also tried to affirm a belief in immortality.

Already aware of the Light in the 1830s – his St Simeon Stylites sees "a flash of light" after a lifetime up pillars "battering the gates of heaven" and asks God to lead "this foolish people…to the light" – he whispers in *In Memoriam* to Hallam's spirit, "Be near me when my light is low," the light being associated with faith two stanzas on rather than with a nightlight. He holds that on death "we lose ourselves in light" and Hallam will return in his "after form/And like a finer light in light". Tennyson expressed the metaphysical aspect of the fundamental theme – the soul's quest for Reality as Light and belief in immortality – in *In Memoriam* in such verses as these, that led Sir Harold Nicolson to call him "a morbid and unhappy mystic".[1]

The "stillness of a central sea" of Light surrounds Tennyson's world. It was boundless Being. Tennyson says in a letter to Mr B.P. Blood[2] that he would fall into a trance in which "individuality itself seemed to dissolve and fade away into boundless being".

Tennyson touches on the metaphysical aspect of the fundamental theme in his poem 'Ulysses', which (he wrote) was "written soon after Arthur Hallam's death".[3] Based on Dante's *Inferno*, canto xxvi, it catches Tennyson's need to go bravely forward despite the loss of Hallam. It states the questing of the metaphysical aspect of the fundamental theme in terms of the quest of an old man: Ulysses has left his kingdom in the care of his son and is eager to seek for "newer worlds", "to strive, to seek, to find, and not to yield". In this poem he is urging himself to be forward-looking and envisaging himself as an optimist in his old age.

Tennyson contrasted the Victorian present – its materialism, irreligion and utilitarianism – with the harmonious life of medievals in the past. He shared a cult of the medieval, retreating from the present into an idealized past along with the Rossettis, Carlyle, Ruskin and Morris. At his house, Farringford, in the Isle of Wight he wrote about the Grail, symbol of Reality as Light, in *Idylls of the King*, in which he described the Grail which Lancelot sees as "a light...in the crannies" that "blinded" him "as from a seven-times-heated furnace". While retrieving the past he wrote on national events of the present: the death of Wellington in 1852 and the charge of the Light Brigade at Balaklava (25 October 1854); and his realism in his "monodrama" set in the present, 'Maud', combined Romantic individualism and Neoclassical psychology to present a morbid, hysterical, bellicose hero who reflected the Age in a fusion of Romantic and Neoclassical methods.

The optimism of Tennyson's early years was not borne out, as can be seen by contrasting the two 'Locksley Hall' poems. In 'Locksley

Hall', written in the 1830s, he rejects the materialistic values of his society but decides to remain in England and serve the coming new age. In 'Locksley Hall Sixty Years After' (1886), however, he is disillusioned with his time. Tennyson retracted the earlier poem's belief that human progress was inevitable and dwelt on the decadence of the mid-1880s in a challenge to liberal thought. However, himself aside, Tennyson reflected the optimism of the early Victorian Age and the disillusion of its last years while perpetuating the metaphysical aspect of the fundamental theme.

Browning
Browning had a Congregationalist mother, and his Nonconformism prevented him from going to Oxbridge. It enabled him to write in 'Paracelsus' at the age of 23, in 1835: "Truth is within ourselves.../...To know,/Rather consists in opening out a way/Whence the imprisoned splendour may escape,/Than in effecting entry for a light/Supposed to be without."[4] Truth is a spring and "source within us; where broods radiance vast/To be elicited ray by ray".

As a boy he read Shelley and Keats in his father's library and developed a love for Italy. He visited Italy in 1838 and again in 1844-45. He married Elizabeth Barrett and eloped with her to Italy in 1846, where they lived until her death in 1861. The dramatic monologues he wrote in Italy reconcile the unhappiness of humans with the providence of a benevolent God and look forward to immortality. Browning also satirizes vices, in the Neoclassical manner of the Renaissance dramatists.

In 'My Last Duchess', the vice is jealousy: the Duke explains that he gave orders for his last Duchess to be killed because he was jealous of the smiles she gave the portrait painter.

Browning's certainty of a life after death accords with the metaphysical aspect of the fundamental theme. In 1855, in 'Bishop Blougram's Apology' the Bishop exposes young Gigadibs' rationalism as shallow and concludes: "The sum of all is – yes, my doubt is great,/My faith's still greater – then my faith's enough." And in 'Saul', David's thoughts turn to immortality. In '*Prospice*', written after his wife's death in 1861, he sees dying in terms of the soul's seeing the Light: "a light, then thy breast,/O thou soul of my soul! I shall clasp thee again,/And with God be the rest!"

Browning's dramatic monologues in the mouths of the Italian painters Fra Lippo Lippi and Andrea del Sarto, and on the inventor of the organ Abt Vogler, combine Romantic individualism with Neoclassical psychology. He presents the metaphysical aspect of the fundamental theme in 'Johannes Agricola in Meditation', in which the soul quests for "dazzling glory" and eternity with God.

Arnold

Matthew Arnold was the son of the headmaster of Rugby School, who had a holiday home in Westmoreland; near Wordsworth, whom he came to know. At Oxford he became friendly with the poet Clough and won the Newdigate Prize for his poem 'Cromwell', which refers to the Light: "An inward light, that, with its streaming ray,/On the dark current of his changeless day/Bound all his being with a silver chain." In 1847 he became secretary to Lord Lansdowne, a Liberal cabinet minister who appointed him inspector of schools, a job that enabled him to get married in 1851. Part of 'Dover Beach' refers to the honeymoon, which continued on the Continent. He remained an inspector of schools for 35 years.

His best-known poems are on the metaphysical aspect of the fundamental theme. In 'Empedocles on Etna' (1852), Empedocles commits suicide by throwing himself into the crater of Mt Etna in Sicily after expressing his doubts about the teachings of religion and philosophy and about his own "dwindling faculty of joy". He felt he should be seeing more of the Light than he was seeing: "And who can say: I have been always free,/Lived ever in the light of my own soul? – /I cannot; I have lived in wrath and gloom/Fierce, disputatious, ever at war with man,/Far from my own soul, far from warmth and light." He has a "numbing cloud" on his soul and an "eternally restless mind". His quest for Reality ends in his leap into fire: "Thou sea of fire!/My soul glows to meet you..../Rush over it again,/Receive me, save me!" There is a hint in this last line that he will find immortality.

'The Scholar-Gipsy' (1853), an "elegiac poem" which has a pastoral setting, is based on a legend narrated by Glanvill (or Glanvil) in his *The*

Vanity of Dogmatizing (1661). An "Oxford scholar poor" was forced by his poverty to give up his studies. He joined gipsies and roamed the Oxford countryside with them, learning from their power of imagination, having left "this strange disease of modern life,/With its sick hurry, its divided aims". The Scholar-Gipsy quests for Reality outside civilization, and we must assume that, having left "the world, with powers/Fresh" and waiting "for the spark from heaven", through the powers the gipsies possessed he found the "spark" of Reality, the Light, and that the prospect of immortality was real for him.

'Dover Beach' appeared in 1867. It is full of doubt. Faith recedes like "the grating roar/Of pebbles which the waves draw back", and there is "an eternal note of sadness". The world is "a darkling plain", and relationships can be like "ignorant armies" clashing "by night". There is "neither joy nor love nor light".

In a letter to his mother, written in 1869, Arnold wrote of his own poetic achievement:

"My poems represent, on the whole, the main movement of mind of the last quarter of a century....It might be fairly urged that I have less poetical sentiment than Tennyson, and less intellectual vigour and abundance than Browning; yet, because I have perhaps more of a fusion of the two than either of them, and have more regularly applied that fusion to the main line of modern development, I am likely enough to have my turn, as they have had theirs."

Arnold is saying that he combined Romantic sentiment and Neoclassical intellectual vigour.

In fact, he was on the Neoclassical side. In his prose works he drew attention to the defects of much Romantic poetry – its lack of substance, lack of form and lack of common sense or sanity on occasions – and to the virtues of classical poetry: sobriety, weightiness and unity. The Reform Bill was bringing in an undisciplined democracy, and he believed that literature would maintain a civilized standard in living. In his criticism he tried to set out criteria that would distinguish the best literature from inferior or counterfeit literature.

In *Culture and Anarchy* (1869) he presented culture as the classical ideal of human perfection. Identifying three groups in English society –

Barbarians (the aristocracy), Philistines (the middle classes) and Populace (the masses) – he proposed that the uncultured middle class should receive a liberal education.[5] "The man who tends towards sweetness and light" (a phrase first used by Swift in *The Battle of the Books*) is contrasted with the Philistine who is "the enemy of the children of light or the servants of the idea". Arnold quotes St Augustine: "Let the children of thy spirit...make their light shine upon the earth, mark the division of night and day."[6] *Culture and Anarchy* is on the metaphysical aspect of the fundamental theme because it recognises religion as the highest form of culture and urges Victorians to open to spiritual experience. It treats the quest for Reality and immortality in terms of culture rather than in terms of personal experience.

In 'The Buried Life' (1852) Arnold addressed the "inmost soul", "our hidden self" and wrote of the "longing to inquire/Into the mystery of this heart which beats/So wild, so deep in us – to know/Whence our lives come and where they go." Arnold was on a quest to find Reality within his buried life.

FitzGerald

Edward FitzGerald, a friend of Tennyson and Carlyle, made a free translation of the *Rubaiyat of Omar Khayyam* (1859), quatrains in English which he made into an independent poem by combining lines from different Persian quatrains. We have seen (on p.98) that Khayyam's original verses were Sufi, and evoked the Sufi One. His references to wine were also references to spiritual intoxication, and the "Thou" and "Thee" of the *Rubaiyat* refers to Mohammed or Allah. In view of this symbolism, FitzGerald's poem is on the metaphysical aspect of the fundamental theme.

Hopkins

Gerald Manley Hopkins came into contact with the Oxford Movement when he was at Oxford. He was received into the Catholic Church in 1866 by Cardinal Newman, who had written "Lead kindly light" when on a boat between Sardinia and Corsica in 1833.

While studying to be a Jesuit priest Hopkins wrote in 1876 'The Wreck of the *Deutschland*', inspired by the loss of the *Deutschland* and "two hundred souls", including five Franciscan nuns exiled for their faith, in December 1875. He addressed Jesus as "heart's light", and tried to make sense of how God could allow five nuns to drown. In 1877 he wrote that the grandeur of God "will flame out, like shining from shook foil", and in 'The Windhover' ends with an image of illumination: "Blue-bleak embers, ah my dear/Fall, gall themselves, and gash gold-vermilion." (In other words, a cold heart can suddenly burst alight with the Fire, or Light.) In one of his "terrible sonnets" (1885) he writes of "light's delay", the cause being "dearest him (i.e. God) that lives alas! away".

Hopkins' work reflects the metaphysical aspect of the fundamental theme. As a devout Catholic, he had been on a quest for Reality as Light early in life, and he believed in the immortality of the soul.

The Pre-Raphaelites

The Pre-Raphaelites can be seen as the last Romantics, and as escapist Victorians. They were a group of writers, which most notably included the Rossettis and William Morris, who were inspired by the vivid, simple colours of the Italian painters before Raphael. They turned away from life and tried to create a dream world of colour based on the medieval style. In 1850 they published their work in a magazine, *The Germ*. Dante Gabriel Rossetti's 'The Blessed Damozel' and William Morris's 'The Defence of Guenevere' belong with Tennyson's evocations of the Arthurian time ('Morte d'Arthur' and 'The Lady of Shalott'). They touch on the metaphysical aspect of the fundamental theme's quest for Reality by archaistically recreating the medieval time.

The English Novel

The Victorian novel was about society in the "strange disease of modern life". In plots that were sometimes serialized and are often melodramatic, unreal and full of exaggerated pathos, the main novelists reflected aspects of Victorian society that concerned them. In the tradition of the Renaissance dramatists and Neoclassical writers, they satirized vices – and institutions.

Satire is a "composition in which prevailing vices or follies are held up to ridicule" (*Shorter Oxford English Dictonary*), and it always has a moral basis in an implied virtue. In my coverage of Victorian (and later, modern) novels I have confined myself to a selection of key works in view of the limitations of space. We shall see that all these works conform to a pattern that exposes vices and uses satire. Practically all works by all novelists can be shown to conform to this same pattern, and the works of the writers I cite that I have not selected due to lack of space can be analyzed for vices and satire in the same way.

Dickens

Charles Dickens' father was sent to the Marshalsea prison for debt, and Dickens was withdrawn from school at the age of twelve and forced to do manual work in a factory. At 15 he became a clerk in a solicitor's office and then a shorthand reporter in the law courts. He became a newspaper reporter and covered debates in the Commons. These experiences left him with contempt for the law and Parliament, but admiration for journalists.

In a few novels such as *David Copperfield*, *Oliver Twist* and *Great Expectations*, the quest for Reality has been replaced by a quest to succeed amid appalling social conditions. Like Shakespeare's plays, Dickens' novels condemn vices but link them to wretched social conditions, which he satirizes.

In *Pickwick Papers* (1836-7), the vice is the villainous trickery of Jingle, who takes advantage of the unworldly, idealistic Pickwick, chairman of the Pickwick Club. Dickens satirizes the law through Pickwick's involvement in a breach-of-promise case and his brief stay in the Fleet prison.

In *Oliver Twist* (1837-8), the vice is the thieving of the Jew Fagin (and his implied child abuse and paedophiliac pimping), and the burglary of Bill Sikes. Dickens satirizes the hypocrisy concealing the actual conditions in the workhouse.

In *Nicholas Nickleby* (1838-9), the vice is Squeers' cruel greed in starving and maltreating forty urchins, and the satire is on education at Dotheboys Hall.

In *The Old Curiosity Shop* (1840-1), the vice is the dwarf Quilp's greed in seizing the shop and pursuing Nell and her grandfather to their deaths.

In *Barnaby Rudge* (1841), the vice is Sir John Chester's smooth villainy in fomenting the Gordon riots. Dickens satirizes capital punishment.

In *A Christmas Carol* (1843), the vice is Scrooge's miserliness, and Dickens satirizes the wretched conditions within the law.

In *Martin Chuzzlewit* (1843-4), the vice is the greed of Chuzzlewit's family, and also the hypocrisy of Pecksniff. Dickens satirizes the American Eden Land Corporation, where Martin loses his money.

In *Dombey and Son* (1847-8), the vice is Dombey's arrogance which results in the loss of his fortune, his son and his wife. Dickens satirizes the strictness of the school that killed his son.

In *David Copperfield* (1849-50), the vice is the self-interested egotism of Murdstone, Uriah Heep and Steerforth. Dickens satirizes the law, which allows Heep to flourish.

In *Bleak House* (1852-3), the vice is Lady Dedlock's hypocrisy in concealing the existence of her former lover and her daughter, now called Esther. Dickens satirizes the old Court of Chancery whose legal costs in the case of Jarndyce and Jarndyce absorb the entire estate.

In *Hard Times* (1854), the vice is Gradgrind's practical and ruthless suppressal of the imagination. Dickens satirizes his utilitarianism.

In *Little Dorrit* (1855-7), the vice is the snobbish arrogance of the moneyed, including Dorrit after his release from the Marshalsea and inheritance of a fortune. Dickens satirizes the Circumlocution Office (a notorious bureaucratic government department).

In *A Tale of Two Cities* (1859), the vice is the Marquis de St Évremonde's cruelty to children. He has mortally wounded a boy and imprisoned his brother in the Bastille to ensure his silence. Dickens satirizes the French Revolution.

In *Great Expectations* (1860-1), the vice is moneyed snobbishness and arrogance which causes Pip to be ashamed of his humble origins and of his benefactor Magwitch, once he comes into money. Dickens satirizes the respectability money brings by having Pip's money come from an escaped convict, Magwitch.

In *Our Mutual Friend* (1864-5), the vice is the moneyed snobbish arrogance of Bella once she has come into money. Harmon's father's fortune was made by his being a dirt-contractor. Through the dirt/money symbolism Dickens satirizes the financial system.

In *The Mystery of Edwin Drood* (1870), which was unfinished at Dickens' death, the vice is the hypocrisy of John Jasper, Edwin's uncle and precentor of the cathedral, who foments enmity between Edwin and Neville and pursues Rosa. Dickens satirizes the cathedral hierarchy through Jasper's behaviour.

In all these novels Dickens writes from an ideal virtue and satirizes the vices of those who fall short of this virtue; villainy, trickery, thieving, greed, miserliness, hypocrisy, arrogance, self-interestedness, suppressal of the imagination, snobbishness and cruelty. This list of Dickens' vices can be compared with Chaucer's vices and Shakespeare's flaws. As in the case of the Renaissance and Neoclassical writers, Dickens reflects the fundamental theme's focus on virtue by showing characters in whom it has fallen short.

Thackeray

William Makepeace Thackeray shows how English society is built on money. He satirizes the vices of vanity, snobbishness, pretentiousness and hypocrisy.

In *Vanity Fair* (1847-8), named after the fair in the town of Vanity in *The Pilgrim's Progress* which is run by Beelzebub, though set in the time of the Napoleonic Wars, the vice is Becky's ambition to rise in society, her love of self which is vanity. At the same time Thackeray satirizes the vanity of worldly society.

In the semi-autobiographical *Pendennis* (1848-50), the vice is the snobbishness of Major Pendennis and the moneyed pretentiousness of Blanche. Thackeray satirizes aristocratic society.

In *The History of Henry Esmond* (1852), the vice is the snobbishness of Beatrix that looks down on Henry for not having a fortune, and Lord Mohun's egotism. Thackeray satirizes the financial system that respects money.

In the earlier *The Memoirs of Barry Lyndon Esquire, by Himself* (1852, first published as *The Luck of Barry Lyndon* in 1844), the vice is Barry's hypocritical villainy. Thackeray satirizes the British aristocracy.

In *The Newcomes* (1853-5), the vice is the snobbish moneyed pretentiousness of Barnes Newcome and the arrogance before the virtuous Col. Newcome loses his fortune due to the failure of Bundelcund Bank.

Thackeray's novels are on the fundamental theme as they imply a standard of virtue and satirize those whose vices of moneyed arrogance, snobbishness and hypocrisy cause them to fall short of the ideal.

The Brontë Sisters

Emily Brontë's *Wuthering Heights* (1847) is on the metaphysical aspect of the fundamental theme as it reflects the One as reconciling two opposite or (in Blake's sense) contradictory states of the soul.

Like *yin* and *yang*, the stormy, destructive passions of Wuthering Heights oppose the gentle, prosperous, rational way of living at the Grange. It could be said that there is a Romantic lifestyle at the Heights and a Neoclassical lifestyle at the Grange. Heathcliff loves Cathy, who shares his stormy nature but spurns him. He exacts his revenge by marrying Isabella Linton of the Grange. The love between Heathcliff and Cathy transcends her death in childbirth and becomes infinite, and eternal – a Romantic love that destroys a Neoclassical family.

Heathcliff and Cathy have found a reality, love, that goes beyond death and promises immortality.

Emily's sister Charlotte Brontë, wrote novels of satiric realism mixed with romance. She, too, focused on vices.

In *The Professor* (1846, published in 1857), the vice is the duplicity of the Catholic headmistress. Charlotte Brontë satirizes the all-girls school in Brussels where she was a language student in 1842.

In *Jane Eyre* (1847), the vice is the selfish cruelty of Jane's aunt Mrs. Reed and of Mrs. Rochester (deemed mad). Charlotte Brontë satirizes Lowood Institution (based on the Clergy Daughters' School at Cowan Bridge which she believed was responsible for the early deaths of her two elder sisters in 1825).

In *Shirley* (1849), the vice is Robert's mercenary motives in proposing to *Shirley*. Charlotte Brontë satirizes ruthless employers such as mill-owners.

In *Villette* (1853), the vices are the unscrupulousness of the headmistress and the asperity of Paul Emmanuel. Charlotte Brontë again satirizes the all-girls school in Brussels, to which she returned for a second, unhappy stay in 1843-4.

Charlotte Brontë's novels touch on the fundamental theme by implying an ideal standard of virtue in terms of which some of their characters' vices cause them to fall short.

The only sister of Emily and Charlotte Brontë to survive, Anne Brontë, wrote two novels.

In *Agnes Grey* (1847), the vice is Rosalie's coquettish ambition, which contrasts with Agnes' modest gentleness. Anne Brontë satirizes being a governess to unruly children.

In *The Tenant of Wildfell Hall*, the vice is Huntingdon's drunken debauchery (based on Anne Brontë's brother Branwell's, according to Charlotte Brontë), from which Helen has fled with her son to become

Lawrence's tenant.

The novels' only contact with the fundamental theme is through these vices.

George Eliot

A freethinker who rejected Christianity and marriage, George Eliot wrote realistic novels of rural life whose powerful emotions mixed with a keen intellect and psychological analysis. She, too, focused on vices in terms of an ideal virtue.

In *Adam Bede* (1859), the vice is Hetty's vanity which leads her to turn away from Adam and be seduced by Arthur, the young squire, who then breaks off relations with her. After discovering that she is pregnant, she is convicted of infanticide, nearly hanged and sentenced to transportation. George Eliot satirizes the injustice dispensed by the legal system.

In *The Mill on the Floss* (1860), the vices are Maggie's father's obstinacy, her brother's controlling rectitude and her own rebelliousness. She secretly takes up with the son of lawyer Wakem, who ruins her father as a result of litigation. Her brother Tom discovers her connection with the lawyer's son and turns her out of the house. There is a flood, she tries to rescue her brother and the two are drowned. George Eliot satirizes the social and legal system that bankrupted Maggie's father.

In *Silas Marner* (1861), the vice is the theft of the miserly Silas's gold by the squire's younger son. His elder brother fathers a child, Eppie, who Silas adopts. The gold is found and Eppie refuses to leave Silas when her father claims her. George Eliot satirizes the social system that allows that squirearchy to behave with such self-interest.

In *Felix Holt the Radical* (1866), the vice is Harold's abuse of the money he has inherited, to which it turns out he is not entitled, the inheritance passing (implausibly) to Esther and Felix. George Eliot satirizes corrupt electioneering.

In *Romola* (1862-3), which is set in Florence at the end of the 15th century, the vice is the treachery of Tito Melema, who robs and abandons his childhood benefactor, marries Romola and betrays her father. Through her trials Romola is purified. George Eliot satirizes the religious preaching of Savonarola, who does not live up to his prophetic mission.

In *Middlemarch* (1872), the vice is the pedantry and meanness of Casaubon, who Dorothea marries before she draws close to Ladislaw. She marries Ladislaw after Casaubon's death, renouncing his fortune in accordance with a codicil that she must forfeit it if she ever marries Ladislaw. George Eliot satirizes the Tory attitudes of Chettam and the Cadwalladers in relation to the Reform Bill championed by Ladislaw, who becomes an MP at the end of the book.

In *Daniel Deronda* (1874-6), the vices are Gwendolen's mercenary self-centredness in marrying Grandcourt for his money, and his cold, selfish arrogance. The idealistic, Jewish Daniel Deronda becomes her spiritual adviser, and after Grandcourt is drowned in Genoa she is mortified to discover that Deronda is to marry a Jewess and devote himself to a Jewish National Home. George Eliot satirizes the social order that regards marrying for money as acceptable.

George Eliot touches on the fundamental theme by focusing on vices in terms of an ideal virtue.

Trollope

Anthony Trollope wrote novels of English upper-middle-class life and institutions. He, too, exposes vices in terms of an ideal virtue.

In *The Warden* (1855), the vice is the bullying of Archdeacon Grantly who insists that his father-in-law, the Warden of the charitable Hiram's Hospital, Harding, should defend himself after a local surgeon, Bold, has informed the national press that he has lived off the hospital's income at the expense of the 12 bedesmen. Not wanting to fight, Harding resigns and receives a new position, and Bold marries his daughter, restoring harmony. Trollope satirizes the politics surrounding charitable institutions.

In *Barchester Towers* (1857), the vice is the ambition of Mrs. Proudie, wife of the new bishop, who selects Mr Quiverful over Harding for the position of Warden of Hiram's Hospital; and of the chaplain Slope, who tries to becomes Dean and marry the widowed Mrs. Bold (Harding's daughter) before he is eventually dismissed by Mrs. Proudie. Trollope satirizes diocesan politics.

In *Framley Parsonage* (1861), the vice is the clergyman Mark Robarts' ambition for preferment, and his ruin after guaranteeing bills in return for a prebendal stall. He appeals to Lady Lufton, whose son loves his sister Lucy. She wants her son to take up with the daughter of Archdeacon Grantley but comes to see Lucy's true worth when Lucy nurses Mrs. Crawley. She pays Robarts' debts. Trollope again satirizes diocesan politics.

Trollope's many novels touch on the fundamental theme by focusing on vices in terms of ideal virtue.

Hardy

Thomas Hardy, an architect who went to London and lost his religious faith, met his wife on an architectural mission to Cornwall. He wrote novels that reflected "the strange disease of modern life", the absence of God and the indifference of Nature. He wove a love story with the lives of simple villagers at a time when the old rural way of life was being replaced by a more mechanised one.

Hardy saw man in a web of destiny, what he called in *The Dynasts* (1904-8) the indifferent "Immanent Will" which brings disasters. This Will is a providential Reality that is less than benevolent and through hostile circumstances destroys the hero. In Hardy, the metaphysical aspect of the fundamental theme's quest for Reality that promises immortality has gone into reverse: the "Immanent Will" seeks out individuals and destroys them through disastrous circumstances, and there is no promise of immortality. In short, Hardy presents a reversal of the metaphysical aspect of the fundamental theme.

In most of his novels he nevertheless focuses on vices that imply an ideal virtue and touch on the fundamental theme. In his works, the vices reveal themselves in relationships.

In *Under the Greenwood Tree* (1872), the vice is the capriciousness of the schoolmistress Fanny Day, who rejects a farmer and the vicar in charge of the school for Dick Dewy, the son of a local "tranter" (carrier), a match opposed by her father. Dick and his father are rustic musicians and singers in Mellstock church and are replaced by a new organ. Hardy satirizes the replacement of the old rustic way of life by mechanisation.

In *Far from the Madding Crowd* (1874), the vice is Troy's mistreatment of Bathsheba, owner of the farm, who has preferred Sergeant Troy (the former lover of one of Bathsheba's servants) to farmer Boldwood and the shepherd Gabriel Oak. Troy disappears and Boldwood pledges to marry her – and kills Troy when he returns, leaving Bathsheba to marry Oak. A set of hostile circumstances destroys Boldwood and Troy. Hardy satirizes the impact on the old rustic life of an irresponsible soldier with a modern attitude.

In *The Return of the Native* (1878), the vice is the treachery of the publican (former engineer) Wildeve, who marries Thomasin to hurt the capricious Eustacia Vye; and of Eustacia, who marries Clym Yeobright and unintentionally causes his mother's death. Wildeve and Eustacia run away and both are drowned. Hardy satirizes the impact on the old rustic life on Egdon Heath of an irresponsible ex-engineer with a modern attitude.

In *The Trumpet Major* (1882), the vice is the boorish boasting of Festus, who is a rival for Anne Garland of Overcombe Mill, along with the dragoons' trumpet major John Loveday, a miller's son, and his sailor brother Bob, who wins her. John leaves with the dragoons and dies in battle in Spain. Hardy presents the impact of "modern" dragoons on the thriving rural society during the Napoleonic Wars.

In *The Mayor of Casterbridge* (1886), the vice is Henchard's obstinacy after he drunkenly sells his wife and child to a sailor for 5 guineas.

Mortified, he gives up drink, works hard in his corn business and becomes the mayor of Casterbridge. After 18 years his wife returns with a daughter he believes to be his, but who is in fact the sailor's. He quarrels with his assistant Farfrae, his wife dies, his corn business is ruined and the scandal of the sale of his wife is revealed. He resumes drinking. Farfrae now has his business and house and becomes mayor of Casterbridge, and Henchard works in his yard. Farfrae eventually marries Henchard's stepdaughter, and Henchard dies in a hovel on Egdon Heath. A set of hostile circumstances destroys Henchard. Hardy satirizes the death of the old rustic life in the face of the modern attitude and business skills.

In *The Woodlanders* (1887), the vice is the snobbishness of Grace Melbury after she returns from finishing-school and sees herself as the social superior of her betrothed Giles Winterbourne. She marries a doctor, who leaves her for a widow. When the doctor appears with the widow, Grace seeks refuge in Giles' cottage. Giles moves out, builds himself a shelter of hurdles and dies. Grace and the doctor are reconciled and move away. Marty, a village girl who has always loved Giles, looks after his grave. A set of hostile circumstances destroys Giles. Hardy satirizes the impact on the old rustic life of the modern outlook that includes sophisticated finishing-schools.

In *Tess of the D'Urbervilles* (1891), the vice is Alec D'Urberville's lust, which motivates his two seductions of Tess. She confesses the first episode to Angel Clare on their wedding night – having written him a letter and pushed it under his door two or three days earlier which, through a hostile circumstance, Angel never found as it slid under the edge of the carpet – and he abandons her and goes to Brazil. She is in dire straits and becomes Alec's mistress again when he returns as an itinerant preacher. Angel returns full of remorse and finds her living with Alec in Sandbourne. Appalled that Alec has damaged her relationship with Angel twice, she stabs Alec and flees with Angel to the New Forest and after a trek is arrested at Stonehenge. A set of hostile circumstances destroys Tess, who is hanged for the murder of Alec. Hardy's last sentence is: "'Justice' was done, and the President of the Immortals (in Aeschylean phrase) had ended his sport with Tess." Hardy satirizes the injustice of the legal system that executed Tess.

In *Jude the Obscure* (1894-5), the vice is the coarse barmaid Arabella Donn's duplicitous mistreatment of Jude Fawley: she feigns pregnancy and then deserts him. Jude has been working as a stonemason at Christminster (Oxford), and studying in the hope of attending the university. He has an affair with his cousin Sue Bridehead, who later marries Phillotson. Sue compares the family to the House of Atreus, and Jude compares it to the House of Jereboam – stating a theme of Hellenism and Hebraism, ideas in Arnold's *Culture and Anarchy*. The eldest of the three children hangs the two babies, then himself, leaving a note saying, "Done because we are too menny." Jude starts drinking and returns to Arabella, and dies. Jude's last words are about the Light: "Wherefore [i.e. why] is light given to him that is in misery, and life unto the bitter in soul?" A set of hostile circumstances involving Jude's affair with his cousin Sue (reflecting Hardy's affair with his cousin Tryphena Sparks) destroys his three children by Arabella and then Jude himself.

Hardy is understanding towards vices. He writes of the consequences of actions, showing that sinners are unhappy people even though "the wages of sin is death". He touches on the metaphysical aspect of the fundamental theme in negative. The paradox in his works is that his focus on vices implies an ideal virtue, but his providence, the "Immanent Will", is almost malevolent and destructive. His contemporaries castigated *Jude the Obscure* as malevolent, describing it as "dirt, drivel and damnation" and "grimy" and "indecent". Edmund Gosse, in his review of *Jude the Obscure*, asked, "What has Providence done to Mr Hardy that he should rise up in the arable land of Wessex and shake his fist at his Creator?" Several of Hardy's other works came in for similar treatment. The Victorians themselves sensed that something had gone wrong with Hardy's moral outlook.

James

Henry James, an American with an Irish grandfather, spent a year in England, France and Italy in 1869-70, moved to Paris in 1875, settled in London in 1876 and moved to Rye in 1898. His novels are about the contrast of the new American and older European character, and all his mature novels identify vices in relation to an implied virtue in the Victorian (and earlier Renaissance) tradition.

In *Washington Square* (1880), the vice is the handsome but broke Maurice Townsend's mercenary fortune-hunting, his motive for his relationship with plain, shy Catherine Sloper, which ends unsuccessfully.

In *The Portrait of a Lady* (1881), the vice is Gilbert Osmond's money-seeking, mercenary fortune-hunting motive for his marriage to Isabel Archer, the "lady", who has rejected the advances of the more suitable Lord Warburton and Caspar Goodwood.

In *The Bostonians* (1886), the vice is Olive Chancellor's feminist, pro-suffragette loathing of men, which she attempts to instil in Verena Tarrant – who is won by the anti-feminist young lawyer Basil Ransom.

In *What Maisie Knew* (1897), the vice is Maisie's parents' self-interested, corrupt neglect of her after her father marries her governess and her mother marries a younger man, Sir Claude. When both marriages collapse, both parents have new lovers, and Maisie's new governess falls for Sir Claude. Maisie views the manipulative adults around her with honesty and innocence.

In *The Turn of the Screw* (1898), the vice is the fantasies involving communicating with the dead of Bly, the governess of the two children she is teaching, Miles and Flora, who she defends against the evil child-snatching of the apparitions of the dead ex-valet Peter Quint and the dead ex-governess Miss Jessel. She defends Flora from Miss Jessel's ghost but Miles dies as she battles for his soul with Peter Quint. Was she delusional or were the apparitions real?

James's trilogy was post-Victorian in its dating, but its content is rooted in the Victorian Age. The main vice involves the lack of truthfulness in relationships.

In *The Wings of a Dove* (1902), the vice is Merton Densher's money-seeking, mercenary, fortune-hunting motive for professing to love the rich but terminally ill Milly Theale, a motive which is shared by his secret lover Kate Croy. They hope that Milly will provide for them in her will, and though Milly does so, Densher's conscience will not allow him to accept the money and his relationship with Kate ends.

In *The Ambassadors* (1903), the vice is Strether's misjudgement of Chad Newsome's relationship with the Comtesse de Vionnet. Strether has been sent to Paris by Chad's mother as an ambassador to bring Chad home, but he takes Chad's side, believing the relationship is virtuous. Chad's mother sends her daughter, the cold Sarah Pocock, as a second ambassador to bring both Chad and Strether home. They both refuse to return. Then Strether discovers by accident that Chad's relationship is not virtuous, and he leaves Paris disillusioned.

In *The Golden Bowl* (1904), the vice is the impecunious Italian prince Amerigo's money-seeking motive for being engaged to the rich but innocent heiress Maggie Verver, whose relationship with him is like the flawed bowl of the title, first seen in a London antique shop, which is made of gilded crystal, not solid gold. Unbeknown to Maggie, Amerigo is the lover of her friend Charlotte Stant, by whom he has a son. Maggie tries to marry Charlotte off with her father, on whom she is emotionally dependent. After the golden bowl comes into her possession its flaw is revealed. The bowl is deliberately broken and Maggie learns the truth about Amerigo and Charlotte. Having lost her innonence, she will marry Amerigo after her father and Charlotte have returned to America.

James touches on the fundamental theme by presenting vices in relation to an implied virtue, but many of his novels are about quests for the truth of a social situation rather than Reality. In this they are within the Neoclassical tradition.

American Transcendentalism
Ralph Waldo Emerson, formerly a Unitarian Minister – Unitarians rejected the Trinity and the divinity of Christ and asserted that God is One – went to England and met Coleridge and Carlyle, who had both

interpreted the German Transcendentalism of Kant and Fichte. He returned with his own brand of Transcendentalism, a blend of Romantic individualism and of Taylor's Neoplatonism.

The Transcendentalists around Emerson saw all creation as One, and believed with Emerson that wisdom flows into the mind from Nature. In 1838 Emerson referred to the "impersoneity" of the Transcendental or divine indwelling. He argued that the Light renews religion: "Nature never fails. Instantly the divine Light rekindles in some one or other obscure heart who denounces the deadness of the Church and cries aloud for new and more appropriate practices." In one of his poems he wrote: "Love it, though it hide its light;/By love behold the sun at night."[7]

Thoreau, a disciple of Emerson's, moved into a cabin on land owned by Emerson in 1845 and kept a journal, in which he wrote: "I perceive that I am dealt with by superior powers." He was referring to the influx of the Light.

Walt Whitman was also inspired by Emerson's Transcendentalism. He saw the poet as a prophet. He believed in the splendour of the common man and democracy, and his *Leaves of Grass* – revised and enlarged from 12 poems in 1855 with 21 more poems added in 1856 and 122 more in 1860, and subsequently revised and rearranged many times – addressed the citizens of the United States. It urged them to be generous and asserted America's spiritual destiny, speaking directly to readers.

Leaves of Grass touches on the metaphysical aspect of the fundamental theme in the section 'Whispers of Heavenly Death', in poems like 'Darest thou now O soul,/Walk out with me toward the unknown region?' and the promise of "some solemn immortal birth", which describe the quest for Reality and the promise of immortality. In poem after poem Whitman sang of the oneness of all things, of the unity of the phenomena of Nature. (The title, "leaves of grass", comes from a line suggesting the unity of the universe, that leaves of grass are counterparts to stars: "I believe a leaf of grass is no less than the journey-work of the stars.") He was aware of all ages and countries: "These are really the thoughts of all men in all ages and lands, they are not original with me."

All those writing in the Transcendentalist tradition – Emerson,

Thoreau and Whitman – were inspired by the metaphysical aspect of the fundamental theme.

The Early American Novel

Nathaniel Hawthorne was of Puritan ancestry. He wrote of Puritan moral dilemmas and focused on vices in relation to an implied virtue.

In *The Scarlet Letter* (1850), which is set in the 17th century, the vice is minister Arthur Dimmesdale's abandonment of his secret lover Hester Prynne to public odium in Boston. (She is branded with A for adulteress on her forehead and put in a pillory.) He is identified and tortured by her husband when he arrives after being held by Indians for two years. Arthur confesses at the pillory before dying in Hester's arms.

In *The House of the Seven Gables* (1851), the vice is Judge Pyncheon's persecution of his cousin Clifford Pyncheon, intriguing for him to be unjustly imprisoned for many years for a crime he did not commit and continuing his persecution on his release.

In *The Blithedale Romance* (1852), the vice is the outwardly philanthropic social reformer Hollingsworth's selfish inhumanity at Blithedale Farm, near Boston, in rejecting Xenobia, who drowns herself, and in marrying her half-sister Priscilla.

In *The Marble Faun* (1860), the vice is the murder by Count Donatello (who looks like Praxiteles' Marble Faun) of a stranger who has been stalking the young American art student Miriam. Donatello loves her and she assents to the murder. He comes to see that his "sin" has "educated" him and he surrenders himself to justice.

Herman Melville wrote about physical quests and focused on vices in relation to implied virtue.

In *Typee* (1846), the vice is the credulousness of the innocent Tommo and Toby who jump ship in the Marquesas and try to find the Happy Valley of the Happars, an Eden, but find instead the cannibalistic Typees.

In *Moby-Dick, or, The Whale* (1851), the vice is Captain Ahab's self-regarding destructive revenge as he obsessively seeks the white whale that bit off his leg. In the course of his pursuit his ship, the *Pequod*, is destroyed. The white whale is a symbol of a Manichaean, demonic God in which Melville believed – a similar belief in malevolence to Hardy's. Like Hardy, Melville presents the metaphysical aspect of the fundamental theme in reverse: a quest for a Reality that turns out to be demonic.

Mark Twain (the pseudonym of Samuel Langhorne Clemens) wrote humorous adventure stories and also focused on vices in relation to implied virtue.

In *Tom Sawyer* (1876), the vice is Injun Jo's murder of the town doctor and incrimination of the drunken Muff Potter. Tom and his friend Huckleberry Finn see the murder and Tom's evidence frees Potter after a trial. Later Tom and Becky Thatcher leave a school picnic and are lost in a cave. Tom sees Injun Jo, who is later found dead. His treasure is divided between Tom and Huckleberry.

In the picaresque *Huckleberry Finn* (1884), the vice is the deceptive confidence trick of "the Duke" and "the Dauphin" who sell Jim, the runaway slave, into captivity. Tom Sawyer appears and helps Huckleberry rescue Jim – who, it transpires, had already been freed.

In his earlier *Life on the Mississippi* (1883), an autobiographical work on being a river pilot, Twain describes Romanticism as: "silliness and emptinesses, sham grandeurs, sham gauds and sham chivalries". ("Gauds", "gaudy things", suggest gaudiness.) In Twain the balance between Romanticism and Neoclassicism has tilted towards realistic Neoclassicism.

Echoes of the fundamental theme can be found in these three early American novelists.

The French Novel
The French novels of the 19th century were realistic and focused on vices that implied virtue.

Victor Hugo focused on the vice of cruelty.

In *Notre-Dame de Paris* (1831, *The Hunchback of Notre-Dame*), the vice is Frollo's cruelty towards Quasimodo, the hunchbacked son he hid in Notre-Dame.

In his *Les Misérables* (1862), the vice is the police officer Javert's cruelty towards Jean Valjean, who is persecuted for 20 years during an economic depression.

Stendhal (the pseudonym of Henri Beyle) focused on vices in his two main novels.

In *Le Rouge et le Noir* (*Scarlet and Black*, 1830), the vice is Julien Sorel's revenge for being denounced as an adventurer by Mme de Rênal, whom he shoots.

In *La Chartreuse de Parme* (1839), the vice is the self-interest of the Prime Minister of Parma, Count Mosca, in his dealings with Gina and Fabrice.

Honoré de Balzac's *La Comédie Humaine* includes some 80 titles which he classified into *Etudes de Moeurs* (Studies of Manners) and *Etudes philosophiques* (Philosophical Studies).

In *Eugénie Grandet* (1833), the vice is Charles's greed and betrayal of Eugenie.

In his *Le Père Goriot* (1834-5), the vice is greed as old Goriot's daughters, and Rastignac, extract money from their families, bankrupting old Goriot in the process.

Gustave Flaubert used realism to criticize the vicious influence of Romanticism.

In *Madame Bovary* (1857), the vice is Emma Bovary's glamorising of the ordinary, which was to Flaubert a consequence of the Romantic perspective which needed to be criticized. His story of the adulteries and suicide (described in repulsive detail) of a doctor's wife who grew bored in a monotonous provincial Normandy town, was deemed offensive to public morals. Flaubert was tried and acquitted.

Émile Zola's many naturalistic, realistic novels also focus on vices and human appetites.

French Symbolist Poetry

French Symbolist poetry grew out of the Romantic poetry of Lamartine, who planned, but only wrote a tiny bit of, a sentimental Christian epic, *Les Visions*, of which one part was called '*La Chute d'un Ange*' (*The Fall of an Angel*, 1838). It is about an angel's love for a woman which dooms him to remain on Earth as a soul with immortality. This touches on the metaphysical aspect of the fundamental theme.

Parnassianism was a revolt against Romanticism that actually strengthened some of the Romantic tendencies, including writing out a personal feeling. The Parnassians were influenced by Théophile Gautier, who was closely associated with "*L'art pour l'art*" ("art for art's sake"), which he set out in the Preface to his novel *Mademoiselle de Moubin* (1835). The leader of the group of French Parnassian poets was Leconte de Lisle. Reacting against the emotional extravagance of Romanticism, he taught his group of poets to practise restraint, precision and objectivity. Their carefully composed, static verse looked back to Greece and Rome.

Out of this movement grew *Symbolisme* (Symbolism). The Symbolists operated between c.1880 and 1895 and reacted against the realist and naturalist tendencies in literature and against the precision and objectivity of the Parnassians. Baudelaire, Verlaine, Rimbaud and Mallarmé looked backed to Nerval.

The first Symbolist was Alfred de Vigny. The theme of his work is the quest for Reality. He saw Jehovah as laying burdens on great men which isolate them from humanity ('Moïse'), and as damning the purest of the angels when he descends from Heaven out of pity ('*Eloa*'). He suggested that Jesus was abandoned by God on the Mount of Olives ('*Le Mont des Olivieres*'). His work avoids Romantic pity and optimism, and emphasizes endurance.

Charles Baudelaire was classical in clarity and form, but Romantic in morbidness, isolation and rebellious individualism. His *Les Fleurs du Mal* (1857), which contains most of his 160 poems, is about his obsession with death and decay, his generally joyless attitude to sex and his despair, boredom, disgust and Satanism. But underneath this surface Baudelaire contrasted the spiritual and the physical, God and the Devil. He was on a quest for Reality and immortality that he never really found.

Paul Verlaine left his young wife, Mathilde Mauté, associated with Rimbaud and shot and wounded him in an arm during a quarrel in Brussels. During his subsequent imprisonment he was converted to Catholicism, which he expressed in *Sagesse*.

The precocious, rustic and boorish Arthur Rimbaud turned his back on literature at the age of nineteen. He had by then written '*Le Bateau Ivre*', in which he pictures himself as a ship being tossed on a sea (although when he wrote the poem he had never seen the sea), and his prose poems *Les Illuminations*, in which he presented a newly discovered visionary world. '*Une Saison en Enfer*' was his farewell to literature, after which he went out as a trader to Abyssinia and gave himself to the material world, taking rifles and salt to communities in unexplored regions. He had tried to reach truth through sensual experience in his poems, but considered he had been unsuccessful. He was too young at nineteen to quest successfully for Reality, but his work undoubtedly touches on the metaphysical aspect of the fundamental theme as it is about the beginning of the quest.

Stéphane Mallarmé, a teacher of English in provincial *lycées*, lived in Paris with his German wife. He pursued perfection by renouncing the actual. In '*Prélude à l'après-midi d'un faune*' (1865) his faun was uncertain of the existence of nymphs he saw. He wrote, "After finding Nothing I have found Beauty." The Beauty was almost certainly the Light, as it was for Keats.

Paul Valéry's "Pythoness" asks "*Qui m'illumine?*" ("Who illumines me?") "Come," he writes, "the divine light (*la lumière la divine*) is not the fearful lightning....It will teach us....Dark witnesses of so much light seek no longer." The divine message of the oracle indicates that Valéry's work was on the metaphysical aspect of the fundamental theme.

The Symbolist movement turned decadent in a novel by Joris-Karl Huysmans, *Against Nature* (*A rebours*, 1884), which shows the influence of Baudelaire. The hero, Des Esseintes, is an aesthete who turns away from society to live alone among beautiful works of art – until his doctor orders him back into the world. He then begins to sense a cure in religion. The book touches on the metaphysical aspect of the fundamental theme of the quest for Reality, which Des Esseintes replaces with a quest for aesthetic reality. Des Esseintes' spiritual odyssey is a decadent variation of the metaphysical aspect of the fundamental theme.

The Symbolist movement was reflected in art by the Dutch painter, Vincent van Gogh, whose pulsing universe of energetic corn, fertile sun and bursting stars evoke the One as a force which opened people's eyes to the infinite. Van Gogh wrote: "I am painting the infinite,"[8] and his letters[9] show a quest for Reality, the infinite, from 1873 to his death in 1890, during a life spent painting symbols that would have appealed to the Symbolist poets.

German Literature

Franz Grillparzer's Neoclassical tragedies written during the Romantic time presented a vice in relation to an implied virtue. The vice is ambition, accompanied by weakness of will against the power of circumstances. To Grillparzer, character flaws and circumstances combine to bring about tragedy, a Neoclassical perspective.

Arthur Schopenhauer's *Die Welt als Will und Vorstellung* (*The World as Will and Idea*, 1819) asserted that humankind has an intuition of Reality, which he called Will. It is the unconscious force of Nature and manifests as human self-consciousness once egoism has been overcome by asceticism and chastity. He held, pessimistically, that the world is illusory, as are God, free will and the immortality of the soul. Schopenhauer touches on the metaphysical aspect of the fundamental theme of the quest for Reality but he never found the Light and did not believe in immortality, and came up with a different description of Reality from that of the metaphysical aspect of the fundamental theme.

Friedrich Nietzsche began as a disciple of Schopenhauer. In *Die Geburt der Tragödie* (*The Birth of Tragedy*, 1872) he challenged the classical, serene, Apollonian tradition and argued for an ecstatic

Dionysiac view of art that allowed for passion and pessimism. In *Unzeitgemässe Betrachtungen* (*Thoughts out of Season*, 1873-6) he criticized German culture's complacency. In *Also sprach Zarathustra* (*Thus Speaks Zarathrustra*, 1883-92), *Jenseits von Gut und Böse* (*Beyond Good and Evil*, 1886) and *Der Wille zur Macht* (*The Will to Power*) he rejected Christian morality and put in its place the Superman who revises all values and has a will to power.

Nietzsche's works touch on the metaphysical aspect of the fundamental theme, the quest for Reality, but in place of the Reality as Light is the perception of the Superman, a corruption of the metaphysical aspect of the fundamental theme.

Russian Literature

The early 19th-century Russian writers were in thrall to Byron's freedom-seeking. They combined Romanticism and realism, and focused on Neoclassical vices in relation to an implied virtue.

Aleksandr Pushkin introduced Byronic Romanticism to Russia after he was exiled from St Petersburg to a remote southern province for writing political poems on freedom. In his poem '*Kavkazsky plennik*' (The Prisoner of the Caucasus, 1822) he wrote of a freedom-lover who rejected social life in the capital and sought freedom as a Russian officer in the Caucasus, where he had a love affair with a Circassian girl.

In his poem '*Yevgeny Onegin*' (*Eugene Onegin*, 1823-31, published in 1833), the vice is Onegin's egotism, his petty, selfish nature, his attraction to Byronic ideas that he cannot reconcile with his life. Pushkin exposes the vanity of civilized life which disillusions Onegin.

Pushkin had a wide knowledge of world literature and (in Dostoevsky's words) had "a universal sensibility" that could imagine itself into the minds of people of different races and historical epochs – a Universalist sensibility that fell short of writing about the quest for Reality and immortality. He was killed in a duel by a French officer who had made advances to his wife.

Mikhail Lermontov was also a devotee of Byron. He was shocked by Pushkin's death and wrote an elegy, 'Death of a Poet', criticizing the aristocracy at court for allowing such duels to happen. As a result he also was exiled to the Caucasus.

In his novel *A Hero of our Time*, the vice is Pechorin's egotism as he describes his disillusionment, rebellion and freedom.

Lermontov returned from exile but was soon exiled again to the Caucasus, this time to an infantry regiment there. He was also killed in a duel with a fellow officer, at the age of 27.

Nikolay Gogol was a realistic Romantic who was at odds with the world.

In his play, *The Government Inspector* (1836), the vice is the corruption of the officials of a provincial town who bribe and dine a man they mistakenly believe is an incognito inspector sent by the government. The outcry was such that Gogol went into exile in Rome.

In Gogol's story 'The Overcoat' (or 'The Greatcoat', 1842), the vice is stealing, the robbing of Bashmachkin's overcoat, to acquire which he, a poorly-paid book-keeping scribe, had made great sacrifices. As a result of the theft he dies of a broken heart. Dostoevsky said of all Russian realists, "We all came out from under Gogol's greatcoat".

In his *Dead Souls* (1842), the vice is Chichikov's swindling as he buys dead serfs (or "souls" as they were called in Russia) whose deaths had not yet been registered, an asset of "living serfs" he planned to pawn in a bank to raise money. Gogol burnt the second volume of the book at the insistence of a fanatical priest, and died ten days later, half-mad.

Ivan Aleksandrovich Goncharov wrote of sloth.

In *Oblomov* (1859), the vice is Oblomov's apathetic indecision in his bachelor apartment and disdain towards getting out of bed, as a result of which he loses the woman he loves, Olga, to his energetic, practical friend Stolz.

Ivan Turgenev exposed Nihilism, the younger generation's rejection of all traditional beliefs and values.

In *Rudin* (1856), the vice is the failure of Rudin (who is partly modelled on Bakunin) to live up to his words, his spellbinding belief in progress.

In *Fathers and Sons* (1862), the vice is Bazarov's Nihilistic denial of all principles and feelings.

In his story 'The Hamlet of Shchigrov District' the vice is the Hamlet's self-conceit.

Fyodor Dostoevsky was arrested as a member of a socialist group, the Petrashevsky Circle, sentenced to be shot with twenty others and after a mock-execution, in the course of which he expected to have only minutes to live, was exiled to Siberia for four years' hard labour. In his cell he read the *New Testament*, the only book allowed, many times and discovered a new faith in Christ. He called himself "a realist in the higher sense – that is, I portray all the depths of the human soul". This is a Universalist aim. Dostoevsky was on a quest for Reality in which the viewpoint of Alyosha in *The Brothers Karamazov* overcame the viewpoint of the doubting Ivan. In his realistic novels Dostoevsky focused on vices in relation to an implied virtue.

In *Notes from the Underground* (1864), the vice is the Underground Man's rationally self-interested revenge which leads him to want to pay back those who have humiliated him, including Lisa.

In *Crime and Punishment* (1866), the vice is Raskolnikov's murder of his landlady. He believes that a humanitarian end justifies an evil means, using the logic of the Superman, an idea whose bankruptcy is demonstrated when Raskolnikov turns to Christianity during his imprisonment.

In *The Idiot* (1868-69), the vices are egotistical sensuality, acquisitiveness, murder, self-love and hatred, which Myshkin, scorned for his "idiocy" (epilepsy) despite his Christ-like compassion, generosity and innocence, is unable to prevent. In a world of money, power and sexual conquest his goodness spreads unhappiness and brings disaster to all he meets, and leads to his reverting to "idiocy" in a sanatorium.

In *The Possessed* (or *The Devils*, 1871-72), the vice is the revolutionary group's murder of Shatov and Stavrogin's persuading of Kirilov to kill himself and leave a note confessing responsibility for all the revolutionary group's crimes.

In *The Brothers Karamazov* (1879-80), the vice is the patricide of Smerdyakov, the illegitimate son of old Karamazov, at the encouragement of Ivan, another of his sons, who has repudiated God's world whereas his brother Alyosha believes in achieving universal harmony through feeling. Ivan's story, 'The Grand Inquisitor', is on the quest for Reality and therefore on the metaphysical aspect of the fundamental theme.

Count Leo Tolstoy lived on his estate but preferred the social life of Moscow and St Petersburg. He became a soldier and travelled abroad. He, too, focused on vices in relation to an implied virtue.

In *War and Peace* (1865-69), which covers the Napoleonic wars of 1805-14, the vice is resisting evil by war (which is seen as an unconscious current that drags everyone along to a bellicose outcome), contrary to the illiterate peasant Platon Karataev's doctrine of non-resistance to evil which impresses Pierre.

In *Anna Karenina* (1875-77), the vice is Anna's adulterous love for Vronsky which challenges Russia's hypocritical high society.

In *The Death of Ivan Ilych* (1886), the hero discovers the Inner Light when confronted by death. This novel is about the quest for Reality as Light, and the promise of immortality; and is on the metaphysical aspect of the fundamental theme.

In *Resurrection* (1899), the vice is Nekhlyudov's seduction of a young girl who in consequence becomes a prostitute, is convicted of a crime she did not commit and is redeemed by his love when, conscience-stricken, he follows her to Siberia, determined to marry her. She marries someone else but Nekhluydov is also redeemed.

All these Russian novels touch on the fundamental theme by examining vices in relation to an implied virtue and reflecting the quest for Reality.

The plays of Anton Chekhov, a doctor, marked the decadent end of the pre-revolutionary Russia of landed states. His characters view their lives with melancholy and boredom, make commonplace conversation to disguise their futility and sense a storm brewing, the revolution. Chekhov was like a realistic painter. His plays are like still lives of men and women with paralyzed wills and no practical ideals, who are full of illusions.

In *The Seagull* (1896), the vice is lack of will, which causes Tregorin and other characters to desire more than they can possibly achieve, and to succeed in nothing.

In *Uncle Vanya* (1897), the vice is Vanya's paralysis of will that prevents him from replacing his dreams, illusions and broken ideals and leaves him feeling helpless.

In *Three Sisters* (1901), the vice is the three sisters' lack of will to convert their longings into reality.

In *The Cherry Orchard* (1904), the vice is the characters' lack of will to convert their longings into reality.

Chekhov's plays are based on "real life" as is lived by ordinary people. But he, too, focused on vices in relation to an ideal virtue.

Drama

Like Chekhov's plays, the drama in other countries of the late 19th and early 20th centuries also examined vices in relation to an implied virtue.

Henrik Ibsen, the Norwegian dramatist, wrote plays about the vice of not telling the truth to comply with social convention, as a result of which past events return to haunt and destroy his main characters.

In *The Pillars of the Community* (or *Pillars of Society*, 1877), the vice is Consul Bernick's deceit or "lie" in relation to a past event, that he made his money and achieved his social position by betraying Lona, sacrificing Mrs. Dorf and Dina, and wrongly blaming Johan, as a result of which he makes a public confession of his hypocrisy and "pretended respectability".

In *A Doll's House* (1879), the vice is Nora's deceit in relation to a past event, that she once forged her father's signature to borrow money from a disgraced lawyer (which she is still repaying) to save the life of her husband Torvald (who is now a bank manager with a horror of debt); and in not telling her husband that her marriage is an intellectual and financial enslavement and that she is a doll in "a doll's house". Her past is exposed to her husband and she leaves him and her children to find freedom in a better world in defiance of convention.

In *Ghosts* (1881), the vice is Helen Alving's deceit in building an orphanage to spend her dead husband's money so that her son Osvald will inherit nothing from his philandering father, and the past event is her husband's transmission of inherited syphilis to Osvald, which symbolizes the family's moral disease.

In *The Wild Duck* (1884), the vice is Werle's deceit in relation to a past event, that Hedvig is Werle's child by his ex-servant Gina, now wife of his son's friend Hjalmar, the revelation of which results in Hedvig's suicide.

In *Rosmersholm* (1886), the vice is deceit in relation to a past event, the suicide in the mill-race of John Rosmer's first wife, as a result of which Rosmer and Rebekka fall into the mill-race together.

In *Hedda Gabler* (1890), the vice is Hedda's deceit in relation to a past event, her relationship with Lövborg and their attendance of pagan rituals, as a result of which she burns Lövborg's manuscript, Lövborg shoots himself with one of Hedda's pistols, Brack sexually blackmails her about the pistol and she destroys herself by shooting herself with the other pistol.

In *The Master Builder* (1892), the vice is Solness's deceit in relation to a past event, the burning-down of Aline's family home "twelve to thirteen years ago", as a result of which Solness climbs a tower and falls to his death.

In *Little Eyolf* (1894), the vice is Allmers' and Rita's not being truthful about a past event, that their child Eyolf was crippled when he fell from a table at the very moment that Allmers lusted sexually for Rita, as a result of which Eyolf longs for death and drowns himself.

In *John Gabriel Borkman* (1896), the vice is Borkman's deceit in concealing a past event, his five-year imprisonment, as a result of which after his rehabilitation in the bank he chooses death in the cold.

Ibsen's virtue requires that there should be no deceit or concealment of past events which would destroy the deceiver in a time when social convention was respected.

The Swedish dramatist August Strindberg endured three unhappy marriages and had a religious longing for salvation and absolution which he put into Expressionist works such as *To Damascus* (1898-1901, 3 parts) and *The Dance of Death* (1901), in which the quest for Reality can be found. His psychological and symbolical approach would influence O'Casey, O'Neill, Shaw and Pirandello. Strindberg exposed vices in relation to an implied virtue.

In *The Father* (1887), Agamemnon and Clytemnestra lurk behind the conflict between the Captain (Strindberg) and Laura (his first wife, Siri), and the vice is Laura's infidelity which leads to the doubts of the Captain/Strindberg about the paternity of his children, causing the Captain to have what appears to be a fatal stroke at the end.

In *Miss Julie* (1888) – Miss Julie herself was first played by Strindberg's first wife Siri – which is about the struggle between a neurotic mistress and a gross valet, the vice is the valet's cruelty which leads to Miss Julie's leaving with a razor in her hand to commit suicide, asking if she can expect to receive "the gift of grace".

George Bernard Shaw, was a Fabian socialist whose primary concern was to expose social ills in the tradition of Dickens. In his *The Quintessence of Ibsen* (1891) he revealed his debt to Ibsen. In Shaw's plays there is a vice in relation to implied virtue, and this is linked to a social ill, a defect in the capitalist system.

In *Widowers' Houses* (1892), the vice is Trench's snobbishness in not accepting Blanche as an equal because her father is a slum landlord who has been corrupted by the capitalist system – and his later snobbish acceptance of Blanche in an arrangement that has Lady Roxdale as ground landlord and himself as mortgagee.

In *Man and Superman* (1903), the vice is Ann's blatant matrimonial pursuit, driven by the Life Force, of John Tanner, author of *The Revolutionist's Handbook* and quester for Reality, who is compelled to submit to her matrimonial drive.

In *Major Barbara* (1905), the vice is the corrupting worldly power of the philanthropic benefactor, a quester for Reality who quotes Plato, who donated a shelter for the East End's poor to the Salvation Army; and Barbara's father's worldly power to which Barbara reconciles her spiritual ideals when her fiancé, a classical scholar, agrees to work for him.

In *Pygmalion* (1913), the vice is the dictatorial and thoughtless behaviour of Henry Higgins, who, to win a bet, undertakes to teach Eliza Doolittle, a Cockney flower-seller, to speak like a Duchess, as a result of which she triumphs over the class system, rebels against his tyranny and achieves freedom and independence.

In *Heartbreak House* (1919), the vice is Boss Mangan's destructive power which has brought a spiritually-bankrupt generation to the brink of the First World War, to the dismay of 88-year-old Captain Shotover, a quester for Reality who has sought "the seventh degree of concentration".

Shaw's plays touch on the metaphysical aspect of the fundamental theme of the quest for Reality in as much as one of the characters is generally on that quest but is hampered by the vice of other characters and the social ills of the capitalist system.

The Dublin-born Oscar Wilde was known for his shrewd social observation and dazzling epigrams which turn conventional practice on its head, making vice out to be a virtue and – the pun is not deliberate – *vice versa*. Despite his outrageous attitudes his plays continued to expose vices in relation to an implied virtue.

In *The Importance of Being Earnest* (1895), the vice is the deceit of two men-about-town who both have *alias*es and pursue ladies, the cousin of one and the ward of the other, until they are found to be brothers, one of whose *alias*es is in fact his real name (Ernest). The plot is as improbable as Shakespeare's *The Comedy of Errors*, in which there are twin sons named Antipholus and twin slaves named Dromio.

Wilde did not pursue the metaphysical aspect of the fundamental theme of a quest for Reality but his plays do conform to exposing vices in relation to implied virtue.

The Irish J.M. Synge had, in Paris, met Yeats, who suggested he went to the Aran Islands to write of Irish peasant life. In his plays he exposed vices in relation to an implied virtue.

In *The Playboy of the Western World* (1907), the vice is Christy Mahon's daredevil boasting that he split his bullying father to the chine, which wins him admiration among the ladies until his father appears, having merely been hit on the head.

The Irish Sean O'Casey received encouragement from Yeats' friend, Lady Gregory, at the Abbey Theatre. His plays deal with the dangers of Irish nationalism, and expose vices in relation to implied virtue.

In *Juno and the Paycock* (1924), the vice is the blustering bravado of

Jack Boyle and Joxer Daly.

In *The Plough and the Stars* (1926), the title being a reference to the flag of the Irish Republic, to create which the Easter rising of 1916 took place, the vice is Nora's deceit in burning a letter informing her husband Jack that he has been promoted Commandant of the Irish Citizen Army and is to lead a reconnaissance attack on Dublin Castle, as a result of which Jack leaves their tenement and is killed in the Easter rising.

Literary Summary

The main references to the metaphysical aspect of the fundamental theme in world literature during the Victorian Age are as follows:

- The infinite that surrounds the universe is in: Tennyson; Arnold; Emily Brontë; and Emerson.
- The metaphysical Reality seen as Light is in: Tennyson; Emerson; and Thoreau.
- The order of the universe can be found in: Tennyson; Emily Brontë; Emerson; and Tolstoy.
- The oneness of known humankind can be found in: Emerson; and Whitman.
- The similarities in cultures and civilizations are emphasized in: Tennyson's *Idylls of the King*; Arnold's poems on Sicily ('Empedocles') and Iran ('Sohrab and Rustum'); Whitman; the Pre-Raphaelites; and Pushkin.
- The universal being (or self) that opens to the Light behind the rational, social ego is in: Tennyson; Dostoevsky; and Tolstoy.
- Universal virtue is in: Pushkin; and in English, American, French and Russian novelists.
- The promise of the immortality of the universal being is present in: Tennyson's *In Memoriam*; and Tolstoy.
- The inner transformation or centre-shift from ego to universal being is found in: Whitman; and Dostoevsky.
- The quest of the purified soul is in: Tennyson's *Idylls of the King*; Arnold's 'The Scholar-Gipsy'; and Melville's *Moby-Dick*.
- The sensibility that approaches Reality through more than one discipline can be found in: Tennyson (poetry, epic, verse drama,

letters); Browning (poetry, long dramatic poems, verse drama); Arnold (poetry, literary and cultural criticism and work as inspector of schools); Dostoevsky (novels, stories, diaries); and Tolstoy (novels, educational reform and writings on Christianity).

- The new perspective of unity in history, religion, philosophy and science, international politics and literature can be found in: Darwin's *The Origin of the* Species (unification of science, 1859); and in the writings emanating from the World's Parliament of Religions (unification of religion, 1893).

The Victorian Age perpetuated the metaphysical aspect of the fundamental theme by mixing Romanticism and Neoclassicism, and by focusing on vices. This combined tradition was handed down to the creators of Modernist literature.

9

Modernist Literature

The Modernist movement in the arts was dominated by Picasso in painting, Stravinsky in music and Pound in literature.

The Modernist movement in literature turned away from the Victorian poets and their successors the Georgian poets to the work of the French Symbolists. The Georgian poets – the term "Georgian" had been used by Rupert Brooke and Edward Marsh to reflect a new outlook in English poetry that began with the reign of George V in 1910 – wrote of everyday life and Nature, which they experienced in the course of weekends spent in the country.

The American-born Ezra Pound and T.S. Eliot turned their backs on poems about Nature, Romantic escapism and art for art's sake. They wrote with intelligent realism and sought to reflect metropolitan concerns about the state of Western civilization and the collapse of the old order in Europe during the First World War. They experimented in their forms and metres, used words precisely and emphasized brevity. They juxtaposed images, and were regarded by the Georgians as an alien (American) invasion. However, they revived the metaphysical aspect of the fundamental theme.

Imagism
The Modernists gathered round the originality of T.E. Hulme and then the forceful and dominating personality of Ezra Pound.

The Modernist movement in English poetry surfaced in a group presided over by the philosopher T.E. Hulme, who had rooms at 67 Frith Street in London's Soho. Ezra Pound, a striking figure with yellow hair, a red beard, a troubadour's hat and a gold ear-ring, an American expatriate who had come to London in 1908, joined this group. He was soon the leading figure of Imagism, which in 1912 asserted that, by analogy with the sculpture of Jacob Epstein and Henri Gaudier-Brzeska, the visual image was a poetic statement. To Pound a poet must be clear and precise, eliminate all abstract words – he did not approve of the abstractions of Milton and Wordsworth – and be hard and concrete. Pound and his associates H.D. (Hilda Doolittle), Richard Aldington and F.S. Flint revolted against imprecise thinking and Romantic optimism. Pound drew up the first Imagist manifesto and edited the first Imagist anthology, *Des Imagistes*.

In April 1909 Pound met the Dublin-born W.B. Yeats, who had moved to London and, after being influenced by the Pre-Raphaelites, turned to the French Symbolists. He had been taken by Yeats' ex-mistress Olivia Shakespear and her daughter Dorothy to Yeats' London lodgings at 18 Woburn Buildings. Yeats came to be within Pound's circle, and Pound and Yeats lived together at Stone Cottage, Coleman's Hatch, near Ashdown Forest in Sussex for three winters and springs from 1913 to 1916,[1] during which Pound acted as Yeats' secretary to answer business letters[2] and married Dorothy Shakespear. (Yeats had been staying in Sussex with Olivia Shakespear's brother, his wife and her daughter by a previous marriage, Georgie Hyde-Lees, in their cottage at Coleman's Hatch. He decided to winter in the same village and rented the nearby Stone Cottage, which had four rooms. Georgie Hyde-Lees later became Yeats' wife.) Pound nicknamed Yeats "the Eagle".

In 1912 the widow of Orientalist Ernest Fenellosa asked Pound to be his literary executor, and in 1913 Pound was presented with Fenellosa's papers. He used this body of work in his early versions of Chinese poetry and seized on the Chinese ideogram as representative of the image, for the appearance of a Chinese character resembled its meaning. Thus the ideogram for man looked like a man. Pound was soon editing translations of Japanese Noh plays which were in Fenellosa's papers, and brought out two volumes of Japanese Noh plays in 1916-17. Yeats was very excited by them and wrote four verse plays of his own, modelled on Noh. Pound urged Yeats to adopt a leaner style. He regarded Yeats as a Symbolist rather than as an Imagist: "'Is Mr Yeats an imagiste?' No, Mr Yeats is a symbolist, but he has written *des Images* as have many good poets before him."[3]

T.S. Eliot's 'The Love Song of J. Alfred Prufrock' had apparently been passed to Pound by Conrad Aiken,[4] Eliot's Harvard friend. In 1914 Pound met Eliot, who called on him on 22 September 1914 and showed him 'Prufrock' at 5 Holland Place Chambers, just round the corner from Church Walk, Kensington where Pound and his bride Dorothy Shakespear had taken a flat on the same floor as the Aldingtons. Pound told him, "This is as good as anything I've ever seen," and introduced him to Wyndham Lewis, Hilda Doolittle and other Imagists.[5] In 1914 Pound moved on to Vorticism, a movement that saw the image as a vortex or whirlpool full of rushing associations, leaving Amy Lowell to lead the Imagists.

English Modernist Poetry

Pound looked back to Dante, and in 1915 he wrote the first canto of his long poem, *The Cantos*, which echoed Dante's verse form. The Modernist movement in English poetry was now dominated by Pound and Eliot. Both turned to the French Symbolists and held up Jules Laforgue as a model.

Eliot

With Pound's encouragement Eliot had brought out two volumes of poetry in 1917 and 1919 while working as a bank clerk for Lloyds Bank. In October 1921 he was on the verge of an emotional collapse. His doctor prescribed three months' rest, and Eliot lived in the Albemarle Hotel in Margate (facing "Margate sands") and then in a sanatorium near Lausanne, where he completed his experimental poem, 'The Waste Land', which Pound edited, reducing it by nearly a half (from around 800 to 433 lines). Eliot dedicated the poem to Pound, referring to him as "*il miglior fabbro*" ("the better craftsman"), the term Dante used of his own master, Arnaut Daniel.

Eliot brought the metaphysical aspect of the fundamental theme back into English poetry. 'The Waste Land' conveys this aspect of the fundamental theme through the Arthurian myths of the Fisher King, whose lands are waste, and of the Grail, which can restore the lands to fertility as explained in Jesse Weston's *From Ritual to Romance*. The poem reflects the breakdown of Western civilization following the First World War and contrasts past moral grandeur and contemporary moral decline. It presents a quest through "modern" (i.e. 1920s) society for truth, but the Reality that is the Light, symbolized by the Grail, is missing and the chapel that once held the Grail is empty, its door swinging in the wind. The metaphysical aspect of the fundamental theme of the quest is present, but its quarry cannot be found. The poem is about the collapse of awareness of the Reality of the metaphysical aspect of the fundamental theme.

Eliot himself remarked that 'The Waste Land' was not so much "an important bit of social criticism" as "the relief of a personal and wholly insignificant grouse against life; it is just a piece of rhythmical grumbling".[6] This remark, which was reported by the American poet and academic Theodore Spencer and recorded by Eliot's brother, Henry Ware Eliot, and is printed as an epigraph in Valerie Eliot's edition of the manuscripts, has the effect of diminishing the poem from a prophetic statement about Western civilization to a "grumble" about his neurotic first wife during an emotional crisis connected with her that left him in a Swiss sanatorium.

Eliot developed from the bleakness of 'The Waste Land'. The end of that poem held up the self-discipline of Eastern values (*"Datta"*, *"Dayadhvam"*, *"Damyata"*), and inner contemplation took him to belief in Christianity in 'Ash Wednesday' ("Teach us to sit still"). In his *Four Quartets* (1935-41) he sees the Light as "the still point", "a white light still and moving" ('Burnt Norton'). In 'East Coker' he tells his soul to "be still" "so the darkness shall be the light". In 'Dry Salvages' the Light is "the point of intersection of the timeless/With time". 'Little Gidding' ends "the crowned knot of fire/And the fire and the rose are one". The fire recalls Rolle's "fire of love", and the rose suggests Dante's "sempiternal rose". Both are aspects of the One Light.

Eliot refers to the Light explicitly in 'Choruses from "The Rock"': "O Light Invisible, we praise Thee!/Too bright for mortal vision/O Greater Light, we praise Thee for the less,.../O Light Invisible, we worship Thee!"

Eliot's poetic work can be seen as a Dantesque journey from the Hell of 'The Waste Land', where the Reality is absent, to the Purgatory of 'The Hollow Men' and 'Ash Wednesday' and the serene Paradise of the *Four Quartets*. It is worth pointing out that the "familiar compound ghost" of 'Little Gidding' seems to be Ezra Pound ("compound"/Pound).[7] His poetic work presents the infinite Light, an orderly universe (in the *Four Quartets*) and similarities of cultures (*Notes Towards the Definition of Culture*). He hints at immortality ("hints and guesses") and indirectly urges virtue by turning away from the follies and vices presented in 'The Waste Land'. He combines sense and spirit as did the Baroque Universalist poets.

Eliot's prose works show how deeply he reflected on the metaphysical aspect of the fundamental theme. His essay 'The Metaphysical Poets',[8] written in 1921, the year of his emotional crisis that led to 'The Waste Land', reflects intensely on the School of Donne, and is Vorticist in its view of the image: "this telescoping of images and multiplied associations". In this essay he set out his theory that in the 17th century, about the time of English Civil War, "a dissociation of sensibility set in, from which we have never recovered". He argued that the bifurcation split thinking and feeling in poets – hence the thinking of the Neoclassical poets and the feeling of the Romantic poets – whereas in the works of Donne, written before the split, thought and feeling were unified. Eliot had developed the idea of a dissociation in reviews between 1917 and 1920, and he continued to pursue this idea.

In fact, the bifurcation of sensibility pre-existed the English Civil War and manifested itself as far back as the Roman time and before: in writers who focused on the quest for Reality and writers who focused on social follies and vices. The quest for Reality of the Metaphysical poets is caught in his eight Clark lectures of 1926 and his Turnbull lectures of 1933, now collected as *The Varieties of Metaphysical Poetry*. These lectures place Eliot's metaphysical theme firmly at the forefront of his cultural criticism, for example *Notes Towards the Definition of Culture* (1948), which emphasizes the importance of religion to civilizations. In his work Eliot caught the quest for Reality.

Yeats

Yeats had joined the Theosophical Society in 1887, and was a member of the Order of the Golden Dawn. In his early works he symbolized the mystic marriage in the joined rose and cross (for example, in 'To the Rose Upon the Rood of Time', 'The Lover Tells of the Rose in His Heart' and 'The Secret Rose'). He visited Florence and Ravenna with Lady Gregory in 1907, and for the rest of his life yearned for Renaissance Italy and the Byzantine culture.

In *The Tower* (1928), named after a ruined Norman castle at Gort which he had bought, is 'Sailing to Byzantium', in which he recalled the Italian and Sicilian mosaics he had seen in 1925 and encountered during his study of Byzantine art. He appeals to the "sages standing in God's holy fire/As in the gold mosaic of a wall", and writes of a Byzantine Emperor listening to a golden bird on a "golden bough". (Yeats wrote in his diary for 30 April 1930 that in Byzantine art "birds of hammered gold singing in the golden trees" offered "their backs to the wailing dead that they may carry them to paradise".) In 'Byzantium' (1930) he writes of "flames that no faggot feeds" on the Emperor's pavement, suggesting a vision of the Light.

Yeats was a visionary rather than a mystic like Eliot, and in *A Vision* (1925-37) he reflects his wife's automatic writing when in trance and brings together imagination, history and the occult to assimilate phases of the moon, the great wheel and the great year of the ancients. *A Vision* is an attempt to present unified history in terms of a dubious scheme that owes its existence to his wife Georgie's automatic writing and which many therefore believed to be mumbo-jumbo. It is nevertheless an attempt to present the metaphysical aspect of the fundamental theme of the quest for Reality in terms of trance.

Pound

Ezra Pound, the force behind Eliot and Yeats, also pursued a quest for Reality. In his work *An Introduction to the Economic Nature of the United States*,[9] he stated the true terrain of poetry:

"For forty years I have schooled myself...to write an epic which begins 'In the Dark Forest', crosses the purgatory of human error, and ends in the light and '*fra i maestri di color che sanno*' ['among the masters of those who know']".[10]

He seems to have been thinking of the Light experienced in the "moment of metamorphosis" which occurs when the everyday world ("quotidien", i.e. quotidian) approximates to the "divine or permanent world" (letter to his father, 11 April 1927).

In *A Vision*, which begins with 'A Packet for Ezra Pound', Yeats reports that Pound told him that in *The Cantos* there would be a hundred cantos on two themes, "The Descent into Hades from Homer" and "A Metamorphosis from Ovid". Its structure would be "like that of a Bach Fugue". "There will be no plot, no chronicle of events, no logic of discourse." Just two themes and "mixed with these, mediaeval or modern historical characters". Having written his first canto in 1915, Pound brought out *A Draft of XXX Cantos* in 1930, sections of his long poem which preoccupied him for 57 years, from 1915 to 1972; for most of his lifetime.

I believe that in *The Cantos* Pound erred too much on the side of brevity and conciseness. The cantos contain many passages of beauty but lack Dante's driving narrative. Wordsworth (in *The Prelude*) and Tennyson (in *Idylls of the King*) were careful to have an understandable narrative. In short, Pound's imagistic method was not well suited to his theme of civilization. Consequently the metaphysical aspect of the fundamental theme's quest for Reality, which Pound expressed so clearly in his letter to his father, does not come across. It is buried within the work, only latently present. Eliot moved away from experimentation, and passages in *Four Quartets* contain almost prosaic narrative. Pound should have made a similar move away from experimentation. Today *The Cantos* seems fragmentary and obscure. Their unity is not immediately apparent to a discerning informed reader.

The metaphysical aspect of the fundamental theme lurks behind some of Pound's poems but is not readily apparent. 'Homage to Sextus Propertius' is a comment on the British Empire of 1917, distanced through Propertius and the Roman Empire, but this is not readily apparent. 'Hugh Selwyn Mauberley' is about the British literary culture of 1919, but seems more concerned with social satire than with Mauberley's quest for Reality. Nevertheless, Pound is a Universalist writer. His "Dark Forest" echoes Dante's "dark wood", and he reflects an orderly universe. His many references to different cultures in *The Cantos* emphasize the similarities of cultures (the Chinese and the European, for example). He holds up an ideal of virtue, sometimes by presenting a vice, and his "Descent into Hades" suggests a quest for immortality.

Pound's literary essays suggest the fundamental theme's quest for Reality by focusing on medieval writers who were aware of the medieval quest: Arnaut Daniel, Cavalcanti and Dante (through his essay, 'Hell').

T.E. Hulme's Attack on the Infinite

Hulme wrote more than 20 short Imagistic poems, five of which were published in *New Age* (January 1912) and reprinted at the end of Ezra Pound's *Ripostes* (1912). (Pound wrote, "The first use of the word 'Imagiste' was in my note to T.E. Hulme's five poems, printed at the end of my *Ripostes* in the autumn of 1912.")[11] Bergson's theory of art, his view of "intensive manifolds", led Hulme to invent Imagism. After his early death in 1917 the Romantic poet and critic Herbert Read collected his papers and published them posthumously as *Speculations*.

Speculations includes an essay on 'Humanism and the Religious Attitude', which held that there were opposed conceptions of man: the religious and the humanist. The religious attitude, which dominated from Augustine to the Renaissance and can be found in Byzantine art, sees man as limited and imperfect, and in terms of absolute values as endowed with original sin. The humanist attitude, which dominated from the Renaissance to the early 20th century, sees man as fundamentally good, not imperfect, and in its relative values evil and sin disappear. Hulme held that on the evidence of a change of sensibility found in modern art, the humanist period was coming to an end. The humanist attitude was being replaced by an anti-humanist, religious attitude in which man will again be subordinated to absolute values, i.e. the Light. These absolute values hold that man is not perfect but is capable of approaching perfection. This essay of Hulme's reflects the metaphysical aspect of the fundamental theme's quest for Reality in terms of the absolute values of the Light.

In his essay 'Romanticism and Classicism', Hulme held that "after a hundred years of Romanticism, we are in for a classical revival" in which fresh and surprising metaphors of fancy would replace imagination. (In his poem 'Autumn' Hulme wrote: "I walked abroad,/And saw the ruddy moon lean over a hedge/Like a red-faced farmer." The moon as farmer is an example of such a fresh, surprising use of fancy.) Hulme prophesied that a period of dry, hard, classical verse was coming. Man would be seen as a Neoclassical "fixed and limited animal whose nature is absolutely constant. It is only by tradition and organisation that anything decent can be got out of him." The Romantic view that "man is intrinsically good, spoilt by circumstance", he argued, has been replaced by the Neoclassical view that "he is intrinsically limited, but disciplined by order and tradition to something fairly decent." The fixed part of man, Hulme maintained, believes in God, and when there is lack of belief, then man becomes a god as in Dostoevsky's *Possessed*, and instead of belief in Heaven there is belief in a heaven on earth. The Romantic, thinking that man is infinite, "must always be talking about the infinite". This essay is also about the metaphysical aspect of the fundamental theme's quest for Reality as God.

Hulme's attack on Renaissance humanism was also an attack on the Romantic concept of man as being by nature good. His return to the religious attitude also involved a return to classicism, or Neoclassicism.

However, Hulme was not right about the infinite, as Graham Hough complained in *Image and Experience*, in which he criticizes Hulme. He identifies many fallacies and contradictions in 'Romanticism and Classicism' and rightly finds fault with Hulme's attack on the infinite, which was to characterize his new classical-religious attitude. Hough points out that the religious attitude in Dante's *Paradiso* owes much to the infinite. I have contrasted Neoclassicism and Romanticism, and Hulme has come down on the side of Neoclassicism and against Romanticism.

When I met Ezra Pound in Rapallo in 1970 he told me, "T.E. Hulme said to me in 1915, 'Everything a writer has to say can be put on half a side of a postcard, and all the rest is application and elaboration.' Have you got that application and elaboration?" Hulme, who Eliot described as "the most fertile mind of my generation",[12] would have approved of the brevity of my consideration of the essence of each writer in this book.

Modernism, Classical or Romantic?

Hulme had an impact on both Pound and Eliot (whose conversion to Christianity owed something to Hulme's abandoning of secular philosophy for religion). Both Pound and Eliot regarded themselves as being classical and anti-Romantic, in Hulme's footsteps.

Eliot's theory of the "dissociation of sensibility" saw a split between Neoclassical thinking and Romantic feeling that widened after the mid-17th century, of which there was no trace in the work of Donne, for whom a thought was a feeling. This "back-to-Donne" position was anti-Romantic. In *The Sacred Wood* (1920), 'Hamlet and his Problems', Eliot set out his theory of the objective correlative, a classical theory: "The only way of expressing emotion in the form of art is by finding an 'objective correlative'; in other words, a set of objects, a situation, a chain of events which shall be the formula for that particular emotion; such that, when the external facts, which must terminate in sensory experience, are given, the emotion is immediately evoked."[13]

Yeats was less sure about his own Neoclassical allegiance. He wrote, "We were the last Romantics," and saw himself as a late flourishing of the Romantic tradition before Pound began to classicize him in 1913. His interest in his wife's automatic writing, which led to *A Vision*, reflected a Romantic view of an infinite sea of consciousness in which automatic writing is possible.

In fact, Pound, Eliot and Yeats, all Universalist poets in questing for Reality, all displayed Romantic features while striking classical attitudes in their criticism. Frank Kermode, in *Romantic Image*, demonstrates that Romantic poetry can be identified by its focus on organic as opposed to mechanical form, on the image as opposed to statement and on the poet's isolation as opposed to his membership of society. These three criteria can be readily detected in the organic form of Eliot's 'The Love Song of J. Alfred Prufrock' and 'The Waste Land', and Pound's *The Cantos*; in the Imagists' use of the image and Yeats' images of dancer and tree; and in the isolation of Eliot's Prufrock, lingering before ascending the stair, in Pound's Hugh Selwyn Mauberley "out of key with his time", in Yeats' Major Robert Gregory, an airman alone in the clouds, and in Yeats himself sitting alone in his Norman tower.

The blend of "Classicism" and "Romanticism" in Modernist English verse is a Universalist trait. Universalism consciously blends "Classicism" and "Romanticism". Pound, Eliot and Yeats were unaware of the true nature of their blend, believing they were "Classical" when in fact they were just as much "Romantic". They all wrote on the metaphysical aspect of the fundamental theme's quest for Reality perceived as Light, or Fire: Pound's Dantesque journey from Dark Forest to Light, Eliot's "the fire and the rose are one" and Yeats' sages standing in God's "holy fire". Being Universalists, Pound, Eliot and Yeats were both "Classical" and "Romantic".

Georgian Poets

Outside Modernism the metaphysical aspect of the fundamental theme's quest for Reality was replaced by secular poetry as many of the other poets of the period wrote about Nature and reflected rural everyday life in a Georgian continuation of Victorian tradition: Edward Thomas, Edmund Blunden, W.H. Davies, Walter de la Mare and John Masefield. Thomas Hardy belongs with them, having stopped writing novels after the adverse critical reception for *Jude the Obscure* and confined himself to poetry, but the "Immanent Will" of his novels is present in his profound sense of the One, that Nature and humans are part of one process, as when the "darkling thrush" sings of Hope "whereof he knew/And I was unaware". This poem, 'The Darkling Thrush' touches on the Reality of the metaphysical aspect of the fundamental theme, as does 'Afterwards', in which he imagines what people will say about him after he has died. The same applies to D.H. Lawrence, whose many rural poems co-exist with 'The Ship of Death', which is about "the long journey to oblivion" in which the "frail soul" bids farewell to his own self and heads for eternity.

Robert Frost, a friend of Edward Thomas, met Georgian poets before the First World War, settled in New Hampshire and blended the colloquial and traditional in his troubled woodland verse, looking to Wordsworth and Emerson. He avoided the experimentation of the Modernists. His quest for Reality as the One reflected the One of Wordsworth and Emerson.

Graves

Robert Graves was a Universalist who wrote 140 books within several disciplines by the time he died. He was a poet, wrote historical fiction, compiled a classic interpretation of Greek myths and made a historical study of poetic inspiration, *The White Goddess*, which held the Muse poets address to be a form of the goddess worshipped in pre-Christian times. His war memoirs, *Good-Bye to All That* recount how he was badly wounded at the Battle of the Somme when a shell fragment went through a lung and left him sick for ten years. His poetry has Georgian forms but its content is deeper and more painful and displays a tension between Romantic intensity and Modernist clarity, order and analysis.

Graves touched on the metaphysical aspect of the fundamental theme but his quest for Reality was replaced by a quest for the goddess of the Muse and classical mythology. He despised the industrial civilization that had led to the First World War, and left it to live in Majorca. His poetry gave him relief from his own sickness and that of Western civilization, and in his body of verse and writings within several disciplines can be found a progressive quest that did not end in his finding Reality.

English Modernist Prose
Modernism had an impact on the English novel.

Joyce and Hemingway
In 1914 Pound began a collaboration with James Joyce, who was then teaching English in Trieste and had just brought out *Dubliners*. Pound wrote to Joyce in Trieste and not long afterwards saw *A Portrait of the Artist as a Young Man* (1916) into print, and later *Ulysses* (1922). Both were semi-autobiographical reconstructions of Joyce's inner life. (Pound and Yeats intrigued a grant from the Royal Literary Fund for Joyce in 1915, and soon afterwards another grant from the civil list.)

A Portrait of the Artist as a Young Man is a quest for Reality as Stephen Dedalus rejects Father Arnall's "Hellfire Sermon" and becomes an unbeliever (*"Non serviam"*, "I will not serve"), and turns to aesthetic truth: Reality as an "epiphany" or moment of revelation. Joyce defines the epiphany in *Stephen Hero*, an early draft of *A Portrait of the Artist as a Young Man*: "By an epiphany he meant a sudden spiritual manifestation."[14] Joyce described the sudden revelation of the whatness of a thing,[15] the moment in which "the soul of the commonest object...seems to us radiant".[16] Thus Stephen sees a wading girl and: "Heavenly God! cried Stephen's soul, in an outburst of profane joy."[17] Joyce comments, "Her image had passed into his soul forever."

The epiphany was inextricably linked with the image:

"The radiance of which [Aquinas] speaks in the scholastic *quidditas*, the whatness of a thing. This supreme quality is felt by the artist when the esthetic image is first conceived in his imagination. The mind in that mysterious instant Shelley likened beautifully to a fading coal. The instant wherein that supreme quality of beauty, the clear radiance of the esthetic image, is apprehended luminously by the mind which has been arrested by its wholeness and fascinated by its harmony is the luminous silent stasis of esthetic pleasure, a spiritual state." [18]

In *A Portrait of the Artist as a Young Man* Joyce presents a quest for Reality that does not succeed as Stephen becomes an artist for whom Reality is the revelation of an image. Truth is in the symbol rather than in the metaphysical Light. The work is therefore a variation on the metaphysical aspect of the fundamental theme. It interprets Reality in Imagistic terms as Joyce attempts to synthesize the Symbolist and Realist novel.

Ulysses follows Leopold Bloom, a Jew who works in advertising, and his wife Molly during one day in Dublin, 16 June 1904 (the anniversary of Joyce's first walk with Nora Barnacle, who became his wife). The whole book is an epiphany of Bloom.

As in 'The Waste Land', structure is artificially provided by a myth: Homer's *The Odyssey*. The actions of Bloom reflect the deeds of Odysseus, those of Molly reflect the deeds of Penelope and those of Stephen reflect the deeds of Telemachus. A modern public bath, funeral, newspaper office, library, pub, maternity hospital and brothel all correspond to episodes in *The Odyssey*. In *Ulysses* Joyce tried to catch the flow of images in consciousness, a technique that does not enhance readability.

Like *A Portrait of the Artist as a Young Man*, *Ulysses* touches on the fundamental theme but again rejects the quest for Reality within everyday events and substitutes artistic reality, epiphanies and sequences of images. In Joyce the quest for Reality has turned aesthetic and pursues an Imagistic revelation within the moment.

Pound also helped Ernest Hemingway, who had come to Paris in 1921. He went to tea with Pound at 70 bis Rue Notre Dame des Champs, and soon Hemingway was teaching him to box with boxing gloves. Pound drew attention to Hemingway's early work and helped launch his first novel.

Hemingway's novels present the quest of the metaphysical aspect of the fundamental theme in a debased, disillusioned, social light.

In *The Sun Also Rises* (or *Fiesta*, 1926), the quest of Lady Brett Ashley and her group of disillusioned hangers-on merely involves the social reality of having a good time at each fiesta.

In *A Farewell to Arms* (1929), Lieutenant Henry's quest in the First World War involves a love affair with a British nurse.

In *For Whom the Bell Tolls* (1940), Robert Jordan's quest is for a social reality, the Republican cause in the Spanish Civil War.

In *The Old Man and the Sea*, the old man's quest is for a marlin, and is similar to Captain Ahab's quest for Moby-Dick.

In Hemingway's works, the quest for Reality has become a quest for a hard-drinking good time, a cause, a prize. I met Hemingway in Spain in 1959 after a bull fight and was struck by the sensitivity and watchfulness of his eyes, which missed nothing.

The English Novel

Meanwhile English novelists had touched on the fundamental theme by presenting vices in relation to an implied virtue, like the Renaissance and Victorian writers, or by presenting quests for a social reality.

The Polish novelist Joseph Conrad (Teodor Josef Konrad Korzeniowski), a sailor who wrote about voyages, resumed the tradition of exposing vices in relation to an implied virtue. He was encouraged by the English novelist John Galsworthy, who met him during a long sea voyage on which Conrad was one of the ship's officers.

In *The Nigger of the Narcissus* (1897), the vice is the troublemaking of Donkin, who tries to incite the crew to mutiny.

In *Lord Jim* (1900), the vice is Brown's treacherous massacre, which leads Jim, still expiating his involuntary jump, to deliver himself to Chief Doramin and death.

In *Typhoon* (1902), the vice is Captain MacWhirr's lack of imagination in steering his ship through the typhoon and confiscating the money of his 200 Chinese passengers.

In *Heart of Darkness* (1902), the vice is Kurtz's tyrannical exploitation of the African natives in the Congo's ivory country, his human sacrifices and placing of natives' severed heads on stakes.

In *Nostromo* (1904), the vice is the corruptibility of the Italian Capataz de Cargadores ("*Nostromo*", "our man") who sails off with treasure from a South-American silver mine.

In *The Secret Agent* (1907), the vice is Verloc's revolutionary ruthlessness in causing his wife's simple-minded brother to blow himself up while targeting Greenwich Observatory. (There are Verlocs behind contemporary Muslim suicide-bombers.)

E.M. Forster wrote comedies of manners that satirized the English abroad. He dealt with personal relationships and conflicting values, and exposed vices in terms of implied virtue.

In *Where Angels Fear to Tread* (1905), the vice is the young widow Lilia's mother-in-law's snobbishness towards the Italian dentist Gino, who Lilia marries, and her mother-in-law's disastrous determination to wrest Gino's son by Lilia from him after Lilia's death in childbirth.

In *The Longest Journey* (1907), the vice is the snobbery of Agnes, who is horrified at the prospect of a scandal when she learns that Rickie has a half-brother who is living with his aunt, and prevents Rickie from telling him that they are related.

In *A Room with a View* (1908), the vice is the snobbery of Miss Bartlett, Lucy's chaperone, who criticizes the Emersons' generous exchange of rooms as indecorous and removes Lucy to England after her first embrace with George.

In *Howards End* (1910), the vice is the business-minded lack of imagination and snobbery of Helen Schlegel in relation to the cultured

Wilcoxes, in contrast to her sister Margaret who marries Henry Wilcox, whose virtues of "neatness, decision and obedience...keep the soul from becoming sloppy".

In *A Passage to India* (1924), the vice is the snobbery of the British in India who (with the exception of Fielding) side with Adela Quested against the Indian Muslim Dr Aziz.

H.G. Wells, a Cockney who was apprenticed to the drapery trade and had struggled to free himself from poverty, became a Universalist at home in several disciplines. He imported the scientific and historical thinking of the day into his work, and his scientific fantasies, such as *The Time Machine* (1895), *The Invisible Man* (1897) and *The War of the Worlds* (1898), all reflected the breadth of his knowledge.

In *The History of Mr Polly* (1910), Alfred Polly quests for freedom (a dream shared by Wells himself) by burning down his shop and holding court at the Potwell Inn. In this work Wells replaced the fundamental theme's quest for Reality with a quest for freedom.

In *The Outline of History* (1920, revised in 1931), Wells attempts a unified view of the history of the world, a Universalist approach.

His last social-historical work is pessimistic: *Mind at the End of its Tether* (1945).

D.H. Lawrence, a sickly miner's son, was close to his mother. He wrote chronicle novels that reflected his working-class background. In his novels the elemental is contrasted with the social, and men and women are seen as part of the natural unity of the universe; and some are aware of the infinite. (See pp.407-8.) However, in his work the quest for Reality became a quest for total and mystical sexual union, and his novels are about the flux of emotions and feelings within relationships against the rhythm of the seasons. His characters therefore seem disjointed, and his episodic structures give his novels the appearance of being Modernist – sequences of episodes rather than images.

In *Sons and Lovers* (1913), the quest is Paul's quest for a replacement for his emotional closeness to his mother in first Miriam and then Clara.

In *The Rainbow* (1915), the quest is Ursula's for true union with Anton during her developing consciousness.

In *Women in Love* (1920), the quest is Ursula's quest for a full union with Rupert Birkin (a portrait of Lawrence), who demands a complete relationship with loss of self.

In *Aaron's Rod* (1922), the quest is Aaron's quest through Bohemian and upper-class society.

In *The Plumed Serpent* (1926), the quest is Kate's quest via the cult of Quetzalcoatl into the complete relationship and loss of self demanded by Cipriano.

In *Lady Chatterley's Lover* (1928), the quest is Constance Chatterley's quest for a complete relationship with Mellors across the class barrier.

Lawrence has secularized the metaphysical aspect of the fundamental theme by replacing the quest for Reality with the quest for full sexual union.

Virginia Woolf presents a scheme of consciousness and fluid characterization through shifting moods and recollections. In her works the quest for Reality is replaced by a quest for a social, secularized reality.

In *Mrs. Dalloway* (1925), the quest is Mrs. Dalloway's quest to buy flowers for her dinner party.

In *To the Lighthouse* (1927), which is set in the Hebridean Isle of Skye but draws on the Godrevy Lighthouse that is visible from St. Ives in Cornwall, where she had a rented holiday home at Talland House for ten years from 1882, the quest is James Ramsay's quest to visit the lighthouse which, like the lighthouse in Shakespeare's sonnet 116, is an "ever-fixèd mark,/That looks on tempests and is never shaken" and has come to symbolize Mrs. Ramsay's stability and security.

In *The Waves* (1931), which is told through a stream of consciousness describing the rising and setting of the sun over waves, the quest is for the truth about a group of friends who reflect on themselves and each other.

Aldous Huxley pursued the metaphysical aspect of the fundamental theme's quest for Reality in his prose works, *The Perennial Philosophy* (1946) and *The Doors of Perception* (1954), which focused on the use of the drug mescaline as a way of inducing "mystical" experience, a work that was taken up by the Beat Generation who sought Beatitude through drugs. He was Universalist in considering the mystical experience in different cultures and times and in predicting that a world state is ahead in his satirical novel *Brave New World*, which takes place in the 7th century AF (After Ford). This work satirizes a society in which a scientifically-induced, Communist-style happiness denies individual freedom.

In *Brave New World* (1932), the quest is Bernard Marx's quest for individual freedom by rebelling against the world state's caste system – he, an Alpha Plus, brings a Savage (the lowest caste) back to London in contravention of the rules.

In *Eyeless in Gaza* (1936), the quest is Beavis's quest for mystical wholeness in intellectual middle-class England.

T.E. Lawrence

The metaphysical aspect of the fundamental theme was asserted in broodings about the desert in an autobiographical book by T.E. Lawrence ("Lawrence of Arabia"), *The Seven Pillars of Wisdom* (1926) and its abridgement *Revolt in the Desert* (1927). Written on the model of Doughty's *Arabia Deserta* (1888), it describes how Lawrence, an archaeologist digging in the Near East, joined the British Army and during the First World War led the Arab revolt against the Ottoman Turks, dressing as an Arab and uniting the warring tribes to capture Damascus by promising them independence after the war. But he was a

British intelligence agent, and his promises were overruled. In disgust he declined all honours and entered the Royal Air Force under an assumed name (T.E. Shaw).

His book reflects his quest for Reality among the Arabs amid deserts and battles as he quests for Arab independence. Death and the Arab belief in immortality are never far away.

American Modernism

Pound, Eliot and Hemingway all had American roots, and the principles of Modernism passed into the American novel.

Scott Fitzgerald, a friend of the critic Edmund Wilson, wrote topical novels that caught the Jazz Age of the 1920s. The titles of his first two novels, *This Side of Paradise*, which is about the disillusionment and moral disintegration of America after the First World War (after the publication of which he married Zelda Sayre), and *The Beautiful and Damned*, echo the paradise and damnation of the Christian Reality. His main relationships in his work are self-dramatizations of his own marriage to Zelda. He exposed vices in relation to an implied virtue.

In *This Side of Paradise* (1920), the vice is the greed and status-seeking of Rosalind Connage (Zelda), who ends her relationship with Amory Blaine (Fitzgerald) and marries a wealthy man instead.

In *The Beautiful and Damned* (1922), the vices are the idleness and futility of Anthony Patch amid a round of decadent parties and, after he is disinherited by Adam, his status-seeking in taking legal action to recover his fortune.

In *The Great Gatsby* (1925), the vice is Gatsby's shady financial dealings involving drugs, on which his fortune has been based, as he romantically and destructively woos the love of his life, Daisy Buchanan.

In *Tender is the Night* (1934), which is set on the Riviera, the vice is the idleness, drink and dissipation of the expatriates which is the context of the story of an American psychiatrist and his schizophrenic wife.

William Faulkner of Mississippi wrote about the decline of the Old South rather than the quest for Reality, but exposed vices in relation to an implied virtue.

In *The Sound and the Fury* (1929), which is influenced by Modernist experimentation, the decline of the South is seen through different consciousnesses in the manner of Virginia Woolf, including the stream-of-consciousness of a thirty-three-year-old idiot, Benjy, whose impressions are jumbled up. The vice is Quentin's theft of $7,000 from Jason which contributes to his own suicide and the dissolution of the Compson family.

In *Sanctuary* (1931), the vice is Popeye's inhumanity which leads him to murder Tommy, rape Temple with a corncob, murder her gangster boyfriend Red and influence her into lying for him in court.

French Modernism

The French poet Guillaume Apollinaire was a French Modernist poet who wrote without using punctuation and experimented with typographical form, shaping poems like downward lines of rain, a tuning-fork, a star and a cannon. He was wounded in the head by a shell in 1916 and, his resistance lowered, died of Spanish flu in 1918. He is credited with synthesizing classical intellectuality and form, and Romantic intuition and feeling. His poem 'Zone' suggests that he was aware of the quest for Reality, but much of his work, like '*Sous le pont Mirabeau*' (which Juliette Greco later sang all over the world) is about the fleetingness of time in the manner of Keats.

Marcel Proust turned the quest for Reality into a quest for past memories in his seven-volume *Remembrance of Things Past* (*A la recherche du temps perdu*, 1913-27), which is dominated by the (then) new psychological theory of the unconscious.

In *By Way of Sainte-Beuve* (*Contre Sainte-Beuve*, 1954), Proust claimed that the artist releases the creative energies of past experience from the hidden unconscious.

In *Remembrance of Things Past*, Proust's aim is to seek for truth, but the quest for Reality of the fundamental theme becomes a quest to experience the past and recapture lost time.

André Gide was on a long quest for Reality. His early tales, set in the castle at La Roque his mother had inherited and at the Rouen and Cuverville of his cousins, revealed his early quest for his cousin Madeleine Rondeaux, who he married. After going through a Symbolist period he kept a journal about his quest for God, *Numquid et tu?* (1927), which was unsuccessful as he was thrown back on constructing his own ethic, being true to himself. *The Coiners* (*Les Faux-monnayeurs*, 1926), his only full-length novel, contained numerous characters and plots and was constructed like a fugue in the Modernist, Poundian manner, with themes rising, submerging and rising again in new patterns.

Gide's final phase left personal issues behind and addressed the world's problems. In *Voyage au Congo* (1927) he took the side of outcasts, demanding better conditions for criminals and women, and condemned French colonialism and exploitation in support of the underprivileged. In 1936 he visited the USSR with strong pro-Communist feelings, and returned disillusioned. In his latest work he put in Theseus's mouth, "For the good of humanity to come I have accomplished my work." Gide had worked his way through to a Universalist position.

German Modernism

Thomas Mann followed the metaphysical aspect of the fundamental theme by contrasting artists on a quest for Reality with the deadening bourgeois culture in which they operated.

In *Buddenbrooks* (1901), the quest is Hanno Buddenbrook's quest to experience the transcendental Reality in Wagner's music, which causes him to lose the will to live and to succumb to fever in his bourgeois family.

In *Tonio Kröger* (1903), the quest is Tonio Kröger's quest for Reality as an artist, and his ensuing suicide is a result of the bourgeois culture in which he lives.

The Prague-born Rainer Maria Rilke wrote of the metaphysical aspect of the fundamental theme. His *Book of Hours* (1905) confronted death through his subjective emotion. He mentioned being "cloaked" from "light's rays", and of angels seeking "you in the light" and "light's realm". Rilke was imagining what a Russian monk might feel and was writing as an imaginative poet rather than as a mystic. He became more objective after becoming the sculptor Rodin's secretary from 1902 to 1906. *The Notebooks of Malte Laurids Brigge* (1910) was a Danish nobleman's (i.e. Rilke's) quest through a variety of experiences to discover unrealized parts of his own personality.

Rilke's *Duino Elegies*, which were set in the Duino Castle near Trieste while Rilke was the guest of Princess Marie um Thurn und Taxis (begun in 1912 and finished in February 1922), were a quest for Reality during the decay of old forms, a search for spirituality that led to a joyful affirmation of life after years of writer's block and depression – a similar journey to T.S. Eliot's. Rilke was addressing an Orphic adept in this work, and again was writing as an imaginative poet rather than as a mystic. However, he clearly had knowledge of the metaphysical aspect of the fundamental theme when writing of the "terrible" angels, and of the invisible. "We are the bees of the invisible," Rilke wrote in the *Duino Elegies*, meaning that we transform the visible into the invisible through sensory perception.

In Rilke's work the metaphysical aspect of the fundamental theme became a quest for a Reality that had spiritual meaning for the isolated poet – a quest for an angel – and Rilke spoke of a monism that included immanence and transcendence.

The Prague-Jewish Franz Kafka was influenced by and contributed to Expressionism, a movement in German literature after the First World War that emphasized the inner significance of things, not their external forms: states of mind rather than life in action – in Kafka's case, a mental state of anxiety before unspecified and overwhelming forces. Kafka's work, published after his death by his friend Max Brod, was about the quest for Reality, which he turned into allegory: an isolated, bewildered, threatened individual named K, his own initial, aware of an unspecified guilt in a world that is full of unease.

In *The Trial* (1925), K quests to be free from a mysterious power that pursues and persecutes him, an analogy for Reality or Being.

In *The Castle* (1926), K quests for, and seeks, the mysterious power, again an analogy for Reality, without success or approval.

Hermann Hesse's mystical novels are all about the metaphysical aspect of the fundamental theme.

Siddhartha (1922) is about the spiritual quest – a quest for Reality – of two Hindu friends, and deals with oriental mysticism as a young Indian, Siddhartha, meets the Buddha, but has to work out his own destiny through a love affair and the temptation of riches.

Der Steppenwolf (1927) is about the quest of a man with a dual personality, who is half-man and half-wolf.

Narziss und Goldmund (1930) is set in the Middle Ages and is about Goldmund's search for the meaning of life and self-realization through sensual and artistic satisfaction in contrast to the spiritual peace of the monk Narziss, who helped him.

The Glass Bead Game (*Das Glasperlenspiel*, 1943) is about a philosophical Utopia in 2000 controlled by an *élite* that is semi-monastic. It is a *Bildungsroman* about Knecht's quest: his education as a youth, his decision to join the Castalian Order, his mastery of the Glass Bead Game, and his rise to the role of *Magister Ludi*, "Master of the Game", controller of the Order's administrators.

Modernism was flagging by now, running out of steam, and the post-Modernist world had no one movement that could replace it. Yeats made two judgements on Pound's Modernism. The first was in early 1913 when he wrote to Lady Gregory, "In his own work he [Pound] is very uncertain, often very bad though very interesting sometimes. He spoils himself by too many experiments and has more sound principles than taste."[19] The second was in his preface to *The Oxford Book of Modern Verse* in 1936: "When I consider his [Pound's] work as a whole, I find more style than form; at moments more style, more deliberate nobility and the means to convey it than in any contemporary poet known to me, but it is constantly interrupted, broken, twisted into nothing by its proper opposite, nervous obsession, nightmare, stammering confusion."

In short, the Modernist experiment had not just run its course, but had failed. Poets and novelists would have to find a way forward that did not depend on images alone, but reverted to the narrative used by Milton in *Paradise Lost*, Wordsworth in *The Prelude* and Tennyson in *The Idylls of the King*. (In 1936 there was tension between Yeats and Pound, who had criticized Yeats' most recent play *The King of the Great Clock Tower*, but this second passage truly reflects Yeats' long-held view of Pound's work.)

Literary Summary

The main references to the metaphysical aspect of the fundamental theme in world literature during the Modernist period are as follows:

- The infinite that surrounds the universe is in: Eliot; Yeats; and Rilke ("We are bees of the invisible").
- The metaphysical Reality seen as Light is in: Eliot; and Yeats.
- The order of the universe can be found in: Hulme (*Speculations*); Eliot; Pound; Yeats; and Hesse.
- The oneness of known humankind can be found in: Eliot; and Hesse.
- The similarities in cultures and civilizations are emphasized in: Pound's *Cantos*; and Eliot's cultural and social essays.
- The universal being (or self) that opens to the Light behind the rational, social ego is in: Eliot; T.E. Lawrence; and Hesse.
- Universal virtue is in: Ibsen; Shaw; and Forster.
- The promise of the immortality of the universal being is present in: Eliot; T.E. Lawrence; and Hesse.
- The inner transformation or centre-shift from ego to universal being is found in: Eliot; and Hesse.
- The quest of the purified soul is in: Joyce (*A Portrait of the Artist as a Young Man*); and Eliot.
- The sensibility that approaches Reality through more than one discipline can be found in: T.E. Hulme (poetry, essays,

philosophy); T.S. Eliot (poetry, verse drama, cultural history, social essays, literary criticism); Yeats (poetry, verse drama, autobiography, Rosicrucianism, patterns of unified history in *A Vision*, letters); Ezra Pound (poetry, literary criticism, cultural and social essays, letters); H.G. Wells (literature, history, science); Aldous Huxley (literature, mysticism); Robert Graves (poetry, historical fiction, mythology, history of poetic inspiration); and Hesse (novels, poems, criticism, philosophy).

• The new perspective of unity in history, religion, philosophy and science, international politics and literature can be found in: Eliot (*Notes Towards the Definition of Culture*, 'Little Gidding'); Yeats (patterns of unified history in *A Vision*); H.G. Wells (unification of history in *The Outline of History*, 1920); and writings emanating from the World's Congress of Faiths and World Spiritual Council (unification of religion, 1936 and 1944).

The coherence of the Modernist movement in literature, which owed much to Pound, was now dispersed, and fragmented groups reverted to the Victorian and Georgian tradition and produced a pluralistic, largely secular literature with no central control that sometimes resembled anarchy. The metaphysical aspect of the fundamental theme was in the background, the foreground belonging to secular literature.

10

Literature in the 20th-Century Anarchy

The Anarchy under the English King Stephen (1135-1154) was a time when the barons made war on each other and there was a lack of central authority. The poetry and fiction from the 1930s to the end of the 20th century was a time when writers belonging to a variety of traditions made war on each other, and the central authority provided by Modernism and the criticism of T.S. Eliot was not renewed.

At a time when religion was collapsing, poetry and fiction became increasingly more secularized, with many writers seeing only a social reality, and the metaphysical aspect of the fundamental theme did not appear as strongly in their works as it had in the 19th century. In the 20th century there was a plurality of traditions as individual literary "barons" and their followers looked back to past masters and continued their *genres* just as after the Renaissance various academicist painters looked back to Raphael or other masters and formed "a school of Raphael" or of other masters.

English Literature

In the last two-thirds of the 20th century English literature had a plurality of traditions and a predominance of secular writers, who had the effect of marginalizing the metaphysical aspect of the fundamental theme.

English Poetry of the 1930s

The 1930s English poets turned their backs on Modernism and wrote on industrial, social themes. Their verse had a left-wing political involvement, naively idealizing the Soviet Union before Stalin's purges, taking sides in the Spanish Civil War and reflecting the attitudes of the Popular Front in France, drawing on the rhythms of Hopkins and the plainness of Hardy. The near-Marxist quartet of W.H. Auden, Stephen Spender, Cecil Day Lewis and Louis MacNeice were nicknamed "the pylon school" because of the industrial imagery in works such as Spender's 'The Pylons' (1933). Skyscrapers, power stations, arterial roads, petrol stations, trains and trams featured in their work. The metaphysical aspect of the fundamental theme lurks in the background. It can be found in MacNeice's 'Prayer before Birth' ("a white light/In the back of my mind to guide me") and in Auden's 'As I walked out one evening' ("You cannot conquer Time").

Auden left England with Christopher Isherwood and settled in America on the eve of the Second World War, and was converted to Christianity in 1940. His 'New Year Letter' of 1941 suggests a Christian view of Reality: "O Dove of science and of light." Auden wrote a quest sequence. In 1961 he wrote in 'The Quest Hero':[1]

> "The Quest is one of the oldest, hardiest, and most popular of all literary *genres*. In some instances it may be founded on historical fact – the Quest of the Golden Fleece may have its origin in the search of seafaring traders for amber – and certain themes, like the theme of the enchanted cruel Princess whose heart can be melted only by the predestined lover, may be distorted recollections of religious rites, but the persistent appeal of the Quest as a literary form is due, I believe, to its validity as a symbolic description of our subjective personal experience of existence as historical."

The quest is one of Auden's favorite motifs, but in his work the quest has a temporal, worldly goal and has ceased to be a quest for Reality.

Verse Drama
The 1930s saw a revival in verse drama which partially reflected the metaphysical aspect of the fundamental theme. T.S. Eliot's plays touched on the quest for Reality and exposed vices in relation to an implied virtue.

> In T.S. Eliot's *Murder in the Cathedral* (1935), the quest is Becket's Christian quest for Reality, and the vice (or sin) is Becket's spiritual pride in considering yielding to the temptation of sainthood – and, of course, Henry II's ill temper.

> In *The Family Reunion* (1939), the quest for Reality is Harry's Orestes-

like quest for purification through the Eumenides or Furies, and the vice is Harry's murder, or the illusion of murder, of his wife.

Eliot followed these plays with three drawing-room comedies mixing profound ideas with shallow social chatter.

In *The Cocktail Party* (1950), which is based on Euripides' *Alcestis*, the quest for Reality is that of Celia, the husband Edward's mistress, who is sent by a psychiatrist on a mission which leads to her martyrdom amongst savages, and the vice is the husband Edward's self-centredness.

In *The Confidential Clerk* (1954), which is based on 1890s farces such as *The Private Secretary*, the vice is the deception of Sir Claude Mulhammer in smuggling his illegitimate son Colby into the house as his confidential clerk, hoping that his wife will take a liking to him and allow him to live with him as her adopted son.

In *The Elder Statesman* (1959), which is based on Sophocles' *Oedipus at Colonus* (also *Oedipus Coloneus*), the vice is Lord Claverton's egotistic disregard for others during his climb up the social ladder, during which he ran over a corpse and never faced the police to clear himself, and had a brief affair.

Meanwhile, inspired as much by the German dramatist Bertolt Brecht as by Eliot, Auden and Isherwood wrote three verse plays: *The Dog Beneath the Skin* (1935); *The Ascent of the F6* (1936), a quest to the summit of a mountain where the central character discovers not Reality but his mother; and *On the Frontier* (1938). Eliot's example inspired some Christian writers to produce verse plays: Ronald Duncan's *This Way is the Tomb* (1945); Norman Nicholson's *The Old Man of the Mountains* (1946); and Christopher Fry's verse plays.

In Fry's *The Lady's Not for Burning* (1948), which is set in the Middle Ages, the vice is the cruelty of those in authority in Cool Clary, notably the Mayor and the Chaplain, in reflecting the widespread belief in witchcraft among the people. They seek to burn Jennet as a witch and torture the war-weary soldier Thomas Mendip to stop him from suicidally confessing to murders he did not commit.

The Post-1930s English Novel

The English novel of the 1930s abandoned experimentation and returned to exposing vices in relation to an implied virtue.

Graham Greene's novels show quests for Reality within a Catholic context, in which moral good and evil are distinguished from ethical right and wrong, and he exposes vices in relation to an implied virtue.

In *The Power and the Glory* (1940), the quest for Reality is that of a whisky priest, the last priest in Mexico during the Mexican Revolution, who is determined to continue his office as he is hunted by the lieutenant; and the vice is the lieutenant's persecution of the priest and the Church.

In *The Heart of the Matter* (1948), the quest is Scobie's quest for Reality which is tarnished by his own actions and results in suicide, and the vice is his deceiving of his wife Louise in his affair with Helen and in concealing the suicidal nature of his death.

In *The End of the Affair* (1951), the quest for Reality is that of Sarah whose affair ends in her becoming a Catholic, and the vice is Bendix's deceiving of Henry, her husband.

In *The Quiet American* (1955), the quest for Reality is that of Pyle who seeks to Westernize Vietnam, and the vice is Pyle's bicycle-bomb massacre.

In *A Burnt-Out Case* (1961), the hero is called Querry (suggesting "query" and "quarry"), and the quest for Reality is Querry's journey into a *leproserie* (leprosy hospital), while the vice is the selfishness of those who conform to their religion, such as Dr Colin and Rycker, who have trapped their wives into living in Africa to suit themselves.

Greene's "entertainments" focus less on the quest than on vice.

In *Our Man in Havana* (1958), the vice is Wormold's deception in passing off vacuum-cleaner plans as plans of a nuclear installation.

Mexico, Sierra Leone, Vietnam, the Belgian Congo (now the Democratic Republic of the Congo), Cuba – Greene's settings in different continents convey his Universalist awareness of the oneness of humankind and the progress of a soul in a worldwide context.

Evelyn Waugh also presented quests for Reality within a Catholic context. However, whereas Greene combined Christian themes with a popular thriller or detective-story form, Waugh (who was received into the Catholic Church in 1930 by Father D'Arcy, the man who received Greene into the Church in 1926) used preposterous comedy in which the quest is undermined and replaced by a secular alternative, and he exposes vices in relation to an implied virtue.

In *Decline and Fall* (1928), Paul's quest for Reality is undermined and replaced when he is sent down from Oxford for being the innocent victim of drunkenness and is forced to abandon his career in the Church to teach in a school until he is unjustly imprisoned; and the main vice is Margot's self-interested framing of Paul to take the rap for her role in the white slave trade.

In *A Handful of Dust* (1934), whose title was taken from Eliot's 'The Waste Land', the quest for Reality is undermined and replaced by Tony's journey up the Amazon; and the vice is Lady Brenda Last's unscrupulous adultery and demands for alimony which threaten his family property, Hetton.

In *Scoop* (1935), Waugh's satire on Fleet Street based on his experiences in Abyssinia for *The Daily Mail*, the quest for Reality is undermined and replaced when the inexperienced William Boot is mistakenly dispatched to cover a war in Ishmaelia (Abyssinia) for *The Beast*; and the vice is the cynical arrogance of the ignorant Lord Copper, owner of *The Beast*, who sends William Boot rather than John Boot, who later gets the credit for William's scoop.

In *Brideshead Revisited* (1945), the theme of which Waugh described as "the operation of divine grace on a group of diverse but closely connected characters", the quest for Reality is undermined and replaced by Charles Ryder's quest for the social reality of the Catholic family, and the vice is Sebastian's decline into the early stages of alcoholism.

In all these works of Waugh's, the quest for Reality is undermined and replaced by a secular, social alternative as a result of the workings of a godless society.

George Orwell (pen-name for Eric Blair) was born in Bengal. He was educated in England and served with the Indian Imperial police in Burma before returning to work in low-paid jobs in London and Paris. His early work was in the tradition of Defoe's, and had a strong autobiographical, left-wing journalistic, documentary trend. Orwell drew on his own experiences of down-and-outs, tramps and hop-pickers, book-sellers, the unemployed, volunteers in the Spanish Civil War and insurance clerks. His political satires on totalitarianism were in the tradition of Swift.

In Orwell's satirical work the quest for Reality is replaced by a quest for an ideal society which is corrupted by a new tyranny, and vices are exposed in relation to an implied virtue.

In *Animal Farm* (1945), the animals drive out the farmer and the pigs take over and quest for a perfect society or social reality, which becomes a new tyranny; and the vice is Napoleon's (Stalin's) ruthlessness.

In *Nineteen eighty-four* (1949), the quest for an ideal society has led to the totalitarianism of Big Brother (Stalin), and Winston Smith's struggle against it to win individual freedom leads to his being arrested by the Thought Police and brainwashed into accepting the tyranny; and the vice is O'Brien's use of torture and brainwashing to compel Winston to comply with the tyranny.

In these two satires Orwell was a political writer for whom only social reality counted, along with retrieving memory of the past which the dictatorship constantly suppressed to facilitate the acceptance of its tyrannical policies.

Angus Wilson wrote novels about the failings of liberal humanism.

He wrote about the middle classes with irony and compassion, using episodic plots reminiscent of Dickens, and exposed vices in relation to an implied virtue.

In *Hemlock and After* (1952), the vice is Bernard Sands' urge towards cruelty which he is shocked to discover in himself (yet exposes an equivalent abnormality in an acquaintance, who is driven to suicide as a result).

In *Anglo-Saxon Attitudes* (1956), the vice is Gerald Middleton's laziness as a scholar and husband until his honesty restores his integrity as a scholar.

In *The Middle Age of Mrs. Eliot* (1958), the vice is Meg Eliot's hubristic contentment before she is widowed and reduced to comparative poverty.

Wilson wrote another four novels. I met him in Libya and during a walk by the sea discussed whether a novelist should have a distinctive voice. He was adamant that a novelist should not have a voice: "I can't read Graham Greene any more because I know what his voice is going to say." Wilson's work does not reflect the quest for Reality as his reality is social, but he does have a sense of virtue in his works.

Anthony Powell wrote five novels about seedy London in the 1930s, and then between 1951 and 1975 brought out a sequence of twelve novels, *A Dance to the Music of Time*, which was named after Poussin's painting (which is in the Wallace Collection, London). The sequence secularizes the fundamental theme.

In *A Dance to the Music of Time* the hero, Nicholas Jenkins, describes the fortunes of people whose lives were disrupted by the Second World War. The quest for Reality has become a quest for social reality, and the vice is Kenneth Widmerpool's power-seeking which propels him from being a widely ridiculed figure to exercising sinister authority.

I met Powell in Japan in 1964, and he told me that he had plenty of material but that the problem was organising it, and it was clear from our conversation that he would not be looking beyond social reality.

English Neo-Romantic Poets of the 1940s

After 1945 the Pound-Eliot tradition was abandoned by English poets. The Neo-Romantic poets looked back to the Oneness of Nature and man found in Wordsworth and Coleridge and replaced the social poetry of the 1930s. The Neo-Romantics began as the New Apocalypse, whose poets were anthologised in *The White Horseman*, 1941. They were shaped by Herbert Read, Dylan Thomas and George Barker, all poets of the image rather than statement – a clash of images that contradict each other but reveal unity – who sought to escape the colloquial diction and topical, urban imagery of Auden.

Dylan Thomas brought out volumes of poetry from 1934 to 1952, and derived linguistically from Joyce, rhythmically from the *Bible* and psychologically from Freud (whose view of the unconscious provided the scientific basis of Surrealism). He sang of a cruel world with a childhood innocence and fascination for birth and death.

There are hints of the metaphysical aspect of the fundamental theme's quest for Reality in Thomas. His 'Vision and Prayer' sequence (1945) is about the inner Light. In a poem typographically arranged as a cross, he writes: "Now I am lost in the blinding/One. The sun roars at the prayer's end." 'Poem on his Birthday' (1951) refers to God as "Him/Who is the light of old". In 'Poem for October' (1951) he begins, "It was my thirtieth year to heaven", reflecting an awareness that everyday life takes place within a deeper context that may offer immortality. Thomas reflects the One in 'The force that through the green fuse drives the flower/Drives my green age". Another Romantic,Vernon Watkins, writes "O dark, interior flame".

Surrealism was behind the Neo-Romantic development. This was brought from France to England in an essay by Herbert Read and in the early work of David Gascoyne, whose *Journal* (1937-9) speaks of "men, convinced at last of the existence of a true Light", and of the Future of this Century burning "with an extraordinary, unseen and secret radiance".

Gascoyne's poems progressed from Surrealism to Hölderlin, whose poetry, Gascoyne asserted, "reaches into the future and the light". Gascoyne, like Hölderlin, became an inspired poet-seer whose poems were produced by "the Platonic doctrine of inspiration". His 'Metaphysical Poems' begin with a quotation from the Egyptian *Book of the Dead* about Osiris Ra, "the Increated Light", and in '*Lachrymae*' he writes: "Slow are the years of light and more immense/Than the imagination."

The poet who commits the "promethean crime" of glimpsing Paradise, of stealing the "Fire" (or Light), can be rewarded with madness, as was Hölderlin, and in Gascoyne's case "the strain which no human mind can stand" led him to an amphetamine-dependency which blocked his inspiration and the access of the Light. This Gascoyne told me when we had dinner together after the launch of my *Selected Poems, A Metaphysical's Way of Fire*, at which he had spoken. He told me, "I am an autodidact" (i.e. self-taught) and talked of the impact Surrealism had had upon him. The metaphysical aspect of the fundamental theme's quest for Reality can be found in Gascoyne's metaphysical works.

Kathleen Raine, who also spoke at the same launch along with Gascoyne, wrote in her poem 'The World', "It burns in the void." An admirer of the visionary work of Blake and Coleridge, she was interested in the Light, as I know from my conversations with her and letters she wrote me, but gave no indication that she had seen it herself as distinct from receiving symbols in her imagination. Raine wrote of archetypal myths and symbols, drawing on a metaphysic, but fell short in the diction of her poetry, which was not adequate to her metaphysic. Nevertheless, her work reflects the metaphysical aspect of the fundamental theme's quest for Reality.

John Heath-Stubbs was a friend of Sidney Keyes, who died before he was 21. Heath-Stubbs was at Oxford during the first years of the Second World War, and later taught in Egypt. He drew on classical mythology and confronted death in 'The Divided Ways' and 'Epitaph', which says he wrote "In a classical romantic manner which was pastoral". "Classical romantic" suggests he was a Universalist, and having met him and talked with him a few times I concur in this view. After he became blind, I tried to guide him in the right direction several times, grappling with his fierce independence. He wrote *Artorius*, an epic poem about the Muses in relation to King Arthur, and the metaphysical aspect of the fundamental theme is touched on in his work.

It may seem that because I have known Neo-Romantic poets (Gascoyne, Raine and Heath-Stubbs), my championing of Universalism is out of Neo-Romanticism. But that is not the case, for Universalism combines both "Romanticism" and "Classicism", as we have seen and as we shall see in greater detail in Part Two.

Empson and the Neoclassical Movement of the 1950s
In the 1950s there was a classical, or rather Neoclassical, reaction against Neo-Romanticism. It began with William Empson, who was held up in an article by John Wain in *Penguin New Writing* (1950), along with Graves, as being a model for poets to follow. Empson was one of my predecessors as a Professor of English Literature in Japan. I was told in early 1964 that the university he taught at from 1931 to 1934[2], Tokyo Bunrika Daigaku (Tokyo University of Literature and Science), had been renamed Kyoikudaigaku (Tokyo University of Education), my main University, and that a particular room I taught in was a room where Empson had taught.

Empson was first known for his critical works, *Seven Types of Ambiguity* (1930) and *Some Versions of Pastoral* 1935). He brought out *Poems* (1935) and *The Gathering Storm* (1940), a title Churchill later used for one of the six volumes of his *The Second World War*. Ironically his poem 'Sonnet' refers to "the loony hooters", warmongers, and seems to target Churchill. Empson's poems were influenced by Donne, whose example he followed in referring to the science and mathematics of the day and in setting his readers puzzles as in *Bacchus* (an example of his "clotted poetry"), where puns allow the poem to be read in three different ways as being about: the myth of Bacchus; fermentation; and history as progressive stages of drunkenness. The trouble is, the poem became the puns, and the original aim of the poem disappeared.

Like Dryden, Empson wrote with conversational exactness and compressed restraint, and he wrote with more pessimism than the 1930s poets. Despair, helplessness, torment can be felt in many of his poems, and he wanly urges in 'This Last Pain', "And learn a style from a despair." In 'Aubade', Empson, in bed with a Japanese lady in Tokyo, is woken by an earthquake that fills him with fear but which symbolizes the earthquake of wars, depression and revolutions that then threatened society.

Empson's tutor at Cambridge, I.A. Richards, held that poetry, unlike science, makes pseudo-statements that do not take us to scientific "truth" but enable us to integrate our inner lives. In 'The Last Pain' Empson takes Richards' premise that all poetic and religious language is pseudo-statement and asks if the poet's "large dreams" can inspire us in our living, and decides they can.

Empson was influenced by life-renouncing Buddhism, which he had encountered in Japan and China, and was against the Christian concept of Hell and damnation that brought eternal pain. The fundamental theme of a search for Reality can be found in Empson's work, but the Reality is more an imaginative creativeness than a mystical union with the One. I met Empson in 1960, a genial, urbane man sitting alongside his acolyte, Christopher Ricks, and I was struck by the Buddha-like serenity and calm of his demeanour.

Empson's classical lead was taken up by the Movement poets of the mid-1950s, of which Wain was one. Kingsley Amis, Philip Larkin, Thom Gunn and Donald Davie contributed to the new approach. They shared a new attitude to the audience, most of them being connected with universities. "The Movement" was a label given to the new poets by the *Spectator* in 1954. Three anthologies brought them together. The first was *Poets of the 1950s* edited by D.J. Enright in Japan (1955). The second was Robert Conquest's anthology, *New Lines* (1956), which gave them a platform in the West. The third was *The New Poetry*, a Penguin edited by A. Alvarez (1962).

The main Movement poets made manifesto-like statements. Kingsley Amis wrote in Conquest's anthology in 1955:

"Nobody wants any more poems on the grander themes for a few years, but at the same time nobody wants any more poems about philosophers or paintings or novelists or art galleries or mythology or foreign cities or other poems. At least I hope nobody wants them."

In 'Against Romanticism' he complained regarding Neo-Romanticism, "Over all, a grand meaning fills the scene." In 'A Bookshop Idyll' he asks, "Should poets bicycle-pump the human heart/Or squash it flat?" Larkin wrote in Conquest's anthology, "[I] have no belief in 'tradition'

269

or a common myth-kitty or casual allusions in poems to other poems or poets." He saw the aim of poetry parochially, as to "keep the child from its television set and the old man from his pub". Davie wrote in 'Remembering the Thirties': "A neutral tone is nowadays preferred." The reaction against the Neo-Romanticism of the 1940s meant that if poetry now became a puzzle of puns and a minor rather than a major art, that was a price worth paying to deliver the new mood, which demanded no grander themes and everything on a smaller scale.

The Movement tone was self-controlled. Like the American Yvor Winters, the Movement poets believed that a poem should be expository and anti-sentimental, and that it should present a situation and offer a judgement with which the reader was invited to agree or disagree. However, they came across as pedantic and as avoiding emotion. They grumbled at the prospect of social change, as did Larkin, whose work has been described (by Christopher Logue) as "genteel bellyaching". The Movement poets' provincialism lost contact with the European values championed in the essays of T.S. Eliot. They were reacting against the unnecessary obscurity of the Modernists and the sloppy Bohemianism of the Neo-Romantics. They chose traditional forms and subjected their feelings to a moral discipline. They did in poetry what the analytical philosophers did in philosophy. The trouble is, the universe was left out of analytical philosophy, and the Movement left a comparable hole where the grander themes had once been, which Universalism now seeks to fill and occupy.

Almost immediately, Cambridge poets who came to be known as The Group, who included Ted Hughes, Peter Redgrove, Edward Lucie-Smith and George MacBeth, reacted against the Movement and wrote poems of emotional violence. If the Movement was genteel, The Group were anti-genteel and wrote about the violent deaths of animals and confronted the horrors of Auschwitz and Hiroshima. I had dinner with George MacBeth after a reception in Turret's Bookshop in Kensington, and was struck by his inclination to pose and his insistence on skipping late at night down Dean Street, Soho. I corresponded with Ted Hughes for much of the last decade of his life, and found him full of probing truth and questing wisdom.

The Group had swung some way back from Neoclassicism towards Neo-Romanticism, into the in-between central ground that

Universalism occupies when it combines "Romanticism" and "Classicism", Neo-Romanticism and Neoclassicism.

The English Angry Young Men of the 1950s
1956, the year of the Movement, was also the year the term "Angry Young Men" burst upon the English literary scene.

Lower-class provincial settings and rejection of "highbrow" attitudes can be found in works by Arnold Bennett and H.G. Wells. William Cooper's *Scenes from Provincial Life* (1950) focused on the provinces, and provincialism was taken up in two novels by John Wain and Kingsley Amis. Both novels were about opting out of middle-class situations and rejecting highbrow culture as "phoney", and though there is no trace of the quest for Reality, both exposed vices – snobbery and pretentiousness – in relation to implied virtue.

In Wain's *Hurry on Down* (1953) the vice is the snobbery encountered by Charles Lumley when he leaves university and rejects his lower-middle-class origin by working in odd jobs, a "come-down".

In Amis's *Lucky Jim* (1954), the vice is Professor Welch's cultural snobbery and pretentiousness in his musical evenings and paper on Merrie England.

Amis adopted philistine and subversive, anti-Establishment attitudes, and these were replicated in his friend Philip Larkin's poems in *The Less Deceived* (1955). Larkin trumpeted a dislike of Mozart and "a mild xenophobia", perhaps echoes of rejecting German culture during the war.

Other novels reflected the new defiance. Iris Murdoch's *Under the Net* (1954) also presented a hero who tried to escape his environment and break down conventions. (See p.276 for her later novels.) The underrated Desmond Stewart's *The Unsuitable Englishman* (1954) was set in Medea (Iraq) and followed an Englishman who works as a chauffeur for an Arab in semi-colonial Iraq. It exposed vices in relation to implied virtue, the main vices being the snobbishness, hypocrisy and deceit of Hugh Flodden of the British Foreign Office.

In May 1956 the working-class Jimmy Porter in John Osborne's play *Look Back in Anger* sneered at the gentleman's code and respect for one's neighbour, and attacked the Christian basis of Western civilization and the political Establishment. Jimmy seems to be a revolutionary, but he is really just turning the stock responses of magazines on their head and turning them into targets. Osborne does not pursue the quest for Reality but he exposes vices in relation to implied virtue.

In *Look Back in Anger*, the vice is the middle-class snobbery of Alison's parents, who look down on the working-class Jimmy.

In *Look Back in Anger* Osborne reflects Tennessee Williams' attitude to women, and Shaw's soliloquies, and his later plays owe much to Brecht, for example *Luther*, the construction of which recalls Brecht's *The Life of Galileo*. Osborne's play led to the journalistic label "Angry Young Man" being applied to the new writers. The term was probably taken from the Irish Leslie Paul's *Angry Young Man* (1951) and was first used as a catch-phrase for the new writers by the press officer of the Royal Court theatre in 1956 to promote Osborne's play. In *Luther* it is likely that Osborne was attempting a self-portrait of a revolutionary. After nine more plays Osborne ironically ended up longing for the past which his own anger had contributed to sweeping away.

Other works followed which focused on working-class heroes. John Braine's *Room at the Top* (1957) is about working-class Joe Lampton's marriage into the middle class and his social climb. The novel exposes vices in relation to an implied virtue.

In *Room at the Top*, the vice is Joe Lampton's ruthlessness in moving from one woman to another to advance his social climb.

For some years during the 1950s Alan Sillitoe had lived in Majorca, where Robert Graves encouraged him to write a novel set in Nottingham (D.H. Lawrence territory). Sillitoe's *Saturday Night and Sunday Morning* (1958) lets the English proletariat into English literature for the first time and shows the working class to have a deadening life of repetitive work and escapism at the weekends.

In *Saturday Night and Sunday Morning*, the vice is Arthur Seaton's defiant, amoral hedonism as a rogue male who is having simultaneous affairs with two married sisters ("all I'm out for is a bloody good time") during his weekend leisure hours, funded by overtime at his bicycle factory.

In Sillitoe's *The Loneliness of the Long Distance Runner* (1959), the vice is the borstal boys' defiance of the Governor in refusing to win the race they both want to win.

Arnold Wesker's trilogy brought in "kitchen-sink drama". It is about the Jewish East-London Communist Kahn family over two decades: Sarah, the matriarch, and her children Ada and Ronnie. All three plays expose vices in relation to implied virtue.

In *Chicken Soup with Barley* (1958), the vice is Ronnie's disillusionment about brotherly love. (When I met Wesker at Oxford's Randolph Hotel in 1959 he was asked "What is socialism?" and he replied, "Brotherhood", to tumultuous applause from those gathered round him.)

In *Roots* (1959), the vice is Ronnie's fiancée Beatie's inability to express herself without quoting Ronnie's idealist, socialist ideas second-hand, until she begins speaking for herself after being dumped by Ronnie.

In *I'm Talking about Jerusalem* (1961), the vice is the unrealistic and naïve belief of Ada and Dave that Dave can be a craftsman-carpenter, until economic and social reality end their dream.

Other dramatists who appeared in this new wave which centred round the Royal Court theatre included John Arden, Shelagh Delaney, Brendan Behan, Eugene Ionesco, Samuel Beckett and Harold Pinter. I will dwell on the last two.

Samuel Beckett, who was brought up as an Irish Protestant, acted as Joyce's amanuensis in 1928-29, taking down passages of *Finnegans Wake* Joyce dictated when his sight was failing[3] and assisting with the translation into French of the 'Anna Livia Plurabelle' section of *Finnegans Wake*. Living in Paris, he had written in French. *Waiting for Godot* was written in 1948-49 and put on in France in French in 1953 and in London in English in 1955.

> In *Waiting for Godot* two tramps wait for a local landlord, Godot, who never appears and may not exist. The title may be an echo of Clifford Odets' one-act play, *Waiting for Lefty* (1935), Lefty being a trades-union organiser who does not appear because he has been murdered. There are echoes of Kafka in Beckett's work, and the play is probably an Expressionist allegory for waiting in the world for God, and God's absence.

In 1958 I met Patrick Magee, an actor in the play, who told me that Beckett had told him that behind "Godot" were the French words "goder" ("puckered, wrinkled") and "godiche" ("clumsy, oafish"), that "Godot" suggests that God is a wrinkled oaf. (Beckett is alleged to have told Roger Blin, who acted in and directed the first French production of the play, that "Godot" came from French slang for "boot", *"godillot"* or *"godasse"*, as boots are very important to tramps.)

Beckett's work was immediately seen as being within the tradition of the "Theatre of the Absurd" (see p.288). Beckett's tramps are allegorically on a quest for Reality, and the metaphysical aspect of the fundamental theme is present in all Beckett's works although the Reality is not found.

In a similar but very different vein, and not as interesting, the Jewish Harold Pinter wrote plays in which simple-minded working-class people menace each other. In Pinter's plays there is no quest for Reality, but vices are exposed in relation to implied virtue.

> In *The Birthday Party* (1958), in which a pianist is threatened by two intruders who accuse him, Kafka-like, of unexplained crimes, the vice is the two intruders' threatening behaviour, which terrifies Stanley.

> In *The Caretaker* (1960), in which two brothers take in a tramp, tell him he is now their caretaker and menace him, the vice is Mick's bullying menace, his jeering at Davies, the caretaker, which frightens him, and

his smashing of the Buddha before he and Aston evict Davies.

Within the cluster of novels, poems and plays of the new writers, Colin Wilson's prose *The Outsider* (1956) offered a rebellious generation a host of socially alienated rebels from the past. He had researched the book in the British Museum (while camping on Hampstead Heath), and was encouraged there by the deputy superintendent of the Reading Room, novelist Angus Wilson. *The Outsider* came out in the same week as *Look Back in Anger*, and Wilson was immediately labelled an "Angry Young Man". *Religion and the Rebel* (1957) gave the unrest of social alienation a metaphysical context.

Colin Wilson's philosophical and cultural works are all on the metaphysical aspect of the fundamental theme of the quest for Reality, and the writers he discussed in *The Outsider* were all on such a quest. His friend Stuart Holroyd's *Emergence from Chaos* (1957) inspired the writing of *The Outsider*. I had dinner with Holroyd in 1958, and can vouch for their immersion in the metaphysical aspect of the fundamental theme, which Wilson also expressed in some of his creative works. However, Wilson stopped short of confronting the Light, which I know from my discussions with him after 1960 he had not experienced by the mid-1990s.

Later English Novels
The Alexandria Quartet (1957-60) of Lawrence Durrell is about the quest for Reality.

The four novels, *Justine, Balthazar, Mountolive* and *Clea*, are set in Alexandria just before the Second World War, the first three novels on the same events seen from different angles in space and the last one going forward in time. The narrator, L.G. Darley, is a novelist as is the British intelligence agent Pursewarden, a genius who utters many nuggets of wisdom. Both of them are on a quest for Reality in the cultures of the ancient world in which Darley's mistress Melissa is Greek, and the Jewish Justine, the destructive wife of Coptic-Egyptian Nessim, becomes his mistress. These characters, together with the British Ambassador, Mountolive, and the artist Clea, are interconnected in political and sexual intrigue in a world of palaces and millionaires, brothels and whores.

The Alexandria Quartet is a Universalist work, feeding off different Middle-Eastern cultures and seeking the truth from different angles as the same events are viewed from differently positioned consciousnesses.

Iris Murdoch worked as an academic philosopher. She used her novels to work out philosophical problems in concrete situations, combining realistic naturalism with romantic fantasy, symbolism and myths. She offers a world constructed imaginatively from her thinking about life rather than a world she has observed in the Aristotelian manner, and the multiple permutations of characters' relationships may suggest cerebral rather than realistically observed pairings. Such artistic considerations aside, her works show a preoccupation with the nature of good and evil, virtue, the religious life (*The Bell*, 1958), the sacred and taboo (*A Severed Head*, 1961), sexuality and determinism. She has written on existential freedom in *Sartre*, and on metaphysics in *Metaphysics and Morals*, and I know from correspondence with her that she was extremely interested in the metaphysical Light. Her themes in her novels are on the quest for Reality, the soul and the possibility of immortality, even though the surface dialogue may not suggest this.

William Golding, a Royal Navy lieutenant commanding a rocket ship during the war, wrote fables about individuals' struggle with the human condition from a Christian metaphysical position. All his novels are about the quest for Reality and a human condition which he approaches from a human nature tainted by original sin.

Lord of the Flies (1954) shows how children who have crash-landed on a desert island and are without self-control revert to innate cruelty and domination, barbarism and superstition, and suggests that as a result of original sin the Devil (the "Lord" of the title) is present within their allegedly innocent hearts.

The Inheritors (1955) is about *homo sapiens'* brutal extermination of his Cro-Magnon ancestors.

Pincher Martin (1956) is apparently about a man lost overboard who clings for hours to a rock, feeling guilty, but at the end of the book we learn that he was drowned almost instantly, that it is not clear where his dying ends and his after-life begins, and that the rock symbolized his clinging to his selfish desires which prevented him from being open to God's mercy, that he may be a blasphemer condemned to eternal life. In other words, we discover that the whole book was a metaphor, and perhaps feel cheated. Golding said, "Pincher is simply in Hell."

Free Fall (1959) is about man's fallen condition, original sin and grace. It begins with the question "When did I lose my freedom?"

The Spire (1964) is about the building of Salisbury Cathedral in the Middle Ages, about the Dean, a man of faith, building a lasting steeple, which is a symbol of his pride and is doomed.

These and his last novels all touch on the metaphysical aspect of the fundamental theme.

Muriel Spark, a devout Catholic, wrote about the eternal significance of all human choices. Her works are on the metaphysical aspect of the fundamental theme's quest for Reality.

In *Memento Mori* (1959), old people receive anonymous telephone messages, "Remember, you must die." God, through Death, is asking them to improve their lives to prepare their souls for judgement, but they cling to their petty vices.

In *The Prime of Miss Jean Brodie* (1961), an egotistical teacher looks after her set of innocent sixteen-year-olds, one of whom has an affair with the Catholic art master, becomes a Catholic and later a nun, and arranges Miss Brodie's dismissal for being interested in Fascism. Her vice, or rather sin, is her betrayal, but she later writes the religious 'The Transfiguration of the Commonplace'.

In these works the quest for Reality is given a Catholic slant.

Frank Tuohy, who had Irish roots, took a social view of his characters and had a heightened sense of place. He was in the

Maupassant – some claim Chekhov – tradition, and his stories were (in his own words) "a painful bite down on the rotten tooth of fact". Though he was better known as a short-story writer, he wrote novels set in Brazil and Poland. They explored social reality rather than conveyed the quest for Reality, a subject I often discussed with him between 1964 and just before his death in 1999, and they exposed vices in relation to implied order.

> In *The Ice Saints* (1964), in which a young English girl visits her elder sister who is married to a professor in People's Poland, the vice is the duplicity of a Pole with whom she falls in love during the post-Stalinist thaw in the Communist state.

He wrote no more novels after that, destroying work that did not reach his high standards. I knew him very well indeed – he and I went to China together in 1966 and returned with news of the Cultural Revolution, and we stayed in touch – and I was aware of the beginning of his writer's block in Japan in the mid-1960s when he would "go shopping" rather than try to write. In Tuohy's scaled-down output, the quest for Reality was replaced by social reality.

History

In his massive 12-volume *A Study of History* (1934-61), the British historian Arnold Toynbee presented the pattern of world history in terms of civilizations. He changed his mind about the number of civilizations, from 21 in 1934 to 23 in 1954 and 30 in 1961, and criticisms can be made of his choice of civilizations and of the rigid timing of phases within his pattern. But his work was a Universalist attempt to understand the history of all humankind as a unified whole which includes the quest for Reality, and his focus on the unity of humankind deserves respect. My own study of 25 civilizations,[4] though very different in many ways, is indebted to his Universalist concept.

One of the most significant Universalists of the 20th century was Winston Churchill, the statesman who resisted Hitler during the Battle of Britain, coined the term "Iron Curtain" and called for a United States of Europe. His many-sided activities included his political orations, four works of history before his *History of the Second World War* (for which he was awarded the Nobel Prize for Literature) and his *History of the English-Speaking Peoples*, two autobiographies, two biographies and his many paintings. Churchill was aware of the oneness of humankind and of the similarities in cultures and civilizations.

American Literature
Post-Modernist American literature touched on the fundamental theme.

The Novel
John Steinbeck wrote about landless rural workers during the Great Depression of the 1930s. In his novels the quest for Reality became a battle with social reality. He exposed vices.

In *Of Mice and Men* (1937), which is about two itinerant farm labourers, one of whom is a giant with the mind of a child, the vice is the weak-minded giant's petting of the landowner's wife, which results in his being shot.

In *The Grapes of Wrath* (1939), which is about a farming family's migration from the dust bowl to the "promised land" of California, the vice is the greed of those (such as the bank representatives) responsible for the Great Depression and its consequences. (Steinbeck wrote: "I want to put a tag of shame on the greedy bastards who are responsible for this.")

In *East of Eden* (1952), the vice is the unscrupulous egotism of Cathy, who shoots her husband Adam and returns to prostitution.

The American expatriate Henry Miller, a friend of Durrell's, mingled metaphysical speculation with sexually explicit passages. His *Tropic of Cancer* (1934) and *Tropic of Capricorn* (1939) both touch on a quest for Reality amid all the sexual variety.

Robert Penn Warren is best known for *All the King's Men* (1946), which exposes corruption. In this work, the vice is the corruption of Southern politician Willie Stark.

After the Second World War a multiplicity of American novelists appeared. They had little in common, and seemed more secular and less concerned with the metaphysical aspect of the fundamental theme: Vladimir Nabokov (of Russian extraction but a US citizen since 1945); Mary McCarthy; Bernard Malamud; William Burroughs (a drug addict); Saul Bellow; Norman Mailer; Joseph Heller; Truman Capote; Philip Roth; John Updike; and many others. The quest for Reality was by and large replaced by social reality in their works, and many dealt with modern man in urban America. They all exposed vices. Like the barons under the English Anarchy, they all stood apart from each other, writing of American values as they saw them in relation to their own particular ethnic groups.

Drama

The American dramatist Eugene O'Neill was influenced by Ibsen and Strindberg. His early work was experimental and Expressionist, and he adapted Aeschylus's *Oresteia* to the years following the American Civil War in presenting a New-England family that destroys itself. In his plays the quest for Reality is a quest for social reality, and he exposes the vice of illusion.

In *The Iceman Cometh* (1946), the vice is the illusions (or "pipe dreams") of down-and-out alcoholics in Harry Hope's Bowery saloon, who are encouraged by the salesman Hickey. (The play draws on Gorky's play *The Lower Depths*, which presents society's dregs living in a doss-house and nourishing their illusions to make their wretchedness endurable.)

In the semi-autobiographical *Long Day's Journey into Night* (1956), the vice is the illusions of the drug-addicted Mary Tyrone and her alcoholic son Jamie, observed by the consumptive Edmund (O'Neill).

In *A Moon for the Misbegotten* (1947), the vice is the illusion of the tormented and dissolute James Tyrone that leads to his being forced to leave his farm by Hogan.

Tennessee Williams wrote plays of sexual frustration that exposed vices in relation to implied virtue.

In *The Glass Menagerie* (1944), the frustration is of Laura's mother, an ex-Southern belle, and the vice is the deceit of the gentleman caller, Jim, in not revealing that he is engaged.

In *A Streetcar Named Desire* (1947), the frustration is of Blanche Dubois, and the vice is the brutality of Stanley Kowalski.

In *The Rose Tattoo* (1950), the frustration is of Serafina, an Italian-American woman who is widowed, and the vice is her husband Rosario's deceit in having a long-term affair with Estelle, which has consequences for the next generation.

In *Cat on a Hot Tin Roof* (1955), the frustration is of Maggie, and the vice is the alcoholism of her husband Brick.

There is no quest for Reality, just frustrated women and despairing, dissolute men who have lapsed from virtue.

Arthur Miller, who was influenced by Ibsen and Greek tragedy, wrote plays about contemporary America. There is no quest for Reality, but his plays exposed vices in relation to implied virtue.

In *All My Sons* (1947), which is about a manufacturer of defective aeroplane parts, the vice is Joe's ruthlessness in shipping defective aircraft cylinder heads during the Second World War, which resulted in the death of 21 pilots.

In *The Death of a Salesman* (1949), the vice is Willie's attachment to money and the false social values of the American Dream, which cause him to kill himself in such a way that his two sons will benefit from his life insurance policy.

In *The Crucible* (1952), in which the 1692 Salem witchcraft trials provide a parallel for the 1950s McCarthyist, anti-Communist show trials in the US, the vice is bigotry.

In *A View from the Bridge* (1955), a tragedy of family honour and revenge with the lawyer Alfieri acting as a Greek chorus, the vice is

Eddie's betrayal of his wife's two cousins, as a result of which one of them kills him.

Poetry

The quest for Reality can be found in American poetry.

Robert Lowell, who attached himself to Ezra Pound after writing to him on 2 May 1936 ("I want to come to Italy and work under you and forge my way into reality"),[5] wrote of his ancient New-England stock and his marital anguish in complex imagery that satisfied the New Criticism. He suffered from spells of manic illness and drank heavily, but the quest for Reality can be found in bits of his verse.

John Berryman wrote of the first New-England poet, and the first poet of the New World, Anne Bradstreet. The quest for Reality can be found in his *77 Dream Songs*. He committed suicide like his father. Theodore Roethke, whose father was a horticulturalist, wrote of vegetable growth and decay. There are hints of a quest for Reality in his work. William Carlos Williams, a friend of Ezra Pound in his student days, echoed Modernism in his experimental forms. He wrote about "the secret gardens of the self" and mystically saw that "man is himself a city".

The Beat poets sought Reality through drugs: Allen Ginsberg in *Howl* and other long poems, Gregory Corso, Gary Snyder and Lawrence Ferlinghetti. They sought Beatitude through improvisation and drew on the perceptions of Zen Buddhism. The English poet Michael Horovitz, a devotee of Blake with whom I have had conversations, followed in their footsteps. I have always made it clear that the Light is of course best approached without drugs.

Jack Kerouac's prose *Dharma Bums* (1959) – "dharma" suggests the Buddhist teachings and truth – is about the quest for Beatitude, or Reality, as restless wanderers used drugs to reach the enlightened state of the Buddha. The book spoke for the Beat Generation, but I stress again, the Mystic Way of the tradition was drug-free, and the quest for Reality originally had nothing to do with drugs.

French Literature

Post-1930s French literature looked back to the Graeco-Roman classics and dwelt on individual freedom in a development of Existentialism that was in part a reaction to the Nazi occupation of France during the Second World War.

Mythologists

Before and during the Second World War French writers reinterpreted the Greek myths in plays: André Gide's *Philoctetes* (1899), *Le Prométhée mal enchaîné* (1899, *Prometheus Illbound*, or *Misbound*, 1953, also referred to as *Prometheus Drops his Chains*), *Le Roi Candaule* (1901), *Oedipus* (1931) and *Theseus* (1946); Jean Cocteau's *Antigone* (1922), *Orpheus* (1926) and *The Infernal Machine* (1934); Jean Giraudoux's *Amphitryon 38* (1929), *The Trojan War Will Not Take Place* (1935) and *Electra* (1937); Jean Anouilh's *Eurydice* (1941), *Antigone* (1942) and *Medea* (1946); and Jean-Paul Sartre's *Les Mouches,* or *The Flies* (1943).

The Greek myths they reinterpreted all reflected the quest for Reality, and therefore the quest lurks behind their works even though their reinterpretations are different from the original myths. For example, Sartre's flies presented a parallel for the Nazi occupation, the plague of flies being German troops, rather than merely presenting the legend of Orestes. The same is true of Anouilh, who was also dealing with the problem of resistance to an unjust, all-powerful authority. These works present the Greek myths in modern terms.

In Anouilh's *Eurydice*, Orpheus is a café violinist who meets a touring actress in a railway station, falls in love with her, but loses her when he persistently questions her about her previous lovers. She is returned to him by Monsieur Henri on the condition that he will not look at her face until morning. Henri's relevance to the plot is solely because he is in the position of Pluto, the ruler of Hades.

In these plays the underlying plot of a Greek myth controls the action just as the myth of the *Odyssey* controls the action in Joyce's *Ulysses*.

It can be argued that in literature there has been an over-dependence on myth. *The Oxford Guide to Classical Mythology in the Arts, 1300-1990s* lists over 30,000 works of art in which authors and poets have used specific Greek myths since 1300, dramatically underlining how each age reinterprets the Greek myths.

Existentialists

Existentialism, a group of loosely associated philosophers, put the individual at the centre of the universe and denied obstructions such as human nature (Sartre's "existence before essence"). It held that each man chooses or makes himself, and his freedom makes his life authentic. Humanist Existentialists such as Sartre quested for the reality of the individual's existence and freedom of choice, not for the Reality of the One behind the universe.

The French Jean-Paul Sartre, one of the later Existentialists, is the best known. In his *L'Être et le néant* (*Being and Nothingness*, 1943), Sartre points to human dread before "Nothingness and awareness of freedom during the experience of Being", by which he means "existence". (In my philosophy and terminology, Being is infinite timeless Reality while the phenomena of the finite universe make up Existence. My meaning of "Being" is very different from Sartre's.) In this work of philosophy Sartre controversially asserts that man is a "useless passion" ("*passion inutile*").

In Sartre's philosophy the universe is gratuitous. In his *La Nausée* (*Nausea*, 1938), M. Roquentin looks at a tree root in a park and feels disgust, nausea at the gratuitousness of existence. He does not see the One, but gratuitousness. His quest for Reality in his philosophy is a quest to feel his own existence, which can lead to nausea, self-disgust. The freedom of one's existence has replaced Reality. In his trilogy *Les Chemins de la liberté* (*The Roads to Freedom*, 1947-50) – *The Age of Reason, The Reprieve* and *Iron in the Soul* – Sartre's Mathieu discovers his freedom when fighting the Nazi occupation. His play, *Huis clos* (*No Exit*, 1945), is set in Hell, where the newly-dead grasp that "Hell is other people". Sartre's work touches on the metaphysical aspect of the fundamental theme but the quest for Reality has become a quest to experience one's individual existence and freedom. Sartre had a Univeralist sensibility but stopped short of developing a Universalist philosophy.

The French-Algerian Albert Camus, the most recent Existentialist, brought an absurdist slant to Existentialist literature. In his philosophy, *Le Mythe de Sisyphe* (*The Myth of Sisyphus*, 1942) he presents an indifferent universe in which life is absurd – purposeless, incomprehensible and bewildering. His novel *L'Étranger* (*The Outsider*, 1942), is about the motiveless shooting of an Arab on an Algerian beach by an alienated and unfeeling hero, Meursault, who is guillotined for his crime. Meursault does not quest for Reality. Rather, he commits an absurd act in an absurd universe, to establish the absurd nature of the human condition. (In his focus on the human condition Camus is close to Dostoevsky.) His play *Caligula* (1944) examines dictatorship from an existential point of view. His last two novels, *La Peste* (*The Plague*, 1947), with its doctor driven to save human lives in a meaningless world, and *La Chute* (*The Fall*, 1957), with its question "Who is laughing at man?", continue the absurd theme.

His history, *L'Homme révolté* (*The Rebel*, 1951), deals with the quest for social reality and justice from a moderate rather than Marxist position in relation to revolutionary intellectuals' attempts to better the human lot. A philosopher, historian, literary novelist and dramatist, Camus had a Universalist sensibility that operated in several disciplines, and in his work the quest for Reality has become a quest for social justice and an exposure of an absurd universe and his philosophy fell short of the Universalist vision of infinite order.

Religious Existentialists such as Gabriel Marcel, took up Kierkegaard's existential leap into faith. In works from *Être et Avoir* (*Being and Having*, 1935) to *Le Mystère de l'Être* (*The Mystery of Being*, 1951) Marcel followed Kierkegaard and Jaspers in rejecting analysis. He held that Being cannot be analyzed but is an experience to be lived and explored. To Marcel Being is Reality, the experience of God.

Sartre, Camus and Marcel all looked back to the German Existentialism of Martin Heidegger and Karl Jaspers. Heidegger studied phenomenology under Edmund Husserl and enquired into the meaning of Being in *Sein und Zeit* (*Being and Time*, 1927). He insisted that the philosopher reveals the One by using a poet's intuition, then rationalises it so that the One can be understood by the reason. In *Philosophie* (1932) Jaspers seeks to reveal "Being": man's direct concern with his own existence.

Heidegger and Marcel quested for the Reality of the One in some of their work, whereas Sartre, Camus and Jaspers quested for individual freedom in a meaningless, absurd universe. These three did not know the Light, and presented the rational, social ego's quest for freedom, which, if unbridled, leads to murder, rather than the soul's "esemplastic" perception of the One. They did, nevertheless, raise fundamental questions about the meaning of life which are relevant to the metaphysical aspect of the fundamental theme.

European Anti-Literature

A new European anti-literature undermined the literary conventions, adding to the anarchy of the 20th-century literary scene.

The Anti-Novel

The new novel, *nouveau roman* or anti-novel, undermined story, plot, character, form, style, meaning, chronology and analysis of thought and feeling. It undermined the traditional hero, replacing him with the anti-hero who does not act, to whom things happen.

It may have begun with Samuel Beckett's *Molloy* and *Malone Dies* (1951), though Nathalie Sarraute's *Tropismes* had appeared in 1938. Identity was undermined and withheld in the German-Swiss Max Frisch's *Stiller* (1954, *I'm Not Stiller*, 1958), in which the quest for Reality became a quest for identity as Herr Stiller denies his identity in a series of notebooks. Facts were withheld in Alain Robbe-Grillet's objective novels *Le Voyeur* (1955) and *La Jaloisie* (1957). I heard him speak in Oxford in 1961, and attempt to explain why he described objects in such detail, why objectivity was desirable. His technique-first approach did not throw light on the quest for Reality, and, indeed obfuscated social reality. Chronology is muddled up in Claude Simon's *Routes des Flandres* (*The Flanders Road*, 1960). In film, its counterpoint was the obsessive *L'Année dernière à Marienbad* (1961), in which something has happened in Marienbad but the confused narrative makes it hard to understand what.

The "chaosisation" of the novel reached a climax with B.S. Johnson, one of whose "false-directional" novels was a bundle of chapters that could be shuffled up by the reader and read in any order. I met him in 1963 just before he died and asked him what his main ambition was, and he said, "I am concerned to push the technical experiments in the novel to their upmost."

And this was the problem with the new novel. It was technique-first.

The quest for Reality had been replaced by technical experiment, and the content was arid and unrewarding.

The Anti-Play
An equivalent "anti-theatre", or Theatre of the Absurd, came into being.

The Italian Luigi Pirandello, drawing on his wife's insanity, wrote of the incoherence of personality, the relationship between self and persona, actor and character. He dwelt on the lack of communication between people and the boundaries between the sane and the insane, and challenged naturalism.

In his *Six Characters in Search of an Author* (1921), Pirandello destroyed dramatic structure and created a new one in which characters seek an author. Again, the quest for Reality has been replaced by a technique-first quest to understand personality.

The Spanish Andalusian Garcia Lorca wrote surreal poetic dramas for peasant audiences before he was murdered by pro-Franco Nationalists during the Spanish Civil War.

In *Blood Wedding* (1933), a bride flees with her lover on her wedding day, and her husband and lover kill each other. They are trapped in a conflict between their primitive passions and civilization's code of honour, and as in Hardy's novels are unable to avert their fate. The doomed pair violate an implied virtue, their vice being infatuation.

The German Bertolt Brecht sought to alienate audiences so that they did not feel sympathy with his characters, but rather made moral judgements on their deeds. His notion of epic theatre replaced Aristotle's unities with a series of loosely-connected episodes. There were no dramatic climaxes, and songs commented, chorus-like, on the action.

In *The Life of Galileo* (1937-9), Galileo's quest for Reality is based on scientific reason and his new telescope, as opposed to faith. In this work the quest for Reality has been replaced by a secular scientific proof, acknowledgement that the stars move across the night sky.

The "anti-play" blended with the Theatre of the Absurd in the work of Eugene Ionesco around 1950. Ionesco caricatured the real and emphasized the absurdity of existence. He surreally exteriorised fantasies as in *The Lesson*, in which a slow learner is stabbed by a teacher teaching the word "knife". Beckett's *Waiting for Godot* (see p.274) was in this tradition.

The Anti-Film
It is worth pointing out that the Swedish film director Ingmar Bergman's intense films undermine the traditional story and contain heroes to whom things happen. They nevertheless touch on the metaphysical aspect of the fundamental theme. The heroes of his two main films travel, a reflection of their quest, and Death is a character in one, and dead parents appear as characters in the other. Bergman was brought up in the religious home of a Lutheran pastor and when a boy was haunted by the art he saw in rustic Swedish churches. He brought his father's faith and Christian imagery into *The Seventh Seal*.

In *The Seventh Seal* (1956), which is set in the Middle Ages during the plague, Antonius, a knight returning from a crusade with his squire, quests for God as he journeys back to his castle and his wife past medieval scenes: the plague, a painting of a Dance of Death in a church, flagellation and witch-burning. Death had appeared where he landed with a chessboard, inviting him to make a move. Every so often throughout the film Death appears inviting another move. Death wins the game the morning after he has reached his castle and wife, and leads him off to the next world in a final *Totendanz* or Dance of Death. Antonius is a hero to whom things happen, and he is on the receiving end of Death's game of chess.

In *Wild Strawberries* (1957) Professor Borg, travelling to receive an honorary degree, quests for Reality as he dreams of seeing his own funeral and, in a later dream, his dead wife and her lover. He remembers going with his wife to a place where wild strawberries grow and sees his dead father and mother waving to him from the other side of the bay.

Borg is a hero to whom dreams and memories happen, and he is on the receiving end of the people he meets and his honorary degree.

In both films there is a questioning of the meaning of life in the face of death, and the Reality is not achieved. Bergman stopped short of a Universalist outlook.

Russian Literature

In Russia, Boris Pasternak, a critic of Stalin, wrote *Doctor Zhivago* (1957) about the fortunes of a doctor during the Soviet Revolution.

Zhivago is on a quest for Reality, judging by his poems at the back of the novel, but it is his immediate historical situation and social reality that predominates. Pasternak presents vices in relation to an implied virtue, and the main vice is Strelnikov's genocidal liquidation of villages for Party reasons.

The Russian novelist Aleksandr Solzhenitsyn stood against Communism, and like Dostoevsky, championed Christianity. He was imprisoned under Stalin, and his *One Day in the Life of Ivan Denisovitch* (1962) was about survival in his labour camp, where he developed stomach cancer. His *Cancer Ward* (1968) reflected his ordeal.

In *The First Circle* (1969) Solzhenitsyn presents a vice in relation to an implied virtue: the co-operation of the scientists working in the prison research institute with the tyrannical prison system. They could have made a moral choice to refuse to co-operate and be sent back to a labour camp.

Solzhenitsyn's *The Gulag Archipelago* (1973-5) exposed the history and geography of the Soviet labour camps. As a result he was deported to West Germany in 1974 and settled in the US. There he began *August 1914* (1971) and a series of novels opposing the Communist view of Soviet society. In Solzhenitsyn's works, the quest for Reality has been replaced by the quest for an alternative to Soviet tyranny: a benevolent authoritarian regime drawing on traditional Russian Christian values.

In his essay *Warning to the Western World* (1976) he warned the West that it could be swamped by Soviet expansionism. With hindsight this was not an accurate prediction as by 1989 the Soviet Union had lost the Cold War, which to Solzhenitsyn it seemed in the mid-1970s to be winning.

*

We have seen that all the works I have summarized reveal a pattern that exposes vices and uses satire. Poets, dramatists and novelists of the last 500 years have consistently written on the social aspect of the fundamental theme and conform to a very coherent pattern.

We have seen that in the 19th and 20th centuries the quest for Reality has become enmeshed in historical, social content, and has often been replaced by social reality. However, the evidence I have presented shows that it is still present in the best post-1930s works, despite their largely secular outlook which has turned the quest for Reality into a quest for personal social advancement or betterment of social conditions.

The evidence I have presented shows that during the 19th and 20th centuries the quest for Reality was present in novels of conflicting types or *genres* – historical, picaresque, psychological, comedies of manners, epistolary, apprenticeship (*Bildungsroman*), *roman à clefs*, anti-novels, coterie novels, detective, mystery and thriller novels, Westerns, fantasy and prophetic novels, proletarian novels and colonial novels – and in conflicting styles: Romantic, realistic, naturalistic, impressionistic, Expressionist and avant-garde. The same is true of plays, and the quest for Reality can be found in poems of many *genre*s – epic, satire, epigrams, lyrics, odes, pastoral poetry, tragedies, comedies, histories, orations and philosophical dialogues – and forms: sonnets, metric compositions, free verse.

We have seen that in secular times such as our own the metaphysical aspect of the fundamental theme's quest for Reality has struggled to co-exist with a secular approach that sees characters and poetic personas in relation to social reality and socially measurable standards of virtue.

Literary Summary

The main references to the metaphysical aspect of the fundamental theme in world literature during the 20th-century anarchy are as follows:

- The infinite that surrounds the universe is in: Eliot's *Murder in the Cathedral*; the Neo-Romantics (Heath-Stubbs, Dylan Thomas); Durrell; and Solzhenitsyn.
- The metaphysical Reality seen as Light is in: Dylan Thomas; and David Gascoyne.
- The order of the universe can be found in: Iris Murdoch; and Solzhenitsyn.
- The oneness of known humankind can be found in: Heidegger; Eliot; and Churchill.
- The similarities in cultures and civilizations are emphasized in: Greene's overseas novels; Camus (in *The Rebel*); and Churchill's *History of the English-Speaking Peoples*.
- The universal being (or self) that opens to the Light behind the rational, social ego is in: Heidegger; and Eliot's plays.
- Universal virtue is in: Greene; Waugh; Orwell; and Solzhenitsyn.
- The promise of the immortality of the universal being is present in: Greene; and Waugh.
- The inner transformation or centre-shift from ego to universal being is found in: Jaspers; and Pasternak.
- The quest of the purified soul is in: Durrell; and Golding.
- The sensibility that approaches Reality through more than one discipline can be found in: Arnold Toynbee (universal world history, classical history, Western civilization, world religion, world travel); Churchill (history, autobiography, biography, political oration, statesman, statecraft, painting); Sartre (philosophy, novels, drama, essays); Camus (novels, drama, philosophy, history); Empson (criticism, poetry, letters); Kathleen Raine (poetry, cultural criticism/statement of tradition in *Defending Ancient Springs*, Eastern thinking on India); David Gascoyne (poetry, journal fiction, literary criticism); John Heath-Stubbs (poetry, epic poetry, plays, anthologies, critical study of later Romanticism); E.W.F. Tomlin (philosophy, literature,

travel); Colin Wilson (social criticism, philosophy, fiction, criminology); Ted Hughes (poetry, fiction, letters, occasional prose, mythological and critical Universalism in *Shakespeare and the Goddess of Complete Being*); Lawrence Durrell (poetry, novels, travel books); Iris Murdoch (philosophy, metaphysics, novels); and William Golding (novels, drama, poetry, essays).

• The new perspective of unity in history, religion, philosophy and science, international politics and literature can be found in: 20th-century books on world history (e.g. Arnold Toynbee, unification of history in *A Study of History*, 1934-61; J.M. Roberts, *History of the* World); the Second Vatican Council (religious unity within Christianity) – since the 19th century the work of religious unification has been taken away from individuals by institutions; Universalist philosophy and metaphysical science (e.g. through the Scientific and Medical Network); the creation of the UN in 1945 (unity in national relations); and Universalist literature.

In Part One we have considered the metaphysical and secular aspects of the fundamental theme from a historical perspective. In Part Two we move to the present and consider the perpetuation of the quest for Reality today, in our secular time.

PART TWO

Chiaroscuro:
Universalism's Reconciliation and Synthesis of the Metaphysical and Secular Traditions and Revival of the Fundamental Theme

"What in mee is dark
Illumin, what is low raise and support;
That to the highth of this great Argument
I may assert Eternal Providence,
And justifie the wayes of God to men."

Milton, *Paradise Lost*, book 1, lines 22-6

"Behind each shadow reigns a glorious sun."

Nicholas Hagger, *Collected Poems*, pp.9, 849

1

Universalism's Reconciliation of the Two Traditions and Sensibilities

We have seen that in very early times there were two traditions side by side. In the early stages of civilizations the metaphysical quest for Reality was predominant in literature, and was its core. As civilization progressed the ancients' view of the universe turned secular and literature developed to examine secular love and the vices of human nature and character. But just when the secular seemed to have replaced the metaphysical, the quest for Reality, the core, returned. This pattern was repeated again and again, and can be found in the Baroque time after the Renaissance and in the Romantic time after Neoclassicism.

The Two Traditions and the Graeco-Roman Culture

Our perception of the two traditions has been clouded by the pervasive and continuing influence of the Graeco-Roman tradition in Western culture. In the Prologue (p.9) I wrote of the figures of Light and Shadow in the pediment at Copped Hall, Essex. The two classical figures and the Latin motto beneath them bear witness to the strength of the classical tradition in the Western world in 1895. Our Western world was then, and still is, seen as a continuation of a world that began in Greece and was passed on to Rome. The classical Greeks addressed most of the intellectual and spiritual problems that have always confronted humankind in philosophy, literature and myths, and we are the spiritual descendants of the thinking and highly-developed civilizations of Greece and Rome. Our literature has descended from the Greeks and the Romans, who between them discovered all the literary forms and stylistic devices that have been used in European literature: tragedy, comedy, epic, lyric and pastoral, satire, essays and philosophical treatises, oratory and rhetoric, all of which can be found in use in the literature of England, France, Italy, Spain and Germany.

The classical tradition of Graeco-Roman literary forms and stylistic innovations spans from the early Greeks to our present time. It is important to understand that the term "classic" originally meant "of the highest class" (Latin *classicus*) and "good enough to be used as a standard". In the early 17th century it came to be used of all Greek and Latin literature, and the "classical tradition" came to mean Graeco-Roman literature. We thus speak of a Chair of Classics or Classical Studies. We have seen that many writers of all labels and descriptions have been influenced by the Graeco-Roman classical tradition. We have seen that these include the classical writers of the Renaissance and the Baroque writers who succeeded them, and also the Romantic poets who loved Italy and Greece and (in the case of Keats, Shelley and Byron) lived and died there.

Both metaphysical and secular traditions have been imbued with the gods and myths of the Graeco-Roman tradition. When we know what we are looking for, these two traditions can be discerned very clearly behind the ubiquitous classical tradition that overlays both in so many works. They are two contraries in literary culture. In some times they co-exist side by side, in other times they are enmeshed and intertwined, and in other times now one, and then the other, is dominant like a pattern in a carpet. We can thus speak of the ever-changing pattern of the metaphysical and secular aspects of the fundamental theme in literature.

Four Reconciliations of the Two Traditions
We have seen that since the Renaissance there have been four reconciliations of the metaphysical and secular traditions, all of which were inspired by Universalists who all wrote English poetry.

Baroque Metaphysicals
The first was during the first half of the 17th century when European Metaphysical Baroque poets tried to unite the medieval and Renaissance outlooks of spirit and sense. We have seen that the Metaphysical style was parallel to but distinct from the Baroque style, and that many of the European poets of the 17th century were both Metaphysical and Baroque. They were Metaphysical in dwelling on the perplexities of experience and the longing of the soul to be freed from the body, and Baroque in being concerned with the difference between appearance and reality, between the religious impulse and the

new science.

The Baroque Metaphysicals' blend of medieval spirit and Renaissance sense unified the metaphysical and secular traditions for a while and created the literary Baroque (see ch.5). Thus Donne wrote about spirit in his later Divine Poems and sermons and about sense in his earlier poems of the 1590s. Herbert combined spirit with a strong physical sense as in 'The Collar'. ("I struck the board, and cry'd, No more./I will abroad.") So did Marvell, in 'A Dialogue, Between the Resolved Soul, and Created Pleasure' and 'A Dialogue between the Soul and Body', and most notably in 'The Garden', in which Marvell's soul glides up into a tree amid the sensuous paradisal fruit and flowers of the garden at Nun Appleton. 'The Garden' is a Universalist poem that includes the soul, the reflective mind with its "green Thought in a green Shade" and the Natural world of the universe, and blends them.

In all three poets the quest for Reality as Light can be found alongside the poetry of vices in relation to an implied virtue: Donne's 'Good Friday, 1613. Riding Westward', which is about the journeying "Soul", and his 'Satyres' and 'The Second Anniversarie' ("Forget this rotten world"); Herbert's 'The Affection' and his more satirical 'The Pearl'; and Marvell's two Dialogues and 'An Horatian Ode upon Cromwell's Return from Ireland', in which he is alert to public vices and virtue.

Victorians

The second reconciliation was during the 19th century when the English Victorian poets tried to unite the Neoclassical and Romantic outlooks. They combined the Romantic love of Nature and the past with a social conscience that reacted against the wretched conditions of the Industrial Revolution and the Crimean War. Tennyson's *Idylls of the King* sits alongside 'Locksley Hall' and 'The Charge of the Light Brigade' and elements of both Neoclassical and Romantic outlooks can be found in *In Memoriam* and 'Maud'. Browning's facing of death and peering for the infinite in '*Prospice*' sits alongside the social 'My Last Duchess', and his dramatic monologues on Fra Lippo Lippi and Andrea del Sarto combine both elements. Arnold's Romantic, brooding 'Dover Beach' and 'The Scholar-Gipsy' sit alongside the social criticism in his *Culture and Anarchy*. The reconciliation of Neoclassical and Romantic outlooks in the Victorians was Universalist.

Modernists

The third reconciliation was in the early 20th century, when the Modernists tried to unite the Neoclassical and Romantic outlooks, and the metaphysical and secular traditions. T.E. Hulme thought of himself as a Neoclassical writer, arguing (see p.241) that "after a hundred years of Romanticism, we are in for a classical revival" (*Speculations*). He devised Imagism as a way of being objective and escaping Romantic feeling while avoiding seeing people in terms of their social, rational selves. Imagism thus became a kind of half-way house between Neoclassicism and Romanticism. Pound and Eliot declared themselves as Neoclassicists. Pound wrote that his main principle was "direct treatment of the 'thing' whether subjective or objective", and, of his Imagism, that "an 'Image' is that which presents an intellectual and emotional complex in an instant of time". He added that "the perfect symbol is the natural object".[1] This was a realistic, classical view of the symbol.

Eliot stated in his essay 'Hamlet' (1919),

"The only way of expressing emotion in the form of art is by finding an 'objective correlative'; in other words a set of objects, a situation, a chain of events which shall be the formula of that *particular* emotion; such that when the external facts, which must terminate in sensory experience, are given, the emotion is immediately evoked."

Eliot thus focused on the object.[2] In 'Tradition and the Individual Talent', also written in 1919, he questioned Wordsworth's Romantic view of emotion:

"We must believe that 'emotion recollected in tranquillity' is an inexact formula. For it is neither emotion, nor recollection, nor, without distortion of meaning, tranquillity. It is concentration, and a new thing resulting from the concentration, of a very great number of experiences."[3]

However, Yeats was under no such illusion and wrote in 'Coole Park and Ballylee' in 1931 "We were the last romantics – chose for theme/Traditional sanctity and loveliness," thinking of the poets of the 1890s before Pound influenced him into being more Modernist and Neoclassical.

It now seems that Hulme, Pound and Eliot were late flowerings of the Romantic tree, along with Yeats. Frank Kermode in *Romantic Image* argues persuasively that the Romantic poets lived for the image which was a truth out of space and time; that they endured isolation or estrangement from their fellow men to perceive it; and that they expressed the image in organic form – and that the Modernists, despite their protestations of Neoclassicism, did so too. Many of the early Romantics yearned to escape from the dream of the image into self-destructive acts, like Yeats' Major Robert Gregory, an artist who joined the Royal Flying Corps and was killed on the Italian front in 1918.

The Modernists united consciously Neoclassical critical attitudes – the objectivity of Imagism and Eliot's objective correlative – with their innate Romanticism, of which they were barely aware: their escape from the present into the past as in Pound's *Cantos* and Eliot's 'The Waste Land', their focus on images in organic form and their isolation and estrangement from society as in the case of Pound's 'Hugh Selwyn Mauberley'. So Hulme's objective poems are in Romantic images, Eliot's 'The Waste Land' is a sequence of images and sits alongside the *Four Quartets*, which is a Neoclassical statement. Pound's imagistic *The Cantos* sit alongside the social Neoclassicism of 'Hugh Selwyn Mauberley'. Similarly, Yeats' Romantic images of tree and dancer in 'Among School Children' – "O chestnut-tree, great-rooted blossomer/Are you the leaf, the blossom or the bole?/O body swayed to music, O brightening glance,/How can we know the dancer from the dance?" – sits alongside his 'Easter 1916', which is about the social Irish nationalist uprising.

This blend of Neoclassical and Romantic outlooks was Universalist in effect if not in intention: although not all the Modernists were fully aware of the Romantic roots of their outlook, including T.E. Hulme, they all produced a blend of Neoclassical and Romantic verse while believing they were being Neoclassically imagistic and objective.

All these reconciliations were Universalist. They all combined spirit and sense: the Metaphysicals' preoccupation with the soul and body from Donne to Marvell; the Victorians' obsessions with the soul (for example, in Tennyson's *In Memoriam*) and criticism of materialism; and the Modernists' images of truth, glimpses of spiritual Reality in the objectivity of 'The Waste Land'. The first of these reconciliations can be seen as Baroque, the second and third can be seen as Neo-Baroque. In these last two reconciliations there is a dialectic: thesis (Neoclassicism), antithesis (Romanticism) and synthesis (Universalism).

A fourth reconciliation and dynamic is being played out in our time.

Literary Universalism's Contemporary Synthesis

A new, fourth, dialectic began in the 1930s and lasted into the 1950s: the Neo-Romanticism of Dylan Thomas, John Heath-Stubbs, Kathleen Raine and others (thesis), and the Neoclassical reaction that began with Empson and led to the Movement (antithesis). Out of these contraries of thesis and antithesis will come a new synthesis to combine them.

What form will this synthesis take? The Romantic writer reveals his ego confessionally, as did Rousseau, but also reveals his soul and shows his spirit reaching to the invisible world beyond the senses, as in the case of Marlowe's *Dr Faustus*. The Neoclassical writer hides his social ego behind the ego of man, but it is the social ego he is interested in and the surface of social life, as in the case of the Movement poets such as Larkin. The Neoclassical looks for social types (the greedy man, the lawyer) as Ben Jonson did, and it is on these that he bases his observation of vices. Universalism's synthesis will unite the focus on the soul's Romantic perception of the infinite and the Neoclassical focus on the social ego of the English Movement.

We need to be clear as to what literary Universalism is in our time (as opposed to the times of the three earlier reconciliations). It incorporates outlooks from Universalism in other disciplines, a tendency that has been evident in every century during the last 4,600 years. As we have seen in the literary summaries at the end of each of the ten chapters in Part One, writers have focused on the universe as being an ordered unity within, and influenced by, the infinite metaphysical Light (an expression of philosophical Universalism). They have seen the experience of the Light known to mystics as the common experience of all world religions (an expression of religious

Universalism). They have focused on the history of humankind as a unity as in Toynbee's *A Study of History* (an expression of historical Universalism). They have seen all humankind as governable by one political entity (an expression of political Universalism).

Universalist writers have reflected all these attitudes in their literature, seeing the literature of all countries as one, an interconnected unity, one supra-national literature. They show humankind as questing for the Light within a unified, ordered universe that is pervaded with and surrounded by the infinite. All writers who have reflected the metaphysical aspect of the fundamental theme, the quest for Reality, can be claimed as Universalists. They include Homer, Virgil, Dante and Milton in epic poetry; and Marvell, Coleridge, Tennyson and Eliot in lyric and reflective poetry. Writers who have expressed social vices in relation to virtue include Horace, Chaucer, Shakespeare and Pope.

Universalist writers blend intuitional and rationalist approaches to the One. They convey their sense of order in the universe: the Greek world of Homer and the Roman world of Virgil are presided over and ordered by the gods. The world of Dante is ordered by God. Shakespeare asserted the "great chain of being", whose disruption disturbs the order of the universe. Marlowe conveyed order in terms of Heaven. Wordsworth wrote of the "Wisdom and Spirit of the Universe", which ordered Nature and the human soul. Shelley wrote of his sense of order in 'Adonais': "The One remains, the many change and pass." Eliot saw order in "the still point of the turning world" in 'East Coker'. Dostoevsky presented nihilists who attempted to overthrow order in *The Possessed* (or *The Devils*). Tolstoy wrote of how a war shook the fundamental order in society.

Universalist writers write of their experience of the One. Universalist poems and stories catch the unity of the universe; they include sudden revelations of Being in the moment. Verse plays relate order through the One behind the universe, which in Shakespeare is linked to the divine right of kings. Universalism's focus on Being takes art beyond secular existence to the unity of humankind and the destination of the immortal soul.

Is there any sign of such a Universalist synthesis in our own time? It has to be said that English poetry since the Movement has been fragmented. Within the contemporary Anarchy, prominent poets

300

operated like semi-independent barons with a few followers. No one style or adherence has dominated, and many individual poets have imitated, or carried forward the tradition of, recent poets. Ted Hughes wrote in the free-verse animal tradition of D.H. Lawrence; the Irish Seamus Heaney wrote in the tradition of Yeats, but without Yeats' reach into the other world and history; Geoffrey Hill wrote in the stress-line tradition of Eliot with considerable obscurity but without displaying Eliot's metaphysical focus on the quest for Reality as Light; Larkin in the homely tradition of Hardy, but without Hardy's sensitivity to the detail of country life and the weather; and Robert Lowell wrote in the tradition of, depending on your point of view, Pound or Eliot. Christopher Ricks said to me during a long conversation about English literature round the city of Oxford in June 1993 (at that moment sitting in a small tea-room opposite Examination Schools where he would lecture as Professor of Poetry in twelve years' time), "There are many traditions." And this is certainly true of the pattern of imitation in post-1960s English poetry.

Universalist poets try not to depend solely on imitation even though imitation is part of the Neoclassical canon. They confront the universe and write about Nature, as did Wordsworth. To write solely to continue the tradition of a past poet is etiolated. The equivalent in art is (as I pointed out on p.259) the artists of the School of Raphael, who followed the tradition of Raphael and produced academicist, undistinguished paintings.

Neoclassical critics, with one eye on the Neoclassical tradition of imitation, might say that my work is in the tradition of, and therefore "imitated", the work of the Victorian synthesizer, Tennyson: that the poems in my volume, *The Gates of Hell*, are in the tradition of his *In Memoriam* and 'Maud'; that my poems on Afghanistan and Iraq are in the tradition of his 'The Charge of the Light Brigade'; and that my two epics are in the tradition of his *Idylls of the King*. In so far as Universalist poetry reflects Neoclassical criteria, which it partly does (as well as partly reflecting Romantic criteria), there may be some truth in the assertion that my roots can be traced back to Tennyson (as well as to Marvell and Eliot).

Be that as it may, imitation, long a feature of Neoclassical thinking and criticism as we shall see on pp.316-9, has been a feature of much of the criticism and poetry since 1960. Poets' academicist references in their poems to the works of others are greeted with approval. The trouble is, poems during this time have tended not to take a fresh look at the universe and have been about the sensible world without any hint of the Romantic infinite.

We can approach a coming Universalist synthesis in English poetry through its view of the imagination. This is best stated by contrasting the Romantic and Neoclassical views of the imagination and then stating the blend that can be expected.

The metaphysical and Romantic view of imagination is that it is a creative power received in the soul from beyond this world, a faculty that perceives unity, glimpses and connects images and fuses together feeling, vision and thought. The imagination operates in a trance-like "other mind" into which flow symbolic communications from the eternal world, suggesting in Coleridge's words "the translucence of the Eternal in and through the Temporal". (To the Romantics, genius is the operation of the creative power of the imagination from the beyond.)

The secular and Neoclassical view of the imagination is that it is Fancy, a decorative verbal playfulness, an associative faculty that works through metaphors, which reason uses to make a statement and embroider poems. Its source is the rational, social ego and can be seen at work in Larkin's imitation of an image in Milton, "Why should I let the toad *work*/Squat on my life?" (Here "toad" is decorative and "squat" associative.) In novels the faculty of imagination transmutes experience, associating it with another set of events which is what happens when the novelist attributes his own experience to a character into whose shoes he steps. (The Neoclassical, social view of genius is that it is a natural ability or quality of mind that takes a work written by a high talent and improves it to make something new. This view, stated by Christopher Ricks in his last Professor-of-Poetry lecture at Oxford in May 2009, represents a derivative view of creativity, it is part imitation and part improvement.)

In the contemplative blend of the metaphysical/Romantic and secular/Neoclassical views, the Universalist synthesis, the rational, social ego reflects on the soul's reception and synthesizing, of symbols and the Light, Reality. In the new Baroque vision, Romantic infinity (the Light) is synthesized with Neoclassical harmony, just as the historical Baroque vision combined harmony and dynamic movement. It unites the temporal self of the social ego to the deeper, timeless, universal being within the self which reflects the One, which it integrates in tranquillity with the social world, with emotions, feelings and thoughts. The blend of Romantic and Neoclassical views is accompanied by a blend of image and statement. A Universalist poem is a statement in images, or an image composed of images that makes a statement. (The Universalist view of genius, blending the metaphysical/Romantic and secular/Neoclassical views, is that the rational, social ego contemplates influxes received within the self's universal being from beyond and turns outward to relate the inner inspiration to the world, looking for a model that resembles what the soul has seen and, on finding it, improving it.)

The Universalist synthesis, then, is a blend of Romantic infinity and Neoclassical harmony, of symbols from the beyond and natural images, of inspired creative power and workman-like improvement of past works, of image and statement.

It must be emphasized that the Universalist synthesis in our time is immediately rooted in the Modernist synthesis (and less immediately in the Victorian synthesis of Tennyson), see pp.297-9. As Eliot survived into the 1960s, the two have overlapped and for a short while ran concurrently. Eliot can be regarded as the first to attempt a Universalist synthesis in our time. As we saw on pp.236-7, his quest for Reality can be traced from the despair of 'The Waste Land', through 'The Hollow Men' and the Christian 'Ash Wednesday' to *Four Quartets*, which refers to the Light as Fire. He exposed the social vices of the people in 'The Waste Land', such as "the young man carbuncular". He reconciled the metaphysical in the course of his work: the metaphysical perspective of the Metaphysical poets in his criticism and his Neoclassical objectivity and social perspective in 'The Waste Land', which are reconciled in his philosophical Universalism in the *Four Quartets*. Eliot challenged the West's secular perspective in his social criticism, for example *Notes Towards the Definition of Culture*, and he was very alert to the cultural tradition in his essay 'Tradition and the Individual Talent' (1919), which halts "at the frontier of metaphysics or mysticism".

Eliot wrote truly on the restoration of a tradition and its strands in the course of synthesis:

"Surely the great poet is, among other things, one who not merely restores a tradition which has been in abeyance, but one who in his poetry re-twines as many straying strands of tradition as possible."[4]

It can be argued that Pound rather than Eliot was the Grand Old Man behind the contemporary attempt at a Universalist synthesis. As we saw on p.239, his Dantesque focus on finding himself in a Dark Forest and journeying to the Light, and on the twin themes of the Descent into Hades and Metamorphosis, make *The Cantos*, for all their lack of narrative and consequent obscurity, is a Universalist work combining the vision of the infinite and astute social observation of past cultures. Arguably Pound rather than Eliot was the first to attempt a Universalist synthesis as he influenced Eliot as early as September 1914 and wrote his first canto in 1915.

Robert Graves approached the Romantic infinite through the mythological in his study, *The Greek Myths*. He worked out the anthropological and mythological background of the tradition of the visitation of the Muse in *The White Goddess*, as we saw on p.244, and wrote two novels about the Roman Emperor Claudius. His work combines the "Romantic" and "Classical".

The Neo-Romantic Kathleen Raine seems to have attempted a similar blend while remaining on the Romantic side. Her *Collected Poems* uses language that is both mythological and concrete, and combines the personal and the universal. Her criticism, the essays in *Defending Ancient Springs* (which includes an essay on David Gascoyne and the prophetic role) and *The Inner Journey of the Poet* (the title essay suggesting the quest for Reality) stand alongside her scholarly studies of Blake, Thomas Taylor the Platonist and Yeats.

Her main theme which is also in her *Autobiographies* is the sterility and bankruptcy of our secular culture which expects poets to illuminate the personal and social realities of our time but not any other Reality.

Our secular culture repaid her with neglect, but alongside her restatement of the Neoplatonist, Hermetic tradition in verse (an occult tradition in relation to the Christian tradition), and her founding of *Temenos* (a journal covering comparative religion), is *India Seen Afar*, a blend of Indian Hindu metaphysics with the social conditions of contemporary India. Her poetry is from the soul and ignores the social ego, but despite her opposition to secularism she hints at a blend of the metaphysical and secular now and again, although she does not fully achieve it.

David Gascoyne, who was eight years younger than Kathleen Raine, had Universalist tendencies. His precocious *Journal*, written in France just before the war, mentions the Light as we saw on p.266. He wrote 'Metaphysical Poems' (a group in *Poems 1937-1942*) and wartime poetry, such as 'A Wartime Dawn'. Having thrown off the influence of Surrealism he wrote *Hölderlin's Madness* and then followed Hölderlin into a form of madness caused by amphetamine dependency, unconsciously acting out Wordsworth's "We Poets in our youth begin in gladness;/But thereof come in the end despondency and madness".

Although I am focusing on poets it is worth noting in passing that some non-poet thinkers were influential Universalists during the 1950s. The philosopher E.W.F. Tomlin, the author of *Great Philosophers of the East* and *Great Philosophers of the West*, and of a book on Eliot, *T.S. Eliot, A Friendship*, was a Universalist at home in philosophy, history and literature, and wrote travel books. He was on a quest for Reality that had taken him to the metaphysical "Absolute", which he rooted in the secular world.

There is a case for regarding Colin Wilson as a Universalist as he has been on a life-long quest into all levels of Reality. Besides social criticism and philosophy that is closer to Continental than to English models his quest took him into criminology and expressed itself in fiction.

It could be argued that the poet Lawrence Durrell was groping for a Universalist reconciliation of the metaphysical and the secular, Romanticism and Neoclassicism, in his prose *Alexandria Quartet*, which draws on the ancient cultures of Egypt and represents some of their metaphysical ideas. There is certainly a blend of the metaphysical and the social in that quartet.

I believe that during the 1990s, while he was corresponding with me, Ted Hughes, then Poet Laureate, a poet who emerged during the 1950s, also attempted a reconciliation between the Romantic and the Neoclassical. He had brought out *Shakespeare and the Goddess of Complete Being*, which identified a basic structural pattern in Shakespeare's *Venus and Adonis* and *The Rape of Lucrece* (which Hughes saw as "a metaphysical poem") and in 14 of Shakespeare's mature plays. This work includes a heading "Shakespeare takes up the spiritual quest", which suggests that Shakespeare focused on the metaphysical aspect of the fundamental theme. Whether or not the pattern Hughes claimed to have found is deemed to exist in Shakespeare's works, Hughes himself was on a "spiritual quest" for Reality. He had read my *Selected Poems* and my 'Preface on the New Baroque Consciousness', and he knew my work *The Gates of Hell*. He had been secretly writing what would become *Birthday Letters* (1998), about his social relationship with Sylvia Plath, for some while, and in 1997 he brought out his loose "translation" of passages in Ovid's *Metamorphoses*, *Tales from Ovid*, which suggested the metaphysical in mythological form. (I had begun writing my verse play *Ovid Banished* when he wrote and told me of his work on Ovid, a weird case of synchronicity that may be explained by our common Universalism.) He was very interested in my Universalism and wrote to me in 1997 that he would have liked to have attended my lecture in Aldeburgh, Suffolk calling for a Universalist revolution in thought and culture, but had been going through some "heavy seas" (an early reference to what would become his last illness). These two works of Hughes', placed alongside each other, reflect Neoclassicism and Romanticism, the secular and metaphysical.

The generation of British poets that succeeded the Neoclassical Movement poets moved some way towards reconciling their work with the Romantic tradition. In 1982 an anthology of these poets, *The Penguin Book of Contemporary British Poetry*, appeared in which the editors Blake Morrison and Andrew Motion claimed that a shift of sensibility had occurred in British poetry which demanded a reformation of public taste to appreciate their work. The poets it contained, it was claimed in the Introduction, showed greater imaginative freedom and linguistic daring than the previous generation, and had adopted the attitude of an anthropologist or alien invader to make the familiar strange with outrageous similes. They had shunned plain speech, had renewed interest in narrative and had inclined to relativism rather than Larkin's empirical moral outlook. A number of different schools and tendencies were at work, but their new interest in narrative, preference for metaphor, use of wit and reassertion of sympathetic imagination and decorative fancy suggest that they were groping towards a Universalist position even though their work did not incorporate the Romantic infinite and was uniformly secular rather than metaphysical. It has to be said that not one of the poems in the anthology transcends the secular or hints at the metaphysical.

Of these poets, Seamus Heaney combined sympathetic imagination and imitation in 'Ugolino', which is based on Dante's *Inferno*, cantos xxxii and xxxiii. His bog poems, for example 'The Tollund Man', 'Punishment' and 'The Grauballe Man', have a Universalist sense of history and timelessness and reveal Irish roots. However, although Heaney was technically very accomplished his poems were secular memories decorated with fancy and fell short of the Universalist sense of the infinite and metaphysical.

Andrew Motion, who had written a book on Keats, imagined himself into the shoes of a First-World-War soldier in 'Bathing at Glymenopoulo', using Keats' sympathetic imagination rather than the inspiring power of creative imagination of Wordsworth and Coleridge. In his work he was very interested in the First and Second World Wars, and there were suggestions that he was approaching a Universalist consciousness.

Craig Raine's best-known poem was 'A Martian sends a Postcard Home', in which an alien sees everyday life in outrageous images and makes wrong deductions about what people are doing. His works include *History, the Home Movie*, which expressed bits of history in images. Again, his imagination was groping towards a Universalist position, but his poems were universally secular.

The same applies to a younger poet not included in the Penguin anthology, Simon Armitage, and to Motion's successor as Poet Laureate, Carol Ann Duffy (who surprisingly reckoned in a poem that the modern Achilles is the footballer, David Beckham, who had just damaged his Achilles' tendon).

A number of the new poets, then, moved away from Neoclassicism but had not moved away from secularism and only wrote about the personal and social reality of everyday life without relating it to the quest for Reality.

My own work effects this Universalist synthesis of the metaphysical and secular in a quest for Reality. It may be helpful if I am more specific. In my early poetic volume *The Gates of Hell* a soul turns away from the world, glimpses the infinite Light and receives symbols from the beyond. This work documents the beginning of the Mystic Way, which leads from attachment, through purgation, to illumination. In 'The Silence' ("a string of baroque pearls") a soul is transformed from living through the rational, social ego to living through the deeper universal being, and comes to grasp that the universe is orderly. In 'A Metaphysical in Marvell's Garden' the personal experience of the rational, social ego merges into objective consciousness and awareness of the metaphysical Light. Many other poems of mine do this, for example 'Clouded-Ground Pond'. Many of my poems balance infinity and harmony, symbols and natural images. Some make a statement through images, others present images to make a statement. The Preface to my *Selected Poems, A Metaphysical's Way of Fire*, which first unveiled this approach, is called 'On the New Baroque Consciousness and the Redefinition of Poetry'. In my *Collected Poems* this preface is titled 'On the New Baroque Consciousness and the Redefinition of Poetry as Classical Baroque', to make it clear that poetry is being redefined as "classical Baroque". I think of my Universalist poems as "baroque pearls".

The perception of a universal order can be found in my *Classical Odes*. 'The Silence' is Romantic in emphasizing the infinite whereas *Classical Odes* is more Neoclassical, though acknowledging the infinite. The "pearls" are now more regular, less misshapen. The two works together effect the Neo-Baroque Universalist reconciliation. My two poetic epics have tried to reconcile conflicts of the social world of war with the reconciling metaphysical One – *Overlord*, during the Second World War; and *Armageddon*, during the War on Terror. Both make statements in images, or present an image composed of images that makes a statement. In both, the heroes visit Hell and Heaven, and I have both opened to inspired creative power (see pp.339-42) and used

Dante's work as a model to be improved. In all these works I have tried to blend Romanticism and Neoclassicism, or the metaphysical and secular, in Universalist poetry.

The Universalist Sensibility

Universalist poets have a distinctive sensibility. Sensibility is the "capacity to feel, openness to emotional impressions" (*Concise Oxford Dictionary*). The secular sensibility is discerned in its openness to secular, humanistic, emotional impressions, whereas the metaphysical sensibility is identifiable by its sensitivity to intellectual activity – "intellectual" coming from the Latin "*intellectus*" and denoting perception of a Reality received in the mind, the Light. The intellectual faculty is distinct from the "rational" faculty which is of "the reason".

It can be said that there are three different kinds of sensibility:

The metaphysical and Romantic sensibility, which includes the faculty that perceives Reality received in the mind, the Light and symbols.

The secular and Neoclassical sensibility, which includes the faculty of reasoning and openness to secular, social and humanistic emotional impressions.

The Universalist and new Baroque sensibility, which includes a combination of intellectual perception of Reality and openness to secular, social and humanistic emotional impressions and rational activity.

Eliot examined the metaphysical sensibility from the 13th to the 19th centuries in *The Varieties of Metaphysical Poetry* (a collection of his Clark lectures of 1926 and Turnbull lectures of 1933). In his Turnbull lecture 'Toward a Definition of Metaphysical Poetry' he defined metaphysical poetry as poetry that "elevates sense for a moment to regions ordinarily attainable only to abstract thought", which has an "intellectual quality".[5] He continued: "With the more intellectual forms of mysticism, the *beatitudo*, or the experience of Theresa or John of the Cross, it may come in contact." In other words, "metaphysical poetry" approaches the infinite Light, and is open to intellectual perception of a Reality that is beyond or behind physical reality. Elsewhere[6] he says: "The metaphysical poets are those who seek something beyond or after nature, refinements of thought or emotion: ergo, they are metaphysical." They seek a Reality "beyond or after nature". Eliot identified three metaphysical moments in European literature when the relation of thought and feeling changed due to a new metaphysical outlook: the 13th century (Dante and Calvalcanti); the 17th century (Donne and Crashaw); and the 19th century (Laforgue and Corbière). To Eliot, 17th-century "Metaphysical poetry", in the sense first used by Dryden and adopted by Johnson, had its roots in Dante and pointed forward to French symbolism, and Eliot was Univeralist in looking with approval on the metaphysicality of poets other than the 17th-century "Metaphysical poets", such as Lucretius, Dante and Goethe. His sweep is wider than the 17th-century Metaphysical poets, and in writing of "sense" and "thought" and of seeking "something beyond or after nature" he appears to be challenging secularism. It is a moot point as to whether he was arguing in 1933 that the secular should be incorporated and reconciled within his metaphysical vision.

In our time very few apart from Eliot and the writers referred to on pp.303-6 have challenged the secular perspective and sensibility. There are not many poets writing within the metaphysical tradition today, and so the Universalist synthesis is in its earliest stages and the contemporary Universalist sensibility is therefore still being formed. The metaphysical has declined in our secular time. The physicist Stephen Hawking has claimed that the universe can be understood in terms of physics without needing an infinite. Richard Dawkins' interpretation of neo-Darwinism has led him to pay for an advertisement on the side of London buses, "There's probably no God". Many critics and poets pride themselves on their atheism. The metaphysical aspect of the fundamental theme's quest for Reality found in Eliot has temporarily fallen into relative disuse.

Secularization has affected all the arts. Performance has taken the place of substance. Sensationalist shock art – an unmade bed and PR gimmicks – have crowded out traditional standards, which have collapsed. In our secular time revealing truth is less important than capturing attention. In painting, the landscapes of Constable have given way to works that no longer show the serenity, unity, composure and the tranquillity of Nature, and to disjointed abstract spatial art. The distorted works of Francis Bacon, who I sometimes met in the Colony Club, Dean Street, Soho, are now admired and sell for colossal sums. The musical symphonies of Beethoven and Brahms compete with atonal music, the syncopated cacophony of Schoenberg. Novels teem with the chaotic everyday events of personal and social reality and have a humanistic outlook. In poetry sturdy works such as Milton's *Paradise Lost* and Tennyson's *Idylls of the King* vie for attention with poems about secular living, common memories of boyhood, poems about the death of a wife or about breast cancer, and doodle poems. It is as though the works in the National Portrait Gallery, the classics of classical music and the metrical works from Chaucer to Tennyson have been replaced by secular humanist works that ignore any Reality that is not personal and social.

The philosopher Descartes wrote in his Preface to the French edition of the *Principles* that

"all philosophy is like a tree, whose roots are metaphysics, whose trunk is physics, and whose branches, which grow from this trunk, are all of the other sciences, which reduce to three principal sciences, namely medicine, mechanics and morals".

Descartes was stating the Universalist Aristotelian-Christian synthesis of metaphysics, physics and the sciences. European culture can be seen as a once-unified tree whose trunk is the Christian religion and branches represent philosophy, history, literature (and art, sculpture and music) and were once kept alive with metaphysical sap. Now the branches have become brittle, having lost their unifying metaphysical power which used to lubricate the tree from their roots in the One, and the fruit of high culture is shrivelled. Eliot held that cultural disintegration was taking place: "The artistic sensibility is impoverished by its divorce from the religious sensibility, the religious by its separation from the artistic."[7]

The Universalist sensibility revives the concept that all the diverse disciplines of a civilization are like unified branches of a metaphysical tree-trunk invigorated by metaphysical sap. It conveys a philosophical, cross-disciplinary view of the universe that assimilates history and is reflected in literature. It consists of the same components I attributed to literary Universalism on pp.299-300. In philosophy it focuses on the unity of the universe and the universality of humankind, and recognises the infinite (*to apeiron*) of the early Greeks. In history it focuses on the civilizations of all humankind as did Arnold Toynbee. In comparative religion it focuses on the common essence of all world religions. In international political relations it focuses on global governance and world government. It admits all these strands to literature and reconciles sense and spirit, the finite and the infinite, the temporal and the eternal in works that can be described as Neo-Baroque, and in sweeping epics that convey the unity of the universe in terms of the metaphysical One.

The Universalist writers in the last 2,700 years can be identified by their being at home in several disciplines. The Universalist sensibility expresses its approach to Reality in several *genres* or disciplines, and in the eleventh bullet point of each of the literary summaries at the end of each chapter in Part One I have identified the following Universalists:

Homer (poetry, epic); Xenophanes of Colophon (poetry, philosophy); Parmenides of Elea (poetry, philosophy); Plato (philosophy, teaching in Academy, statecraft, letters); Aristotle (philosophy, logic, sciences, *Poetics*); Demosthenes (political orations, statesman); Julius Caesar (history, military leader, ruler, dictator, statecraft); Cicero (political oratory, philosophy, law); Virgil (poetry, epic); Horace (poetry, criticism); Ovid (poetry, *Ars amatoria*, *Metamorphoses*, poetic letters from Black Sea); Omar Khayyam (astronomy, algebra, philosophy, jurisprudence, history, medicine, alchemy, poetry); Dante (poetry, philosophy, statecraft, diplomacy); Petrarch (poetry, epic poetry, essays, letters, ambassador); Chaucer (poetry, romance/*Troilus and Criseyde*, translation, page, courtier, soldier, squire, diplomat, customs comptroller, Knight of the Shire, Clerk of the King's Works); Leonardo (painting, sculpture, architecture, musician, science, mathematics, engineering, inventions, anatomy, geology, cartography, botany, writing); Michelangelo (painting, sculpture, architecture, poetry, letters, engineering); Ficino (Platonic scholarship, philosophy, letters); Sir Thomas More (*Utopia*, statecraft, diplomacy); Erasmus (writing, Biblical scholarship, theology, languages, diplomacy); Sidney (poetry, novel/*Arcadia*, *An Apologie for Poetrie*, letters); Shakespeare (plays, poems, sonnets); Marlowe, (plays, poetry, translation); Donne (poetry, sermons, work as Dean of St Paul's); Milton (poetry, polemical writing, work as Cromwell's Latin secretary); Marvell (poetry, work as MP); Dryden (poetry, plays, criticism, translation); Pope (poetry, unfinished epic *Brutus*, prose 'Epilogue to the Satires', translation); Swift (poetry, novels, polemical essays); Johnson (poetry, literary criticism, lexicography in compiling the first dictionary, novel); Voltaire (novel/philosophical satire, history, epic poetry, drama, criticism, letters); Goethe (poetry, drama, literature, theology, philosophy, science); Blake (printing, engraving, art, poetry); Coleridge (poetry, literary criticism, philosophy); Wordsworth (poetry, letters, prefaces); Shelley (poetry, verse drama, *A Defence of Poetry*, letters); Tennyson (poetry, epic, verse drama, letters); Dostoevsky (novels, stories, diaries); Browning (poetry, long dramatic poems, verse drama); Arnold (poetry, literary and cultural criticism, work as inspector of schools); Tolstoy (novels, educational reform, writings on Christianity); T.E. Hulme (poetry, essays, philosophy); T.S. Eliot (poetry, verse drama, cultural history, social essays, literary criticism); Yeats (poetry, verse drama, autobiography, Rosicrucianism, patterns of unified history in *A Vision*, letters); Ezra Pound (poetry, literary criticism, cultural and social essays, letters); H.G. Wells (literature, history, science); Aldous Huxley (literature, mysticism); Robert Graves (poetry, historical fiction, mythology, history of poetic inspiration); Hesse (novels, poems, criticism, philosophy); Arnold Toynbee (universal world history, classical history, Western civilization, world religion, world travel); Churchill (history, autobiography, biography political oration, statesman, statecraft, painting); Sartre (philosophy, novels, drama, essays); Camus (novels, drama, philosophy, history); Empson, who qualifies as a Universalist although on the Neoclassical side (criticism, poetry, letters); Kathleen Raine, who qualifies as a Universalist although on the Romantic side (poetry, cultural criticism/statement); David Gascoyne (poetry, journal fiction, literary criticism); John Heath-Stubbs (poetry, epic poetry, plays, anthologies, critical study of later Romanticism); E.W.F. Tomlin (philosophy, literature, travel); Colin Wilson (social criticism, philosophy, fiction, criminology); Ted Hughes (poetry, fiction, letters, occasional prose, mythological and critical Universalism); Lawrence Durrell (poetry, novels, travel books); Iris Murdoch (philosophy, metaphysics, novels); and William Golding (novels, drama, poetry, essays).

By listing these writers, I have stated a broad Universalist tradition. This list is not exhaustive, but in varying degrees all on this list have a Universalist sensibility and outlook.

Universalism revives the metaphysical vision and therefore the metaphysical tradition; the quest for Reality and therefore the metaphysical aspect of the fundamental theme. We have seen that the quest for Reality, the Light, has its shadow side: a secular view of vices in relation to an implied virtue, which it reconciles.

I return (see p.9) to the pediment at Copped Hall, Essex and its two figures of *lumen* (Light) and *umbra* (shadow), and the message below its sundial: *Me umbra regit vos lumen*. The sundial says, "Shadow rules me (i.e. the sundial), light rules you (i.e. all mortals who look at the sundial)".

It can be argued that there are two interpretations of Copped Hall's sundial. It can be seen as contrasting the metaphysical Light (*lumen*) and the phenomenal world that has manifested from it (which Plato called "shadows"). It can also be seen as contrasting secular life in sunlight (*lumen*) and its time-ruled consequence of death (shadow). The motto of the sundial can be interpreted as declaring to Universalists, "Shadow rules me, metaphysical Light you". At the same time it can be interpreted as declaring to secular sceptics, "Shadow rules me, sunlight rules you". Both metaphysical Universalists and secular sceptics are ruled by light, but by different kinds of light: Universalists by the metaphysical Light of the One, secular sceptics by physical sunlight.

It can be said that we mortals who gaze up at the sundial interpret the motto to fit our own outlook. The ripened grain may evoke the metaphysical vision through the Eleusinian mysteries, at the climax of which a reaped ear of corn was dramatically revealed to symbolize spiritual growth. The ripened grain may also refer to us mortals' bodily dependence on wheat, which is turned into bread, and assert, as suggested on p.9: "Light rules us mortals as we depend on ripened grain."

The modern battle of the books is between literary Universalism, which holds in literature that life has a meaning and purpose in relation to the One, and secular scepticism, which holds the materialist view that life is an accident and death is the end. This book calls for a revolution in thought and culture to reinstate the Universalist tradition in our globalized time.

2

A Defence of Universalist Poetry

I pointed out on p.295 that the four post-Renaissance reconciliations of the metaphysical and secular traditions have all been undertaken by Universalist poets writing within the English poetic tradition. It is time to defend Universalist poetry against contemporary assumptions that poetry can only be secular, and this will mean taking a closer look at what is meant by "poetry" and at the Neoclassical and Romantic traditions. I can then sharpen the basis of the two main components of Universalist poetry.

Poetry as Heightening

There have been many attempts to define poetry. There are many competing theories of poetry, and as many definitions as there are types of poetry, prosodic metres and speech-rhythms, and poetic *genre*s. A universal definition is elusive, and it has been held that poetry is impossible to define.

The word "poetry" comes from the Greek *poiesis* ("making"), which was first used by Herodotus. In early agricultural societies poetry may have been the language of ritual, of magical spells recited to guarantee a good harvest, and prose may have derived later. Poetry's voice is different from the conversational voice of habit. Poetry and prose use language in different ways, which raises the question of how poetry differs from prose and whether they are similar ways of communicating. Traditionally, poetry is the Muse-inspired language of the soul. Wordsworth held that it is distinguished from prose by its regular metre. According to a Neoclassical idea, poetry's punctuation into lines gives it a different appearance on the page from that of prose. It has been widely said that prose appeals to rational thought and poetry to the feelings, a distinction that can be found in their Latin roots: *prosus* means "going straight forward" and *versus* "returning". The Latin suggests that prose is a straightforward appeal to rational thought whereas poetry "returns" to the feelings.

There is widespread agreement that poetry consists of heightened forms of perception, experience, meaning and consciousness that are expressed in heightened language. It is a heightened mode of consciousness, and requires technical devices such as alliteration, similes, metaphors and other figures of speech that heighten feelings. Some poets (such as George Herbert) make a virtue of their plain, puritanical style and achieve their heightening by varying their tone and pace and by using other less colourful devices of versification.

The Tradition of Classical and Neoclassical Imitation
The classical, and Neoclassical, view of poetry is that it is an imitation of the external world, and that all poetic works conform to established *genre*s. The view that poetry is imitation, or mimesis, was first expressed by Aristotle, who wrote in the Introduction to *On the Art of Poetry* (*Poetics*, c.335-322BC):

"Epic and tragic poetry, comedy too, dithyrambic poetry, and most music composed for the flute and the lyre, can all be described in general terms as forms of imitation or representation."[1]

Aristotle analyzed imitation in these *genre*s and laid the foundation for classical (and therefore Neoclassical) literary criticism.

Horace's *On the Art of Poetry* (*Ars poetica*, c.19-18BC) did not discuss poetry as an imitative art but he was aware of imitation in the genesis of a poem: "I would lay down that the experienced poet, as an imitative artist (*doctum imitatorem*), should look to human life and character as his model, and from them derive a language that is true to life" (lines 317-18). In this work, and in his 'Epistle to Flores' (19BC) and his 'Epistle to Augustus', Horace abandoned his earlier satirical approach to poetry for a more philosophical outlook, holding that the secret of good writing is wisdom, that poetry should be edifying as well as delight. The edification is apparent in the common sense he displays while teaching the writing of poetry. He states 30 maxims young poets should follow. "Choose a subject that is suited to your abilities, you who aspire to be writers."[2] "The foundation and fountain-head of good competition is a sound understanding."[3] "Poets aim at giving either profit or delight, or at combining the giving of pleasure with some useful precepts for life."[4] Horace had followed his own advice in his *Odes*, which were intimate and reflective and had nothing in common with Pindar's lofty, heroic, passionate, dazzling odes. Horace's tone in his odes was serious and serene, sometimes ironic and melancholic and sometimes gently humorous.

Longinus's *On the Sublime* (1st century AD), a Greek work of literary criticism designed to correct the views of his neo-contemporary Caecilius of Calacte, also saw poetry as imitation. Longinus's work is about "grandeur", excellence in language and the power of a great spirit to stimulate ecstasy (as distinct from bombast, conceits or sentimentality). Longinus held that although grandeur or greatness of thought is said to be innate or inborn – "genius, they say, is innate; it is not something that can be learnt"[5] – it can be acquired by imitation of models, by emulating great authors such as Homer, Demosthenes and Plato, if the imitator handles passions well and uses appropriate techniques. Again, this is a classical and Neoclassical view, a reinforcing of the view of poetry as imitation.

The classical view was taken up within English literature by Sir Philip Sidney, whose *An Apologie for Poetrie* (which was written in 1579-80, published posthumously in 1595 and reissued in the same year as *The Defense of Poesy*) was the best work of Elizabethan literary criticism. Sidney referred to Aristotle's mimesis as both "representing" and "counterfeiting". An oration defending poetry against charges that it is a worthless waste of time, the *Apologie* argued that poetry teaches the rules of good government and makes a case for poetry as the best medium for giving moral teaching to future rulers. Sidney maintained that poetry, the earliest form of literature, holds a mirror up to Nature and teaches virtuous action better and more attractively than philosophy or history, both of which were first written down in verse.

Sidney answered objections to the different kinds of poetry and addressed the low repute of poetry in England during his time, which he blamed on idle readers and mercenary poets. Writing in the 1580s just before Shakespeare and Marlowe, he bemoaned the poverty of contemporary drama, and his criticisms of the Elizabethan scene ring hollow as we look back on the later Elizabethan time and judge it to have been a literary Golden Age. Sidney also pleaded for the social value of imaginative fiction such as his own *Arcadia*. T.S. Eliot pointed out that[6] *Arcadia* is dull and few of Sidney's poems warrant a return, except for a few sonnets, and it has to be said that his Neoclassical criticism lacks the authority of coming from a poet of the first rank.

The classical view was continued by Ben Jonson, who consciously imitated Horace and Catullus in his poems[7] and whose characters are types as we saw in Part One.

Dryden also practised imitation of the classics, notably Horace, and also of Shakespeare (in *All for Love*, which is subtitled "written in imitation of Shakespear's stile"). In his *An Essay of Dramatic Poesy* Dryden held that the representation of Nature is an "imitation of common persons and ordinary speaking" in which plot, characters, and description "are exalted above the level of common converse".[8] In the prefixed "account of '*Annus Mirabilis*' to Sir Robert Howard", Dryden writes of the imagination and fancy in a very Neoclassical way:

"The first happiness of the poet's imagination is properly invention, or the finding of the thought; the second is fancy, or the variation, deriving, or moulding of that thought, as the judgment represents it proper to a subject; the third is elocution, or the art of clothing and adorning that thought, as found and varied in apt, significant and sounding words. The quickness of the imagination is seen in the invention, the fertility in the fancy, and the accuracy in the expression."

This Neoclassical view sees imagination as finding, moulding and clothing a thought, and as Dryden imitated classical authors, his imagination found a thought in a classical text that could be imitated.

Pope in his 'An Essay on Criticism' (1711) also advocated imitation: "Learn hence for ancient rules a just esteem;/To copy Nature is to copy them." (139-40.) "True wit is Nature to advantage dress'd;/What oft was thought, but ne'er so well express'd." (297-8.) Pope saw imitation as extending to the sound of verse: "But when loud billows lash the sounding shore,/The hoarse rough verse should like the torrent roar." (368-9.)

Dr Johnson maintained in his 'Preface to Shakespeare' (1765) that there is a timeless, universal critical standard, and in his earlier *Rasselas* (ch.10) he had stated his belief that the poet records the typical.

In our time the view of Neoclassical poetry has been taken up by William Empson in *Seven Types of Ambiguity*, which held that uncertainty or overlap of meaning could enrich poetry; and by Yvor Winters, in *In Defense of Reason*, which held, "The poem is a statement in words about a human experience."[9] Neither discussed imitation, having moved Neoclassical thinking forward to linguistic considerations and regarding poetry as a rational, moralistic statement, but they would both have agreed with Aristotle's view of poetry as imitation, as, we have seen on p.302, would the Neoclassical critic Christopher Ricks.

The Tradition of Romantic Inspired Imagination

The Romantic view of poetry is that it does not imitate the external world but is an expression of the creative power of the imagination that inspires a vision that transcends the merely personal; and that poems do not conform to Neoclassical *genre*s but grow organically.

The imagination is a "mental faculty forming images of external objects not present to the senses" (*Concise Oxford Dictionary*), but the inspired imagination suggests that the images *are formed* from beyond the senses. The inspired imagination is inadequately dealt with in the *Shorter Oxford English Dictionary*'s five definitions of "imagination" (see pp.416-7). It falls under the fourth definition, "productive" imagination, "forming concepts beyond those derived from external objects", rather than the third definition, "reproductive" imagination, "conceiving the absent as if it were present", which includes making poems out of memories. But "productive" imagination can involve "imagining" oneself into the shoes of others as in John Wain's poem (see p.417), whereas in inspired imagination it receives images from beyond the senses, and is a power that takes over the poet's mind. The *Shorter Oxford English Dictionary*'s definition stops short of saying this, referring to "the creative faculty; poetic genius". We saw on p.302 that "genius" has Neoclassical/social and Romantic/metaphysical interpretations and senses; that there is Neoclassical genius that improves and Romantic genius that is inspired.

The ancient world knew that the imagination could be inspired from the beyond. The Indian *rsi*s, inspired poets at the time of the *Rig Veda*, knew the metaphysical Light (*tapas*), as we saw on pp.23-4. Greek thought and poetry claimed that when the god Apollo takes possession of a poet, the poet enters a transcendent ecstasy or frenzy, a "poetic madness". In Homer's *Odyssey* (22.347-48) the bard Phemius admits that the god has put songs into his heart.

This view of inspired imagination can be found in Plato's *Ion*:

"For all good poets, epic as well as lyric, compose their beautiful poems not by art, but because they are inspired and possessed. And as the Corybantian revellers when they dance are not in their right mind, so the lyric poets are not in their right mind when they are composing their beautiful strains; but when falling under the power of music and metre they are inspired and possessed....The poet is a light and winged and holy thing, and there is no invention in him until he has been inspired and is out of his senses, and the mind is no longer in him: when he has not attained to this state, he is powerless and is unable to utter his oracles."[10]

Plato often refers to poetic madness (for example, in *Laws* 719c, *Symposium* 197a and *Phaedrus* 244-45).

In his *Republic*, bk 10 Plato asserts that literature and the visual arts copy reality, meaning the objects and circumstances of the visible world, which is itself an imperfect copy of ideal objects and states that exist beyond this world. The imitation or mimesis of poetry and the arts is therefore of imperfection, and, Plato maintains, poetry and the arts teach nothing of value about life. He argues that poetry appeals to the less rational part of our nature and strengthens the lower mind. Believing that a ratiocinative culture was more evolved than inspired poetry, Plato excluded poets from his ideal republic.

Classical literature is full of references to inspiration. Virgil invokes a Muse in *Aeneid* 1, and Ovid refers to the inspiration of the poet in *Ars Amatoria* (3.549) and *Fasti* (6.5). Longinus, besides writing of imitation, says in *On the Sublime* that the reader is transported as if into divinity.

Milton invokes the Muse in *Paradise Lost* (for example, 9.24). In this work the Muse is a source of enlightenment like the Protestant Inner Light and is compared to the Spirit that inspired Moses when he received the Ten Commandments.

The view that poetry is the expression of the inspired imagination evolved through the 1800, 1802 and 1815 editions of Wordworth's 'Preface to the *Lyrical Ballads*'. The 1802 version challenged Neoclassical poetic diction and called for language to reflect the speech of "humble and rustic life" as "the poet is a man speaking to men". In championing the language of the most humble in society, Wordsworth was mounting a revolt against the social order that put rustic life at the bottom of its class structure. Wordsworth acknowledged inspiration:

"All good poetry is the spontaneous overflow of powerful feelings....It takes its origin from emotion recollected in tranquillity: the emotion is contemplated till, by a species of reaction, the tranquillity gradually disappears, and an emotion kindred to that which was before the subject of the contemplation, is gradually produced, and does itself actually exist in the mind."

Wordsworth had written of the imagination in some of his works. In *The Prelude* he wrote that an infant's mind "Doth like an agent of the one great Mind,/Create, creator and receiver both,/Working but in alliance with the works/Which it beholds. – Such, verily, is the first/Poetic spirit of our human life." (Bk 2, 257-261.) He referred to "Imagination, which, in truth,/Is but another name for absolute power/And clearest insight, amplitude of mind." (Bk 14, 189-191.) And again: "Imagination having been our theme..." (Bk 14, 206.) In the 1815 version of the 'Preface' he wrote, answering Coleridge, that imagination creates as well as associates: "The Imagination also shapes and *creates*; and how?...Consolidating numbers into unity, and dissolving and separating unity into number, – alternations proceeding from, and governed by, a sublime consciousness of the soul in her own mighty and almost divine powers." Wordsworth saw imagination and fancy as differing in degree, not kind.

Coleridge's *Biographia Literaria* (1814-17) was first written as a Preface to his own verse, with the partial intention of modifying Wordsworth. Chapter XIII replies to Wordsworth's ideas regarding the imagination and fancy, which he saw differently:

"The Imagination then, I consider either as primary, or secondary. The primary imagination I hold to be the living power and prime agent of all human perception, and as a repetition in the finite mind of the eternal act of creation in the infinite I AM. The secondary I consider as an echo of the former, co-existing with the conscious will, yet still as identical with the primary in the *kind* of its agency, and differing only in *degree*, and in the *mode* of its operation. It dissolves, diffuses, dissipates, in order to re-create; or where this process is rendered impossible, yet still, at all events it struggles to idealize and to unify. It is essentially *vital*, even as all objects (*as* objects) are essentially fixed and dead.

"Fancy, on the contrary, has no other counters to play with, but fixities and definites. The Fancy is indeed no other than a mode of memory emancipated from the order of time and space; and blended with and modified by that empirical phenomenon of the will, which we express by the word choice. But equally with the ordinary memory it must receive all its materials ready made from the law of association."

Coleridge, who was familiar with the philosophy of Plato, Aristotle and German transcendental metaphysics, decoupled imagination and fancy. He argued that imagination is different from associationism. He confessed in 'Dejection: an Ode' that he had been devastated by the disappearance of "my shaping spirit of Imagination". T.S. Eliot, quoting Coleridge's "Haply by abstruse research to steal/From my own nature all the natural man" in 'Dejection', claims that Coleridge's loss of his imagination was due to his study of metaphysics. He says, "It was better for Coleridge, as poet, to read books of travel and exploration than to read books of metaphysics and political economy."[11] Having written my own book on metaphysical philosophy,[12] I would disagree. It is possible to take time out from being a poet to set out the Oneness of the universe and then return to poetry with one's sense of unity strengthened. It is clearly wrong for a poet to spend excessive time researching metaphysics, but it is beneficial for him to do this in moderation.

Shelley's *A Defence of Poetry*, written in Pisa in 1821, defended the inspired imagination. He was replying to Peacock's assertion that there was "no longer a poetical audience among the higher class of minds" and that "the poetical reading public" was "composed of the mere dregs of the intellectual community" and must rest on "mawkish sentiment with an absolute negation of reason and knowledge".[13]

Shelley contrasted the imagination with reason (which he saw as deductive and experimental). He emphasized the unconscious power of the imagination over the conscious will in poetic composition. He saw the power of the imagination as rising from within, and as poets "imagine and express this indestructible order" they are "the institutors of laws, and the founders of civil society", or "the unacknowledged legislators of the world". "Poetry lifts the veil from the hidden beauty of the world". "The great instrument of moral good is the imagination."

Shelley saw Homer as the first and Dante as the second epic poet, ignoring Lucretius, whose spirit was held back by the sensible world ("Lucretius had limed the wings of his swift spirit in the dregs of the sensible world"), and also ignoring Virgil, who "with a modesty that ill became his genius, had affected the fame of an imitator" (in accordance with classical literary-critical theory), "even whilst he created anew all that he copied". (According to Shelley, Virgil was being modest in claiming to be a mere imitator, but Virgil may also have been positioning himself in the classical and Neoclassical tradition of Aristotle's imitation. However, Asconius Pedianus, in his *Life of Virgil*,[14] denies that Virgil confessed to being an imitator, saying that "Virgil used to rebut the charge of plagiarizing Homer with the following remark: 'Only let such critics try to do the same themselves. They would soon find that it is easier to steal his club from Hercules than to steal a line from Homer.'")

In 'Epipsychidion' (January/February 1821) Shelley saw the imagination as the Light: "[True Love is] like thy light,/Imagination! which from earth and sky,/And from the depths of human fantasy,/As from a thousand prisms and mirrors, fills/The Universe with glorious beams, and kills/Error." (The "prisms and mirrors" may have been suggested by light glinting on the Arno which ran alongside the Lung'arno Galileo in Pisa, where Shelley lived from 1820 to 1822.)

Shelley defended the Romantic view of poetry as inspiration:

"A man cannot say, 'I will compose poetry.' The greatest poet even cannot say it; for the mind in creation is as a fading coal, which some invisible influence, like an inconstant wind, awakens to transitory brightness; this power arises from within....But when composition begins, inspiration is already on the decline, and the most glorious poetry that has ever been communicated to the world is probably a feeble shadow of the original conception of the poet."

Shelley symbolized inspiration as the west wind in his 'Ode to the West Wind'. He was very good on the process of creation. Having created two epic poems myself I concur with his view that "Milton conceived the *Paradise Lost* as a whole before he executed it in portions. We have his own authority also for the muse having 'dictated' to him the 'unpremeditated song'."[15]

Keats wrote of the imagination in his letters, as we saw in ch.7. He explored the sympathetic imagination and "negative capability", a search for truth or reality without any impulsive reaching after fact: "when a man is capable of being in uncertainties, mysteries, doubts, without any irritable reaching after fact and reason".[16] There are passages in his letters about the meaning of "truth" and the imaginative inner life. But Keats was very young and was anti-fact. He did not want to know "how change the moons,/Or hear the voice of busy common-sense" ('Ode on Indolence'), and it was enough for him to lose himself in the "setting sun" or "a sparrow" before his window (letter to Bailey, 22 November 1817) without "any irritable reaching after fact and reason".

However, a number of facts would have deepened his reflection: where the goldfinch next to the sparrow came from and how many of the other birds pecking at seed or nuts were visitors from abroad. Keats' Romantic criticism is exposed as ignorant on these points, and Neoclassical fact and reason can deepen and enhance the totality of a contemplative vision and strengthen a contemplator's sense of the workings of the One. Matthew Arnold, whose criticism took up more of a Universalist position, put his finger on this aspect of Keats' outlook in his essay *The Function of Criticism*: "The English poetry of the first quarter of this [i.e. the 19th century], with plenty of energy, plenty of creative force, did not know enough."

Later Romantic critics such as Hazlitt and Carlyle reinforced this Romantic view of poetry as inspired imagination. Carlyle in *The Hero as Poet* (1840), which focuses on Dante and Shakespeare, saw the workings of imagination in terms of the Light: "Can the man say, *Fiat lux*, Let there be light; and out of chaos make a world? Precisely, as there is light in himself, will he accomplish this." He added that "the seeing eye...discloses the inner harmony of things."[17]

A Romantic critic of the 20th century, Herbert Read, whose philosophy of Romanticism contributed to his "synthesis of romantic intuition and intellectual order",[18] also stressed the inspired imagination. In 1936, for example, he wrote, "We think we know how one kind of poetry originates – in inspiration....[The poet's] deepest and most original interpretation is likely to come by way of the imagination." [19]

Read disagreed with the Neoclassical view of poetry Dryden stated in his prefixed account of '*Annus Mirabilis*':

"The Composition of all poems is or ought to be of wit; and wit in the Poet, or wit-writing...is no other than the faculty of imagination in the Writer, which, like a nimble Spaniel, beats over and ranges through the field of Memory, till it springs the Quarry it hunted after; or, without metaphor, which searches over all the Memory for the Species or Ideas of those things which it designs to represent. Wit written, is that which is well defined, the happy result of Thought, or produce of Imagination."

Read said in 'Poetic Diction' (1926) that Dryden wrote "wit written", not poetry from the imagination: "Such art is not poetry."[20] He felt that Dryden's verse was from thought, not from the imagination.

In his essay *Form in Modern Poetry* (1932) Read disregarded Milton, Dryden and Pope:

"The main tradition of English poetry...begins with Chaucer and reaches its final culmination in Shakespeare. It is contradicted by most French poetry before Baudelaire, by the so-called Classical phase of English poetry culminating in Alexander Pope, and by the late Poet Laureate [Robert Bridges]. It was re-established in England by Wordsworth and Coleridge, developed in some degree by Browning and Gerard Manley Hopkins, and in our own day by poets like Wilfred Owen, Ezra Pound and T.S. Eliot."[21]

In *The Use of Poetry and the Use of Criticism* (1933) T.S. Eliot was shocked by this rejection of Milton, Dryden and Pope. He took Dryden's side ("I cannot see why Dryden's and Wordsworth's minds should have worked any more differently from each other than those of any other two poets"),[22] and his reconciling position is a Universalist one.

Eliot, who combined classicism and Romanticism in his work, perhaps sensed the difficulty of labelling himself as a Neoclassical or Romantic poet a year later in *After Strange Gods* (1934):

"Romanticism and classicism are not matters with which creative writers can afford to bother overmuch, or with which they do, as a rule, in practice greatly concern themselves. It is true that from time to time writers have labelled themselves 'romanticists' or 'classicists', just as they have from time to time banded themselves together under other names. These names which groups of writers and artists give themselves are the delight of professors and historians of literature, but should not be taken very seriously; their chief value is temporary and political – that, simply, of helping to make the authors known to a contemporary public; and I doubt whether any poet has ever done himself anything but harm by attempting to write as a 'romantic' or as a 'classicist'. No sensible author, in the midst of something that he is trying to write, can stop to consider whether it is going to be romantic or the opposite. At the moment when one writes, one is what one is, and the damage of a lifetime, and of having been born into an unsettled society, cannot be repaired at the moment of composition."[23]

However, Eliot is off beam. We saw on p.238 that he attributed the difference between Neoclassical thought and Romantic feeling to "a dissociation of sensibility" in 'The Metaphysical Poets' (1921) that split the "felt thought" of Donne. But the thought was inextricably linked to the classical and Neoclassical social emphasis within the fundamental theme, and the feeling was inextricably linked to the quest for Reality within the metaphysical aspect of the fundamental theme. Eliot was not correct in siting the split between the two after Donne as the split occurred in the classical world, if not before. It was inconvenient for his theory of "the dissociation of sensibility" that "classical" and

"Romantic" should be conflicting critical labels, and though a Universalist himself, he did literary criticism a disservice by dismissing the difference after his disagreement with Read. Read's condemnation of Dryden was valid in terms of his Romantic view of the Neoclassical approach of Dryden, and would have won the sympathy of Kathleen Raine, who regarded Auden as a journalist in not being influenced by his inspired imagination.

Kathleen Raine saw poetry as inspired imagination in her essays in *Defending Ancient Springs*. In her essay 'On the Symbol' (1964) she wrote brilliantly on William Empson's positivism:

"What William Empson, in his subtle, brilliant, and influential critical writings gave his generation was a theory of poetry consistent with the positivist philosophy which flourished in Cambridge; the Cambridge of Darwin and the Cavendish Laboratory, of Russell and Wittgenstein and their successors. His theory of ambiguity lacks nothing in conceptual subtlety but dispenses with the imagination and disregards the metaphysical roots of poetic thought. I still admire the brilliance – though the brilliance is often perverse – of his theory of ambiguity and of complex words; yet I see now what then I only felt, wherein it fails as a full description of poetry; for all the complexities and ambiguities and relationships which he discerns are upon the same plane of the real. There is one type of complexity which he fails to consider, that resonance which may be present within an image of apparent simplicity, setting into vibration planes of reality and of consciousness other than that of the sensible world: the power of the symbol and symbolic discourse....I have since come to understand that what such theories as we then held, together with the kind of poetry we were bidden to admire, precisely lacked (in comparison, that is, with Spenser or Shelley, Milton or Yeats), is, in the metaphysical sense, intellectuality."[24]

Her main thrust applies equally to Empson's mentor, I.A. Richards, and to his disciple, Christopher Ricks, who omitted both Kathleen Raine and David Gascoyne from his edition of *The Oxford Book of English Verse*.

Kathleen Raine gives an account of being inspired:

"When I was young, I looked for, and constantly discovered, the numinous in and through nature; and only in middle life did I first experience in an overwhelming degree one of these archetypal epiphanies. The vision was of the Tree of Life, with many associated symbols, all suddenly and clearly and simultaneously presented to my mind. For a long time I lived on that vision, to which I could return, so I discovered, not with the same overwhelming awe as the first time, but clearly enough, at any time, to contemplate aspects of it which I had at first seen or had forgotten. Others have come since, some in dream, some not....Physical perception may sometimes be the vehicle of imaginative vision, but is not necessarily so....The 'visionary gleam', as Wordsworth himself discovered, may be entirely absent from the sensible world."[25]

There is much in Kathleen Raine's criticism that I agree with. However, she was extremely insistent that the language of poetry is the Romantic language of the soul, and that there is no place for rational thought. She wanted me to be an extreme Romantic, and did not fully understand my reconciling Universalist position. As we have just seen, it won't do for Read (or Wordsworth before him) to exclude Milton, Dryden and Pope from the English literary tradition, and to put forward a one-sided Romantic view of the tradition. In the same way, it won't do for Kathleen Raine to exclude Dryden, Auden and Empson from the English literary tradition.

Eliot was a Universalist critic because he admitted both sides in his essays, and his taking Read to task for his one-sidedness is a measure of his centrist, Universalist position. Empson was one of my predecessors in Japan, and having had many conversations with his disciple, the Neoclassical Ricks (who can wear a centrist hat when he chooses as can be seen in the bulk of his selections in his edition of *The Oxford Book of English Verse*), and Empson's opponent, Kathleen Raine, I have arrived at Eliot's position between the two contraries, a centrist, Universalist reconciler's unitive position.

And so I affirm that the tradition of English literature contains both views of poetry and their traditions: poetry as imitation and poetry as inspired imagination.

Universalism's Inspired Imitation: The Basis of Universalist Poetry

We saw on p.179 that in *From Classic to Romantic* W. Jackson Bate showed that there was continuity between Neoclassical and Romantic literature. Bate contended that the supplanting of Neoclassical taste and aesthetic judgement by Romantic taste and aesthetic judgement was connected with "the broader shift in European thought which it reflects".[26] This work, presented as the Lowell Lectures in Boston in 1945 and dedicated to the contemporary philosopher I most admire, Alfred North Whitehead, can be seen as reconciling Neoclassicism and Romanticism by viewing them in terms of a historical progression, a perspective Whitehead surely approved.

Nevertheless, as we have just seen, the 18th-century Neoclassicism to which Bate refers was quite late in a long tradition of Neoclassical imitation. The 19th-century Romanticism was a later surfacing of a tradition of inspiration known in ancient India and Greece, and the reconciliation of the two traditions has been renewed every few decades, as can be seen from the four post-Renaissance reconciliations. In short, the continuity of 18th-century Neoclassicism and 19th-century Romanticism does nothing to explain away the fact that the two traditions have been opposed for at least 2,400 years, and that in our time they are still opposed, despite the Victorian and Modernist reconciliations.

Universalist poetry takes up where balanced Victorians such as Tennyson and balanced Modernists such as Eliot left off. It reconciles anew the conflicting metaphysical and secular traditions and Neoclassical and Romantic traditions and attitudes, the contraries or opposites that stem from that conflict and dividing line. Pairs of opposites within the Neoclassical and Romantic positions can be listed as thesis (Neoclassical positions) on the left and antithesis (Romantic positions) on the right in a dialectic whose synthesis is a combination of both thesis and antithesis:

- imitation, and inspired imagination;
- harmony, and the infinite;
- natural images, and symbols;
- genius that improves, and genius that is inspired;
- poetry as statement, and poetry as image;

329

- traditional stanzaic form, and organic form;
- poetry from the rational, social ego, and poetry from the soul;
- objective poetry, and personal poetry;
- materialist reality, and Reality as Light;
- personal and social reality, and metaphysical Reality;
- personal memory, and contemplation;
- the historical, and the timeless;
- the temporal, and the eternal;
- secular outlook, and metaphysical outlook;
- poetry of society, and poetry of the beyond;
- poetry of language, and poetry of the universe;
- structure (including grammatology and deconstruction), and symbolism;
- poetry of vices in relation to implied virtue, and poetry of the quest for Reality.

In other words, Universalist poetry reconciles the metaphysical-Romantic tradition of the infinite with the secular-Neoclassical tradition of the finite. Secular-Neoclassical poets who write from their rational, social ego and have not opened to their universal being that perceives the infinite are ignoring a long tradition of taste and aesthetic judgement that reveals the truth about the universe through the unity-seeing and synthesizing perception Coleridge called "the esemplastic... imagination". Secular poets who have not undergone the inner development required to perceive the metaphysical and therefore deny the metaphysical turn their backs on one half of the literary tradition. The defence of Universalist poetry against secularism is that it includes the *entire* poetic tradition in its synthesizing reconciliation, and is a truer expression of the whole being than is secular-Neoclassical poetry, which is an expression of *part* of the poetic tradition and is written from the rational, social ego, and excludes the deeper being.

The main perception of Universalism is that while poetry can erupt volcanically from the inspired imagination (or be received as symbols from the Light like dew) it can also be a measured, technical imitation of models of past works and improvement on them.

Both activities can be found in one work, though not necessarily at the same time. I have said that the fourth Universalist synthesis and reconciliation is at an early stage, which does not make practical illustration easy. I need to demonstrate imitation and inspiration at work in specific poems to clinch my argument. In the last chapter I focused on the reconciliation of the metaphysical and secular traditions in my work, and I can best illustrate the reconciliation of the traditions of Neoclassical imitation and Romantic inspiration by returning to my work. I must stress that my work offers just one approach to Universalist reconciliation, and that other writers will offer different approaches. Neoclassical statement and Romantic image are opposite ends of a unified spectrum, and extracts can be expected to incline to statement or image depending on their context in the work from which they are taken.

The blend of imitation of the external world and inspiration can be found in my early work, *The Early Education and Making of a Mystic*, which combines scenes from the outside world with glimpses from the beyond. I planned to have a hundred scenes, but in fact there are 42. The poem is subtitled 'Fragments of a Spiritual Odyssey', and is the beginning of my quest for Reality. I believe my model for imitation was Wordsworth's *Prelude*, and the inspiration in my imagination was to make sense of illumination.

This blend of imitation and inspiration was carried forward into 'The Silence', which at one time was also to be a hundred poems. It narrates an Angry Young Man's revolt against his English surroundings, his turning away from society and his finding of serenity and inspired illumination among the giant Buddhas of Japan. The poem is an inspired quest for Reality in a Modernist sequence of images, my main model for imitation being Eliot's 'The Waste Land' and the narrative thrust and glosses of Coleridge's 'The Ancient Mariner'. The inspiration in my imagination was to show that an inner transformation is necessary for Reality, the Light, to be experienced: a partially involuntary undermining of the rational, social ego (the "Reflection") and a shift to a new centre within the universal being and future self ("Shadow"), from which a new self grows like a stem pushing through from a seed:

"The lift went down a well
Into a mine of gleaming diamonds

And golden gods with Egyptian heads were drawn past my closed
  eyelids.
Through falling masonry I rushed up into the shaking street –
And seeing the city crumbled into a thousand ruins,
And the dancing dead, I did not cry out or weep,
Wandering in the girdered rubble of an old personality.
And when i awoke, i was a floor below my thoughts,
Looking out at the dawn as from a tiled bungalow –
And suddenly, nourished by silence
My seed-case burst into a thousand I's
And a central stem broke through the tiled crown of my head. Hallelujah!
  in a dazzling universe i had no defence,
round that round white light, life and night were one
and i was afraid, for i did not know
                       if the sun reflected
my reflecting sun."

                       ('The Silence', 1219-1235.)

After inner transformation is the prospect of growth:

"To outgrow all ideas
Save the important one,
The upward thrust of the sap
To a form of pagan height
And the quiet, stout-timbered shrine,
Or in the fading light,
At one with his fellow man,
The giant Buddha's calm."

                       ('The Silence', 1331-1338.)

Poems in *The Gates of Hell* describe the soul's development from attachment to detachment, purgation, inspired illumination and the unitive vision. They show a transformation from ego to universal being and inspired encounters with the Light. My models for imitation were Catullus's Roman poems and Tennyson's *In Memoriam*. The inspiration in my imagination was to show the inner waste into which Reality can break as Light. In 'Visions: Golden Flower, Celestial Curtain' there is an eye-witness account of experiencing the Light of Reality and the inspired imagination:

"That weekend I lay down and breathed at twilight,
Looked into my closed eyes, saw white light flowing
Upwards..., a tree of white fire, flickering.
Then a spring opened in me, for an hour bright
Visions wobbled up like bubbles: from a great height
A centre of light, a gold-white flower, shining
Like a dahlia, the centre and source of my being;
A chrysanthemum; a sun; a fountain of white
Light; strange patterns; old masters I was not certain
I had seen before; old gods. I was refreshed, after this
I fell on my knees in the dark, and breathed "I surrender"
To the white point. It changed into a celestial curtain
Blown in the wind, like the aurora borealis.
I feel limp, an afterglow in each moist finger."

In the 147 poems within this work Neoclassical social reality and the Romantic infinite are combined, as they are in *The Gates of Paradise*. All the poems in these works are Universalist poems.

'A Metaphysical in Marvell's Garden' (1973) describes a visit to Fairfax's grounds at Nun Appleton in Yorkshire where Marvell wrote his metaphysical poem 'The Garden' in 1651. Contemplation takes over and there is a shift to the inner:

"Here shed body like a sheepskin jacket,
Discard all thought as in a mystery school.
By this nun's grave sit and be the moment,
A oneness gazing on the heart's green pool.
A universe unfolds between two stone columns
And takes a leafy shape of clouded ground.
The sun-lily floats. Question its waters,
It will trickle through your fingers and be drowned.

The South Front sundial says in coloured glass
"*Qui Est Non Hodie*". I am a bowl.

In the North Hall the piano-tuner
Ping ping pings and trembles through my soul...."

There is an inspired glimpse of hidden Reality as the natural world
becomes tides of energy:

"With drowsed eyes glance at solid grass and be
In whirlpools of energy like a sea.
Breaths heave the light, and answering currents pour
Through spongy stones and stars, or seaweed tree.
Now see with eye of mind into swelled form,
Imagine sap wash, oak wave in acorn.
Knowers are one with known, and are soaked by tides
That foam and billow through an ebbing lawn."

The soul has been seen as a "climbing rose", and souls are now seen as
being formed on a "great Rose-tree of light" from which thorns
manifest "as petals fall to ground". The contemplating soul gazes down
on galaxies "like curved rose petals". The closing vision turns from
Fairfax's daughter to the present and reconciles soul, society and
universe (and Neoclassical and Romantic):

"May you be
A rose-sun-leaf-ground-cloudy fire-gold heart."

The inspiration in my imagination was to show the relevance of Reality,
the Light, to the everyday life of a child. My model for imitation was,
of course, Marvell's 'The Garden'.

Around 1980 I underwent a development in the course of writing the
poems in *The Fire-Flower*, and my poems became more classical. In
The Rainbow in the Spray and *Question Mark over the West* I combine
the Light of Reality with specific social settings. In 'Cambridge Ode:
Against Materialism' I consider three hundred years of materialism and
the imagination's reaction against materialism, and reconcile the two in
an image of two fields separated by a gate. When the gate is open there
is only one field:

"And between two fields railed-in with iron, I stare
At gates in the hedge, where thought and shade are green,
Swing back their rust, and in one field declare
Against Materialism! by my hedgerow screen."

The inspiration in my imagination was to show that Newton's search for an expanding force of light that counteracts gravity may have been a search for the workings of metaphysical Reality, a sea of mind-and-matter that counteracts Cambridge rationalism. My model for imitation was a passage in David Castillejo's *The Expanding Force in Newton's Cosmos*.

In 'Night Visions in Charlestown' I contrast the "dark night" of three hundred years of science with the inspired imagination's flight of the soul to the future and a vision that leaves the soul "aglow". The inspiration in my imagination was the soul's flight to the coming Age of Light. In this future age Universalism and knowledge of the universe are widespread, there is a united Europe, and the soul is routinely filled with Light. My model for imitation was the "flight of the soul" in Plotinus's writings.

In 'A Mystic Fire-Potter's Red Sun-Halo', the harbour in Charlestown, Cornwall, becomes an image of the soul. Just as the narrow bridge there dips to let ships into the inner harbour, so the inner harbour of the soul opens to the sea of Being. The inspiration in my imagination was to show an artist who lived by the Light. My model for imitation may have been Eliot's 'Portrait of a Lady' – for its narrative approach rather than its treatment of the lady. In my Cornish sonnets the sea symbolizes the creative power of the imagination which pours onto the rocky land.

In 'Out on the Alone or, The Mystery of Being' a fishing-trip becomes an image for leaving the world of land and confronting Being. The inspiration in my imagination was to show that Being and immortality can be glimpsed in solitude. My model for imitation may have been Cowper's 'The Cast-Away'.

In 'Question Mark over the West', which was written at the height of the Cold War, I look at the stars, and in the Plough, which is shaped like a question mark, I see a natural image for the soul's questioning about the future of the West. I focus on "the moon-like One". The inspiration in my imagination was the threat of Soviet Communism, seen as a hammer and sickle within the Plough hanging over the idyllic country life in the West. My model for imitation was probably the impact of the Roman civil wars on the settled countryside, as reflected in poems by Virgil and Horace.

Universalist poetry reconciles the mystic and visionary traditions in English verse, which are quite different as I explained in a letter to Kathleen Raine.[27] The mystic tradition sees the soul as progressing from attachment to purgation, illumination and a unitive outlook, well-documented stages along the Mystic Way.[28] Poets in this tradition have seen the Light, notably Dante, St John of the Cross and Eliot. The visionary tradition, which is essentially Romantic, expresses visions seen in the imagination as in Coleridge's 'Kubla Khan' and in Yeats' "Rough beast, its hour come round at last" that "Slouches towards Bethlehem to be born". My work finds room for both traditions, sometimes in different places and at different times, but, as in 'Visions: Golden Flower, Celestial Curtain' (see p.333), sometimes both at the same time. In a number of poems like this one I have recorded my eye-"witness-accounts" of my first mystic glimpses of Light and of the visionary symbols that came with it – my contact with the Muse that brought experience of both traditions.[29]

I have said that Universalist poetry reconciles the mystic and visionary traditions, and that Kathleen Raine, who spoke for the visionary tradition in our time in her books on Blake and Yeats, reproved me for introducing the language of the world, of statement, in these poems alongside the language of the soul, of image, not realizing that my aim was to bring about a blend of her Romantic tradition with the Neoclassical tradition she despised. (See pp.327-8.) She wanted me to write like an extremist Romantic, not realizing that I was trying to create an enduring union of inspiration and imitation, and of the Romantic and Neoclassical styles.

Sometimes inspiration can burst into consciousness, like a large apple falling through leaves from a tree. Sitting on the Lung'arno Mediceo by the Arno in Pisa in May 1993, within view of the wall behind which Shelley wrote *A Defence of Poetry* in March 1821 and spoke of poetry's lifting the veil from the hidden beauty of the world, I had a glimpse – a profound revelation – in which, for about ten seconds,

I saw two vast finished works of mine in an image and knew that I should undertake them immediately: my epic poem *Overlord*, and *Classical Odes*. This revelation was a compelling instance of Romantic inspiration in the imagination, and I recorded it in two poems, 'By the Arno, Pisa' and 'After the Pisan Arno'.[30]

In the case of *Overlord*, I had visited Ezra Pound in Rapallo in 1970,[31] and had discussed with him my intention to write a poem in 12 books. I had often returned to the idea during the next 23 years. I looked at Homer, Virgil, Dante and Milton, and Pound's *Cantos*, and having considered to what extent there should be imitation I resolved to narrate the end of the Second World War from D-Day to, and after, the fall of Berlin, our Troy. I had put off making a start – like Milton, who first had the idea of writing *Paradise Lost* during his Italian tour of 1638-39 but did not start the poem until July 1665; and before him, Virgil, who had put off *The Aeneid* for 20 years.

Coleridge understood the long process of gestation of an epic poem: "I should not think of devoting less than twenty years to an Epic Poem. Ten to collect materials and warm my mind with universal science. I would be a tolerable Mathematician, I would thoroughly know Mechanics, Hydrostatics, Optics, and Astronomy, Botany, Metallurgy, Fossilism, Chemistry, Geology, Anatomy, Medicine – then the mind of man – then the minds of men – in all Travels, Voyages and Histories. So I would spend ten years – the next five to the composition of the poem – and the five last to the correction of it. So I would write haply not unhearing of the divine and rightly-whispering Voice, which speaks to mighty minds of predestinated Garlands, starry and unwithering." (Letter to Joseph Cottle, early April 1797.)[32]

I was aware of Pound's *Pisan Cantos* (1948), which were written in a US Army Disciplinary Training Centre near Pisa after his arrest in Genoa in 1945, and now knew I had to write about the Second World War, the outcome of which had dominated Europe for the past 50 years.

In the case of *Classical Odes*, the inspiration in my imagination was to show the passing of an old way of life and the emerging of a new one. My model for imitation was a line in Tennyson's 'The Passing of Arthur', "The old order changeth, yielding place to new." I drew on Herodotus and Pausanias, who both visited classical sites, and on Virgil and Horace, who wrote of everyday life in the countryside. I found

Horace's four books of odes as a classical model for the odes I had glimpsed. They were very different from Pindar's odes, and, having considered to what extent there should be formal imitation I resolved to create my own stanzaic form in accordance with my glimpse of the revealed finished work, which I took to be a call to let the culture of Europe back into English literature, a cause dear to Eliot's heart.

My 318 Classical Odes, which are addressed to posterity, combine history located in specific historical, social places, and the beyond that can be approached from them, blending image and symbol, Neoclassical and Romantic. I show Western civilization as a waste land in decay, and new forms emerging, including the new Europe, and relate the quest to specific places. I seek Neoclassical proportion and balance, and in this work swung Neo-Baroque poetry back towards classicism while consistently revealing the Romantic One. My method is caught in the ode, 'In Cornwall: A New Renaissance':

"Why do I do this, spend my time each day
Drafting a poem, polishing it twice?
I sharpen my thought, hunt for precise words,
Make a statement in language that's concise....
I have a need to keen clarity, search
For new ways to relate to and present
The One in words, as some need prayers in church."

Another example can be found in 'After the Pisan Arno':

"I write to achieve clarity of thought,
About complexity, simplified view,
And to express classical clarity,
Reflect on experience digested, true,
Mind grappling with complex issues, precise
Ending on top with exactness yet dense;
Catch the situation's total content,
Sense first, care for exact verse serving sense."

In *Classical Odes* I aim for clarity of thought and expression in precise, concise language, and put sense first, ahead of complex subject matter.

Kathleen Raine objected to history being introduced into poetry. In *Defending Ancient Springs* she argued[33] that Juvenal's Rome, Dryden's Restoration and Auden's Twenties are dated in a way that the timeless worlds of Dante, Milton, Coleridge and Yeats are not dated as these four make fewer topical references and write from the imagination, not thought. But Yeats' 'Easter 1916' is about a very dated event, and yet is a Universalist work, combining history and the imagination. Lifting the reader from the sensible, historical world into a perception of the One is imaginative, even though the language, reconciling Neoclassicism and Romanticism, conveys the thought of the personal, rational, social ego as much as does the work of Dryden, Pope or Auden.

In my two epic poems the inspiration in my imagination was to reconcile the chaos and havoc of war with the providential workings of the One, and to justify these contraries to man. My models for imitation were Homer's *Iliad*, Virgil's *Aeneid* and Milton's *Paradise Lost*.

Overlord is Universalist because it offers a historical narrative in 41,000 lines of blank verse about the major event of the 20th century, the Second World War, which is central to the world's common culture for everyone has heard of it; and integrates it with a mythological, Dantesque background that arises from the imagination: Heaven's concern at the smashing up of Europe, Christ's determination to support Eisenhower (an American hero), their conflict with Satan and Hell, who support Hitler, and Christ's first attempt at establishing a Thousand-Year Millennial Reign. Eisenhower visits both Hell and Heaven, in the footsteps of (if not in direct imitation of) visits to the Underworld by Homer's Odysseus and Virgil's Aeneas. The conflicts of war are reconciled with the One:

"God saw no dualism, just the One
Whose positive and negative forces,
Plus and minus charges, both Light and Dark,
Like day and night, and life and death, both form
A Unity comprising contraries,...
Apparent opposites which complement
The One Whole that God is, and God was pleased
That contradictions were back in balance,

Reconciled within the cosmic design,
With Light just uppermost as it should be." (12.4843-54.)

The same principles are behind my second poetic epic, *Armageddon*, a narrative in 25,000 lines of blank verse about the major event of the 21st century to date: the War on Terror from 9/11 to the retirement of Bush, which is integrated with a mythological, Dantesque background of a second bout of seven years' tribulation and a second establishment of Christ's Thousand-Year Millennial Universalist Reign. The hero, President George W. Bush, hunts down bin Laden, who was in possession of at least 20 nuclear suitcase-bombs stolen from the ex-USSR and sold to him (a fact confirmed by Hans Blix of the IAEA in 2004), some of which he planned to explode in ten American cities – hence the title. Bush visits both Hell and Heaven in the footsteps of the journey to the Underworld of Odysseus and Aeneas, and of Eisenhower (in *Overlord*). There are descriptions of the dead and of the vices they indulged in during their lives. The journey to the Underworld still has a moral dimension. The conflicts of war are again reconciled with the One:

"O Wisdom, you are, like Christ, an ideal
Beyond imperfect men who just aspire
And your Millennium which Christ has brought
Is an aspiration for which the Good
Work and which is for ever undermined
By the Bad in the endless interplay
Between opposing *yin-yang* forces that
Conflict and balance, order-disorder,...
O Wisdom, you have tilted the balance
Just slightly towards peace and against war
Like a cease-fire that's often breached, yet holds.
And now Christ's Thousand-Year Millennium
Has given us recalcitrant humans
A better chance of forming a World State
That keeps the peace and restores paradise
In outer harmony where souls can grow." (12.3242-62.)

The blend of image and statement can be seen in a later passage:

"Just as a spider spins thread from its glands,
Silks from its spinnerets it chews to break
And weaves and hangs a web with a centre
And twelve spokes radiating out,...
And patient, waits for tiny flying things
To stick on thread where crystal drops of dew,
Condensed balls of atmospheric vapour,
Have formed in evening air; so this poet's
Gut and mouth have spun a twelve-spoked theme and
Hung its structure for Being to condense
As globules like dew on its worked silk thread,
Pure drops of truth manifesting from air,
The metaphysical condensed to form.
I wait for images to fly in and
Become entangled on its sticky mesh,
Tremble clear droplets under rosy sky,
The delicate filigree tracery
Of its design whose symmetry pleases
But is a practical, working form that
Has been shaped to catch truths and symbols that
Feed the spider-like imagination.
I hung my twelve-book web and caught my catch." (12.3459-83.)

Again and again while writing *Overlord* and *Armageddon* I heard passages drifting into my mind, seemingly from beyond, the workings of inspiration, and I scribbled them out as fast as I could to keep up with what I was being given. I said on p.336 that the ten-second revelation of *Overlord* and *Classical Odes* took place across the Arno from the site of the house Shelley occupied in the summer of the year he wrote in 'Adonais' after the death of Keats (when to and fro between Pisa and San Guiliano): "The One remains, the many change and pass;/Heaven's light forever shines, Earth's shadows fly;/Life, like a dome of many-coloured grass,/Stains the white radiance of Eternity." In his *A Defence of Poetry*, which he composed there, as I said on pp.322-3 Shelley wrote well of the inspiration Milton experienced in conceiving and writing his epic: "Milton conceived the *Paradise Lost* as a whole before he executed it in portions. We have his own authority for the muse having 'dictated' to him the 'unpremeditated song'." I can remember David Gascoyne saying of a particular poem, "It came from the beyond." In my experience writing epic poems is as much a process of inspiration as of imitation of the works of others or of research sources.

I have been demonstrating that the basis of Universalist poetry – its contextual glue – is inspired imitation, but I should point out that the same is true of short stories. The thousand and one stories in my *Collected Stories* also blend inspiration and imitation. Many detail aspects of the quest for Reality, and many follow Boccaccio and Chaucer in describing the follies and vices of our time. They present, to echo Johnson's description of the wit of Metaphysical poets in his 'Life of Cowley', "a combination of dissimilar images" in which "the most heterogeneous ideas are yoked by violence together", and in so far as they adhere to, and carry forward, Johnson's description of Metaphysical wit, they can be regarded as stories in the 17th-century Metaphysical tradition. Their blend of Romantic and Neoclassical inspired imitation is Universalist.

Contemporary Universalist poetry's inspired imitation unites the contrasting metaphysical and secular themes and the contrasting Neoclassical and Romantic aesthetic views and styles, blending theme, form, style, image and statement into a new phase of unified creativity.

Universalist Poetry Reflects the Order and Meaning in the Universe
To sum up, what Coleridge called "the esemplastic power of the imagination"[34] shapes bits of experience into one, renews the whole from parts. Imitation of models (such as Homer, Virgil, Dante and Milton) may help, but inspiration, which Shelley symbolized as the west wind, is very important to the genesis of Universalist poems. New Universalist poetry is innovatory (rather than experimental like Modernist poetry, exclusively mechanical like Neoclassical poetry or organic like Romantic poetry). It deals with traditional matter in traditional metres, and eschews free verse, which as Eliot saw[35] is not the way forward. It combines and reflects conflicting styles.

But above all, Universalist poetry approaches order and the One. In the course of his act of writing a poem, the Universalist poet reshapes and restructures the apparently chaotic universe into a structure of order and in doing so approaches – puts himself in readiness for – the One. He receives from the One a glimpse or reassurance that the universe is an ordered whole with a purpose and meaning. This is the reward for the quest for truth and Reality, the metaphysical aspect of the fundamental theme of world literature: reassurance that the universe, and therefore life, is not a materialist accident as secular atheists assert, but is a living, unified power that imbues all forms of life with ordered meaning. Universalist poetry retrieves purpose and meaning from experience and conveys it to a new generation.

The language Universalist poetry uses is a blend of the language of discourse used by the personal, rational, social ego, and the language of the soul which is inspired by the creative power of the imagination, the Light. Universalist poetry reveals, and exemplifies, the Mystic Way's shift from the Neoclassical consciousness of the personal rational, social ego to the Romantic soul – and records the shift in a mixture of statements and images, not exclusively in the abstruse language of the soul.

I took issue on pp.238 and 326-7 with T.S. Eliot's view in 'The Metaphysical Poets' that in the 17th century "a dissociation of sensibility set in", which led to the split between thinking Neoclassical Augustan poets and feeling Romantic poets. I pointed out that this dissociation pre-existed the 17th century. Eliot puzzled over how "felt thought" split into Augustan thought and Romantic feeling, but Augustan thought was part and parcel of the secular Neoclassical, social emphasis, and Romantic feeling was part and parcel of the metaphysical quest for Reality. Eliot was not correct in seeing one Universalist sensibility becoming divided into thought and feeling after Donne.

I have corrected Eliot's "dissociation of sensibility" in this work by seeing a long-standing and deep-rooted division between Neoclassical and Romantic sensibilities. There was not one sensibility at the beginning of the 17th century. There have been two sensibilities ever since the fundamental theme split from questing for Reality into also exposing secular vices in relation to an implied virtue, as Part One has outlined. There have been two sensibilities since the Graeco-Roman time, and Universalist poetry (of which Eliot's own work is an example) reconciles these two sensibilities and restores "felt thought". Once a reconciliation of the two disparate traditions has been effected the resulting Universalist sensibility will of course be unified for as long as the reconciliation lasts.

The greatest poetry points the way to transcendence, or higher Reality. This was so of Dante, Milton and Eliot, and is the aim of all Universalists. It shows the wickedness, terror and beauty of the world but its final message is that all will be well, as Christ asserts in the closing lines of *Armageddon*, after which:

> "My
> Heart leapt at his certain optimism,
> His Epping-Forest vision that despite
> The dreadful things that had beset the West
> Things will be all right, there can still be hope.
> He saw so clearly that all will be well." (12.3730-35.)

Transcendence is the goal of the quest for Reality of the metaphysical aspect of the fundamental theme of world literature.

Poetry is most needed in an age of information overload. As Shelley put it:

> "The cultivation of poetry is never more to be desired than at periods when, from an excess of the selfish and calculating principle, the accumulation of the materials of external life exceed the quantity of the power of assimilating them to the internal laws of human nature."[36] (See p.402.)

Shelley makes a very important point about poetry's cross-disciplinary role in synthesizing the mass of information in the world, which has been deluged with too much information.

The defence of Universalist poetry, then, is that it reconciles secular and metaphysical thematic traditions and the Neoclassical and Romantic stylistic traditions, and through inspired imitation reshapes the chaos of the universe and of experience into an order that enables poet and reader to glimpse and know the One. The reader might not have had this insight and knowledge without the poet's revelation. The Universalist consciousness takes account of all levels of consciousness and layers of the self, not just of the rational, social ego, and its language is therefore a blend of discourse and soul-reflection. Universalist poetry restores the grand themes and unifies the infinite, the universe and the self, as the Universalist Wordsworth saw when he wrote that the imagination unites the universe, Nature and the soul.[37] It returns meaning and purpose to poetry. It restores order and meaning to a vibrant universe that has been temporarily blighted and laid waste by materialism, and is the most profound contemporary inspirer of hope and optimism. Universalism is the way forward for poetry today.

Epilogue

A New Direction for World Literature

We have now considered the two motifs of the fundamental theme of world literature, which are symbolized by the figures of Light and Shadow in the pediment at Copped Hall. I have traced the fundamental theme from c.2,600BC to the 21st century, and have demonstrated from a sample of the most respected works (see p.7) that it is present in every age and time. We have seen that the fundamental theme began as a quest for Reality as Light, or Being, and for the possibility of the virtuous soul's immortality, and that a classical ridiculing and denunciation of vices emerged to exist alongside it in secular times. In my algebraic thinking, $+A + -A = 0$. Quest + vices = fundamental theme.

Algebraic thinking was first introduced to me by the Japanese poet Junzaburo Nishiwaki, often called Japan's T.S. Eliot, who in 1965, sitting opposite me in a *saké* – rice-wine – bar with sawdust on the floor (See p.v), wrote this formula out on a business reply card I happened to have, which now hangs on my study wall. I went to Japan to absorb the wisdom of the East and returned with knowledge of the Light and of this dialectic that reconciles opposites into harmony with the One.

Metaphysical Revolution: Five Reconciliations
The theme of this book has been that further to Eliot's thinking in 'Tradition and the Individual Talent' literature must return to the metaphysical aspect of the fundamental theme, and that there must be a strengthening of the metaphysical outlook to combat increasing secularization. The metaphysical and secular are two contraries in a dialectic whose outcome is a synthesis: Universalism.

In this work, using the "esemplastic" power of the imagination[1] which sees unity and similarities and "moulds" or "shapes" "into one" and not the analytical faculty that sees differences and makes distinctions, I have seen the unity of world literature. I have pursued the same dialectical approach and algebraic thinking that can be found in *The New Philosophy of Universalism*, where Being and non-Being, life and death, the world of time and the world of eternity, the finite and the infinite, and the metaphysical and the scientific are reconciled within the One. In this work, $+A + -A = 0$. Metaphysics + secularism = Universalism.

We have seen that Universalism has reconciled and synthesized five sets of contradictory traditions or approaches:

(1) the metaphysical and secular traditions;
(2) the classical/Neoclassical and Romantic traditions;
(3) rational and intuitional approaches within literature;
(4) linguistic and verbal imitative, and inspired imaginative, traditions;
(5) mystic and visionary traditions.

At present literary Universalism is in a very early stage of a revolution to restore a balance between the metaphysical and the secular. Europe's, and the UK's, metaphysical origins have been marginalised: the European Union is a secularized conglomerate and the UK is the most secular society in Europe. There therefore has to be a "Revolution in Thought and Culture" to reintroduce the metaphysical in the UK and the European civilization to which it belongs so that it exists alongside the secular and makes possible the synthesis of Universalism. In the case of poetry, the mansion of poetry has many rooms, and the secular *genres* can continue to inhabit them, but the metaphysical tradition must reassume its place within the mansion and live alongside them.

To translate this idea into more practical terms, for the synthesis of Universalism to happen there will have to be a Metaphysical Revolution to establish the metaphysical alongside the secular tradition. This Metaphysical Revolution can be detected in the works of a number of contemporary writers who, as I have tried to show (see pp.303-6), have laid the quest for Reality of the metaphysical outlook alongside the personal and social reality of the secular outlook to try and reach a new audience that includes those who have never really encountered the metaphysical and have only a hazy idea of what it means.

Historical Progression to a Univeralist World State and Literary Universalism

This literary Universalism connects with a historical movement towards a political World State, which regards all humankind as a whole. As I have set out in other works,[2] all civilizations may pass within a World State for a while. This political process connects with: historical Universalism, which makes a comparative study of all civilizations; religious Universalism, which focuses on the essence of religions; and philosophical Universalism, which focuses on man's role in the universe (see diagram on p.353). Literary Universalism is caught up in this four-sided political, historical, religious and philosophical movement towards a World State and cannot avoid considering the attempt by a self-interested *élite* to rule the world.

T.S. Eliot recognised in *The Man of Letters and the Future of Europe* (1944)[3] that the man of letters must champion the cultural health of Europe and must scrutinise the actions of key figures for their cultural consequences:

"The man of letters as such, is not concerned with the political or economic map of Europe; but he should be very much concerned with its cultural map....The man of letters... should be able to take a longer view than either the politician or the local patriot....The cultural health of Europe, including the cultural health of its component parts, is incompatible with extreme forms of both nationalism and internationalism....The responsibility of the man of letters at the present time...should be vigilantly watching the conduct of politicians and economists, for the purpose of criticizing and warning, when the decisions and actions of the politicians and economists are likely to have cultural consequences. Of these consequences the man of letters should qualify himself to judge. Of the possible cultural consequences of their activities, politicians and economists are usually oblivious; the man of letters is better qualified to foresee them, and to perceive their seriousness."[4]

Eliot was writing during the Second World War with Fascism and Communism in mind, the *élites* round Hitler and Stalin, but in our "present time" when global developments have overtaken Eliot's perspective of the European civilization the man of letters must scrutinize the conduct of the *élite* running the world today, which I have called "the Syndicate". That was precisely what I was doing in my book, *The Syndicate*: scrutinising and exposing those whose actions can have adverse cultural consequences for Europe and the world. In my later book *The World Government* I attemped to limit the damage of these adverse cultural consequences. Writing within the tradition of Eliot's *Notes Towards the Definition of Culture*, I proposed an improvement in global governance in the form of a limited, partial World State with the legal power to abolish war, that would contain, in the sense of "hold in check", the *élite* I have called the Syndicate and end their destructive cultural impact on the world.

As I have attempted to show in my historical writings,[5] civilizations rise through a metaphysical idea and decline when the idea becomes desiccated like sap ceasing to flow, and the civilization turns secular. (See p.106.) When they have run their course they pass within another civilization. In this context, the "cultural health" of a civilization involves the perpetuation of its metaphysical idea which is vital to its survival.

On the evidence of my historical writings, Universalism is an idea whose time has come. Western civilization is an amalgam of the European civilization and the later North-American civilization, and in my comparative study of the life-span of 25 civilizations,[6] I have shown that, judging from analysis of dead civilizations which have been through similar stages, in both these civilizations there are phases of Universalism ahead. The European civilization is two-thirds advanced – the advent of the European Union marks the beginning of stage 43 out of the 61 stages of the European civilization's life cycle – and is in a secular stage at present, awaiting a metaphysical revival through a form of Universalism. The North-American civilization is only a quarter through – it is currently in stage 15 of the 61 stages of its life-span – and it still has to go through a phase when a "new people" bring in a new metaphysical emphasis. This phase will be equivalent to the appearance of the Renaissance Humanists in the European civilization, and I have argued that in the North-American civilization the "new people" will be Universalists.[7]

The time appears to be right for political, historical, philosophical and religious Universalism, and for their mirroring in literary Universalism. (History, philosophy and literature make a three-legged stool, for the glimpses of Reality that impact on civilizations in history and on metaphysical philosophy are reflected in literature. It is significant that the Muses were inspirers of history and philosophy as well as of poetry.)

Literature's New Direction: Inspired Metaphysical Vision that restores Civilizations' Health

To put it another way, on evidence I have presented elsewhere[8] a healthy civilization is nourished by a metaphysical vision which is expressed in its art. Writers who revive and convey the metaphysical vision keep their civilization healthy. The Universalist sensibility that synthesizes the metaphysical vision and the secular outlook of the society to which it is applied resists the decline of Western civilization and maintains its health.

It is important to grasp that a philosophy of literature based on the metaphysical vision of the fundamental theme of world literature slots into the forward movement of history. It is instructive to see how it slots into the philosophy of history. The philosophy of history explores the direction of historical events, as we saw on p.8. The direction of history is a progress from tribes to villages, city-states, baronial states and nation-states, and to a coming World State, as I have argued in *The World Government*, and is Universalist. The philosophy of literature correspondingly explores the direction of literary events, which reflect the historical movement of the age, and is also Universalist. The direction of literature, which reflects the historical movement of the age, is inextricably linked to the direction of history, whose civilizations, I have just said, need the perpetuation of the metaphysical vision for their enduring health. At present the direction of world literature is increasingly secular.

The new direction for world literature therefore involves a return by poets, dramatists, novelists and cultural essayists to the inspired metaphysical vision, which is received during the quest for Reality and immortality. It involves a renewed focus on the order of the universe and the infinite that surrounds it, and on humankind's brotherhood in relation to the metaphysical Light which bestows historical and religious unity (see pp.1-2).

It follows that the immediate new direction of world literature is to challenge secularization and secular literature with the "Revolution in Thought and Culture" I have called for, that revives the metaphysical so that it co-exists with the secular. Essential to the new metaphysical approach is a growing awareness in poets and other writers that personal and social levels of reality are only part of human experience, and that there is a creative power of Light which is beyond the natural world and which inspires and awakens the imagination with symbols.

Ten Innovations

To sum up, in stating the fundamental theme I have introduced ten innovations. I have:

(1) stated a metaphysical tradition in literature (the quest for Reality);

(2) stated a secular tradition in literature (vices in relation to an implied virtue), which co-exists with the metaphysical;

(3) unified world literature by seeing it as a unity in relation to the dialectic of these two contraries;

(4) restored the metaphysical infinite to literature;

(5) restored the vision of the infinite in literature;

(6) stated a synthesis of the metaphysical and secular traditions, Universalism;

(7) stated a Universalist literary tradition;

(8) reconciled classicism/Neoclassicism and Romanticism in the synthesis of Universalism;

(9) carried the Metaphysical Revolution, the "Revolution in Thought and Culture", into literature;

(10) stated a new direction for world literature.

In these 10 statements, restorations, unifications and revolutions, I have reconciled the contradictions of literature by using algebraic thinking: $+A + -A = 0$.

On the pediment at Copped Hall Light and Shadow sit together, two contraries either side of the unifying sundial, two different sensibilities now reconciled. The reconciliation of the two opposites on the pediment and the synthesis of their two sensibilities is a symbol of unifying Universalism.

A New Discipline

All the different traditions, movements and perspectives within world literature which I have identified in this study, on which the 10 statements, restorations, unifications and revolutions are based, should be treated as one interconnected, indivisible, interdisciplinary flow of 4,600 years of literary activity which has an unmistakable progress and direction. The literatures of different nation-states can no longer be taught in isolation from each other.

In *The New Philosophy of Universalism* I called for a new discipline, Universalism, to focus on the universe, Nature, all the sciences, evolution and the rise of intellectual consciousness, and to seek evidence of universal order as opposed to randomness. There should be a related part of the new discipline in the university curricula: the new philosophy of literature, which will synthesize classicism/ Neoclassicism and Romanticism within Universalism and restore the metaphysical to literature.

This new discipline will include all the literature from the ancient world to the 21st century. It will teach undergraduates about the dialectic in literature that spans 4,600 years and about the periods of synthesis when the metaphysical and secular have drawn together into early, nascent and developing forms of Universalism. The new discipline will answer with arguments based on personal transformation and cultural health, such questions as "Why quest for Reality?", "Why be metaphysical?", "Why turn away from secular, personal and social reality and seek a Reality that is hidden?" and "Why join a Revolution in Thought and Culture to bring in a new perception of truth?"

This new discipline should deal with the contradictions in literature and their reconciliation. It should focus on the unified vision within literature and should cover all creative works and novels in a more comprehensive way than I have been able to do here. There are many books and essays to be written to establish its new approach.

I have stated the tradition of the fundamental theme, and it is now up to the writers of coming generations to place themselves at the service of the tradition and, on whatever continent they are based, make new metaphysical contributions to the maintenance of the literary and cultural health of the world's living civilizations.

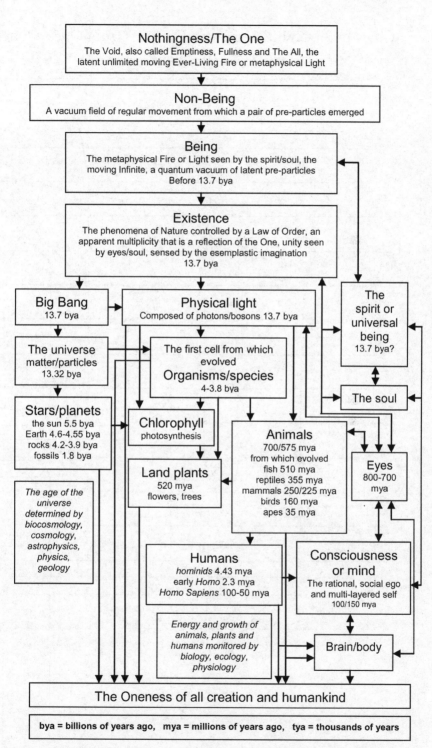

Universalism's View of the Structure of the Universe[1]

Chart of 25 Civilizations and Cultures from One to One

The Fundamental Unity of World Culture

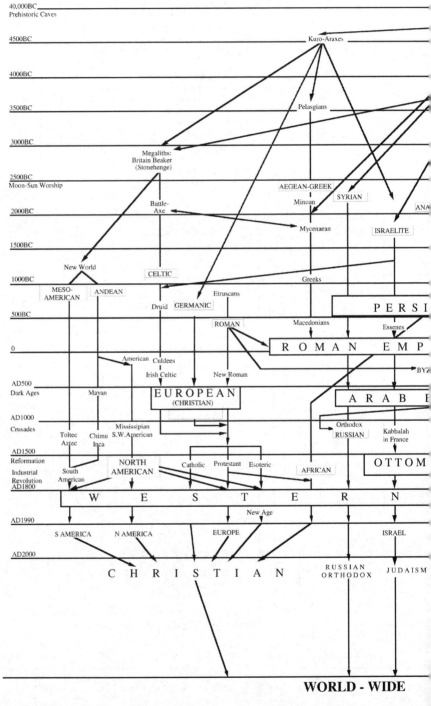

WORLD - WIDE

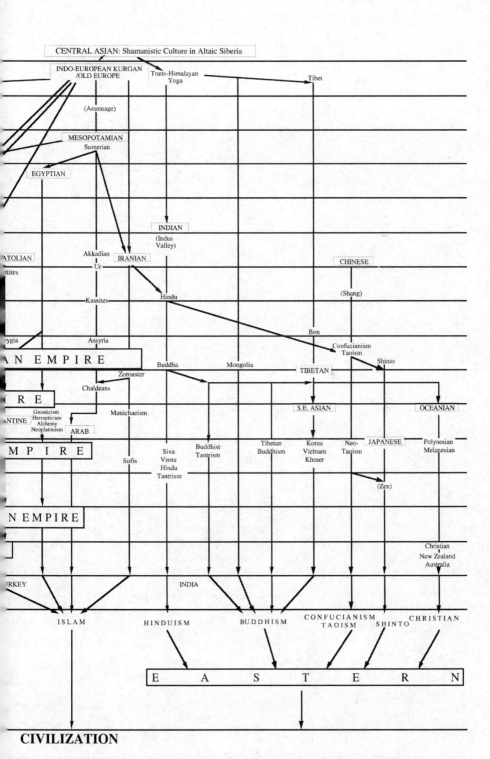

CENTRAL ASIAN: Shamanistic Culture in Altaic Siberia

INDO-EUROPEAN KURGAN /OLD EUROPE

Trans-Himalayan Yoga

Tibet

(Anannage)

MESOPOTAMIAN
Sumerian

EGYPTIAN

INDIAN
(Indus Valley)

ATOLIAN
ttites

Akkadian
Ur

IRANIAN

CHINESE

Kassites

Hindu

(Shang)

ygia

Assyria

Bon

Confucianism
Taoism

AN EMPIRE

Buddha

Mongolia

TIBETAN

Shinto

Zoroaster

Chaldeans

RE

S.E. ASIAN

OCEANIAN

NTINE

Gnosticism
Hermeticism
Alchemy
Neoplatonism

Manichaeism

ARAB

MPIRE

Sufis

Siva
Visnu
Hindu
Tantrism

Buddhist
Tantrism

Tibetan
Buddhism

Korea
Vietnam
Khmer

Neo-
Taoism

JAPANESE

Polynesian
Melanesian

(Zen)

N EMPIRE

Christian
New Zealand
Australia

JRKEY

INDIA

ISLAM

HINDUISM

BUDDHISM

CONFUCIANISM
TAOISM

SHINTO

CHRISTIAN

E   A   S   T   E   R   N

CIVILIZATION

APPENDIX

Close Readings

The Emergence of a Secular Tradition Alongside the
Quest for Reality in English Literature

The following studies were written by Nicholas Hagger at different times between 1974 and 1985, and reflect his thinking during that period. The last two studies, on Swift and on traditional poetic method (a later piece of work written on 3-4 June 1999), question the Age of Reason and modern secular poetry. He has not amended them in the light of the current work, apart from minor tidying up. They illustrate the differences between the Neoclassical and Romantic approaches and sensibilities in English Literature by close readings of key aspects of their works: contraries that Universalism reconciles.

1

Studies of the Approaches and Sensibilities of Classical and Romantic Poets in English Literature

Chaucer's Ironic Praise and Deflation, Ridiculing Follies and Vices of the Incumbents within the Church System

Chaucer's method is a method of praise. In *The Prologue* he applies the same method to each of the 29 pilgrims he describes in detail. He introduces them, says nice things about them, gives us their attitudes, justifies them, and carries us along on a tide of panegyric. Then – was that the bottom of our boat scraping on rocks? – we suddenly realize he has carried us too far, and that we are assenting to his praise of a trait that is not praiseworthy. And so deftly is it done that it is with a slight shock we realize that Chaucer does not believe his own praise, that he is, in fact, being ironical. And in that little shock lies much of his humour.

We can see this movement at work in his portrait of the Friar. He was a merry man, Chaucer tells us, he was licensed to beg, he was a man of great importance. In all the four orders no one spoke with such light familiarity. He had married "younger wommen at his owene cost". Now we realize that he was a womaniser, but Chaucer goes on praising him. "Ful swetely herde he confessioun." And: "He was an esy man to yeve penaunce."

Hey, we think, these are not good qualities to be admired, surely. He takes money, and is it not justified? "For many a man so hard is of his herte/He may nat wepe, althogh him sore smerte,/Therfore instede of wepinge and preyeres/Men moote yeve silver to the poure frères." A preposterous justification. But this is the man, speaking in his own language, justifying himself, and Chaucer still does not give his opinion, at least not overtly. The Friar knew every innkeeper and barmaid

"Bet than a lazar or a beggestere.
For unto swich a worthy man as he
Acorded nat, as by his facultee,
To have with sike lazars aqueintaunce."

No one could believe such exaggerated justifications, Chaucer *can't* believe them. And of course he doesn't. This master of irony has pinned this rogue fixed and sprawling on a wall.

The same applies to the Prioress, with her affected French and manners, her excessive daintiness. It applies to the Monk and his justification for his excessive outdoor pursuits:

"What sholde he studye, and make himselven wood,
Upon a book in cloistre alwey to poure,
Or swinken with his handes, and laboure,
As Austin bit? How shal the world be served?"

It applies, less blatantly, to all the rogues Chaucer shows us, a gallery of characters who are on the make: the Merchant, The Shipman and the Doctor to name but three. Indeed, the problem in *The Prologue* becomes deciding when Chaucer is not being ironic, when he is being straight.

The Knight, is he such a "worthy" man after all, seeing how often Chaucer uses the word "worthy" ironically elsewhere? (He uses it twice each of the Merchant and of the Friar.) Is Chaucer perhaps suggesting that he could not possibly have been to all those battles, that he was a bit of a romancer? Or is there another reason for the "gypoun" being "al bismotered with his habergeoun" – could he be idle, for instance, and just not up to getting it cleaned the evening before all 29 characters put up at the Southwark Tabard? And his son the Squire, is it really permissible that "He slepte namoore than dooth a nightingale"? Or is Chaucer again here praising the unpraiseable?

Chaucer condemns by praise, by appealing to our sense of what is right. His condemnation is very different from, say, what Ché Guevara's condemnation would be. For Chaucer accepts the theological and social structure of 1385, he does not reject the System at all. He merely criticizes – always by implication – individuals who do not live up to their theological and social roles. In his portraits of the Prioress, the Monk and the Friar, Chaucer is not against the Church, he is against three human individuals, and he is able to expose them, and ridicule their vices and follies, with a gentle chuckle. It is this humour that distinguishes him from the intense revolutionary.

Even with the Pardoner, Chaucer is not against an institution. The selling of pardons was, after all, on the way out when he wrote, and the Establishment was as much against them as he was. Chaucer, as one might expect from his many jobs as page to the Duchess of Clarence, courtier, soldier, squire, diplomat, peace-negotiator, customs comptroller, Knight of the Shire (equivalent to an MP) and Clerk of the King's Works, was a natural supporter of the *status quo*.

His condemnation is also very different from, say, Pope's. There is no "abhorrence of vice" in Chaucer, nor desire to correct. He is not a moralist, but a describer, a brilliant painter who catches the implications of abstract character in a vivid description of appearance and dress. Above all he is the master of significant detail, seizing on an unwimpled forehead or an "A" on a bracelet to suggest the true bent of his subject. He is a teller of the truth, one who ridicules the gap between how men ought to be if they are to live up to their job, and how men are. He does it with the ironic praise and chuckle of the experienced Taverner. What a good companion Chaucer must have been at the Tabard Inn.

Chaucer doesn't want to change anything. He doesn't want to overthrow the *status quo*, and he doesn't want his people to change. He likes them with their vices and foibles. He has a humorous attitude towards them that has forgiven them as soon as he has understood them. He must have had the Friar's eyes:

"Hise eyen twinkled in his heed aright
As doon the sterres in the frosty night."

He admires the Parson – perhaps the only character who is definitely offered straight, without irony – but it is hard to believe that Chaucer wanted all men to be like him. He is writing the first character-sketches in our literature, and his condemnation states an attitude, the attitude of a very great artist, and it is that that gives his portrait distance and roundness.

When it comes to the Tales themselves, we have the double irony of characters already praised praising their characters. The Merchant tells us that Januarie was a "worthy knight" in line 2. Only fools stay single, and "To take a wif it is a glorious thing". After that, marriage – the theme of the tale – is praised whenever it is mentioned: "A wyf is Goddes yifte verraily;.../Mariage is a ful greet sacrement." And so on.

We are carried along on this deceitfully benevolent outlook until we find ourselves approving of the outcome of the tale: May, his wife, making love to Damyan up a pear-tree, which Januarie sees. For in a passage which anticipates the mock-heroic 'Rape of the Lock' Pluto intervenes to give the blind old man back his sight. Hey, we think, pulled up short. Something must be wrong. How come that we have agreed that marriage should be praised – to be confronted with this.

Deflation is central in Chaucer's technique. He pumps his characters up with praise, and then pauses to let out a little air. Pope works differently: he pumps Arabella Fermor up until she bursts: BANG. Chaucer is closer to the method of Swift in 'A Modest Proposal'. Look, Swift is saying, the politicians must know what they're talking about, and everyone knows that the Irish are a problem, so what about cutting up the children of the poor and cooking them? There is no blatant exaggeration here: no disproportionate attention on a single hair that has been "raped".

Swift is using the words and attitudes – the very language – of the people he is criticizing and ridiculing, and is arriving at a preposterous conclusion that deflates them. Chaucer likewise uses their language and likewise lets them arrive at a preposterous conclusion that deflates them.

In a study of irony in literature, the methods of Chaucer must be compared with the methods not just of Pope and Swift, but of Dryden, of Horace's light-heartedness and Juvenal's seriousness, and of the novelists Jane Austen, Henry James and Conrad. There are a number of different ways of ridiculing your characters, and Chaucer's way remains as good as any.

Chaucer's *Merchant's Tale*:
Epic Marriage and Early Mock-Heroic Deflation of Blindness

The Merchant's Tale is memorable for its climax, of course: the climax in the pear-tree when Damyan "Gan pullen up the smok, and in he throng." Students, especially girl students, never fail to be delighted at the picture of Damyan being joined in the pear-tree by May, who has to climb on the old, blind Januarie's back to be there; of the love-making up among the pears, and of Januarie, having had his sight restored at the crucial moment, screeching indignantly, "Strugle…ye algate in it wente". Poor Januarie is convinced he saw "thy smok hadde leyn upon his brest". How laughable he is when May convinces him that he should not believe the evidence of his own eyes.

It is the laughter that makes the earlier parts of *The Merchant's Tale* equally memorable, for the irony in this Tale is an extension of the way the Merchant laughs at Januarie. If the Merchant were alive today, and were interviewed on television, and if he confessed to having a "labbing shrewe" as a wife, and were asked for his views on marriage, he would surely reply: "Any man who marries is daft. A man of 60 and a woman of under 30 – ridiculous. The woman is bound to be unfaithful. Surely no man is going to trust her words? Only a raving idiot would." This is the Merchant's, and presumably Chaucer's, attitude towards Januarie.

Januarie is ridiculous until after the wedding, when we focus on May's inevitable infidelity. Januarie ceases to be quite so ridiculous for a while, but becomes utterly laughable when he is conned into refusing to believe the evidence of his own eyes. He is a particularly stupid cuckold from a time when cuckolds were laughed at pretty mercilessly.

The irony reinforces the laughter. "Any man who marries is daft" – "To take a wif it is a glorious thing". "Januarie is ridiculous" – "This olde knight, that was so wis". You can hear the gale of laughter from the audience as the Merchant breaks into his ridiculing tone to simulate an adoption of Januarie's point of view, to pretend to take Januarie's part. How self-importantly Januarie consults all the authorities, with their conflicting claims: Theophrastus and Solomon. How het-up are the examples from the *Bible*: "Lo, Judith…Lo Abigail" (which reflect his increasing self-persuasion and excitement).

What heroic apostrophes to the gods and what invocations to Januarie himself turn the poem into a mock-heroic to rival 'The Rape of the Lock'. How deflatingly banal and meat-like are the animal images that run through this "heroic" Tale, with its attendant divinities (Pluto and Proserpine) in the best epic tradition. "'Bet is,' quod he, 'a pyk than a pickerel,/And bet than old boef is the tendre veel.'" And to cap it all, how hilarious is the picture of Januarie on his wedding night, reading Constantine Afer's *De Coitu*, the *Kama Sutra* of the eleventh century, for love-making tips, cramming himself with aphrodisiacs ("ypocras, clarre, and vernage"), and then kissing May "with thikke brustles of his berd unsofte,/Lyk to the skin of houndfissh, sharp as brere". We can see him chattering like "a flekked pye" so that "the slakke skin aboute his nekke shaketh", sitting "in his sherte,/In his night-cappe". No wonder May "preyseth nat his playing worth a bene".

The Merchant's Tale is memorable because of the mock-heroic tone. It is surely the first example of the mock-heroic *genre* in English literature, and it debunks the solemnity of the epic marriage with a superb sense of the ridiculous. Once we have grasped this we can see why Chaucer has to compare Januarie's garden with the one in the *Roman de la Rose* – which surely did not have a "cliket" to its "wiket" – and why the astrological news (about what constellation is in what sign of the zodiac) is so necessary.

The mock-heroic works by creating a lofty tone for a banal subject, and then deflating it. Small wonder that the young Pope translated *The Merchant's Tale* under the title *January and May*.

Julius Caesar:
Plotting for Power in the Roman Civilization

The key to *Julius Caesar* is the interpretation of Cassius. It is my contention that Cassius is a self-interested, Machiavellian character. From the very beginning he has his sights on ruling Rome. The names Cassius and Caesar are as interchangeable as Brutus and Caesar. He knows it is too dangerous to run the *coup* single-handed, and he contrives it so that Brutus will be blamed if the *coup* fails. He needs Brutus to command the people's assent following the murder of Caesar:

he knows that he himself could not command that assent.

All along, however, he intends to remove Brutus once he has served his purpose. He will murder Brutus. As Nasser was a party to dethroning Farouk, and later took over from Neguib, so Cassius too will be the supreme ruler. No wonder he says in fury, after Antony has insulted him, "This tongue had not offended so to-day/If Cassius might have rul'd".

Brutus, then, is incredibly naïve. He does not grasp that he is being used until the quarrel with Cassius, when he begins to glimpse the truth: Cassius's "itching palm". No wonder Brutus is "sick of many griefs". His idealism and nobility, his belief that Rome should be liberated from his friend Caesar, lead up to the incredible blunder of allowing Antony to address the mob unchecked. Surely even Brutus would have been in the wings to listen, instead of leaving the stage (the Forum) free for Antony.

Antony too is after power. His scorn for Lepidus makes that clear. "Is it fit,/The threefold world divided, he should stand/One of the three to share it?" Antony asks. Antony checkmates Cassius, he out-Cassiuses Cassius. And, ironically, the holder of the office to which both Cassius and Antony aspire, the dictatorial Caesar who will not repeal the banishment on Cimber's brother, is revealed, as holders of such tyrannical power often really are, a timid aging man "in his night-gown".

The power that Cassius and Antony seek is an illusion. And this is a very Elizabethan – and Websterian/Jacobean – theme.

The Politics of *Measure for Measure* to Secure Inner Change to Virtue

Above all *Measure for Measure* is a study in politics. The Duke, confronted with a Vienna that has gone permissive, resolves to clean up a city and rid it of its whoring by reviving the death penalty for fathering illegitimate children. So far he is like a Headmaster in a school whose discipline has decayed, or, to use his own image for it, one of the "fond fathers" who have "bound up the threat'ning twigs of birch". He explains his motive in choosing Angelo to do his tightening up for him in a speech to Friar Thomas (Act 1, sc 3):

"Sith 'twas my fault to give the people scope,
'Twould be my tyranny to strike and gall them
For what I bid them do; for we bid this be done,
When evil deeds have their permissive pass
And not the punishment. Therefore, indeed, my father,
I have on Angelo impos'd the office;
Who may, in th'ambush of my name, strike home,
And yet my nature never in the fight
To do in slander."

His choice of Angelo as opposed to Escalus, who recommends Angelo on the first page of the play, shows us that the Duke is a skilful, intriguing politician of the Harold Wilson calibre. For the Duke, as we learn, knows that Angelo will make a "corrupt deputy", for he knows about Mariana and the "examples for his falling". His aim is, obviously, to intrigue a situation in which Angelo shakes the threatening twigs of birch without actually using them. So long as Angelo has committed the offence (with Mariana) for which someone is to die, the Duke feels he has a hold over the situation, and can control it. And control is what government is all about.

And control the situation he does. For whether or not he has read Angelo's character right, whether or not he expects Angelo to go through with the execution of someone when he is just as guilty as the condemned man, he has foreseen that Angelo will abuse his power. And so when it transpires that Claudio is to be executed so that the law shall not be a scarecrow, the Duke, now in disguise, is ready with the solution, to help Isabella save her brother by allowing Mariana to take her place at the meeting. The whole exercise has been carefully thought out in advance, the only unknown (on the evidence of the text) being exactly who Angelo would arrest for fathering an illegitimate child.

When seen like this, the play loses some of its problems. The Duke is using Angelo as a modern prime minister doubtless uses a minister: to introduce an unpopular policy for which he himself will not be blamed. We should not feel sorry for the scholar, Angelo, who is reluctant to accept his new office ("Let there be some more test made of my metal"), for such using is fair game in politics. We should not make a problem of Angelo's unsuitableness for the job in view of his past association with Mariana, for it is precisely that which has led the Duke to choose him. Nor should we make a problem of the fact that the Duke is, at one and the same time, helping Isabella to save her brother and advising Claudio to "be absolute for death". From the start he had no intention of allowing the victim of his new policy to die – Ragozine's head would presumably have fallen anyway – and his advice to Claudio is to be seen as bringing him to an understanding of the truth about himself, which is the business of the comic misunderstanding.

The "cruel striking" of the Duke towards Claudio and Isabella in keeping them in suspense about Claudio's fate is, in fact, an instrument of self-change. For the Duke, like Shakespeare, believes that a tightening up of the law is not enough. The change must take place in the heart of each citizen, and this is to be founded on the idea from which the title is taken: "'An Angelo for Claudio, death for death!'.../Like doth quit like, and Measure still for Measure" (Act 5, sc 1).

We see now why the Duke has let the law "slip" for fourteen years. It is because of this belief that change should come from within, and the outer law should be used as an aid to such inner change. It should not replace it.

The Tempest:
Ariel as Muse to Summon Corrupt Rulers for Forgiveness

The Tempest is a baffling play, at first sight. Here among the Peter-Pan magic of the island, which is probably Bermuda, we find an intense father-daughter relationship, a past wrong – Prospero deprived of his Dukedom by his brother – and a contrived storm to bring a group of people together so that they can be forgiven.

What *is* Shakespeare playing at? This is, after all his last play. And judging from the speech about the breaking of the staff, the drowning of the book, Shakespeare knows it is his last play. Would Shakespeare, the author of *King Lear* and the storm on the heath, have devoted his last work to fairy-tale magic? Surely not. From what we know of him from the *Sonnets*, he would surely have filled the play with the pressure of a personal emotion?

And – and this is what critics seem to have missed, with their analyzes of Prospero/Art versus Caliban/Nature, and the like – he did. *The Tempest* makes sense if it is read as an embittered Shakespeare resenting his forced removal from the London stage by the actor-manager rival of his, Burbage; and Shakespeare's subsequent forgiveness.

As much as Pirandello's work, *Six Characters in Search of an Author*, *The Tempest* is a play about a dramatist working on his characters. Ariel, "an airy spirit", is nothing less than the Muse, or poetic inspiration, of Prospero/Shakespeare. Prospero calls on his Muse to contrive a tempest that will bring his enemies together, and he promises to free his Muse once this is done, i.e. renounce his writing. His Muse obeys and besides being full of poetry about cowslip bells and blossom, acts as a *deus ex machina*, bringing the characters on and taking them off and generally watching over the action, in the course of which he saves the life of the King. As a reward for this last work – his enemies gathered together before him by the idea of a tempest – Prospero duly rewards his Muse with freedom, which necessarily means that he will have to drown his book. That last renunciation speech is therefore a logical consequence of Prospero's dealings with Ariel, and not the digression it is sometimes made out to be.

Caliban, a near-anagram for Cannibal which has led all the critics to write about Montaigne's essay 'On Cannibalism', is the groundling who revolts against his erstwhile master (Prospero/Shakespeare) and worships a new god: in Stefano, the drunken fool, there may be a caricature of someone connected with the Jacobean stage, whether an actor-manager or even a dramatist, or possibly even the Master of the Revels of the time, who had proved unsympathetic to Shakespeare. "You taught me language; and my profit on't/Is, I know how to curse," he grumbles at Prospero. How bitter Shakespeare must have felt at his desertion by the groundlings in the Jacobean climate when free speech was beginning to become a problem.

And this brings us to the tempest which has struck the group on the island – the real tempest that happened after Elizabeth's death, not the imaginary one that Shakespeare asks his Muse to create. Indeed, it is the contrast between these two tempests (one political and real, one imaginary) which is at the heart of the play, and which makes the play so baffling.

The Tempest contains the sense of the passing of an Age. "We have seen the best of our time," Gloucester says in *King Lear* and this sentiment is echoed in Gonzalo's "Our hint of woe/Is common". Gonzalo harks back to the Golden Age. Trinculo says, "If th' other two be brain'd like us, the state totters". There was a feeling that the Golden Age of Elizabeth had passed and that what had replaced it was not as good. The tempest that had swept the old order away had washed up the group of rulers Prospero judges and forgives, who may include the doddering, harmless King James (King of Naples), who is in the hands of wicked men; and in the honest old Gonzalo, someone who had helped Shakespeare in the past: perhaps the Master of the Revels before the last one (who was perhaps the original for Malvolio), now an old man.

The Tempest, then, is a play within a play, like the play performed by the Player King that Hamlet watched. The outer play is about the aging Shakespeare producing those he needs to forgive and renouncing his writing. The inner play is what Ariel, his Muse, gives us: the tempest that has changed Shakespeare's life by compelling his retirement. We need to investigate the historical facts surrounding this retirement in the light of what *The Tempest* itself tells us.

But even without our being in possession of the full facts we have here a basis for interpreting Prospero's character. There can be no flat, monotonous delivery; no withdrawn, worn-out, emaciated old man looking in disgust on the general proceedings. That interpretation misses the spirit of the play. Prospero should rather be presented in conflict, as a man forced to retire against his will, who is writing one last work and composing himself for peace with his daughter. For in Miranda was there a portrait of Shakespeare's own daughter, Juliet?

Shakespeare's Dissatisfaction in *Sonnets:*
The Tradition of Lost Love

The dating of Shakepeare's *Sonnets* is crucial to their interpretation. Dr Rowse goes for an early dating, 1592/3, and therefore sees the Rival

Poet as Marlowe, the patron as Southampton, and the Dark Lady as Emilia Lanier, who was then 24. Dover Wilson in his Cambridge University edition plumps for 1597/8, later, and therefore sees the Rival Poet as Chapman, the patron as William Herbert, The Earl of Pembroke, and the Dark Lady as perhaps Mary Fitton, who visited Herbert and became pregnant by him on 16 June 1600. It may be that the sonnets are in two groups, one written early and one written later and that both Rowse and Dover Wilson are partly right.

Dover Wilson rearranges the sonnets to make a chronological narrative of the affair. Shakespeare persuades his patron to have an heir, worships his beauty, goes on a journey during which the patron's affair with the Dark Lady begins, suspects the liaison, is ousted from his patron's affection by the Rival Poet, bids farewell to the patron he once loved, and is finally full of reproach towards the Dark Lady. Whether the patron is Mr W.H., or whether Mr. W.H. is merely the publisher's dedicatee as Dr Rowse claims (perhaps a printing error for Mr W.Sh, i.e. William Shakespeare), is immaterial to this essentially autobiographical narrative.

But are the sonnets autobiographical? In spite of Rowse and Dover Wilson, there are still scholars who deny that they are. These take the more traditional Eliotian view that they are literary exercises. (To be fair to Eliot, I believe he said that *some* of them are literary exercises.) One of my pupils went for an interview at a teacher training college and was soundly ticked off for suggesting that the sonnets may be autobiographical. It is worth forgetting Rowse and Dover Wilson and a mixture of the two for a while, and all other daters, datings and commentators, and taking a fresh look at *Sonnets* in the order in which they come down to us and regarding them as evidence of a state of mind to see if what is revealed is consistent with a literary exercise. The answer is, I submit, that the sonnets are anything but a literary exercise. A picture of Shakespeare emerges that shows a very disturbed state of mind.

Shakespeare is obsessed by time. "Time's scythe", "this bloody tyrant Time", "swift-footed Time", "sluttish time", "Time's injurious hand", "Time's fell hand", "Time's thievish progress to eternity", "Time's tyranny", "Time's fool", "Time's fickle glass" – these are just some of the key expressions to be found in sonnets 12, 16, 19, 55, 60,

63, 64, 65, 77, 115, 116, 126. Beauty is "like a dial-hand" on a watch, it is destroyed with "no pace perceiv'd" (104), and this affects Shakespeare's own face, which is getting old. "My storm-beaten face" (34) "beated and chopt" (62) – "Time's pencil" (16) has drawn lines on his brow, and he knows "my days are past the best".

Knowing this he idolizes the beauty of his younger patron, though he knows that it will not last. His patron has an honourable name (36), "birth" (37), "a woman's face" (20) and it will be forgotten unless he has an heir, a child who will have his looks. His beauty is a classical beauty that outshines the beauty of Adonis or Helen (53), but Shakespeare specifically says in sonnet 20 that the relationship was not homosexual: "But since she (Nature) prick'd thee (= selected, with an obvious pun) for women's pleasure,/Mine be thy love (= your platonic love is mine), and thy love's use (= bodily love, sexual intercourse) their (= women's) treasure." Shakespeare says that a man is no use to him sexually: "By adding one thing to my purpose nothing." Shakespeare makes it clear that his patron embodies the ideal beauty of the age – "All their praises are but prophecies/Of this our time, all you prefiguring" (106), and this is surely a straight judgement rather than the flattery of an impecunious actor-poet who depends on his patron's cash.

Time destroys all beauty, and if there is to be no immortality for the patron through children – and between sonnet 17 and 18, Dover Wilson is right, surely something has happened to kill the "heir" theme and blossom a relationship that is more "temperate" than a "summer's day" – then his immortality is to come through Shakespeare's poetry, which, Shakespeare is at times confident, will last for ever. Though this self-belief is to some extent a sonneteer's convention, and Ovid, for one, was proclaiming that he had immortalized a friend in his work, Shakespeare's moods of self-belief ring true. Shakespeare's sonnet 17 will be a lasting "tomb" for his patron, and the end of sonnet 18 (the "summer's day") is: "So long as men can breathe or eyes can see,/So long lives this (i.e. sonnet 18), and this gives life to thee." His patron's "name from hence immortal life shall have..../Your monument shall be my gentle verse,/Which eyes not yet created shall o'er-read" (81).

I have said Shakespeare had "moods" of self-belief, because a look at sonnets 17, 71, 72, 76, 80, 100, 103, 107 give an opposite picture of self-doubt and self-deprecation – or is he merely being falsely modest? "Stretched metre of an antique song" (17), "do not so much as my poor name rehearse.../Lest the wise world.../Mock you with me after I am gone" (71) – after these two passages it is not surprising that Shakespeare should tell his patron that he should be ashamed to love "things nothing worth" (= his sonnets), (72). Shakespeare despises "new-found methods, and...compounds strange,/Why write I still all one, ever the same?" (76.) His "saucy bark" is "inferior far" (80) to the Rival Poet's – *is* this ironical, or is it to be taken straight as an admission of his own shortcomings? – and he feels his Muse deserts him (100) and that "I no more can write!" (103.) Sonnet 107 is "this poor rhyme". If we forget about the dating of the sonnets and regard them as the expression of one state of mind, there is a baffling mixture of self-belief and self-doubt.

Shakespeare was very dissatisfied with his situation. He complains at his "outcast state" (29), i.e. being an actor. He does not like being a slave to his patron (or is the Dark Lady referred to here?): "Being your slave, what should I do but tend,/Upon the hours, and times of your desire?/*I* have no precious time at all to spend,/Nor services to do till *you* require." (57.) The irony here leaps from the page – "my sovereign" he writes in the same poem, i.e. my King, or is it Queen?, i.e. "my lord and master". The same ironical tone is to be heard in sonnet 40 when he says to the gentle thief, his patron, in effect, 'Why don't you help yourself to everyone I love, while you are at it?': "Take all my loves, my love, yea take them all...."

He is dissatisfied with the evil times he lives in, and how Hamlet and Lear ring in our ears as he complains about the Age and its "new-fangled ill" (91): "Tir'd with all these" (evil times) he lists all the abuses of the day, for example censorship, "art made tongue-tied by authority" (66). His patron has to live "with infection" unlike "in days long since, before these last (= days) so bad". (67.) Gossip is a "canker vice" (70) that destroys the rose with sweet odour (54, 94, 95), while gossips "to thy fair flower add the rank smell of weeds" (69). The Age is to blame for his patron's increasingly bad reputation: "But why thy odour matcheth not thy show,/The soil (= age) is this, that thou dost common grow (= like a weed)." The world is "this vile world" (71) and Shakespeare abhors the new, "new-found methods" (76). Shakespeare was in touch with Court diplomacy – "great princes' favourites" (25) and "this written embassage" (26) reflect its language, as do "Policy" (124) and the "suborn'd informer" (125) – and his attitude towards the politics of the day is surely contained in the baffling sonnet 107, which is about "the mortal moon", presumably the death of Elizabeth I. There is a hint that the evil times are over in the phrase "this most balmy time" (107), which may refer to the springtime of James I's clemency if the later dating is adopted.

Shakespeare is dissatisfied that he has wasted time: the "chronicle of wasted time" (106) is evidently one he knew. He knows that lust is "no sooner had/Past reason hated as a swallowed bait" (129). He knows that "love is as a fever" that makes men "frantic mad" (147). Yet "you and love are still my argument;/So all my best is dressing old words new" (76). He despises himself for being involved in the triangle with his patron, and it is often hard to sort out which is the "sweet thief" (= the Dark Lady) (35) or the "gentle thief" (= the patron) (40) who has robbed him. The Dark Lady has "robb'd others' beds' revenues of their rents", i.e. has made love to other married men (142), and Shakespeare is full of disgust at her "black" "deeds" (131). She is a "vulgar thief" (48), yet Shakespeare is like a "babe" running after a "careful huswife" (143). The two "Will" poems (135, 136), which between them mention the word and name Will twenty times, obviously punning on the Christian name of Shakespeare, and probably on the first names of the patron (if William Herbert) and possibly of the Dark Lady's protector as well (if Sir William Knollys, suitor to Mary Fitton), show what a tangle Shakespeare is in. Dissatisfied with his situation, yet powerless to do anything about it so strong is his infatuation for the Dark Lady, Shakespeare reveals a state of mind that is in a complete mess. Even in Bath he is in the "thrall" (154) of his "mistress' eyes" (153).

Some lovely phrases come out of his torment: "summer's honey breath" (65) and "proud-pied April" (98). The waves move towards the pebbled shore, the summer's day shines, but not too hotly, and throughout the sonnets Shakespeare avoids the conventional image – "My mistress' eyes are nothing like the sun" (130, i.e. they cannot be compared with anything as conventional as the sun; not as Shaw wrongly interpreted, they are not as good as the sun). The grave, the glass, usury, the seal, a lease, a tomb, painters, the chest and the jewel, the arrest, the King – all these images carry Shakespeare's discontent and self-disgust. There is a line which runs from Catullus; the exiled Ovid; through Wyatt and Surrey; through Shakespeare; to Tennyson (in *In Memoriam*) and Hardy (in those poems about his dead wife, when in his mind's eye he revisits scenes they have visited together). This tradition is one that celebrates and laments a lost love.

Of course, the way to escape from time, and mess, is not into children ("heirs") or the false eternity of art, though both of these created forms that outlive oneself, and therefore help. It is, quite simply, to experience the Light within the soul, the illumination which it is the business of all religions to uncover in the soul when the conditions are right, and which most English people today – and this is certainly true of the atheists – have yet to know. Shakespeare was not a mystic, and he gives no indication in the sonnets that he even knew what a "jewel" there was in his soul – and so he remains lost in the mess outside, and lacks the standard by which to measure its inadequacy. No Christian eternity or immortality looks like filling the soul which is emptied of the world in the sonnets, and the process of purgation continues in *King Lear*.

The experience of lost love is a purging one that can lead to illumination. Shakespeare's dissatisfaction does not go that far, but there is sufficient dissatisfaction in the sonnets to attest the following proposition: you can dispute the dating, yes, and therefore the identification of the cast; but you cannot deny that there is a very large autobiographical element in the sonnets.

Shakespeare's *Sonnets*: Autobiographical Poetry

Some temperaments emerge from suffering to laugh and mock. Byron emerged from the bitterness and self-pity of *Childe Harold* to write the devastatingly comic satiric epic *Don Juan*. Shakespeare is a different case. His temperament was permanently overwhelmed by his suffering, as a close reading of *Sonnets* reveals. His self-loathing at his lustful side (sonnet 129) and his self-disgust at chasing the "huswife" Dark Lady when he knew she wasn't interested in him, his "frantic mad" lovesick infatuation, developed into the tragedies and *Antony and Cleopatra* –

did the Dark Lady become Cleopatra? – and the serenity of his last plays is very hard won indeed, and contains more than a hint of spiritual exhaustion.

"The man who suffers", to cite Eliot's dichotomy, always touches "the artist who creates". Some temperaments win detachment from their suffering, or repress it; other temperaments are scarred for life and are deepened by it. The difference between the two is not a matter of maturity but a question of superficiality or depth. A Byron plays on the surfaces and is extrovert. A Shakespeare lies awake thinking of Mr W.H. and broods on his "sweet thief", the "robber" of husbands whom he described in terms of the devils of Hell. Shakespeare knew what it meant to expend his spirit, how lust can madden both before *and* after the lustful act, and he recorded his self-disgust with very little irony. Byron probably knew more lust than Shakespeare, but he didn't worry so much about its baser qualities.

Shakespeare took the conventions of the Latin lyric poets – Catullus, Horace and Ovid – and wrote about the seasons, love, joy, friendship and the shortness of life with reference to his patron. But the polite tone turned sour. And in that sourness lies the greatness of *Sonnets*. He followed the conventions, but injected the sweated blood and pain of his own autobiographical experience. He brought the art of the sonnet to its highest perfection, developing the subordinate theme of the first four lines into the subordinate theme of the next four, and then changing the treatment of the overall theme by introducing a separate subordinate theme in the first three lines of the sestet, and developing this in turn into the subordinate theme of the last three lines. Shakespeare brought a musical approach to his own experience, so "the artist who creates" shaped the raw past experience of "the man who suffers".

Sonnets tell a story when properly arranged – see Dover Wilson's rearrangement – but they also reveal an incredible spectrum of human emotions, ranging from extremes of ecstatic love to extremes of hate, from extremes of self-confidence to extremes of self-doubt, from extremes of trust to extremes of suspicion. Each sonnet has to be read in relation to the others and collectively they comprise a definition of the human mind in all its moods: a spectrum of perennial states of mind. It is in these permanent states of mind that these sonnets have their universality. The autobiographical particularity of Shakespeare's experience has been generalised into an image of a state of mind that is universal in its application.

A work of imagination has had high claims made for it; Coleridge attempted to relate the imagination to the organic mind. To the extent that a work of art is make-believe, it is (the artist is trying to persuade us) an image of a general truth. To the extent that it is based on an autobiographical experience and disguised as make-believe – as both *Don Juan* and *Sonnets* were – then it is just as precious an image of a general truth. For it is not merely what the artist speculates the general truth to be, what he tries to persuade us *is* the truth; it is what the artist has lived and therefore what he *knows* the general truth to be, which rises dripping wet from the sea of experience.

Our Age regards autobiographical poetry as "embarrassing". "You don't talk about your own experience over dinner," neo-Augustans say. But poetry, like thought, can be far more private than dinner party conversation, as Hardy's poems addressed to his dead wife show.

There is nothing wrong with being "an autobiographical poet". The poet who imagines another's experience speculates; the poet who records his own experience knows. Knowledge is no less valid than speculation, as any news editor knows. And though truths of speculation differ from truths of knowledge, just as make-belief differs from fact, the lesson of Shakespeare's *Sonnets* is that a poet *can* create a universal image of a general truth out of his suffering, if he is a good enough artist; and that this can have just as much impact as a disguising of his suffering in the form of mocking laughter, *à la* Byron.

Wit in the Metaphysicals

There have been many attempts to define a Metaphysical poem since Drummond of Hawthornden wrote of "Metaphysical Ideas and Scholastic Quiddities" in a letter, and thereby introduced the term that was to be taken up by Dryden, Pope and Johnson. The brevity and conciseness, the strong line and concentration, the "hammering out" of learned conceits after the manner of the imprisoned Richard II – all these have been commented on. So too has the ingredient that cannot be overlooked, wit. Yet I cannot help feeling that no one has really got to grips with the wit.

Since Johnson, I must hasten to add, for in his 'Life of Cowley', Johnson really grapples with the Metaphysical wit. It is not Pope's "True wit", "What oft was thought, but ne'er so well expressed", he says, and it is not "that which is at once both natural and new". Rather it is "a combination of dissimilar images, or discovery of occult resemblances in things apparently unlike". "Of wit, thus defined, they have more than enough," Johnson writes. "The most heterogeneous ideas are yoked by violence together; nature and art are ransacked for illustrations, comparisons and allusions."

Johnson did not like the Metaphysicals, and his view of their wit is disparaging. Eliot did like them, and in 'The Caroline Poets' he writes of wit in the seventeenth century as "a tough reasonableness beneath the slight lyric grace". He was thinking of Milton as much as of Marvell, and in 'The Metaphysical Poets' he writes of Johnson that "by wit he clearly means something more serious than we usually mean today".

It is worth quoting the OED on one of the meanings of "wit": "that quality of speech or writing which consists in the apt association of thought and expression, calculated to surprise and delight by its unexpectedness". Thought and expression aptly associated – that is close to Pope's definition, which Johnson rejected. But "calculated to surprise and delight by its unexpectedness" – now we are getting closer. Johnson surely felt when he condemned the "novelty" of the Metaphysicals' "yoking" that they were out to surprise with the unexpected.

Wit, of course, differs from age to age, and from generation to generation, as do society's standards. What *we* find surprising and unexpected will naturally differ from what the seventeenth century did. In the case of Marvell we can see this wit at work in the shock yoking of love and globe in 'The Definition of Love'. The lovers are at opposite poles, and can only meet if the globe is squashed into a planisphere. Then the image switches to geometry, and instead of making an angle, i.e. intersection, they are parallel lines that will never meet. Fancy seeing love in terms of geometry. Or there is the "vegetable love" in 'To his Coy Mistress' which "should grow/Vaster than Empires, and more slow." Fancy seeing love as a vegetable, like a cauliflower or tomatoes, or even runner beans. Or, yet again, the very aptly expressed association of "The Grave's a fine and private place,/But none I think do there embrace." Fancy associating embracing with a grave, fancy associating "a fine and private place" with a grave. How surprising and unexpected these associations are, and how delightful.

As Love, so Time. Time and Eternity are abstract notions, but how surprising and unexpected to find them linked with a chariot and deserts. And in 'The Garden', how surprising and unexpected to find "th'industrious Bee/Computes its time as well as we," when "time" is an obvious pun for "thyme". Marvell is full of such instances. How surprising and unexpected to find Hope seen as a bird with a "tinsel wing", and, for that matter, the Soul as a bird (or angel) that "whets, and combs its silver Wings". How surprising and unexpected to find the vagina seen as iron gates, and how utterly delightful. And so on. And this is not to mention the conceits. How surprising and unexpected to find courting seen in terms of World and Time, but how dazzling when the idea is developed at length, so that World takes us to the Ganges, the Humber, and Empires, and Time takes us to "ten years before the Flood", to the Conversion of the Jews, i.e. the end of Time because they will never be converted, and to all the hundreds and thousands of years and Ages to be allocated to each part of the body that is being courted.

In his technique, Marvell is a gigantic show-off. "Look what I can do," he says on his poetic tightrope, and we watch amazed as he undresses, balancing on now one foot, then the other, does cartwheels and somersaults along the wire, cavorts high into the air and lands safely, replaces his clothes, and bows low for the inevitable applause. Yet, when he is being most himself, as he is in his philosophical, reflective 'The Garden', how little by comparison he needs to show off and shock or use conceits. The subject matter takes over, he has too much to say to surprise with the unexpected very much.

Of course, Marvell inherits his exhibitionism from Donne, who in his early poems was the most colossal show-off. What a twinkle Donne must have had in his eye as he wrote. Can he have believed a word of how Angels took bodies of Aire? I doubt it, yet what good images he has found for the soul and the body. Can he have believed that our eyebeams thread each other, like needles, and that our souls negotiate above us while we lie back "like sepulchral statues" on a "Pregnant banke" of violets? Surely not. (Yet I once walked with Sir John Eccles, a Nobel prize-winner for discoveries relating to nerve cells, and asked him where our souls were, and he replied that they were above and ahead of us, outside our bodies, and in a rapport outside our bodies – exactly Donne's perspective.)

If we read 'The Extasie' as a preposterous piece of flirtation, how we warm to him, how we are delighted by all the metaphysical and astrological parallels. How surprising and unexpected that two lovers should be seen as "twin compasses", the compass with two spiked points we still use in our geometry classes at school, in 'A Valediction: forbidding mourning', and how aptly expressed the last three stanzas are. Again, how surprising and unexpected that love should be seen as a mine for alchemists in 'Loves Alchymie' – or rather, as the image is developed, as "this vaine Bubles shadow". So much for marriage if "my man/Can be as happy'as I can". And then there is the poem that Eliot quotes, 'A Valediction: of weeping'. How surprising and unexpected that a tear should be seen as a coin, a globe, a moon in successive stanzas. What brilliant showing-off. What a display.

And when it comes to conceits, what of 'The Relique'? How surprising and unexpected that Donne should imagine his lover's bones are seen as a Mary Magdalene's, and how delightfully the idea is developed through the grave imagery of stanza 1. And can we not hear Marvell's "a fine and private place" in the opening: "When my grave is broke up againe/Some second ghest to entertaine/(For graves have learn'd that woman-head/To be to more than one a Bed)"? Yes, the more we look at the early Donne, the more we see the tone that Marvell was later to use. And as with Marvell, when he starts writing in earnest as his religion grows, his tricks become quieter, and subject matter begins to dominate.

Herbert is quite different. He is the honest, plain carpenter knocking up sincere devotional poems. In the two 'Jordan' poems he sets out the principles behind his art. He wants to tell us about a true chair, not a painted one; about facts, not fictions. Not for him the curling metaphors "Decking the sense, as if it were to sell." His is "a plain intention". He would "plainly say, My God, My King," and his virtues are directness, and a far greater fidelity to his devotional subject matter than either Donne or Marvell reveal in their "showing-off" poems. In short, Herbert is not out to surprise us with the unexpected, though he is not averse to using the occasional shock comparison, as in 'The Collar' ("Loose as the winde", "Thy rope of sands"), and 'The Pulley' ("a glasse of blessings", "this jewell").

The wit of the Metaphysicals needs to be looked at again. A study needs to be made of all of them, taking into account the spirit in which they wrote, a spirit which seems to have been overlooked and left buried in the seventeenth century. We must exhume this relique.

The Metaphysicals' Learning

There are many instances where one feels that Donne and Marvell are showing their learning, and that to use Johnson's phrase "to show their learning was their whole endeavour". One thinks of the use of mathematics in Marvell's 'The Definition of Love' and in Donne's 'A Valediction: forbidding mourning' – the parallel lines and the compass – and of the use of chemistry in Donne's 'Love's Alchymie' and 'A nocturnall upon S. Lucies day', the use of contemporary medicine in Marvell's 'A Dialogue between the Soul and Body' and of metaphysics in Donne's 'The Extasie' and 'Aire and Angels'. The poetry of Donne and Marvell contains references to contemporary philosophy, mythology, history, and geography (e.g. the Ganges in the 'To His Coy Mistress').

Perhaps because of this learning, criticism has taken the Metaphysicals very seriously indeed, and has often removed us from the spirit in which the poems were written. Very often the metaphysical mind throws up an image, which it then develops. It lives within the world of the image for the duration of the poem, suspending disbelief for the time of the poem, and walks away from it at the end of the poem. While it is working out its image it may be playing with its private audience. Many of the metaphysical poems were written for a limited circle of friends, and were perhaps flirtations, spoken with a twinkle in the poet's eye.

At the time when he wrote them Donne did not believe the

metaphysical propositions of 'The Extasie' or 'Aire and Angels' in any religious sense. He used them as ideas to flirt with, and as images on which he could hang the structure of a poem.

Donne

Donne began as a lawyer – see the legal imagery of 'The Will' – and in the 1590s he held political posts. He was not then religious: witness the 'Satyre: Of Religion' which can be dated to 1597 or possibly even to 1593. He travelled with Essex on the Islands Voyage to the Azores of 1597: see 'The Calme'. He had already written the Elegies of 1593-6: 'His Picture', 'On his Mistris', 'To his Mistris going to Bed'.

Donne wrecked his political career as secretary to the Lord Keeper by falling in love with Ann More, the under-aged niece of his employer's wife. For this he was thrown into the Fleet Prison in 1601, and the next 14 years were years of poverty and insecurity. By 1617 he had 12 children, of whom five died, and he had no job, but sponged off his friends, notably off his Twickenham patroness Lucy, Countess of Bedford.

The love poems fall naturally into two groups: those in which he is full of belief in love and the "joint soul" – for example 'The Extasie', 'The Canonization', 'The Relique', 'The Sunne Rising', 'The Good-morrow', 'The Anniversarie', 'A Valediction: of weeping', 'A Valediction: forbidding mourning', 'Loves Growth', 'Sweetest Love', 'The Flea' and 'The Undertaking' – and those poems in which he shows an increasingly nihilistic despair. To these belong 'Falling Star', 'Twicknam Garden', 'The Apparition', 'Love's Alchemy', 'Love's Deity', 'A nocturnall upon S. Lucies day', and 'The Will'. The feeling towards women in these poems is bitterly bleak, like the feeling at the end of 'Aire and Angels', which surprises us after so promisingly optimistic a first stanza, so what happened?

There is a problem over the dating of these love-poems, and we can only conjecture whether the sunny poems belong near 1601 and the bleak ones towards 1610. It is one of the unsolved mysteries of English Literature as to what had happened before 'Twicknam Garden', with its characteristic pun on "manna" "my Anna". No trace here of the young man whose world was his shared bedroom, or of his feeling that if one lover cries the other must weep too, since they are one soul.

In 1609 at 37 Donne underwent a religious crisis of the depth of the crisis that Hopkins went through in 1885, the year of 'Carrion Comfort' and those dreadfully suffering sonnets. In the 'Holy Sonnets: Divine Meditations' and the awful 'Batter my heart' Donne felt himself undermined. He had already abandoned the Catholic faith of his family – his two uncles were Jesuits – for Anglicanism, and his quarrel with Catholicism intensified around this time. It is not relieved in 'Good Friday, 1613. Riding Westward' where he is still divided. In 1615 he took orders, and in the 'Holy Sonnet' of 1617, on the death of his wife, he has come through: "I have found thee." He also turned away from the world towards heaven: "Wholly in heavenly things my mind is sett."

In 1623 he was ill and thought he would die. The puns of "Thou hast not done./For, I have more" and "Thou hast done, I have no more" (punning on Ann More) show how God took the place of his wife in his battered heart.

Donne had come a long way by his last poem – if Izaak Walton is right in attributing 'Hymne to God my God, in my sicknesse' to 23 March 1631, eight days before his death. In his youth he had worshipped "Love's Deity", but the courtly love turned religious as his "disgrace" and "shame" humbled him. Those terrible fourteen years of failure burnt away his pride and left him illumined – see the taper imagery in 'The Dreame'. This is part of the pattern of the slow believer. Nothing could illustrate the movement in Donne's soul better than a contrast between the youthful egotism of "This bed they center is" ('The Sunne Rising') in which the Donne of 1603 is a complete island shut away in his room from the universe; and the wonderful "no man is an island" of his sermons, with its implications of being responsible for all men, Dostoevsky's Father Zossima's "All are responsible for all".

Fundamentally Donne was a man who had to lose the world to find his own soul. He lost his career and his wife, and he came to look on his sexual virility with odium. He refers to "lecherous goats," in one of his 'Divine Meditations'. He now saw his youthful *joie de vivre* as being enslaved to Satan. Like a Muggeridge of his day, he forgot his fornications in his sermons from the pulpit of St Paul's – arguably a greater folly than all the worthies did – but what he could not make us forget was his unique talent for taking a concrete object such as the relic and developing it as a poetic idea.

And this is what sets Donne apart from the romantic autobiographical poet. Above all he was concerned with making something outside himself. He used his own experience but he made an objective point in each poem – the hallmark of the classicist.

We do not need Eliot's theory of the "dissociation of sensibility" to understand Donne. He does not represent an age that was whole or which fused thought and feeling. He was simply a man journeying towards God with a gift for stating his experience in objective terms, and he had the curiosity to inquire into the soul: first as it was affected by love, and secondly as it was modified by religion. To such a man in any age, thinking is a passion.

Donne's Journey from the Human to the Divine

Donne's poems reflect a corrupt, rotten world from which the soul must escape, and this metaphysical view of life is treated at first satirically and humorously, with the twinkling eye of the lover, and then seriously as his pessimism becomes almost too great to bear.

In the *Satyres* (1593-7) London society, religion, the law and the court are all corrupted by vice (notably vanity, lust, pride, greed). In the *Songs and Sonets* (1593-1601) Donne decorates his love poems with a "twinkling" use of these vices. (The *Elegies*, 1593-8, are love poems without satire.) However, the titles taunt his sensuality with the idea of the shortness of life and the ever-imminence of death. 'The Relique', 'The Funerall', 'The Will', 'A nocturnall upon S. Lucies day', 'The Legacie', 'The Canonization', 'A Feaver', 'A Valediction: forbidding mourning' – all these titles use the idea of death as a metaphor to suggest the shortness of life.

Donne flatters Sir Robert Drury's family in his eulogy on his dead daughter and receives a rent-free house in the Drury mansion in Drury Lane, just as he flatters another patron, Lucy Countess of Bedford in four verse letters. The least attractive side of Donne is the flattery of his begging letters. The most attractive side of Donne is his satirical, twinkling, flirtatious love (or rather lust) poems.

In the Divine Poems (from 1607) Donne escapes the corrupt world for the soul's love of God, and the soul's human love of the *Songs and Sonets* becomes a divine love. In the 'Anniversaries' (1611-12), on the death of Elizabeth Drury in 1610, the world is rotten, as in the satyres, and the soul longs to escape it and expand after death, as does the "joint soul" in the *Songs and Sonets*.

The sequence of 1607 on the life of Christ reached a crisis in c.1613 with 'Good Friday, 1613. Riding Westward' and 'Batter my Heart', in both of which God comes to Donne, and in the *Holy Sonnets* the sinfulness of the world and shortness of life (themes in the 'Anniversaries') become conditions which the soul must escape. In the last hymns (1619, 1623, perhaps 1631) Donne looks back on his youth and dedicates the energy he spent on profane loves to God.

Donne's excesses in the 1590s taught him that the soul does not belong in a corrupt world. His metaphysical view of life was at first adopted humorously in his poems, and then seriously as he made preparation to jettison his sensual outlook for a path that would take him to becoming the Dean of St Paul's.

Marvell's Reflective Tone

Though Marvell was deeply curious about the conflicts of his time, he retained throughout a sense of reflective quiet: the quiet of the Garden.

As one might expect from a man who was tutor to Fairfax's daughter, then Cromwell's Latin Secretary, and MP for Hull, he was a keen observer of the conflict between Charles I and Cromwell. His 'A Dialogue, Between the Resolved Soul, and Created Pleasure' and his 'Dialogue between Soul and Body' can be read as definitions of the conflict between the Puritan restraints and the Royalist pleasures. In these poems he is very relevant to our permissive time. In the 'Horatian Ode' he maintains his ambivalent attitude towards Cromwell, genuinely praising his achievements while satirizing his excesses in the same vein that Pope used to attack George II in his 'Epistle to Augustus'.

Before this he was interested in the journeys of the pilgrims: witness 'The Bermudas'.

His love poems are a bizarre lot: he seems to have been easily infatuated, and the girl always seems to be out of reach. His "passion's heat" is most argumentative in 'To His Coy Mistress', of course, where he develops his thought from paragraph to paragraph ("Had we....But....Now") and from association to association, breeding idea after idea from the two opening words, "world" and "time". In 'The Fair Singer' and 'The Mower to the Glo-Worms' he is obsessed with a woman who clearly comes between him and what Eliot called "the tough reasonableness" of his verse. In 'The Definition of Love' he is full of a sense of impossibility and despair, and it remains one of the fascinatingly unprovable questions as to whether this poem was written for Fairfax's daughter, whom of course, as tutor, he could not possibly marry.

Though he remained a bachelor, he was obviously fascinated by children. His friend's child, ten-year-old little T.C. (Theophila Cornewall), obviously made a great impact, and it is possible that 'The Nymph Complaining for the Death of her Fawn' was a kind of bedtime story for her. The language of the opening two lines is very much the indignant complaint of a child:

"The wanton Troopers riding by
Have shot my Faun and it will dye."

But behind all the historical clashes and the passion and the people around him, there is the reflective, philosophical tone of 'The Garden'. Set after a lyrical stanza about apples, grapes, nectaren, peach and melons, the stanza beginning "Meanwhile the Mind from pleasure less" comes across with an immense weight. The word "Mind" is mentioned twice, "Thought" once. This is Marvell the thinker, the contemplative, who has at last escaped from Cromwell and Juliana (who "displac'd" his Mind in 'The Mower to the Glo-Worms'), from ambition and the lovers who carve their name on trees. Here by the fountain he was most himself.

Marvell stands for the middle way. He saw from both sides, and remained fundamentally detached, and this did not preclude action as an MP. He was a man of immense wisdom and commonsense, and the wit with which he associated disparate ideas (the grave and embracing

– death and love) is that of a sensibility that has seen the universe as a whole, as one "green thought", and is able to relate and link parts of it in a way that is impossible for less profound minds.

'Lycidas'

'Lycidas' is a conventional poem, to the extent that in it Milton draws on conventional classical mythology: Jove and Arethusa and all the various nymphs and other deities Milton invokes. How then does Milton convey the deep feeling which is surely there, the genuine regret he felt for the early death in 1637 of the young Edward King, on whom Lycidas is based?

The answer is, the regret comes out in the rhythms, which play against the pentameters with a marvellous skill. The first three lines of the poem give us a clue:

"Yet once more, O ye laurels, and once more
Ye myrtles brown, with ivy never sere,
I come to pluck your berries harsh and crude...."

It is the long rhythm and cadence of this opening sentence that catch the tone, for the feeling is pressing through it and expressing itself in the stylistic tricks Milton is so fond of in this poem: the repetition (once more), the apostrophe or invocation (O ye laurels), and the inverted word-order (Yet once more...I come). All these devices help to establish the elegiac tone, and they reappear in many of the twelve subsequent paragraphs of the poem. (They cannot be called stanzas as there is no break between them and they are all of unequal length.)

In keeping with these tricks for strengthening rhythm, Milton uses rhetorical questions and exclamations, and he heightens his mood with a suitably lugubrious word-choice and by alliteration. The rhymes play an important part in achieving a "sad" effect.

It would take several pages to illustrate these devices in full. The poem is dignified and ennobled by its classical trappings. The tone would be far less grand if "King" replaced "Lycidas", and "Cambridge" the various woods and pastures of Sicily; and if "congregations" replaced the idea of "sheep" in the passage where Milton criticizes the clergy. The classical references conventionalize – and distance, universalize. Eliminating the particular facts of 1637 makes the regret universal and cuts it free from its time to work in a world of metaphor where poets are not referred to as poets but as shepherds.

This world of metaphor is crucial to a work of art. It allows parallels, like the parallel between Lycidas and King. It is Milton's achievement that he has combined such deep feeling with such conventional metaphor, the metaphor of the pastoral tradition.

Milton's Siege of Contraries

The good thing about Milton is that he makes his characters in *Paradise Lost* so human, and he does this by giving them a case. I am tempted to write "an irrefutable case", for he has Shakespeare's or Dostoevsky's knack of giving his characters a strong argument.

What I mean is illustrated at the beginning of Book 9. Let us assess the responsibility for the Fall. There are three characters, of course, whose responsibility is in question. Satan seems so sinister and loathsome at first, full of stealth, "involv'd in rising Mist", bulging with "dark suggestions". He comes across as a thoroughly dishonest fellow. But then we begin to see it from his side. We have been told he is "full of anguish driv'n", and now we are told of his "inward griefe". "The more I see/Pleasures about me, so much more I feel/Torment within me, as from the hateful siege/Of contraries," he tells us. Again: "For onely in destroying I finde ease/To my relentless thoughts." We begin to understand his appalling self-division, his inability to enjoy outer pleasures and his compulsion to destroy. Glory, ambition, revenge, envy are all mentioned.

A siege of contraries indeed. We almost feel sorry for him in the black mist, and when he sees Eve at close quarters and is abstracted from his Evil, so that he is "stupidly good", we feel he is very human. But, we are told:

"But the hot Hell that alwayes in him burnes,
Though in mid Heav'n, soon ended his delight,

And tortures him now more, the more he sees
Of pleasure not for him ordaind: then soon
Fierce hate he recollects...."

And he tells us:

"What hither brought us, hate, not love, nor hope
Of Paradise for Hell, hope here to taste
Of pleasure, but all pleasure to destroy,
Save what is in destroying, other joy
To mee is lost."

The hot Hell in his heart, the anguish and inner conflict of his contraries, reminds him that his only pleasure is in destruction. How understandable, we think. What else could the poor fellow do? Can we blame him for the Fall, really?

Then there are Adam and Eve. In the seven speeches between them before Eve goes off to the rose-garden alone, they are both given a strong case. Eve's arguments for going are so clever. They will achieve more by dividing their efforts, they distract each other by being so near each other. In vain Adam reasons with her. God does not mind their smiling at each other, as smiling comes from the Reason, which is good. He grants that "Solitude somtimes is best societie", but warns her of Satan who envies their happiness. He says "The Wife.../Safest and seemliest by her Husband staies" in times of danger. Eve brushes this aside. She is indignant that he should doubt her firmness especially as they are "not capable of death or paine". Adam has to do some quick mollifying. "Not diffident of thee do I dissuade/Thy absence from my sight," he tells her hastily. He says, reasonably, that his advice was to avoid a temptation altogether, as Eve would be angry at the affront. He says that he draws strength from being with her, and that she should feel the same from him.

Then Eve's pleading becomes really subtle. Are they going to be happy if they are for ever afraid of Satan? They have committed no sin, yet, so no harm can befall them. If Satan tempts them, *he* will suffer the dishonour, not they. They will gain the approval of God for coming through their trial. Besides "what is Faith, Love, Vertue unassaid"?

Moreover, should they doubt the "happie State" of Paradise?

In vain Adam points out the danger, that Man's enemy is himself: "within himself/The danger lies." He warns that the Reason may misinform the Will which may choose to yield rather than resist the temptation, and explains that it would be better for her to avoid temptation altogether. If she is to prove her constancy, let her first prove her obedience. We think, how wise he is. And, how reasonable, when he grants her her freedom: "Go; for thy stay, not free, absents thee more;/Go in thy native innocence." Poor Adam, we think, what a handful he has on his hands. Yet *should* he have put his foot down and forbidden her? This would have made him a dictator, and he would have been acting contrary to the Reason he has preached. *Can* he put his foot down after his arguments?

Eve, presumably motivated by the independence which some women find so dear, immediately wheedles and manoeuvres it to look as though Adam has freely granted his permission: "With thy permission then, and thus forewarnd.../The willinger I goe." Permission indeed. What else could Adam do, faced with such demands, and believing as he does? And yet, throughout, how reasonable Eve has been, how difficult to argue against. How understandable, like Satan. As much as Satan's heart, Milton's art is a siege of contraries.

Pope's Exaggeration for Truth

It is not easy to put one's finger on why Pope appeals. The crippled dwarf who depended on his mother, the plodding translator of Homer and imitator of Horace, the arrogance that poured scorn on so many other poets and dunces, the arrogance of the sensitive cripple – these do not make for an attractive portrait. His life was pretty uneventful. He lived in Berkshire until his early twenties (hence the youthful pastorals) and spent the rest of his life quarrelling in Chiswick and Twickenham. No, it is a quality in the writing that endears us to him.

Perhaps more than anyone else, Pope had the ability to present an abstract idea in a concrete form. And in a very vividly concrete form at that. Instead of telling us that critics are worthless compared with poets, he shows us grubs and worms in amber, or a fossil. He does not tell us that the Vice-Chamberlain Lord Hervey (Sporus) is less attractive inside than he is on the outside, he presents him as a butterfly-bug: "Yet let me flap this bug with gilded wings,/This painted child of dirt that stinks and stings...." (Pope calls him Sporus after Nero's castrated lover, seeing Lord Hervey as a hermaphrodite.) To move from the 'Epistle to Dr Arbuthnot' to the 'Epistle to Augustus', he does not tell us that people prefer their authors dead, he says: "Authors like coins grow dear as they grow old;/It is the rust we value, not the gold." This felicity of expression, the couplet stamped out by the rhyme, is also the basis of Pope's wit. Wit is the association of opposite ideas or, as Dr Johnson put it, "when heterogeneous images are yoked by violence together". Pope associates an abstract idea and a concrete idea for a particularly destructive effect.

He exaggerates, of *course*, but then the basis of his satire is exaggeration. Satire ridicules the follies and vices of others, and exaggeration is the best way to ridicule. The whole of 'The Rape of the Lock' is an exaggeration. Pope sets beside the trivial episode of the loss of Arabella Fermor's hair a heroic event complete with gods and battles and an underworld from Homer and Virgil. It is the disparity between the trivial subject and the heroic tone that makes the poem mock-heroic, or "heroi-comical" to use the description of the Frontispiece. Look, Pope is saying gently to Arabella Fermor, use your commonsense, wasn't the quarrel senseless? Let's keep everything in proportion. He says it gently, tenderly, affectionately, not savagely or cruelly, and this is part of Pope's charm.

He could be cruel, though. How exasperated he is in the 'Epistle to Dr Arbuthnot'. Driven up the wall by people who pester him for his recommendation of their tripe, or so he affects to be, how he exaggerates his grumbling. How he poses, affecting indifference to his own reputation. We don't believe he really wants to be left alone that much. Yet we accept the attitude he strikes as it measures his "abhorrence of vice" (Pope's letter to Dr Arbuthnot of 2 August 1734, in which he defends his satirical methods).

And yet two years after this spiteful display he appears in May 1737 as the champion of all neglected poets in arguing with George II. Hiding behind the pretence that he is Horace writing to Augustus – for the title of 'The Epistle to Augustus' is 'The First Epistle of the Second Book of

Horace Imitated' – he satirizes George II with exaggerated, and undeserved praise; as if George had been Octavius Caesar himself. "Great Friend of Liberty!" he addresses this King who had led his country into an unpopular and unnecessary war with Spain, and in a devastating passage at the end:

"Oh! could I mount on the Maeonian wing,
Your Arms, your Actions, your Repose to sing!
What seas you travers'd, and what fields you fought!
Your Country's Peace, how oft, how dearly bought!"

Pope cannot, of course, sing these things. Yet, one can hear him exclaiming in mock innocence, "What have I said that's wrong? I'm only imitating Horace."

Pope used exaggeration as a ruler by which to measure the truth. He is a master of overstatement, which is an American rather than a British characteristic. And the overstatement is like a bulldozer manned by a demolition team. How unfair he is about "Dulness" and the dunces, yet how just is the point he is making if you reduce the scale, convert his overstatement into a statement.

When he gives us straight statement without the exaggerating satire, the effect is of weakened tea. His elegy 'To the Memory of an Unfortunate Lady' contains a delicate feeling for the lady's poverty and her burial in a pauper's grave, just as 'Eloisa to Abelard' feelingly evokes the fate of the would-be lover who has become a nun. But these two works in the middle of Pope's career lack the fire and bite of the two great satires he wrote, the first ('The Rape of the Lock') in his twenties and the second ('The Dunciad') in his fifties, and it is in his satires we look for Pope's true spirit.

Blake's *Songs of Innocence and Experience:*
Two Contraries in the Human Soul

The *Songs of Innocence* and *Songs of Experience* are indeed, as the title page asserts, about the "two contraries in the human soul". The contraries are two sets of virtues: Mercy, Pity, Peace and Love ('The

Divine Image') on the one hand, and Cruelty, Jealousy, Terror and Secrecy ('A Divine Image') on the other hand. The first set, "virtues of delight", are divine, and as the child is created in the image of God, they inform the world of innocence, the world of the small child with its security and joy. All the *Songs of Innocence* are influenced by these divine virtues in some way. The second set of "virtues" are human, and as man creates God in his own image, they inform the world of the growing child's experience, with its disillusionment and growing sense of evil. Thus a baby has divine qualities and human qualities. As it grows older it loses its sense of the divine and acquires negative human emotions which it makes into divine ones; it creates a cruel, jealous God, the qualities of old "Nobodaddy" of the false religion which Blake associates with the Church.

The dialectic is there in the soul from birth – see 'Infant Joy' and 'Infant Sorrow' – and there is no synthesis. Experience corrupts the divine innocence, and so society is built by men more on the negative emotions than on the positive ones: see 'London'. Blake symbolizes the two sets of "virtues" in natural images, for example the tiger (cruelty and terror), and the rose (jealousy); the clod (love) and the pebble (secrecy, i.e. selfish love). To Blake, the human soul is divided, and the only way to achieve a marriage between Heaven and Hell is by accepting the dualism, one side of which includes the positive aspect of Cruelty (Hell) – "energy is eternal delight"; and by accepting the God within as a permanent alternative to the cruel, jealous God without.

*

The revolutionary Blake was greatly influenced by both the American and the French Revolutions. Earth awakening from her chains mirrors the situations in the US and France. Similarly the soul is in the chains of the body; Mercy, Pity, Peace and Love are in the chains of Cruelty, Jealousy, Terror and Secrecy. The Age of Reason's night is over, and "the new dawn" of the Romantic Age is ahead. The Age of Reason was ruled by Urizen ("Your reason"), the cruel, jealous god.

It is wrong to trace Blake's ideas forward to the student revolution of 1968, to the Communist "liberation from chains". Blake saw God within, and he abhorred the God without, and though he protested at the condition of London, he would have loathed the cruelty and jealousy of contemporary Communism, preferring the free individualism of Mercy, Pity, Peace and Love.

Wordsworth's Sub-Rational Soul
Feeling Tranquillity and Gladness

'The Leech-Gatherer, or, Resolution and Independence', 'Lines composed a few miles above Tintern Abbey' and the 'Ode, Intimations of Immortality', arguably the three greatest poems Wordsworth wrote, are curiously parallel. In each Wordsworth is, or says he tends to be, depressed. In each, the title represents an escape from his depression: the independence of the Leech-Gatherer and his courage, the image of Tintern Abbey, which puts him into a trance so that he sees "into the life of things", and his sense of immortality. All three are really the same. The Leech-Gatherer, at one with Nature, is seen through the "living soul", the immortal part of a poet's sensibility.

'Tintern Abbey' is perhaps the most fascinating of the three poems. It is nothing less than a spiritual autobiography. The Abbey itself is first of all an image that enables Wordsworth to escape "the weary weight/Of all this unintelligible world", "the dreary intercourse of daily life". He used to be able to *feel* Nature intensely in 1793 – experience the "visionary gleam" of the Ode – but now the aching joys are no more. Instead is his consolation, his awareness of the Oneness of Nature, the "motion and a spirit, that impels/All thinking things, all objects of all thought". He is content to have graduated to the "still, sad music of humanity".

Nevertheless the loss of his youthful delight echoes through these three poems. The early joys and gladness are replaced with a despair from which comes despondency and madness, and but for the consolation, the escape, all would be very grim indeed.

Wordsworth's Leech-Gatherer is a part of Nature, like a stone, a cloud, a stream. It is as if he has crawled out of the pool like some "sea-beast". He does not think. Wordsworth starts the morning in "gladness", but falls into "despondency" and "dejection" when he begins to think. His "meddling intellect" ('The Tables Turned') is the villain; his "untoward thoughts", which are about the fate of poets, who begin in gladness, "but thereof" – if they live through their reason – "comes in the end despondency and madness".

The Leech-Gatherer's mindless perseverance snaps him out of his depression. The truth is that some poets (like Chatterton) have lived wrongly and have found "despondency and madness", but this is not the fate of all poets, especially not of those who are able to switch off their thinking and unite themselves with Nature, which flows into their souls: the "in-fluence" of natural objects. It is possible to be a Romantic poet and end in gladness, if one's growth is right.

The Leech-Gatherer will be an image for Wordsworth, as Tintern Abbey was for five years an image: of an emotion recollected in tranquillity as a consolation within a depression, in lonely city-rooms. Wordsworth knew that we are a part of Nature, united with Nature, when we see the hare "running races in her mirth" and do not think about the hare. He needed to still the questioning mind which took him away from that knowledge.

There is a distinction to be drawn between feelings and emotions. Emotions are agitations, excitations; feelings are sympathetic, tendernesses for the suffering of others. Emotions are turbulent and stormy, like a wind ruffling a pond. Feelings are tranquil and calm, especially feelings of love; like a pool mirroring leaves that shake, though its surface is calm.

Emotions stir us, feelings mirror humanity with love. Jimmy Porter emotes angrily and negatively in *Look Back in Anger*, but Mother Teresa loved serenely. The consciousness of the mystic has been purified of emotions, and his calm serenity mirrors creation with serene feelings. Our age is an age of emotion, and the mystic has to shelter from its wind if he is to live through feeling.

Wordsworth's Mysticism:
The Unity between Nature and the Human Heart

Wordsworth's mysticism comes across very clearly in the first two books of *The Prelude*. It is a mysticism that sees Spirit (the "Wisdom and Spirit of the universe") as pervading both the world of Nature, the

Lake District of his boyhood, and the feelings of his mind.

All the experiences that haunt him – the moving mountain when he was rowing on Lake Ullswater, the wheeling cliffs when he was giddy from skating, the birds-nesting, the kite-flying and the rest – are to be seen as gifts from the Spirit of the universe, which made the forms we see and the feelings that react to them:

"Thou Soul that art the eternity of thought,
That givest to forms and images a breath
And everlasting motion, not in vain...
           ...didst thou intertwine for me
The passions that build up our human soul."

The "calm/That Nature breathes", the "low breathings" that came after him, the steps "Almost as silent as the turf they trod", the power with which the mountain "Upreared its head" and, like a living thing "Strode after me" – all indicate the personification of this Spirit and Wordsworth's sense of "unknown modes of being". Animated by this Spirit, the forms "do not live/Like living men", but they *do* live and are animated by the One "Being" and "The unity of all hath been revealed". These different manifestations of the One are therefore "Ye Presences of Nature in the sky/And on the earth".

But, and this is the point about Wordsworth, so are his feelings about them. The "grandeur in the beatings of the heart," the gleams "like the flashing of a shield" whereby "the earth/And common face of Nature spake to me" – these have a similar origin in the Spirit. Like the babe who knows the "one dear Presence" of his mother, and whose feelings are intensified by his knowledge of the One so that love "Hath beautified that flower", and who therefore lives in an "active universe", Wordsworth's feelings emanate from One presence, for feeling

      "has to him imparted power
That through the growing faculties of sense
Doth like an agent of the one great Mind
Create....
           Such, verily, is the first
Poetic spirit of our human life."

Again:

"I was left alone
Seeking the visible world, nor knowing why.
The props of my affections were removed,
And yet the building stood, as if sustained
By its own spirit! All that I beheld
Was dear."

As a result, "that universal power...by which the mind/Is moved with feelings of delight, to me/Came strengthened with a superadded soul," and he felt "whate'er there is of power in sound", and "The ghostly language of the ancient earth". He tells us, "A plastic power/Abode with me..../A local spirit of his own,.../but, for the most,/Subservient strictly to external things/With which it communed. An auxiliar light/Came from my mind." In this mystical state of mind "the power of truth/Coming in revelation, did converse/With things that really are; I, at this time,/Saw blessings spread around me like a sea". He tells us, "All my thoughts/Were steeped in feeling." Again, "I felt the sentiment of Being spread/O'er all that moves and all that seemeth still." He "looked/Towards the Uncreated (i.e. Spirit) with a countenance/Of adoration, with an eye of love".

Wordsworth remains aware that he owes his mystical vision to the Lake District. "Ye mountains, and ye lakes," he says, "/And sounding cataracts, ye mists and winds..../If in my youth I have been pure in heart/...and have lived/With God and Nature communing.../The gift is yours". Like Coleridge, his Friend, he serves "in Nature's temple".

We have, then, a triangular relationship. If we draw it as a diagram, at the apex of the triangle is the Spirit and Power of the universe, the One. On the left of the base is the world of Nature, and the forms which it animates. On the right of the base is the feeling of the human heart, which it likewise animates. The relationship along the base is two-way. His feeling needs the world of Nature, and would not exist without it, just as the world of Nature needs his feeling on which to "gleam". Both are held together in the One which includes various "modes of Being", and so there is a unity between the world of Nature and the human heart.

Coleridge: The Life of Imagination

'Kubla Khan' has a very precise geography. The sacred river, Alph, rises as a fountain, runs above ground for five miles, after two and a half miles of which it passes the pleasure-dome, and then it plunges down through caves to the sunless sea or lifeless ocean. *Lifeless* ocean....At one level, the river is not a Chinese or Mongolian river, nor the source of the Nile in Abyssinia, about which Coleridge was reading when he wrote this poem, but a symbol for life, rising in birth and plunging down in death, but continuing after death in the sunless sea of immortality, from which – who knows – the fountain, perhaps with a circular movement, springs. At this level the pleasure-dome midway between birth and death throws a Platonic shadow on the waters of the river, which pass through illusory forms of pleasure on their way to eternity. And the lifeless ocean of souls is a collective unconscious of ancestral voices, the source of prophecy as well as of life.

But the poem is obviously about more than life. It is about the imagination. Alph is a *sacred* river precisely because it represents the imagination which rises in the mind, mixed with rock-like images, runs through an inner fertile stately garden that is full of poetic images – walls, towers, trees – and plunges down into the unconscious parts of the mind, the lifeless ocean from which it came, the source of prophecy; while meanwhile more and more waters of the imagination are flowing through the mind in a never-ceasing flow which fertilises the mind, and makes it wholesome. The pleasure-dome, at this second level, embodies the imaginative pleasure a work of art gives, the delight to which the Abyssinian maid would win Coleridge if he could but remember enough of her song to recreate it in poetry. On this interpretation, Coleridge is remembering a delight, a pleasure, a shadow of the dome of pleasure which stands as a Platonic natural object does to its Idea (the dome), and, identifying with the sacred river of his inspiration which gives him Orphic flashing eyes, he naturally writes of "his floating hair": for it is the inspiration of his imagination that has made his hair float.

The connection between the Abyssinian maid and the dome of pleasure provides the connection between the first three sections and the apparently different fourth section. It provides the unity of the poem. The unity of the piece is clinched, though, when we grasp that for Coleridge the imagination *was* life, that the two principles, life and imagination, are indistinguishable, are unified. In 'Dejection: an Ode' Coleridge writes of "what nature gave me at my birth,/My shaping spirit of Imagination", and associates life and "fountains" when he says he "may not hope from outward forms to win/The passion and the life, whose fountains are within".

The fountains of life *are* the Imagination, and that is the point of 'Kubla Khan'. Or to put it another way (also from 'Dejection: an Ode'), "from the soul itself must issue forth/A light, a glory, a fair luminous cloud/Enveloping the Earth". The sacred river is sacred, and Coleridge inspires holy dread because the geography of 'Kubla Khan' is a geography of the soul.

Keats: Charms and Joys, Agonies and Cold Philosophy

"Do not all charms fly/At the mere touch of cold philosophy?" Keats asks in 'Lamia'. The question sums up Keats' self-division which he puts into a letter to John Taylor (24 April 1818): "I have been hovering for some time between an exquisite sense of the luxurious and a love for philosophy." Elsewhere he referred to the "luxurious" "charms" as "joys", as in these early lines from 'Sleep and Poetry':

"And can I ever bid these joys farewell?
Yes, I must pass them for a nobler life,
Where I may find the agonies, the strife
Of human hearts...."

The "joys" are amply illustrated in the early 'Endymion' (1817), where they take the form of vivid pictures of such detail that they give instructions to a painter who wishes to recreate the scene:

"Many and many a verse I hope to write,
Before the daisies, vermeil rimm'd and white,
Hide in deep herbage; and ere yet the bees
Hum about globes of clover and sweet peas,

I must be near the middle of my story."

"Until they came to where these streamlets fall,
With mingled bubblings and a gentle rush,
Into a river, clear, brimful, and flush
With crystal mocking of the trees and sky."

"...a wailful gnat, a bee bustling
Down in the blue-bells, or a wren light rustling
Among sere leaves and twigs, might all be heard."

"...and listening still,
Hour after hour, to each lush-leav'd rill.
Now he is sitting by a shady spring,
And elbow-deep with feverous fingering
Stems the upbursting cold: a wild rose tree
Pavilions him in bloom, and he doth see
A bud which snares his fancy...."

"...Now,
Where shall our dwelling be? Under the brow
Of some steep mossy hill, where ivy dun
Would hide us up, although spring leaves were none;
And where dark yew trees, as we rustle through,
Will drop their scarlet berry cups of dew?..."

"At this he press'd
His hands against his face, and then did rest
His head upon a mossy hillock green,
And so remain'd as he a corpse had been
All the long day; save when he scantly lifted
His eyes abroad, to see how shadows shifted
With the slow move of time,—sluggish and weary
Until the poplar tops, in journey dreary,
Had reach'd the river's brim...."

The vermeil-rimmed daisies, the bee bustling in the bluebells, the shadows of the poplar trees are pictures of the kind we find in the letters, such as: "I go among the Fields and catch a glimpse of a Stoat or a fieldmouse peeping out of the withered grass – the creature hath a purpose and its eyes are bright with it." (19 March 1819.) They are results of Keats' famous "negative capability" at work – his capability of being negative in the presence of Nature and allowing Nature to be filled with his being – and these pictures are expressed with superb effects; the words, especially the verbs and adjectives, are heightened to appeal to the senses: sight, sound, taste, touch and smell.

We see the appeal to the five senses in the six odes (1819): "My heart aches, and a drowsy numbness pains/My sense..."; "A burning forehead, and a parching tongue"; and the wonderful line about autumn, "Drows'd with the fume of poppies", which gave rise to Leavis's remark about Keats the poppy-drowsy. And it is still much in evidence in 'The Fall of Hyperion' (summer 1819), which appeals especially to taste and smell:

"Methought I stood where trees of every clime,
Palm, myrtle, oak, and sycamore, and beech,
With plantain, and spice-blossoms, made a screen;
In neighbourhood of fountains (by the noise
Soft-showering in my ears), and (by the touch
Of scent), not far from roses. Turning round
I saw an arbour with a drooping roof
Of trellis vines, and bells, and larger blooms,
Like floral censers, swinging light in air;
Before its wreathèd doorway, on a mound
Of moss, was spread a feast of summer fruits,
Which, nearer seen, seem'd refuse of a meal
By angel tasted or our Mother Eve;
For empty shells were scattered on the grass,
And grape-stalks but half bare, and remnants more,
Sweet-smelling, whose pure kinds I could not know.
Still was more plenty than the fabled horn
Thrice emptied could pour forth, at banqueting
For Proserpine return'd to her own fields,
Where the white heifers low. And appetite

More yearning than on Earth I ever felt
Growing within, I ate deliciously;
And, after not long, thirsted, for thereby
Stood a cool vessel of transparent juice
Sipp'd by the wander'd bee, the which I took,
And, pledging all the mortals of the world,
And all the dead whose names are in our lips,
Drank."

However, the "agonies, the strife/Of human hearts" have begun to take over from the charms of the "purple-stainèd mouth".

The 'Ode on a Grecian Urn' (May 1819) has the charms and the joys in pictures – the fair youth, the trees, the music, the near-kiss – but the urn itself has a philosophical message for future generations. "Cold Pastoral!" Keats addresses the urn. The word "Cold" echoes the "cold philosophy" of 'Lamia', which undoes all the magic, empties the "haunted air", and will "Unweave a rainbow". In 'Ode to a Nightingale' there is the charming joy of the nightingale's song and the reality the nightingale has never known, which Keats yearned to escape but which towards the end of his life he was compelled to face:

"The weariness, the fever, and the fret
Here, where men sit and hear each other groan;
Where palsy shakes a few, sad, last gray hairs,
Where youth grows pale, and spectre-thin, and dies;
Where but to think is to be full of sorrow
And leaden-eyed despairs."

In 'The Fall of Hyperion' Moneta says, "None can usurp this height.../But those to whom the miseries of the world/Are misery", and urges the poet to be among those "Who feel the giant agony of the world". In his letter to Charles Brown from Naples (1 November 1820) Keats writes of "the load of WRETCHEDNESS which presses upon me" and he says: "It surprised me that the human heart is capable of containing and bearing so much misery."

Just one thought about time or death, about the agonies of human hearts, and the joys are gone, the rainbow is unwoven, the charms fly.

Only art made sense of the contradiction between the joys and the despair. In his greatest poems, the odes, he found symbols of permanent, eternal changeless states which are unaffected by ephemerality and the passing of time. Both the nightingale and autumn will come again each year, both are (generically rather than individually) unaffected by time and change, as is the Grecian Urn. There is an ideal love in 'Ode to Psyche' – one that is changeless – and in 'Ode to Indolence' he yearns not to know "how change the moons" or to "hear the voice of busy common-sense". In 'Ode on Melancholy' Keats regards Melancholy as the necessary unchangeable condition of all who taste "Joy's grape" – a sort of natural depressive reaction after a particular elated manic mood. Beauty – in the sense of what is changeless – is Truth, and the Truth that both Art and Religion try to achieve is changelessness. (The very poem is a kind of urn which contains, like ashes, Keats' idea of Truth.)

Through such images in his art Keats was able to reconcile the conflict between the joys and the agonies, the charms and the cold philosophy, and in this he is very close in feeling to the world of Shakespeare's sonnets, which perform a similar reconciliation between the joys of the "summer's day" and Shakespeare's troubled look at his own "storm-beaten face".

Shelley and External Knowledge

Shelley wrote in *A Defence of Poetry* (1821) that:

> "The cultivation of poetry is never more to be desired than at periods when, from an excess of the selfish and calculating principle, the accumulation of the materials of external life exceed the quantity of the power of assimilating them to the internal laws of human nature."

This attitude is very relevant to today, when facts and data in the specialized sciences are apt to defeat their own ends by smothering creative ideas beneath a weight of tangible materials. This is not to say that the contribution of modern psychology and philosophy should be limited or restricted. What it does mean is that every age should produce its men who can escape from the binding precedent of facts and footnotes to treat human and metaphysical problems in terms of human experience rather than logical consistency or psychiatric research.

Today there is too much knowledge as an end in itself. The artistic view regards knowledge as contributing to an overall coherence of personality. Shelley speaks of poetry as being "at once the centre and circumference of knowledge; it is that which comprehends all science". It speaks of the One which pervades science and is beyond it. While an attempt to dissociate creative ideas from their encumbering facts may seem facile when the achievements of modern science are so many, the artist's job is always to focus attention on people through his own experience. Much knowledge to him is therefore immediately useless (as Kierkegaard, Blake and Butler all saw).

Many are unsatisfied by lack of documentation, but living is not a process of documentation. It is possible that specialised scholarship accounts for too much of our poetic (and critical) attitude today. As Shelley saw, the poet should make sense of experience to enhance a response to it.

Byron's Freedom or Tyranny: Radical Libertarianism

"Would *he* adore a sultan? he obey
The intellectual eunuch Castlereagh?...
The vulgarest tool that Tyranny could want...."

(*Don Juan*, Dedication, XI, 1818)

In these verses on what Milton's attitude to Castlereagh might have been Byron states the essence of the radical view: Freedom or Tyranny.

No doubt the lines were clear-cut in Byron's day. You were either on the side of Greece, which was struggling to be free, or you were on the side of the tyrannical Turks (the Sultan) who ruled Greece, and who were supported by the Tory Castlereagh. Today the radical is for all Freedom and against all Tyranny. Freedom is, as Solzhenitsyn has said, indivisible, and the radical is for it everywhere. The problem is to identify what is Freedom and what is Tyranny.

To the radical, the old imperialism and colonialism was a form of Tyranny which prevented self-determination. The radical opposed such – albeit benevolent – Tyranny and exploitation, and worked for Freedom. But the trouble is, the alternative today – usually some form of Communism – is just as much of a Tyranny as was the former imperialism. President Carter was right: Human Rights are the criterion. Where the basic Human Rights of freedom to live and work, to speak and think without fear, to move and read at will are present, there is Freedom.

Human Rights are not present under Fascist regimes or Communist regimes. They are not present under white racialist regimes. They are not present under military dictatorships. The trouble is, as in Greece of the 1960s, the military dictatorships are there to keep out the Communists; as in South Africa or Rhodesia, the white racialists are arguably there to keep out the Communists. One Tyranny rules to exclude another, and perhaps worse, Tyranny. In such cases the radical works to exclude both. His ideal is a Free regime with Human Rights for all.

In the post-war world, the list of Tyrannies is long: the Soviet Union and East-European states; China and most of the South-East-Asian states; South Africa and most of the new African and Arab states; Chile and most of the South-American states; Germany, Italy, Spain, Portugal and Japan have been freed from their former National Socialist Tyrannies, as a result of world and colonial wars, or of the deaths of their dictators. Most of the world has been ruled by Tyranny. Only the European and American nations – and Japan – today are free from Tyranny, and they have all been purveyors of Tyranny in the form of colonial wars at some time in the 20th century.

Contemporary domestic politics are about the art of how to govern mass societies. If all their citizens have Human Rights, there is a mass happiness for all, after the manner of the utilitarianism of John Stuart Mill and Jeremy Bentham, who did so much to develop radicalism as a wing of Liberalism of their day. The happiness of the masses in its most active form includes a concern for others which did not exist as much as it should in the 19th century. It excludes the cunning fiddling and materialism that surrounds the Welfare State.

The European of the late 1970s knows that contemporary Europe embodies his vision of Freedom opposed to Tyranny. He stands at the end of a long tradition of struggling against Tyranny for Human Rights. In foreign policy he is against all big power meddling, and he is concerned to see that the Third World is freed from Tyranny; not to be ruled by an alternative Tyranny, but to be free. In doing so he defends principles rather than the interests of any one political party. In domestic policy at any moment he will look at the parties to see which embodies the principle he stands for most. The State is a form of Tyranny if its power becomes too extreme. A degree of power has to be surrendered by the individual to the State for government of a mass society to take place, and this power has to be a moderate amount only if Freedom is to persist and the government is not to become a Tyranny.

The democratic ideal of freedom within the law is the best expression of Freedom today. Anarchism, which rejects all government as tyrannical, is too extreme a form of Freedom. In a free society there are many different talents and abilities which can express themselves freely and which should have an equal opportunity, regardless of birth, inheritance, class and family privilege. Some "social engineering" is necessary to achieve this equality of opportunity, but merit must rule at the end. Extreme right-wing Conservatism is therefore another form of Freedom which is too extreme.

The modern Byron is a "radical libertarian"; which is to say that he believes in representational democracy and the universal suffrage (like the early 19th-century exponents of "radical reform"). He affirms a principle of Freedom which he applies as a measure to each country or society he comes up against. He will avoid the extremes of right and left, and will therefore be a moderate. He will avoid extreme Freedom or extreme Tyranny; he will avoid State Tyranny and extreme non-interfering individual Freedom. Human Rights for all members of a mass society cannot be achieved under these four extremist views, which can be labelled Anarchism, National Socialist Fascism, Communism and right-wing Conservatism.

The modern Byron recognises that all men are brothers, that mankind is equal in Human Rights, though unequal in ability and spiritual gifts. All mankind must therefore be freed from Tyranny, which means living in the peace of a freedom to contemplate and fulfil oneself irrespective of any political system.

Tennyson's Alliteration and Inverted Strong Moving Verbs

Some of the most haunting lines in English poetry are to be found in Tennyson. Take the following, for example:

> "Now sleeps the crimson petal, now the white;
> Nor waves the cypress in the palace walk;
> Nor winks the gold fin in the porphyry font:
> The fire-fly wakens: waken thou with me."

How does Tennyson achieve the obsessive, incantatory tone? He does not use rhyme, and there is no obvious repetition of sounds: the first line and a half contains ow, ē, ĭ, ĕ, ă, ī, or, ā, though the third line is largely composed of or and ĭ and f alliteration. No, it is a combination of two devices: alliteration (s, w, p, f), and the inversion of placing the verb before the noun. Now sleeps, nor waves, nor winks. And later on, now droops, now slides, now folds. They are all strong verbs, and verbs of movement, so that we can *see* the thing happening cinematographically, whether it is a sleeping or a waving or a winking. And the emphasis on the strong verb is heightened by its being placed so early in the sentence. How much weaker the lines would be if he had written: Now the crimson petal sleeps....Nor does the cypress wave in the palace walk.

This use of a precise verb to carry the feeling and the action recurs in Tennyson. We find it in *In Memoriam* cxv:

> "Now fades the long last streak of snow....
> Now rings the woodland loud and long....
> Now dance the lights on lawn and lea."

Again there is the same combination with alliteration, and at that, an alliteration that carries over from previous lines. Here the l alliteration runs through three stanzas.

Consider again:

> "When rosy plumelets tuft the larch,
> And rarely pipes the mounted thrush;
> Or underneath the barren bush

Flits by the sea-blue bird of March." (xci.)

Here it is b alliteration and the inverted strong, moving verb "flits" that achieves the effect. Or again (vii):

"And ghastly thro' the drizzling rain
On the bald streets breaks the blank day."

Again it is b alliteration and the inverted strong, moving verb "breaks".

Lawrence and the Elemental

D.H. Lawrence was a poet of the elemental and instinctive, but I want to dwell on his approach to the elemental and instinctive in prose.

The Rainbow appeared in 1915, when Freud was proclaiming the unconscious sex-drives of the instinctive "*id*", and when Picasso and Stravinsky were rediscovering primitivism in art and music. A new definition of man was in the air: man in terms of his primitive, unconscious instincts as opposed to man as a rational, social being. And in Lawrence, the instinctive is fed by the elemental background of the universe and the seasons, against which his country people live out their lives. Man as part of the natural unity of the universe, fed by nature, a flow of feelings – this is the Lawrentian view.

A new earth is ahead; its symbol being the rainbow, which has nothing to do with the corrupt social world. Imagine what Lawrence would have said to Jane Austen who satirized the idea of admiring a view in *Pride and Prejudice*. Lawrence hated the rationalism of the Garsington lot – Bertrand Russell and the rest – and he pilloried it in *Women in Love*, which contrasts the country elementalism of *The Rainbow* with the sophisticated loss of contact with it of men like Gerald Crich.

The seasons form a background for the drama. "The force that through the green fuse drives the flower/Drives my green age," Dylan Thomas wrote, and there are many instances in *The Rainbow* of a seasonal, floral background to key events in the character's lives.

Like *Wuthering Heights*, which ends with the benign sky and the harebells, *The Rainbow* is above all about man and the elements: the wind, the clouds, the stars and the flora and fauna of farm life on the Derbyshire-Nottinghamshire border.

The universe, when experienced through the emotions as opposed to the intellect, is a unity, but *yin*-and-*yang*-like. Man's feelings are in pairs, opposites: for example, Tom Brangwen perceives Lydia's "ugly-beautiful" mouth.

Those who can see the elemental see it in the Church, like Will. ("The verity was...his connection with the Church, his real being lay in his dark emotional experience of the Infinite, of the Absolute.") Those who cannot, see the social, teaching aspect of the Church, like Anna, and are destructive – Anna Victrix is destructive and victorious over the Church. The elemental and the social are like Blake's contraries, innocence and experience.

The Rainbow is a chronicle of three generations of rural family life. The family derives its roots from the earth, and its freshness from the rhythm of the seasons. Its unconscious elemental life was the great strength of the working class, Lawrence seems to be saying, just as the conscious, social life is the great feebleness of the urban townies of London.

Of course, the unconscious approach is only a partial one. Man is more than his instincts which at their worst lead to the pre-civilized heart of darkness of Kurtz amid his severed heads – or the ice-cold fridge of the cannibalistic President Amin of Uganda.

Look, Stranger at this Figurative Language and Forget the Sea

A poet uses sounds as a composer uses notes. The sounds will probably be chosen unconsciously, as they occur to him intuitively, but an awful lot can be done with basic art. Auden's 'Seascape' should be required reading for all would-be poets who are learning how the sounds are put together.

Consider the first four lines:

"Look, stranger, on this island now
The leaping light for your delight discovers,

Stand stable here
And silent be...."

In this passage Auden is using six sounds: a, i, er, st, l, and d. "Stranger", "stable", we think, and is*l*and after *l*ook, and then *l*eaping *l*ight and de*l*ight. And then, a few lines further on we have:

"Here at the sm*a*ll field's ending p*au*se
When the ch*a*lk w*a*ll f*a*lls to the foam and its t*a*ll ledges
Oppose the pluck
And knock of the tide,
And the shingle scrambles after the suck-
-ing surf,
And a gull lodges
A moment on its sheer side."

Here we have six repeated sounds within two lines, the assonance of chalk/wall and of ledges/lodges, and the full rhymes pluck/suck divided by the semi-assonance of knock. We have the personification of "scramble", which implies a small boy scrambling up the shingle and later sauntering, like the clouds. And there is so much more. The *s*waying *s*ound of the *s*ea", like the alliteration of "And the *s*hingle *s*crambles after the *s*ucking *s*urf", intensifies the already heightened, figurative language, and by the time we reach the end we have encountered just about every figure of speech and are breathless with admiration at the technical brilliance of the poet.

It is then, when we come to add the poem up and see what it amounts to, that we have to admit that it is just about a man standing on top of a cliff listening to the sea. So much verbal dexterity for so simple and straightforward an experience. And it is then that we have to admit that somehow the poem has escaped, and that what we are left with is the brilliance – the technique.

'Look, stranger' is above all a poet's poem. The verbal fireworks come between us and the moment, and do not take us closer to it, as a more straightforward lyric might. They obscure rather than illuminate.

Larkin's Unheroic Social Reality

Larkin has been much praised. He is "the best of the post-Second World War generation of poets," Kenneth Allott writes (*Penguin Book of Contemporary Verse*, p.332), "and the most exciting new poetic voice – with the possible exception of Dylan Thomas – since Auden." Strong words indeed, and now this Oxford friend of Kingsley Amis and unmarried provincial librarian has brought out the latest *Oxford Book of English Verse*, a prerogative granted only to Yeats among other twentieth-century poets.

What makes his voice "exciting"? Or, rather, what *made* his voice appear exciting? For we are used to it now. The novelty is, of course, in the tone. After a decade of Neo-Romanticism which ended with the death of Dylan Thomas (1952), there was a reaction, and the poets of the Movement wrote about an essentially social reality. The tone had appeared in the first novels of John Wain and Kingsley Amis in 1953 and 1954 respectively (*Hurry on Down, Lucky Jim*), before Larkin's first collection, *The Less Deceived* appeared in 1955. 'Church Going, generally acknowledged to be showpiece of the Movement, appeared in that collection, and a glance at the poem's opening reveals the colloquial, atheistic, almost ignorant sensibility of the visitor:

> "Once I am sure there's nothing going on
> I step inside, letting the door thud shut.
> Another church: matting, seats, and stone,
> And little books; sprawlings of flowers, cut
> For Sunday, brownish now; some brass and stuff
> Up at the holy end....
>   Hatless, I take off
> My cycle-clips in awkward reverence."

He is diffident, he refers to "stuff", he doesn't know what the "holy end" is called, he presents an awkward figure in his bicycle-clips. This is the put-upon young man of Kingsley Amis's novels.

"Cleaned, or restored?" he asks of the roof. "Someone would know: I don't." And in those days you were supposed to approve, and think how good – and, of course, *new* – it was to be ignorant of such matters, and culturally a philistine. Like Lucky Jim in his public lecture. "Bored, uninformed", the poet wanders round "this accoutred frowsty barn" superbly mediocre. It is the ideal of some comprehensive schools – a man who is not impeded by anything so useless as a traditional aesthetic sense. Or at least, that is the pose.

"Nobody wants any more poems on the grander themes for a few years," Amis wrote in D.J. Enright's first collection of Movement poets, *Poets of the 1950s* (Japan), "but at the same time nobody wants any more poems about philosophers or paintings or novelists or art galleries or mythology or foreign cities or other poems. At least I hope nobody wants them." And the pitifully provincial direction that contemporary British poetry has taken becomes understandable. "I have no belief in 'tradition' or a common myth-kitty or casual allusions in poems to other poems or poets," Larkin wrote in the same collection, disqualifying Eliot as an influence. "Of the contemporary scene I can say only that there are not enough poems written according to my ideas."

In 1955 this may have sounded like a breath of fresh air. In Larkin, though, the air is only fresh in the poems he writes about other people or country scenes: as in 'Wedding-Wind' and 'At Grass'. Otherwise, there is a stifling sense of suffocation. Larkin feels suffocated by the chores, the unheroic – indeed, anti-heroic – triviality of modern living. In 'Poetry of Departures' he longs to "clear off" and tells us "I detest my room." In 'Toads' he grumbles, quite rightly, at having to work ("Six days a week.../Just for paying a few bills") and wishes he were "courageous enough/To shout *Stuff your pension*!" One cannot imagine this intelligent but very wet poet having the gumption to shout "stuff" anything.

Larkin's wetness is central to his unheroic tone. In 'If, My Darling' he informs us that he is full of delusions and betrayal, and there is a sad classical statement of self-knowledge in these rueful confessions. In 'Mr Bleaney' he imagines his predecessor in the room where he is lodging. He builds up his habits through the 60-watt bulb, the radio he persuaded the landlady to buy, his pools coupons. It is a depressing social reality – nothing ennobles his situation – and then Larkin writes:

"But if he stood and watched the frigid wind
Tousling the clouds, lay on the fusty bed
Telling himself that this was home, and grinned,
And shivered, without shaking off the dread

That how we live measures our own nature….
                    I don't know."

A piece of pure Eliot, and magnificent at that. Here is the true reality intruding on Larkin's grey world and its grey inhabitants, and in this poem Larkin is aware that Mr Bleaney probably lived without glimpsing the true reality beyond "how we live" that reveals "our own nature". He is presenting us with the possibility that Mr Bleaney was a mere automaton whose life was spent inauthentically on little things.

Larkin is at his best when he lifts the drab, mannered self-pity with a sudden Romantic image. In 'Whitsun Weddings' there are two moments when this happens:

"I thought of London spread out in the sun,
Its postal districts packed like squares of wheat…."

"We slowed again
And as the tightened brakes took hold, there swelled
A sense of falling, like an arrow-shower
Sent out of sight, somewhere becoming rain."

These flashes of image go entirely against Movement dogma, which preferred statement to image in accordance with the dubious theories of the Movement guru, Yvor Winters. (His theories about the importance of Elizabeth Daryush – see *In Defense of Reason* – border on the plain cranky.) No poet can afford to be straightjacketed into a theory of what a poem is, and it is refreshing to see Larkin breaking out of the blunt, down-to-earth pose.

Technically, however, Larkin is as Movement as they come. All his poems are carefully architectured, and despite some careless, slipshod rhymes in 'Church Going', they are generally carefully rhymed and metred. The eighteenth century is very evident in the control of the verse and in the sometimes archaic diction of some of the less colloquial poems. The Movement moral is often to be found in the last line – the logical consequence of a rational statement.

Larkin sees himself as continuing the tradition of Hardy. He regards Eliot and Pound as being American invaders, and Yeats as importing an irrelevant Celtic strain into British poetry. The poems we are offered return to the true source of classical English poetry, we are supposed to agree, eliminating the intrusive Romantic tradition from *The Lyrical Ballads* until Dylan Thomas; but including Hardy.

The aims are clear, but does the achievement match up to them? I think the answer must be: No. Both technically and in terms of subject-matter, Larkin's work is unadventurous. He is willing to explore the states of mind he feels in his drab, provincial situations, but he does not take emotional risks, and the moral reflections are a very poor relation of Pope, Swift and Johnson. Having such limited, small goals he achieves: limited, small achievements. I predict that at the end of the 21st century he will be seen to have the stature of a competent dwarf – on par with some of the Georgians. The garland for the giant will be awarded to a poet who had dared more.

In Defence of Autobiographical Poetry

There is a line – I touched on it in 'Shakespeare's Sonnets: Autobiographical Poetry' (see pp.375-6) – that runs from Wyatt and Surrey, through Shakespeare's 'Sonnets', to the Romantic 'I' poem (for example Keats' "I stood tip-toe upon a little hill"), Tennyson's lyrics and Hardy's poems about his first wife. This line is pre-eminently autobiographical. The subject matter of poetry is what it was to the Latin lyric poets, Catullus, Ovid, Horace, the poet's loves and hopes.

At the same time, there is a sensibility which maintains that poetry should be impersonal. Eliot's poem to his second wife is "embarrassing", this sensibility argues; there should be a distance between the author and the subject matter, and this distance only comes through writing about other people. Irony can then come into play, and detachment. Raw knowledge has to be shaped and distanced by the aesthetic mind like clay being shaped by a potter. Despite his apparently personal veneer, Larkin, who in many ways seems to be a descendant of Hardy's without having his sensitivity to Nature, is in this ironic tradition. According to the thinking of this sensibility, Wyatt and Surrey, Shakespeare, Tennyson and Hardy had no business to write the poems they did.

The truth is, there are different sensibilities. One is personal and empirical. It uses its own experience as its material and quests for a metaphysical Reality and creates images of a range of personal feelings which have the complexity of music. The other is impersonal. It is conversational in outlook and does not write in images; it defines man as a social, rational being, and makes statements of moral generalisations like Larkin's 'Church Going'. It does not know what to say to mystics, existentialists and new-wave religionists who define man in relation to a shift from his ego-consciousness to the consciousness of his deeper self. It says "Ah" to intensity about love affairs, and then changes the subject.

The social-rationalist's disapproval of autobiographical poetry is connected with what is a proper subject for conversation. It is sometimes a matter of class. It has nothing to do with the fact that autobiographical poetry is bad or immature poetry.

In a critical democracy there is room for all talents. In a critical dictatorship there is room for only a few. The autobiographical sensibility must not allow itself to be banned because of dictatorial taste.

*

Art works like this: I create an image which is understood by the reader. The image must be generalised and universal. It is in this generalising of emotion that autobiographical poetry is at its best.

Both religious and love poetry are best written through an 'I', as is demonstrated in the "terrible" sonnets of Hopkins and the hate-and-love poems of Catullus.

There are two ways of recording inward feelings. They can either be stated personally as in Tennyson, and perhaps be presented in terms of a realistic image ("And my regret/Becomes an April violet/And buds and blossoms like the rest"); or they can be objectivised into an impersonal symbol, Eliot's "objective correlative", or stated with ironic impersonality. The first produces a personal poetry, the second an impersonal poetry. Both ways are equally valid.

But they are both personal at heart. Seemingly Eliot's impersonal poetry was very personal beneath the impersonality, and the images in 'The Waste Land' were as much about the emotional trauma of his failing marriage as about the decay of Western civilization.

Imagination: The See-Saw of Knowledge and Speculation, and High Classicism

I want to sharpen my distinction between Speculation and Knowledge, the two sides of the imaginative process. (See p.376.) First we need to distinguish Fantasy, Fancy and Imagination.

These three terms were originally synonymous. Later they came to be distinguished. "Fantasy" is now used in a visionary sense, and is to be differentiated from its pejorative meanings in the *Shorter Oxford English Dictionary* which I exclude: "a phantom, an illusory appearance"; "delusive imagination, hallucination"; "a supposition resting on no solid grounds"; imaginary activities produced spontaneously as in daydreams or as a response to stimuli". "Fantasy" is, to quote the *Shorter Oxford English Dictionary* further, "the process, the faculty or the result of forming visionary representations of things not present to the senses". It is the visionary faculty, the faculty that receives visions. In poetry, the "caves of ice" in Coleridge's 'Kubla Khan', much of Shelley, Blake's prophetic works and a good slice of Dylan Thomas (for example the breeding images in 'After the Funeral') exemplify visionary "Fantasy". The images have arisen in the mind and are at the level of high dream (in Coleridge's case in response to the stimulus of opium).

"Fancy", on the other hand, originally a shortened form of "Fantasy", is now used of aptitude for inventing illustrative or decorative imagery. Examples of this can be found in Pope, Byron and T.E. Hulme. In Pope: "Eternal smiles his emptiness betray/As shallow streams run dimpling all the way." In Byron: the 17-stanza-long Dedication to *Don Juan* which decorates its main idea – Byron's criticism of the Lake Poets – with wings (blackbirds, a hawk, a flying fish, Pegasus). In T.E. Hulme: "The moon looked over the hedge/Like a ruddy-faced farmer." The point is, the idea comes first, and fancy is a decoration of the idea, like piped icing on a birthday cake. The streams and the wings and the farmer do not exist in reality, as do the smiles and the Lake Poets and the moon – or as do the caves of visionary Xanadu, and some of the images which breed images that Dylan Thomas has fished up from the depths of his mind. Fancy is verbal playfulness and grace, the associative power of felicitous elaboration. It is a supremely rational quality, for it illustrates thought.

"Imagination" is altogether harder to define. The *Shorter Oxford English Dictionary*, distinguishing it from Fancy, defines it as "the power of giving the consistency of reality to ideal creations". And this is precisely what a novelist does: his creation is an idea to which he gives the "consistency of reality", relating it to the external world. "Imagination" can be a process, an action, a faculty, or a power. It was Wordsworth and Coleridge who redefined the term. Living at the end of an Age of Reason, they were aware that the poetic process was not a rational one, and they needed to ascribe the source of creativity to something other than the reason. This source synthesized raw experience into images, shaped them into form, and fused feeling, vision and thought into a whole, as a potter's hand shapes clay into a pot. "Imagination" was therefore an organic process/action/faculty/ power.

But we can go deeper than this. Consider the following definition of "Imagination" (from the *Shorter Oxford English Dictionary*):

"**Imagination**. ME. [–(O)Fr. *imagination* – L. *imaginatio*, f. *imaginat-*, pa. ppl. stem of *imaginari*; see prec., -ION.] **1**. The action of imagining, or forming a mental concept of what is not actually present to the senses (cf. sense 3); the result of this, a mental image or idea (freq. characterized as *vain, false*, etc.). **2**. The mental consideration of actions or events not yet in existence. **a**. Scheming or devising; a device, scheme, plot; a fanciful project. *Obs.* exc. as a biblical archaism. ME. **b**. Expectation, anticipation – 1654. **3**. That faculty of the mind by which we conceive the absent as if it were present (freq. including memory); the 'reproductive imagination' ME. **4**. The power which the mind has of forming concepts beyond those derived from external objects; the 'productive imagination'. **a.** Fancy ME. **b.** The creative faculty; poetic genius 1509. **5.** The operation of the mind; thinking; thought, opinion. Now *rare* or *Obs*. ME."

The first two meanings are associated with delusion and anticipation, and are not of direct concern here, although the novel *Nineteen eighty-four* might fall within the second meaning. It is the third and fourth meanings I want to look at, the "reproductive" and "productive" imagination. In both there is a "mental faculty forming images of external objects not present to the senses" (*Concise Oxford Dictionary*), but whereas the third meaning concerns absent memories, the fourth concerns invented concepts.

The "reproductive" imagination is to be found in Wordsworth's 'Daffodils'. Wordsworth recalls a specific memory, which is "recollected in tranquillity" resulting in "the spontaneous overflow of powerful feelings". The daffodils "flash upon the inward eye". The image which haunts Eliot, the "hyacinth girl", is another instance of a memory. Such memories of the external world have the force of images because of the strength of feeling attached to them. They are memories of situations in which deep feelings occurred, and therefore they are realistic images rather than symbols. These absent memories are, like the visionary fantasies – which I prefer to think of as visions – not present to the senses, images of Knowledge. They have been known – directly seen as images or visions – and they have been 'reproduced'.

The "productive" imagination is to be found in John Wain's poem about Major Eatherley, the pilot who dropped the Hiroshima bomb, or in Ted Hughes' poem about the jaguar. Wain has formed a concept of what the Major felt, he 'imagined' himself into the Major's shoes, looking outwards rather than inwards, though the starting-point was a memory – of the Hiroshima incident, or perhaps a newspaper cutting the essence of which is at first "reproduced". In the same way Hughes imagines himself into a jaguar's skin, having started from a memory. The "productive" imagination forms images (in works of art) of other beings' consciousnesses. This is the faculty and power used by novelists who imagine their way into other people's minds. Consider *Great Expectations* or *The Brothers Karamazov*; or *Wuthering Heights*. These novels are ideal creations which have "the consistency of reality". In so far as they are make-believe inventions – inventions which appear plausible, certainly – they are speculations. The authors are saying in effect, "This is how I speculate it might have been." To the extent that they are make-believe, they are images of Speculation.

A little thought immediately convinces us that there are very few purely make-believe poems, novels and plays. Most of the Speculations start somewhere in Knowledge. Keats' 'Grecian Urn' and his 'Nightingale' were memories to begin with. *Sons and Lovers* is more Knowledge than Speculation. *Great Expectations* draws on much Knowledge. Even science fiction and television or stage adaptations of the lives of men such as Shakespeare or Clare, which must be largely Speculation, have points of contact with Knowledge. The same is true of Shakespeare's historical plays, which, though being Speculations, are based on sources such as Holinshed or Plutarch, and have some contact with "the consistency of reality", i.e. Knowledge. All the excellent Speculative novels are informed by Knowledge, just as the execution experience recounted in Dostoevsky's *Idiot* is informed by the execution Dostoevsky himself faced in Semyonovsky Square.

The same interplay between Knowledge and Speculation can be seen at work in children's games. The child is father of the man, and the small boy who plays out test matches or soccer internationals with his brother (alias an Australian fast bowler or a German goalkeeper) is not necessarily re-enacting a past match. He is playing an entirely new game, what might have happened if such a ball were bowled or crossed. On the other hand, his Speculation draws on a real match he has seen, on real gestures. He is to some extent imitating and reproducing Knowledge, even though his star is doing new things. Yeats writes of a small girl practising "a tinker shuffle". She is re-enacting a tinker she has seen, and is either reproducing what she has observed, or varying what she has observed to include new things the tinker himself did not actually do – i.e. introducing Speculation into the Knowledge.

The creative powers of the mind – which children often express in spontaneous drama – exercise both aspects of the Imagination: both Knowledge (the visionary dream or the imaged memory of observed fact from the external world) and Speculation (the image of what another being has felt). The first is a report on experience. A poem by Hardy about his wife, which is based on a remembered experience that was deeply felt at the time, is, in effect saying, "This is what I experienced, this is what I know" – though the Knowledge is being shaped and made significant by the power of the Imagination. The second aspect hazards a guess, "This is how I speculate it was." The more "consistency of reality" a work of art derives from Knowledge (i.e. experience of the external world), the more plausible it will appear. The more it departs from Knowledge, and therefore from autobiographical knowledge of the external world, the more irrelevant the make-believe Speculation will appear.

The "reproductive" and "productive" imaginations are linked in each artist, then, which is why the same poet can develop from writing works of extreme Knowledge to works of extreme Speculation in his own career. At the same time, they have produced sensibilities which have come to colour their Ages. The "reproductive" Imagination produces a Romantic sensibility. Like Wordsworth, the poet writes from his heart, from his memories. He sees himself as an individual, and he feels the artist is isolated, he often has a mystical or existentialist outlook. The "productive" Imagination, on the other hand, produces a Neoclassical sensibility. Like Pope, the poet writes from his head. He sees himself as a social being, as belonging to a society, and he frowns on the "self-indulgence" of isolated privacy, he has no time for Outsiders. He has a rational outlook, and writes about others, not himself. In the "reproductive" Imagination, the experience of the individual – like Shakespeare's in his *Sonnets* – is paramount. In the "productive" Imagination, the experience of the individual has to be someone else's.

I have said that the "reproductive" and "productive" imaginations, in individual artists "produce" sensibilities which colour their Ages, but of course it is a two-way process. The Ages colour the sensibilities that flourish within them, and therefore affect which of the imaginations poets will employ. In a Romantic Age, it is hard for the "productive" Imagination to come through, for it is unconsciously blocked by the magazine editors and publishers. In a Neoclassical Age like (until recently) our own, it is hard for the "reproductive" Imagination to come through for the same reason.

Our post-war Neoclassical Age has returned to Reason in poetry. In Britain, the academic Movement admired Yvor Winters' *In Defense of*

Reason, and took an architectural, mechanical view of form, rather than an organic view. It saw art as statement rather than image, and decorated the statement with Fancy. Its "productive" Imagination looked outwards in the form of Speculation rather than focused inwards in the form of Knowledge. The Movement opted for a limp and weak Augustan, rational Fancy and Speculation against organic "Fantasy" (vision) or memory. The 18th century has likewise been held up as a model in the novel, two of whose practitioners (Amis and Wain) were Movement poets.

One effect of this trend has been a devaluation of Knowledge. The absurd notion has arisen in Britain that extreme Speculation – "the guess" – is in some way superior to extreme Knowledge, that Fiction is superior to Autobiography, that it is better to explore other people or the external world than to explore oneself. This notion gathers support from the traditional Augustan canons of Western society, in which it is considered impolite to be too concerned with oneself, in which extroverts are preferred to introverts. It assumes that the traditional, rational, social view of Western human beings is a certainty that will be with us for some time to come. However, we are now living in a time when the ego-centred social man has been recently overthrown for a man with a deeper self to find, through a metaphysical, and perhaps religious, search. I know this sounds a controversial statement to make, but I have argued this fully elsewhere[1] and take the case as proved. It is not widely recognised now, but we are already living in a time when the Western world has undergone a shift in consciousness rather like the change that happened between the Middle Ages and the Renaissance.

The mystic whose theme is his slow finding of the Divine Light will express his visionary "Fantasy" in any Age, as will the Romantic temperament who is haunted by absent memories. In a social, rational, pre-Classical Age, they can expect to be neglected until they develop the "productive" side of their imaginations. However, the shift in Western consciousness is already bringing back Knowledge. As traditional Western civilization disintegrates, the old social, rational view of man has begun to crumble, and the individual is again becoming the focal point of art. As God ceases to be worshipped in social and rational terms, mystics are already expressing their visions that redefine religion in new "Fantasies". As the old Imperialist certainties collapse, new ones are already being created within the European Union. These grow out of haunting absent memories.

Once again, visionary "Fantasy" and memory are becoming permissible subject matter for art. But "Fantasy" and memory are not the goal. To affirm the superiority of Knowledge over Speculation is as absurd as to affirm the inferiority of Knowledge to Speculation. "Fantasy" and memory are only a half-way house on the road away from Speculation and its rule of the head. The road is that perennial search whose destination is the balance between the heart and the head that is High Classicism.*

In this highly desirable state in which heart and head are in balance, the "reproductive" and "productive" imaginations, Knowledge and Speculation, are in a perfect balance. The balance is not achieved very often. To change the image, every generation the see-saw tilts up and down between the two and from time to time it achieves a balance. Eliot's *Four Quartets* are the most recent instance of such a balance.

In Britain, the see-saw, which has elevated the head and Speculation on one side, must elevate the heart and Knowledge on the other side before it can stabilize briefly in the High Classicism of balance. The individual artist who is ahead of his Age and has shown the heart and mystic Knowledge must therefore aim for the High Classicism and balance of Homer, Virgil and Milton, regardless of the sensibility of his Age.

*The balance of High Classicism in this and the next two paragraphs was an early statement of the Universalist synthesis.

2

Implied Virtue: Questioning Reason, Swift's Classical Onslaught on the Age of Reason

The Theme of *Gulliver's Travels:* How the New Utopia of the Age of Reason is Shipwrecked on the Reality of Human Nature

In a sense, the four books of *Gulliver's Travels* are all variants of one book. There is a disaster at sea (a shipwreck in the first three books), Gulliver encounters strange creatures who either mirror or judge the corrupt English "governing animal", and he either detests or likes their society before he makes or takes a boat that returns him to the known world. We may justly suspect, therefore, that there is one theme common to all four books; that it is no accident that, for example, the Lilliputians "are most excellent mathematicians"; that the King of Brobdingnag was "educated in the study of philosophy [= natural philosophy, science], and particularly mathematics"; that the Laputians "cut our bread into cones, cylinders, parallelograms, and several other mathematical figures"; and that the Houyhnhnms' gestures are "not unlike those of a philosopher, when he would attempt to solve some new and difficult phenomenon".

A close reading of the four books does bring out one theme. It takes the form of a horrified attack on the so-called "Age of Reason" of the seventeenth century, the time when philosophers began to explain natural processes in mathematical terms, and the importance of physics and mathematics in philosophy increased while traditional medieval theology declined. The Age of Reason marked the beginning of the conflict between science and religion, and Swift, as an Anglican Dean and a Tory, was very much on the side of religion. As much as Aristophanes did in *The Clouds*, Swift attacked the new ideas of his time, the new political, scientific and ethical theories, and in each of the four books he shows them to be unworkable with all the tendentious skill of the pamphleteer that he was. The new theories do not work out in practice because they leave out of account one consideration that is crucial to a religious mind like Swift's: human nature. Founding their notions of honesty and virtue on the reason as opposed to God, they break down as surely as do the geometrical theories of the Laputians, who are full of speculations but who cannot make the walls of their buildings perpendicular.

Human nature, Swift shows us, is self-interested, hypocritical and proud, and it can be at its proudest (in the pejorative sense of the word) when it is condemning pride. Such is the working of human moral blindness. It is Swift's achievement to have entered our attitudes towards our fellow human beings, and to have grasped, and put across, this paradox: that to hold an ideal does not exempt us from faults which contradict the ideal, and that the very holding of an ideal can cut us off from mankind, make us despise man, make us proud through contempt. It is crucial to grasp that in Swift an ideal cuts both ways. On the one hand, it judges the corruption of the English "governing animal". On the other hand, the very act of judgement, accompanied as it is in Swift by contempt, leads to the sin of pride. We should therefore remember that when the first Minister observes in Brobdingnag "how contemptible a thing was human grandeur", he is himself being "grand" and therefore "contemptible". It is significant that the Brobdingnagian metropolis, *Lorbrulgrud*, means "Pride of the Universe", and that the Empress is "Ornament of Nature, the Darling of the World, the Delight of her Subjects, the Phoenix of the Creation", and inescapably proud in her titles.

Human nature, then, is "corrupt" and "degenerate" in *Gulliver's Travels*, and the ideals that judge it to be so have their hypocritical side, which adds to the corruption and degeneracy. There is therefore, in each of the four books, a focal character who represents a *flawed standard of proud goodness*, who is innocent (or "ignorant", when innocence is treated ironically) and who exposes the gulf between theory and practice in the society under examination. In Book 1 the standard is Gulliver, and the gulf is exposed when, after seeing the "leaping and creeping" that determines appointments to high office in Lilliput (alias Whig England), we are told: "In choosing persons for all employments, they have more regard to good morals than to great abilities." In Book 2 the standard is the King of Brobdingnag, who demolishes Gulliver's idealized portrait of England with a battery of questions towards the end of chapter 6. In Book 3 the standard is

Gulliver again, and Gulliver demolishes the political theories of the "school of political projectors" by explaining what corruption there is in the kingdom of "Tribnia" (an anagram for Britain). In Book 4, the standard is the virtuous Houyhnhnm who is Gulliver's master, who expresses his "abhorrence of the whole species" of mankind after Gulliver's description of the state of England.

Bearing in mind that this one theme runs throughout the four books – how the Age of Reason founders on the reality of human nature – we can now examine each book in turn to see how Swift works out his overall theme. Let us keep at the back of our minds the question: to what extent does the *flawed standard of proud goodness* represent Swift's attitude, which is against the Age of Reason, and to what extent does it come to embody the Age of Reason? For this is the crux of *Gulliver's Travels*. In so far as Gulliver, the Brobdingnagians and the Houyhnhnms embody Swift's point of view, they represent an albeit proud, satiric attack on the corruption of England. But in so far as they ambivalently represent at the same time Utopian qualities advocated by the philosophers of the Age of Reason, they demonstrate the inadequacy of their philosophies and the logical bankruptcy of the new Utopia of the Age of Reason. Thus, if the Houyhnhnms do embody an aspect of the Age of Reason, the theme of *Gulliver's Travels* becomes: how the new Utopia of the Age of Reason is shipwrecked on the reality of human nature.

'A Voyage to Lilliput': The Degenerate Nature of Princes and Ministers
At first sight, the theme of "A Voyage to Lilliput" is the "degenerate nature" of princes and ministers, or, to quote the proverb, "Put not your trust in princes."

'A Voyage to Lilliput' is a record of Gulliver's disillusionment with princes and ministers. At the beginning, when he has recovered from being tied down by strings, he appears to be impressed by Lilliput. The plan to transport him on a machine is bold and dangerous, and "I am confident would not be imitated by any prince in Europe". The Lilliputians are "most excellent mathematicians...by the encouragement of the Emperor, who is a renowned patron of learning". The ladies and courtiers are "magnificently clad". The "country shows" – the "leaping and creeping" which determine who is to be a minister – "exceed all nations I have known, both for dexterity and magnificence". There is a hint of a suspicion that all is not well in Lilliput when we glimpse the self-interestedness of the Lilliputians. The first time is when Gulliver observes that their good treatment of him was "prudent as well as generous" for if they "had endeavoured to kill me" he would have broken his strings, "after which, as they were not able to make resistance, so they could expect no mercy". The second occasion is when they decide not to kill him because "the stench of so large a carcass might produce a plague in the metropolis, and probably spread through the whole kingdom". Both here, and when Gulliver absurdly begs for his liberty from the Emperor, "which I every day repeated on my knees" – showing how vain and proud is the pomp of the tiny monarch – and again during the ridiculous "leaping and creeping", we begin to feel that the Lilliputians are behaving a little too much like the English "governing animal" for our comfort.

However, Gulliver does not appear to see this. The "Man-Mountain" is as gullible as they come, as he never stops intimating towards the end of 'A Voyage to Lilliput', and he merely records what goes on in the society of Lilliput without comment, and certainly without any overt criticism. The account of the disputes between the High-Heels and the Low-Heels, and the Big-Endians and the Little-Endians (which are, of course, based on the disputes between the Tories and the Whigs, and between the Catholics and the Protestants) is given by Reldresal, the Principal Secretary of Private Affairs, and his reported speech means that Gulliver cannot interrupt to say what he thinks of it all. This lack of a reaction on Gulliver's part further strengthens the idea of Gulliver's innocence about the ministers and their conflicts, and it is with evident hindsight that he refers to the "malice" of Skyresh Bolgolam (= the Earl of Nottingham), the High Admiral and his "mortal enemy".

Gulliver's eyes are opened when, after he has destroyed the Blefuscudian fleet, the Emperor demands that he should reduce the whole Empire of Blefuscu into a province and destroy the Big-Endian exiles. This is greeted with the first open criticism in 'A Voyage to Lilliput'. It is in chapter 5:

"And so unmeasureable is the ambition of princes, that he seemed to think of nothing less than reducing the whole Empire of Blefuscu into a province. And from this time began an intrigue between his Majesty and a junta of Ministers maliciously bent against me....Of so little weight are the greatest services to princes, when put into the balance with a refusal to gratify their passions."

Gulliver does not exactly help matters by entertaining the Blefuscudian ambassadors after the signing of the Treaty, and by agreeing to visit the Blefuscudian monarch. Anyone with the slightest sense of diplomacy would know that this gesture might cause Flimnap (= Walpole), the Treasurer, and Bolgolam to whisper that it was an act of disaffection. Gulliver is too innocent to see this. He is too ignorant of the ways of the world. To him, a Treaty is a Treaty, and peace means peace, and so he is surprised at the accusations of disaffection: "And this was the first time I began to conceive some imperfect idea of Courts and Ministers."

Now he is disenchanted. The eight articles he signed, all of which are self-interested from the Lilliputians' point of view, but which he has so far accepted without demure, are now "too servile". The episode of the putting out of the fire, when Gulliver's "fire-hose", charged by a swollen bladder, desecrates the Empress's palace, is recorded without comment or criticism, but it is made clear that by "vowing revenge" instead of being grateful, the monarchy is again falling short of Gulliver's expectations. The round-up of the "learning, laws and customs" of the Lilliputians and "the manner of educating their children" measures the imperfections of England against a theoretically well-organized, if not perfect society – Gulliver is "heartily ashamed" of the English view of fraud, and comments that "begging is a trade unknown in this Empire" – but this seemingly near-perfect society of Whig theory is in practice tainted, corrupted. In the most important paragraph in chapter 6 Swift writes: "In relating these and the following laws, I would only be understood to mean the original institutions, and not the most scandalous corruptions into which these people are fallen by the degenerate nature of man." *Man*, mark you, not Lilliputian. "For," he continues,

"as to that infamous practice of acquiring great employments by dancing on the ropes, or badges of favour and distinction by leaping over sticks, and creeping under them, the reader is to observe, that they were first introduced by the grandfather of the Emperor now reigning, and grew to the present height by the gradual increase of party and faction."

He has seen through, and openly criticized, the leaping and creeping, and it is clear that he is describing a corrupt society whose ideals do not match the reality. "Ingratitude is among them a capital crime," Swift continues. If the ideal of gratitude had been practised by the monarchy, the Emperor would not have plotted against Gulliver, and Gulliver would not have been disillusioned. It is clear that the ludicrous gossip associating the Man-Mountain Gulliver with Flimnap's wife who is only one-twelfth of his size – "a most infamous falsehood" as Gulliver calls it – is a further disappointment for the innocent hero.

Now Gulliver learns about the four Articles of Impeachment (for defiling the Queen's apartment, failing to make Blefuscu a province, and aiding the ambassadors and the Empire of Blefuscu) from "a considerable person at Court", and his knowledge of the ingratitude of these princes and ministers is complete. He has not a good word to say for them:

"I had been hitherto all my life a stranger to Courts, for which I was unqualified by the meanness of my condition. I had indeed heard and read enough of the dispositions of great princes and ministers; but never expected to have found such terrible effects of them in so remote a country, governed, as I thought, by very different maxims from those in Europe."

The Emperor's "lenity" (= lenience) is referred to no less than five times within four pages. The Emperor, we are to understand, is being merciful in agreeing that Gulliver should be blinded (his blindness will typically be useful to the self-interested Emperor) instead of being put to death, and now Gulliver caustically remarks:

"It was a custom introduced by this Prince and his Ministry (very different, as I have been assured, from the practices of former times), that after the Court had decreed any cruel execution... the Emperor always made a speech to his whole Council, expressing his great lenity and tenderness, as qualities known and confessed by all the world."

Shades of Stalin.

"This speech was immediately published throughout the kingdom; nor did anything terrify the people so much as those encomiums on his Majesty's mercy; because it was observed, that the more these praises were enlarged and insisted on, the more inhuman was the punishment, and the sufferer more innocent. Yet, as to myself, I must confess, having never been designed for a courtier either by my birth or education, I was so ill a judge of things that I could not discover the lenity and favour of this sentence, but conceived it (perhaps erroneously) rather to be rigorous than gentle."

He writes that he owes his eyes to his "own great rashness and want of experience: because if I had then known the nature of princes and ministers...I should then with great alacrity and readiness have submitted to so easy a punishment." There is a final dig at the generosity of the Emperor of Blefuscu: "My reception at this Court...was suitable to the generosity of so great a prince." And in the next breath we hear of Gulliver's difficulties "for want of a house and bed, being forced to lie on the ground, wrapped up in my coverlet".

Near the end of 'A Voyage to Lilliput' Gulliver writes: "I resolved never more to put any confidence in princes or ministers, where I could possibly avoid it." This is a far cry from the impressed Gulliver at the beginning, and it is what the princes and ministers have *done* that we ponder at the end, along with Gulliver's sense of his own moral superiority over them, his scorn and undisguised contempt towards them.

If we interpret 'A Voyage to Lilliput' in this way, as a record of a disillusionment, we see that Swift's irony in the book is essentially of two kinds. The first type is found in the first half of the book. Gulliver is not openly critical of Lilliput, but merely records what happens there, and Swift expresses his dislike for the self-interestedness of the princes and ministers and for the absurdities of their corrupt practices by simulating an attitude of approval, which is conveyed through words like "magnificence" and "dexterity". The second type is found in the second half of the book. By now Gulliver has had his eyes opened and is openly critical, and Swift's irony is applied to exposing the full cruelty of the princes and ministers by simulating an attitude of accepting their claim of lenity at face value, and of looking for evidence of lenity, and not being able to find it; in short, simulating the point of view of the innocent.

'A Voyage to Lilliput' describes how human nature has messed up a Utopia, and Swift argues his case with a remarkable blend of irony and "savage indignation".

The King of the Brobdingnagians: A Relative Moral Standard, and a Gigantic Hypocrite

There is nothing like littleness for showing up pride. The more little the proud man is, the more absurd is his pride. The pride of the Lilliputians/English is ridiculous when it is measured by the stature of Gulliver. The pride of Gulliver/the English is ridiculous when it is measured by the physical and apparently moral stature of the Brobdingnagians. In Swift's world, scale appears to be all, and Gulliver, having been the standard by which the Lilliputians' littleness is measured, now finds his littleness measured by the standard of the Brobdingnagians. As Swift observes,

> "Nothing is great or little otherwise than by comparison. It might have pleased Fortune to let the Lilliputians find some nation, where the people were so diminutive with respect to them, as they were to me. And who knows but that (the Brobdingnagians) might be equally overmatched in some distant part of the world, whereof we have yet no discovery?"

The standards appear to be relative, then, as Berkeley's *New Theory of Vision* (1709) maintained all judgements of size are. But is there no absolute good? In Swift, size appears to be indicative of moral stature: the bigger, the better; the littler, the more corrupt. The Lilliputians might seem honest beside creatures one twelfth *their* size, and

Brobdingnagians might seem corrupt beside creatures twelve times their size.

This apparent relativity of standards, and the way Swift shifts his point of view to dwarf the giant Gulliver, are crucial to understanding the Brobdingnagians. For although from Gulliver's point of view the Brobdingnagians represent an ideal society, from the point of view of creatures twelve times their size they may be very imperfect indeed, as, it can be argued, Swift hints they are. In other words, all the relative standards of the Age of Reason are ultimately imperfect, and in this sense there *is* an absolute good, which judges them to be so.

For most of the book, the Brobdingnagians are presented as an ideal. Having been introduced to us as "monsters" and "barbarians" they swiftly become the standard of what is "human", while Gulliver is presented in terms of "any hateful little animal" (such as a weasel, a toad or spider), or in terms of sparrows, rabbits, young kittens and puppy dogs. Gulliver is "exactly shaped in every part like a human creature; which it likewise imitated in all its actions", "in every part of his body resembling an human creature". In other words, Gulliver is like a human, a Brobdingnagian, but he is not one. The "Prince of the Brobdingnagians", the King, observes "how contemptible a thing was human grandeur, which could be mimicked by such diminutive insects as I" which "contrive little nests and burrows". The word "human" there means "Brobdingnagian", and the fact that the Prince observes this to his first Minister suggests that he is undeceived by human pride, as perhaps an ideal Prince should be. Aha, we think, Gulliver won't be disillusioned with *this* Prince.

Gulliver is aware of his own ridiculousness when he is compared with the Brobdingnagian ideal. "There could nothing be more ridiculous than the comparison" between the Queen and himself, and he reflects "how vain an attempt it is for a man to endeavour doing himself honour among those who are out of all degree of equality or comparison with him". In other words, both Gulliver's "courage" and his "honour" appear ridiculous when measured by the Brobdingnagian, and produce "loud laughter", and later the English will appear ridiculous in their self-importance: any "little contemptible varlet" will "put himself on a foot with the greatest persons of the kingdom".

The King of the Brobdingnagians has a "contempt...towards

Europe". The relatively tiny Gulliver tries hard to "celebrate the praises" of England in his speech about British institutions: the Lords, the Commons, the Courts of Justice. It is made clear that he is painting a proudly idealized, untruthful picture to impress the King: "I...gave to every point a more favourable turn by many degrees than the strictness of truth would allow." The King arrives at the truthful picture by his questioning of British (institutions the Lords, Commons, Courts of Justice and the Treasury) and gaming, and by his searching questions he exposes the corruption in England. But, and this is surely the point, how is the King able to probe behind the façade and raise questions about corruption if he is as perfect as we have been led to believe? He would not know about corruption on this scale if he were truly contemptuous of human grandeur, just as the Houyhnhnms of Book 4 do not know what lying means.

The King's verdict on Britain represents a condemnation of Britain by an ideal. British history throughout the years 1600 to 1700 ("during the last century") is "only an heap of conspiracies, rebellions, murders, massacres…" etc. The legislators are qualified in "ignorance, idleness, and vice", and are skilled at "perverting, confounding and eluding" the laws. The British institution "which in its original might have been tolerable" – as were the Lilliputian institutions – is "blotted by corruptions". The "bulk" of the British are "the most pernicious race of little odious vermin that Nature ever suffered to crawl upon the surface of the earth".

We are told, by Gulliver, of "the King's great ignorance in politics". The King is "secluded from the rest of the world", he is "unacquainted" with manners and customs; he has "prejudices" and "a certain narrowness of thinking", "narrow principles and short views". Gulliver reflects "it would be hard indeed, if so remote a Prince's notions of virtue and vice were to be offered as a standard for all mankind". But Swift is being ironical about the King's ignorance – the King *knows* – and at one level Swift clearly *does* intend him to be "a standard for all mankind". The King does not want to know about gunpowder or exploding cannonballs, which are "inhuman ideas" entertained by a "grovelling insect" such as Gulliver, and at this stage the King seems to rule an ideal society which is free from war, and to have no intention of making himself "absolute master of the lives, the liberties, and the fortunes of his people". He despises "all mystery, refinement, and intrigue, either in a prince or a minister", and seems to be the ideal prince. He rules with "common sense and reason,...justice and lenity", and has an educational system based on the ideal subjects of "morality, history, poetry and mathematics" instead of the British subjects of "ideas, entities, abstractions and transcendentals" which lead to more than "one interpretation", i.e. ambivalence, deception and lying. All this lies behind the ironical condemnation of the ideal qualities in terms of British ones, which are ironically praised. The book that Gulliver reads appears to be an ideal one too, from Swift's point of view, for it shows "how diminutive, contemptible, and helpless an animal was man in his own nature", a view of man which, once the irony and the satire in the passage has been allowed for, is clearly religious. The theme of the book is "the weakness of human kind", and both "man" and "human" in this passage means "Brobdingnagian".

But, having nearly convinced us that the King is a standard for Gulliver and the English for all his knowledge of corruption, Swift now tells us that the King has a huge army – or, to be fair, a militia of tradesmen and farmers – of 176,000 foot and 32,000 horse. There have been civil wars, we are told, and the last was "put an end to by this Prince's grandfather". Gulliver is naturally "curious to know how this Prince, to whose dominions there is no access from any other country, came to think of armies, or to teach his people the practice of military discipline". The answer suggests the doctrine of Original Sin and reaffirms Swift's essentially religious view of man: "in the course of many ages they have been troubled with the same disease to which the whole race of mankind is subject; the nobility often contending for power, the people for liberty, and the King for absolute dominion."

In other words, the Lords, the Commons and the monarchy – the institutions Gulliver has covered – are no better in Brobdingnag than they are in England. Admittedly, there has been a peace since the time of the Prince's grandfather, but the history of the Brobdingnagians mirrors the history of England, and the moral indignation of the King towards England is a case of the pot calling the kettle black. In 'An Enquiry into the Behaviour of the Queen's last Ministry', Swift writes, "The art of government...requires no more, in reality, than diligence, honesty, and a moderate share of plain natural sense." The King has "common sense and reason,...justice and lenity" – but no mention is made of his honesty.

So much for Brobdingnag as an ideal society. By his contempt, the King *implies* it is a Utopia, but the reality is different. No wonder he knew all about corruption. The King then, was surely being hypocritical when he was horrified at the idea of gunpowder and of "absolute mastery", for his grandfather was a party to "absolute dominion". So much for the King's "*saeva indignatio*" about "little odious vermin". For by the same standard, the Brobdingnagians are big "odious vermin". All princes and ministers are tarred with the same brush – they are insincere. This is the implication in Swift's disclosures concerning the militia.

The truth about the Brobdingnagians, then, is that they break their own teachings. They say they are undeceived about pride, yet they are proud: witness the pride in the remark about vermin. So at one and the same time they are a standard by which Gulliver/the English can be judged; and they are a mirror of the pride and self-deception of Gulliver/the English. The Brobdingnagians are truly afflicted with "the same disease to which the whole race of mankind is subject", and it is soon apparent that Gulliver has caught this disease. The sailors appear "the most little contemptible creatures I had ever beheld" and though "the comparison [with the Brobdingnagians] gave me so despicable a conceit of myself", he now sees through the eyes of the Brobdingnagians. Observing the littleness of the houses of England, he "began to think myself in Lilliput", and he "looked down upon the servants and one or two friends who were in the house, as if they had been pygmies, and I a giant".

The Brobdingnagians, then, appear to be a moral standard by which the English can be measured, and while we believe they are a moral standard, they have the effect of a moral standard. The King of the Brobdingnagians represents man undeceived by human grandeur, the truly human man in comparison with whom proud British men are like insects or vermin, and British institutions corrupt. Once we grasp that by his words the King of the Brobdingnagians shows himself to be as dishonest and proud as the Europeans he condemns for being dishonest and proud, we realize that we have been deceived by legerdemain, that it *"would* be hard indeed if so remote a Prince's notions of virtue and vice were to be offered as a standard for all mankind". Swift has turned the tables on us very cunningly, and having approved of the Brobdingnagians, we now condemn them. Just as much as the Lilliputians, they embody an aspect of fallen man. They are not ungrateful like the Lilliputians, or un-lenient; their vice is that they preach the opposite of what they practise, or rather, that they practise the opposite of what they preach. They are hypocritical.

Gulliver has not found a Prince or minister who will save him from his disillusion with princes and ministers. And once again the strange creatures he has encountered have turned out to be mirror-images of sinful human nature, with one sin being highlighted. The Brobdingnagians are as repellent as the Lilliputians, and it is the fact that for a while they are presented as a "standard for all mankind" that obscures their repulsiveness and makes for confusion.

Against Rationalism and Scientific Materialism
Book 3 of *Gulliver's Travels* provides a context for the first two books, and points forward to the Houyhnhnms.

After the usual storm, Gulliver encounters the "flying island" of Laputa, which is an inspired anticipation of the flying saucer that puts Swift ahead of Jules Verne as the first Science-Fiction writer. The minds of the Laputians are "so taken up with intense speculations, that they neither can speak, nor attend to the discourses of others". They are, in fact, obsessed with mathematics and music – the King's food is cut into "cones, cylinders, parallelograms" – and at the theoretical level give the impression of being mathematical geniuses.

Unfortunately, the theory is ahead of the practice. In spite of their aptitude for geometry, in Lagado, the capital city of Balnibarbi, the houses are

"very ill built, the walls bevel, without one right angle in any apartment, and this defect ariseth from the contempt they bear for practical geometry, which they despise as vulgar and mechanic, those instructions they give being too refined for the intellectuals [= intellects] of their workmen, which occasions perpetual mistakes".

They are

> "slow and perplexed in their conceptions upon all other subjects, except those of mathematics and music. They are very bad reasoners....Imagination, fancy and invention they are wholly strangers to...; the whole compass of their thoughts and mind being shut up within the two forementioned sciences."

The Laputians are incarnations of rationalism without imagination, and like our own often unimaginative, rational experts today, they are obsessed by news and politics and are "perpetually enquiring into public affairs", and are "curious in matters where we have the least concern". They consequently have no "peace of mind", and are worried by the consequences of their logic, which tells them that the earth will be "swallowed" by the sun.

These fears were entertained by the scientists of the day, and can be traced back to Newton's *Principia*. The Laputian flying island works through magnetism, and in particular through the theories of William Gilbert and the Royal Society of his day, which are set out, complete with mathematical symbols, in chapter 3. So many scientists of the Royal Society are referred to in Book 3 that it is quite clear that the Laputian scholars represent the scientific materialism of the time. There is even a direct swipe at Descartes later on: he "freely acknowledged his mistakes in natural philosophy".

In Book 3, Swift exposes the weaknesses of scientific materialism, the great new "religion" which he, as a Dean of the Anglican Church, evidently despised so much. In the island of Balnibarbi, the theories of the scientists and philosophers never work out. For a start the King should in theory be absolute in power because of his magnetic island, but in practice, he cannot "prevail on a Ministry to join him" – not one Ministry. The Academy of Projectors in Lagado is full of professors who "contrive new rules and methods of agriculture and building, and new instruments and tools for all trades and manufactures, whereby, as they undertake, one man shall do the work of ten" so that "a palace may be built in a week" and "all the fruits of the earth shall come to maturity at whatever season we think fit to choose". The only inconvenience is that "none of these projects are yet brought to perfection, and in the meantime the whole country lies miserably waste, the houses in ruins, the people without food and clothes". Like the economic forecasters of our own day– like the experts who made wrong predictions for the cost of Concorde and the cost of the Swansea Driving Licence building – or like our educational theorists who pooh-pooh ability, the Lagadonian experts find that their theories do not work out in practice.

The 500 rooms of the Academy are full of scatterbrained projects, none more daft than the research on the project "for extracting sunbeams out of cucumbers", which has so far taken eight years. There are dozens of similarly unlikely projects – such as reducing human excrement to its original food, or building houses by "beginning at the roof and working downwards to the foundation" – and there is even a project "for improving speculative knowledge by practical and mechanical operations". There is a project for reducing polysyllables, and another project for abolishing words altogether. We know what Swift thought of scholars.

The "school for political projectors" is equally crazy. There is a scheme for taxing vices and infirmities. Quarrels between political parties are to be solved by cutting brains into two. Plotters are to be identified by various dubious means, including acrostics. In a passage reminiscent of the King of Brobdingnag's outburst against Europeans, Gulliver says that in "Tribnia" (an anagram for Britain), "the bulk of the people consisted wholly of discoverers, witnesses, informers, accusers, prosecutors, evidences, swearers…all under…the pay of ministers and their deputies." Gulliver concludes, "I saw nothing in this country that could invite me to a longer continuance, and began to think of returning home to England."

After that Book 3 becomes even more bitty. Gulliver travels to the port of Maldonada and sails to Glubbdubdrib, the island of Sorcerers and Magicians. It is there that he sees the ghosts of historical figures (as Faustus conjures up Helen), and in a passage reminiscent of his reflection in Book 1, he records with familiar superiority and scorn that he is "surprised to find corruption grown so high and so quick in that Empire, by the force of luxury so lately introduced", and he reflects "how much the race of human kind was degenerate among us, within these hundred years past." He returns to Maldonada and sails to Luggnagg where he meets the Struldbruggs, or Immortals, who are "a mortifying sight".

So how are we to make sense of the whole of Book 3? At one level, Swift is defining man in terms of what he is not; having defined him in terms of dwarves and giants in Books 1 and 2, he is now measuring him in terms of ghosts and immortals. At another level, in Book 3, Swift is showing us how science has tinkered with gravity and with death, and how the logical outcome is that it will overcome both with flying islands, access to ghosts, and longevity. But, he is saying, human nature will not change, and so there will be no Utopia. In other words, Swift is defining man in terms of his scientific reason, and is showing us how limited this is.

The mind of man, Swift is surely saying, which operates through the reason exclusively, becomes unbalanced. It needs the imagination as well. In his view of the need for wholeness, Swift is very close to Blake, whose Urizen and Los represent a private mythology similar to that of the Lagadonians and the Houyhnhnms, and whose enemy was similarly "single vision and Newton's sleep".

When man lives exclusively through the reason, Swift seems to be saying, he lives without God and becomes degenerate and corrupt. The reason is limited in what it is capable of achieving, he is saying, and it can lead us into sillinesses like extracting sunbeams from cucumbers. The reason can invent theories and speculate, but it is often far removed from what will work out in practice. This remoteness is what the Laputians of the Flying Island, the Lagadonians and the rest have in common.

Swift's anti-rationalism in Book 3 is important, because it throws an important light on Books 1 and 2. Now that we look again at the theories of the Emperor of Lilliput and of the King of Brobdingnag, can we not detect the same gulf between theory and practice? Both the Emperor and the King have theories of good government, but the Emperor is far from lenient, though his lenity is extolled, and the King's Utopia, which is implicit in his scathing denunciation of Europeans as "vermin", crumbles when we learn that his history is no different from Europe's. The imperfections in the practice in both Lilliput and Brobdingnag give an impression of hypocrisy or sheer incompetence, or both, and these "corruptions" may be the consequences of a theory of government which regards the reason as paramount.

Book 3 provides a context for the first two books, because it gives them an anti-rational context. It points forward to the Houyhnhnms who are incarnations of Reason itself.

Swift loathed modern ideas as much as he loathed the Whigs. As a Tory and a Dean of the Anglican Church, he regarded the new scientific materialism with savage indignation. He lampoons its various facets in the institutions of his time.

The Rational Virtue of the Houyhnhnm Governing Animal, and Gulliver's Pride
The main point about the Land of the Houyhnhnms is that it is a country where virtue rules vice, where "the governing animal" is virtuous rather than vicious. The Houyhnhnms stand for pure virtue, the Yahoos for pure vice, and man – Gulliver – has the essentially Christian dual nature: limited powers of virtue and a capacity for vice. It is because the "governing animal" in England is so corrupt and degenerate and vicious that Gulliver accepts the appellation of "Yahoo". We must be absolutely clear on this point. The identification of Gulliver as Yahoo is a measure of Swift's satire on England; it is a dig against the corruption of the English rulers. Gulliver has reacted to the Houyhnhnms' reason by loathing individuals and being misanthropic. Swift's identification of Gulliver as Yahoo has nothing to do with disgust or misanthropy on Swift's part, as some critics have maintained.

Swift is of course standing the English situation on its head. In England, man has some reason and some virtue, and horses have brute strength. In Houyhnhnm-land, the horses have the reason and virtue, and "man" has brute strength – and the vices of the English "governing animal". The Houyhnhnms are credited with greater powers than man in the same way that in a work they sired, George Orwell's *Animal Farm*, the pigs are credited with greater intelligence than Mr Jones.

The picture is built up very skilfully. The Yahoos are "disagreeable", are "a herd". The Houyhnhnms' behaviour is "orderly and rational" and their civilization suggests "a people who…must need excel in wisdom all the nations of the world". The Yahoos are soon "detestable creatures" who eat vegetables and meat ("feeding upon roots and the flesh of some animals"), and they have the nose and lips "common to all savage nations". "I confess," Gulliver says, "I never saw any sensitive being so detestable on all accounts; and the more I came near them, the more hateful they grew."

Gulliver naturally identifies himself with the Houyhnhnms at first, but his Houyhnhnm master is convinced "that I must be a Yahoo, but my teachableness, civility and cleanliness astonished him". For the Yahoos are "the most unteachable of brutes". Gulliver has "some glimmerings of Reason". Gulliver begins to accept that he is a Yahoo: "my body had a different covering from others of my kind". Yet his kind is still "that cursed race of Yahoos", and "I expressed my uneasiness at his giving me so often the appellation of Yahoo, an odious animal, for which I had so utter an hatred and contempt". The Yahoos have a "degenerate and brutal nature".

The question then becomes: Who is the rightful governing animal? In all the countries he has travelled in, Gulliver says, "creatures like myself...were the only governing, rational animals". Again, "the Yahoos were the only governing animal in my country". The Houyhnhnm who is Gulliver's master says, "If it were possible there could be any country where Yahoos alone were endued with Reason, they certainly must be the governing animal, because Reason will in time always prevail against brutal strength". Gulliver now finally caves in and accepts the Houyhnhnm thesis. On his ship, he says, he "had about fifty Yahoos under me", and he explains that "a soldier is a Yahoo hired to kill in cold blood as many of his own species, who have never offended him, as possibly he can".

Gulliver explains the state of England to the Houyhnhnm, "extenuating" its faults as he did when he explained England to the King of the Brobdingnagians. He describes the history of the 1688 Revolution, the "ambition of princes", the "corruption of ministers", and the trivial hair-splittings that lead to war, like those of the Big-Endians and Little-Endians in Lilliput. The Houyhnhnm makes the caustic comment that "what you have told me, upon the subject of war, doth indeed discover most admirably the effects of that Reason you pretend to", i.e. that wars prove that man has not a great deal of reason, and Gulliver is soon "smiling a little at his ignorance", as he smiles at the King of Brobdingnag's ignorance. But the Houyhnhnm denounces European man in words reminiscent of the King of Brobdingnag's "little odious vermin":

"My discourse had increased his abhorrence of the whole species....Although he hated the Yahoos of his country, yet he no more blamed them for their odious qualities, than he did a *gnnayh* (a bird of prey) for its cruelty....But when a creature pretending to Reason could be capable of such enormities, he dreaded lest the corruption of that faculty might be worse than brutality itself. He seemed therefore confident, that instead of Reason we were only possessed of some quality fitted to increase our natural vices."

In other words, man pretends to Reason, but as his wars show, he achieves brutality, whereas the Houyhnhnms (whose name is derived from a word meaning "Perfection of Nature") are guided by "Nature and Reason".

Unabashed, Gulliver gives his usual account of English politics. When asked "what species of Yahoo" a Minister of State is, Gulliver says that the Prime Minister (the "First or Chief Minister of State") "never tells a truth but with an intent that you should take if for a lie." The Houyhnhnm now says that Gulliver "far exceeded in shape, colour, and cleanliness, all the Yahoos of his nation" and that he has "some rudiments of Reason". In other words, he has a "good opinion" of Gulliver – relatively speaking, of course – and "the vilest opinion of human kind".

It is at this point that the Houyhnhnms increasingly represent virtue. They are "placed in opposite view to human corruptions" so that Gulliver "began to view the actions and passions of man in a very different light", i.e. the vicious side of man. He resolves "never to return to human kind, but to pass the rest of my life among these admirable Houyhnhnms in the contemplation and practice of every virtue; where I could have no example or incitement to Vice". This is the ideal of the monk, the ideal of contemplative virtue. The Houyhnhnm regards Gulliver as coming from a race that has "some small pittance of Reason" which aggravates "our natural corruptions", and which has "gross defects in Reason, and by consequence, in virtue". Being deficient in Virtue, and understanding human nature better than the Houyhnhnms, Gulliver finds it "easy to apply the character he gave of the Yahoos to myself and my countrymen", for all the Yahoos' "strange disposition to nastiness and dirt" and their being "the most unteachable of all animals".

The "noble Houyhnhnms are endowed by Nature with a general disposition to all virtues, and have no conceptions or ideas of what is evil in a rational creature". The governing animal in Houyhnhnm-land therefore lacks the "controversies, wranglings, disputes and positiveness in false or dubious propositions" that were all too familiar in the politics of Swift's day, and which made the rulers of England resemble the Yahoos. The Houyhnhnms' virtues are: friendship, benevolence, decency, civility, temperance, industry, exercise and cleanliness.

Now comes the familiar Swiftian jolt. At their grand Assembly, the Houyhnhnms "resumed their old debate, and indeed, the only debate that ever happened in their country....The question to be debated, was, Whether the Yahoos should be exterminated from the face of the earth" as "the most filthy, noisome, and deformed animal which Nature ever produced". Some jolt. For this is the language of Nazi Germany, and for Yahoos read "Jews". How can such purely virtuous beings spend all their time debating genocide? Surely something has gone wrong.

One is perplexed. Of course, virtue cannot tolerate vice, we tell ourselves. It is quite natural for virtues to root our vices. Yet the Yahoos *are* living creatures, and "everything that lives is holy", as Blake put it. All creatures have Buddha-nature, even Yahoos, and should the Houyhnhnms not include tolerance among their virtues? The seven virtues of scholastic theology are the three theological virtues of faith, hope and charity, and the four cardinal virtues of justice, prudence, temperance and fortitude. Where is charity in the Houyhnhnms' nature?

The answer is: it is not there – and that is the point. The Houyhnhnm virtue is based on Reason, not God, and therefore it lacks "love", in the Christian sense, and feeling, and, indeed, all sense of "neighbourhood". In one of his sermons Swift wrote, "There is no solid, firm foundation of virtue, but in a conscience directed by the principles of religion", and rational virtue, when taken to its logical conclusion, can lead to the extermination of all who are "vicious" by its standards, as any class-revolutionary dictator or tyrant knows. Stalin and Mao, who between them executed a good few million of their opponents as inferior beings, would both have understood the logic of the beastly Houyhnhnms.

So, with a brilliant reverse, like the sleight of hand with which Swift rang the changes on the King of the Brobdingnagians, transforming him in an instant from a moral standard to a dishonest hypocrite, Swift, the master-magician and conjuror, has pulled off another trick, transforming the saintly horses into genocidal maniacs. So the rational theories that are divorced from God work out in practice. So much for Cartesian ethics and Whig political theories. And we should remember, the word "Whig" comes from a word "Whiggamore", meaning "one who urges on a *mare*". Here, "one who urges on a Houyhnhnm".

Saints do not debate the extermination of sinners, but those who believe that virtue is founded on reason sometimes do, and their corrupt and degenerate nature leads them astray. "Reason alone is sufficient to govern a *rational* creature," Gulliver's master has told him. What rot, Swift is saying in Book 4. The Houyhnhnms, having been a standard of virtue, now become an ideal that is utterly repulsive; not merely an impossible ideal but an utterly undesirable ideal. "Perfection of Nature" indeed. True virtue includes the forgiveness of vice.

Now the Houyhnhnm ethic works itself out inexorably. Gulliver, his master tells him, has "all the qualities of a Yahoo, only a little more civilized by some tincture of Reason, which however was in a degree as far inferior to the Houyhnhnm race, as the Yahoos of their country were to me". The Houyhnhnms, "naturally disposed to every virtue, wholly governed by Reason" have no feelings and express "neither joy nor grief at their departure; nor does the dying person discover the least regret that he is leaving the world". They have no word for "evil". The "sad catastrophe" that befalls Gulliver is inevitable. Practising a form of apartheid as these virtuous racists do, lacking feelings and a concept of evil, the Houyhnhnms can only ask Gulliver-Yahoo to leave.

How blind Gulliver is. Free from vice, he is proud to be a subject of their discourse ("I may add without vanity, that my presence often gave them sufficient matter for discourse") – along with friendship, benevolence, order, economy, Nature, virtue and Reason, of course; and the "vices and follies" of man, with his "small proportion of Reason", who must be "vile as well as miserable". Gulliver thinks his "family, my friends, my countrymen, or human race in general" are really Yahoos, "making no other use of Reason, than to improve and multiply those vices".

"In the midst of all this happiness," Gulliver is told that the Assembly had taken offence at his master's "keeping a Yahoo (meaning myself) in his family more like a Houyhnhnm, than a brute animal", for "such a practice was not agreeable to Reason or Nature". His master must either "employ me like the rest of my species [= Yahoos], or command me to swim back to the place from whence I came". It has to be the second, because the rational Houyhnhnms "feared I might be able to seduce them [= Yahoos] into the woody and mountainous parts of the country, and bring them [= Yahoos] in troops by night to destroy the Houyhnhnms' cattle".

So now the secret is out. The Houyhnhnms *fear* the Yahoos, and the government of this rational "governing animal" is no different from any tyrant's. The fear that motivates the expulsion of Gulliver is the same fear that motivated Ian Smith's confinement under house arrest of Garfield Todd in Rhodesia – lest he seduced some black Africans into the woody and mountainous parts of Rhodesia. And how unfriendly and unbenevolent is the exhortation to Gulliver's master, who was to "command me to swim". To swim indeed. The Houyhnhnms don't give a damn for Gulliver, but think only of themselves and of the security of their state.

Gulliver feels "in my weak and corrupt judgement" that the exhortation "might consist with Reason to have been less rigorous (= severe)". Well he might, for not being able to swim to the nearest island, he has in effect been sentenced to death. We recall the "lenity" of the Emperor of Lilliput – all princes are tarred with the same brush, Swift is saying. He is filled with "grief and despair" and dreads the prospect of returning to live among Yahoos "and relapsing into my old corruptions, for want of examples to lead and keep me within the paths of virtue". Luckily he is allowed to spend two months in making a boat.

Gulliver's master comes to see him off, "out of curiosity, and perhaps (if I may speak without vanity) partly out of kindness". A truer motive might be that the Houyhnhnm wanted to make sure that Gulliver left. Gulliver is touched because the Houyhnhnm lifted his hoof to be kissed, thereby saving Gulliver the necessity of prostrating himself. This, he says, is "a mark of distinction to a creature so inferior as I", but it is also a mark of pride, the vice of the Emperor of Lilliput who expected Gulliver to lie on his face before his small pomp. So much for the "noble and courteous disposition of the Houyhnhnms" – which is far from noble, and far from courteous, having booted Gulliver out. Once again in Swift, the theory and the practice are at variance.

Gulliver now finds the idea of returning to live "in the society and under the government of Yahoos" "horrible", and he craves for solitude so that he can "reflect with delight on the virtues of those inimitable Houyhnhnms, without any opportunity of degenerating into the vices and corruptions of my own species", for which he has a "detestation". When he meets men again, he "was going to leap into the sea, and swim for my life, rather than continue among Yahoos" – and with that pride he condescends to treat them: "at last I descended to treat them like an animal which had some little portion of Reason." "Descended" – the word suggests coming down from a height. How he judges his neighbour. "Judge not that ye be not judged."

Gulliver's contact with pure virtue has led to his contacting the disease of pride. The Yahoos fill him with "hatred, disgust and contempt". "During the first year," he says, "I could not endure my wife or children in my presence", and he converses with his horses "at least four hours a day". Swift tells us that his aim has been "to inform, and not amuse thee" – "to inform and instruct mankind" – and that he has written for "the PUBLIC GOOD":

"For who can read of the virtues...of the glorious Houyhnhnms, without being ashamed of his own vices, when he considers himself as the reasoning, governing animal of his country? I shall say nothing of those remote nations where Yahoos preside, amongst which the least corrupted are the Brobdingnagians, whose wise maxims in morality and government it would be our happiness to observe."

In other words, Swift is trying to make the governing British animal ashamed of his vices – it is the business of the satirist to ridicule the nation's follies and vices – and those vices include, high on the list: pride.

Gulliver has never seen his own pride, and now he is still utterly blind to it. He says, "I may, without breach of modesty, pretend to some superiority" over mankind "from the advantages I received by conversing with...the Houyhnhnms". He wants "to apply those excellent lessons of virtue which I learned among the Houyhnhnms, to instruct the Yahoos of my own family as far as I shall find them docible [= teachable]", and his "reconcilement to Yahoo-kind in general might not be so difficult if they would be content with those vices and follies

444

only, which Nature hath entitled them to". He says that most vice is "according to the due course of things", "but when I behold a lump of deformity and diseases both in body and mind, smitten with *pride*, it immediately breaks all the measures of my patience; neither shall I be ever able to comprehend how such an animal and such a vice could tally together". Gulliver says the Houyhnhnms have no word for pride in their language, and therefore could not distinguish pride in the Yahoos "for want of thoroughly understanding human nature, as it [= human nature] showeth itself in other countries, where that animal [= Yahoo] presides. But I, who had more experience, could plainly observe some rudiments of it [= pride] among the wild Yahoos." How proudly he criticizes Yahoo pride.

The ending is brilliant. Gulliver records that the Houyhnhnms "are no more proud of the good qualities they possess, than I should be for not wanting a leg or an arm". He says, "I dwell the longer upon this subject [= pride] from the desire I have to make the society [= company] of an English Yahoo by any means not insupportable [= tolerable], and therefore I here entreat those who have any tincture [= trace] of this absurd vice [= pride], that they will not presume to appear in my sight." Presume. In other words, Gulliver has set himself above mankind, which must not presume to appear on equal terms with him if it has any trace of pride, and Gulliver at the end is the proudest man on earth.

He cannot see that if he is a Yahoo, then he, too, must be proud. He deceives himself by regarding himself as purely virtuous, and therefore blinds himself to his own pride – as, it can be argued, do the Houyhnhnms, which is why they are not aware of their own pride when they debate the extermination of the Yahoos.

Book 4, then, begins as a journey into a land where virtue rules vice. It ends by showing that Houyhnhnm-land is really a land where pride rules. This ambivalence is very much a part of Swift's satirical method. Houyhnhnm-land is at first an ideal, a standard of virtue by which to judge Europe, but it then becomes an embodiment of the rational virtue in modern philosophy and political theory which Swift disliked and satirized. Swift is therefore not – repeat not – urging us to be like the Houyhnhnms and to detest man as a Yahoo, and any critic who says that he is, has failed to understand the ambivalence of Swift's satire, in which the standard itself becomes judged by another standard. Swift is not a misanthrope doing dirt on life by identifying man as a Yahoo.

He is, as always, an Anglican Dean. The cousin of Dryden and school friend of Congreve, he is showing us a rationalist's Utopia, which like all Utopias, including those of Russia and China, prove to be not such good places as they once appeared after all. And we must remember that in Swift's time the horse was the natural means of transport, that Swift rode a horse, and that by switching the qualities of man and horse he is able to give us a defence of the traditional religious view of man, with his dual nature, by attacking and demolishing the view that in his day threatened to replace it: Whig – we should say liberal – rational virtue, in which the Reason is the measure of all things, including man.

The Age of Reason's Sense of its own Superiority, and its Moral Blindness

We have taken each book of *Gulliver's Travels* in turn, and we have seen how Swift works out his theme. Both Books 1 and 2 are about "the Art of Government", and how the claims made by princes and ministers differ from what happens in practice because of "the degenerate nature of man", and the same goes for Books 3 and 4. The Lilliputians are self-interested and corrupt, the Brobdingnagians have a contempt for all other creatures that is not based on their own actual superiority; the Laputians on the Flying Island and the Lagadonians have lost touch with reality, and the Houyhnhnms are self-interested and proud. For all their contempt, the Brobdingnagians and the Houyhnhnms are little better than the Lilliputian princes and ministers – though they are less corrupt in some ways, they are as corrupt in others, for all the relative standards are ultimately imperfect – and Swift speaks near the end of Book 4 of "those remote nations where Yahoos preside, amongst which the least corrupted are the Brobdingnagians". In other words, the Brobdingnagians are Yahoos in comparison with the Houyhnhnms, and the Houyhnhnms are little better than the Yahoos, only Gulliver is too blind to see it. The Utopias of the Brobdingnagians and of the Houyhnhnms are not Utopias after all.

And this brings us back to the question: does the *flawed standard of proud goodness* represent Swift's attitude, which is against the Age of Reason, or does it embody the Age of Reason? We have seen that it is each in turn; both; that the standard is ambivalent. In Book 4, the notion of rational virtue comes to embody the Age of Reason, and the Houyhnhnm ethic is therefore being satirized; the Houyhnhnm Utopia debunked. In Book 2, on the other hand, we are told very little about the philosophy of the Brobdingnagians – we can only deduce it by implication from their contempt for Europe and human grandeur. Is it not this tone of contempt which Swift is attacking, which he has heard in the philosophers of his time? Is not their arrogance his target, and is that not why we hear little about their philosophy? Is it not the new philosophy's sense of its own *superiority* that Swift is hammering in both Books 2 and 4, the way the new philosophers set themselves up as authorities, and are ready to judge; the pride of all who think they are better or more right than anyone else?

If so, then Gulliver is not immune in Books 1 and 3, for just as in Books 2 and 4 he catches the disease of both the Brobdingnagians and the Houyhnhnms, and on his return to the West despises mankind, so in Book 1 and 3 he expresses attitudes of superiority that are uncomfortably close to those of Books 2 and 4. In his blindness to his own pride, Gulliver is surely very much a child of the Age of Reason, and it is surely the moral blindness and pride of the Age of Reason (which is to be found in Gulliver's attitude to the Lilliputians and the Laputians and Lagadonians as much as in Books 2 and 4) that is Swift's chief target; the pride whose "lenity" and "benevolence" can lead to the inhumane conse-quences of expulsion, or ultimately, even extermination.

In a sense, Swift's world is close to Kafka's. K, Kafka's hero, has reason and rationality, but the Castle is irrational and does not operate by rules. Swift's creations have reason and rationality, and they act with consequences that are irrational and in breach of their own rules because of Original Sin: the flaw in human nature which cannot be changed. In another sense, Swift's world is close to Solzhenitsyn's in *Warning to the Western World*, for he shares with Solzhenitsyn a mistrust of all Utopian creeds which put man in God's place as the "crowning glory" of creation. What a time Swift would have had today with our reasonable and rational Labour government, and its Utopian dreams.

1976

3

Questioning Modern Secular Poetry:
A Defence of Traditional Poetic Method or:
Poking the Hornets' Nest[2]

"Yet let me flap this bug with gilded wings,
This painted child of dirt, that stinks and stings."
(Pope, 'Epistle to Dr Arbuthnot', lines 309-10)

For 600 years (1380-1980) the different branches of English culture all grew out of one healthy Christian trunk like the branches of a tree, and all the disciplines were fed by the same metaphysical sap from the Christian religion. In the Middle Ages, religion pervaded philosophy, painting, music and poetry, the earliest form of literature. Over the years secularization weakened English culture and by the 20th century the English cultural tree was pretty dry.

For 600 years English poets have had something to say, and the intensity, pressure and urgency of their message elevated their verse into poetry. (Verse is metrical patterns with rhyme heightening their effectiveness, whereas poetry has an additional quality that is hard to define but which has much to do with the poet's vision.) The sap of European culture imbued their lines, leading to reflections on time and eternity and on the metaphysical nature of the universe. Shakespeare wrote of the lark at heaven's gate in *Cymbeline*. Marvell saw the soul gliding like a bird into a tree in General Fairfax's Garden in Nun Appleton, Yorkshire. Milton justified "the wayes of God to men" in *Paradise Lost*. Pope vindicated "the wayes of God to men" in his 'Essay on Man'. Wordsworth wrote of the "Wisdom and Spirit of the universe" in his *Prelude*, and of "a motion and a spirit, that impels/All thinking things, all objects of all thought,/And rolls through all things" in 'Tintern Abbey'. Shelley wrote in 'Adonais', "The One remains, the many change and pass." Similar sentiments can be found in the poets of the European tradition, such as Dante and Goethe. What the poet had to say was often lofty and elevated, sometimes sublime. Shelley wrote in his *A Defence of Poetry* that "a poem is the very image of life expressed in its eternal truth".

For 600 years the mainstream of poetry has involved metre and rhyme or blank verse, which act like banks beside a river, as borders that order, without which there would be an anarchic flood. Within the restrictions of these banks poets paddle with the flowing currents of spiritual energy. The Greek and Latin iambic measures entered English Literature with the Normans and the Renaissance, pushing out the Old English alliterative line of stresses. St Godric (who died c.1170) was the first to reject Anglo-Saxon forms. From Chaucer to Tennyson readers knew clearly where they were technically, whether a line scanned well or badly and rhymed well or badly. Shakespeare had his irregularities but these were exceptions rather than the rule. The Metaphysicals, Milton, the Augustans and the Romantics all used the stanza, blank verse, the heroic couplet and the formal ode. The Victorians held the line with the dramatic monologues of Browning and lyrics of Tennyson, though Matthew Arnold loosened his verse and Hopkins introduced feet of one stress with sprung rhythm.

As poets used forms that enabled readers to know precisely where they were their verse could take on reflective philosophical weight as they communicated what they had to say. This weight can be found in Shakespeare's soliloquies and Platonist sonnets, Donne's probing of metaphysical truth, Milton's speeches about God, Pope's *Essay on Man*, Wordsworth's autobiographical *Prelude* and Keats' great odes about the ephemerality of life. There was a general awareness that humans have a spiritual and divine spark as well as a social mind and body. After the freeing rhythms of Whitman and Pound, Eliot and Lawrence, Yeats held the line in the 20th century with reflective poems about life and death, and Eliot himself returned to profound philosophical considerations in his formal *Four Quartets*. The word-drunk Dylan Thomas sang about the mysteries of time and death, Betjeman surveyed life in his strictly formal poems. Larkin and the Movement poets (for all their rationalism and concern with statement rather than image) used their formal concerns to reflect on society. For 600 years it has been possible to understand the content and method of Chaucer, Shakespeare, Milton, Pope, Coleridge, Shelley or Tennyson without requiring any fundamental change in the nation's poetic taste. Just as the domes of Islamic mosques express the beauty of God in art over a thousand years, so the poets of the British tradition created their own testaments to divine beauty in their life's work.

The collapse of religious belief in the late 20th century, and of belief in immortality, has had consequences for "the traditional" poetic method. For poetry then becomes a record of the world of the self, which is dark and lacking in the beauty of the cosmos. Since 1980 many practitioners of English verse have had nothing to say and they have moved away from the readily comprehensible forms, preferring that words should be put down on paper as they happen to come out instinctively, without the shaping constraints of stanzas or metrical form. A climate of "anything goes" has arisen. Metre and rhyme were largely abandoned and with them a 600-year-old tradition of poetic method. Rooting himself in Lawrence's free verse, in Eliot's early stress poetry and in American free verse practised by William Carlos Williams, Roethke and of course Sylvia Plath, Ted Hughes (with whom I corresponded from 1993 until his death in 1998) encouraged this tendency and some of his poems seem to be written in "chopped-up prose" (though pentameters, 5-feet lines, can be found by piecing short lines together). In 1982, the introduction to the *Penguin Book of Contemporary British Poetry*, co-written by Andrew Motion, the new Poet Laureate, and Blake Morrison, stated: 'A body of work has been created which demands, for its appreciation, a reformation of poetic taste.' Verse without metre and rhyme, with irregular lengths of lines, sometimes (but not always) using rhythm, requires a different kind of understanding. (Of Motion, Michael Schmidt wrote approvingly in *Lives of the Poets*, "He has a subtle ear for speech so that the poems seldom settle into metre." The implication is that any poet who is alert to speech does not need to use metre, and that metre is a crutch for bad poets. This is a wrong view of poetry that is a necessary consequence of the reformation of taste.)

The effect has been to make it harder for readers to know what is going on and for practitioners of this alternative method to approach reflective, philosophical themes, for the new-way verse forms are slight and sometimes have only one or two words per line. Practitioners have in effect demanded that the old way of responding to poetry for 600 years should be unlearned – poetry like Chaucer's, Shakespeare's, Milton's and Wordsworth's which is rooted in English culture and appeals to the soul – and that appreciation of the new way should focus on word-choice, sounds and image and applaud its slight subject matter and lack of depth. It is as if painters were to have a revolution against the traditional art of portrait-painting and declare that doodle-cartoons are now the norm, that there needs to be a 'reformation of taste' so that the public can appreciate the new art and that the advantages of the cartoon should be stressed so that portraits can be ignored in future. Pope understood the thinness behind such thinking and lampooned banality in his *Dunciad*.

I could now invite you to consider half a dozen typical examples of the new-way poetry, which new-way critics have praised for their power; lyric beauty; intense emotion; biting satire; punning eloquence that makes the language sing; and intense imagery, inventiveness and jewelled language.

I decline to offer selections from these new-way versifiers (whose permission I would have to seek) as I am defending the old way; but informed readers will readily be able to supply their own examples from the best-known new-way poets. "Old-way" sensibilities see such metreless, rhymeless offerings differently, as evidence of the bankruptcy of the new-way secular-humanist vision.

In the majority of new-way poems, language is decorative rather than descriptive – meaning is sacrificed to decorative effects – and its source is the rational ego and memory, the world of the self which has lost contact with the soul. It is therefore shallow. In the great majority, meaning, grace and beauty are not obviously apparent. A comparison to, or rather contrast with, the two Poets Laureate of the 19th century, Wordsworth and Tennyson, shows what a huge decline in communication of meaning through language there has been in the last hundred years, and that the beauty of the best verse of Wordsworth and Tennyson is missing. Many of the new-way works deliberately do dirt on the sacred; all amount to a kind of anti-poetry that is now held up as the norm and defended by the poetic Establishment, for the new-way versifiers of my half-dozen examples would include two Poet Laureates, a Chairman of the Literature Panel of the Arts Council and the Oxford Professor of Poetry.

The new way of writing is user-friendly to poets. Whereas Yeats on at least one occasion spent all morning hunting for a rhyme and Betjeman spoke of the surprising simile that can be thrown up during the search for a word within the constraint of rhyme, a two-or-three-words-per-line poem without metre or rhyme (which is spurned as "predictable") and precious few other rules can be dashed off in a minute or two at a bus-stop or while waiting for tea in a café. Ease, brevity and convenience have brought followers to this disposable, sketchy kind of art. A reader may be forgiven for feeling unable to judge the result as the criteria by which its worth can be deemed are not obviously apparent.

I have come to hold grave reservations about free verse. Eliot wrote that there should be a ghost of a pentameter behind the arras of free verse, and he had strong opinions on the matter: "There is no freedom in art"; "No verse is free for the man who wants to do a good job....Only a bad poet could welcome free verse as a liberation from form." Lawrence's free-verse poems seem unsatisfactory, dashed off in varying lengths of lines that do not really lodge in the memory.

The great drawback of the new metreless, rhymeless way is that it produces poems that cannot be remembered, and are therefore unmemorable. Memory, the ability to remember, is fundamental to a shared rooted culture. Consider the following passages which, by contrast, *can* be remembered and *are* memorable:

"When icicles hang by the wall,
And Dick, the shepherd, blows his nail,
And Tom bears logs into the hall,
And milk comes frozen home in pail,
When blood is nipp'd and ways be foul,
Then nightly sings the staring owl,
'Tu-who;
Tu-whit, tu-who' – a merry note,
While greasy Joan doth keel the pot."

Shakespeare, *Love's Labour's Lost*, v.ii

"About, about, in reel and rout
The death-fires danced at night;
The water, like a witch's oils,
Burnt green, and blue and white."

Coleridge, 'The Rime of the Ancient Mariner'

"The One remains, the many change and pass;
Heaven's light forever shines, Earth's shadows fly;
Life like a dome of many-coloured glass,
Stains the white radiance of Eternity...."

Shelley, 'Adonais'

Rhyming lines from Shakespeare, Coleridge and Shelley drop into the memory like a stone into a well, and are retained without effort. But none of the new-way verse lends itself to memory and retention. After several readings a poem by Hughes or by other new-way versifiers fails to lodge in the memory. Sir Philip Sidney pointed out in his *An Apologie for Poetrie* (1579-80) that "verse far exceedeth prose in the knitting up of the memory..., one word...begetting another as, be it a rhyme or measured verse, by the former a man shall have a near guess to the follower". In Sidney's terms the unguessable new-way verse is closer to prose.

Another drawback of the new-way verse is that it diminishes the standing of both the poem and of the poet. For 600 years the poet was a cross-disciplinary reflector who held the mirror up to human nature and the universe and, as one who often embodied the central idea of his culture, reflected on the state of his civilization as a leading figure in it and often the embodiment of its central idea and its culture. Now the poet has become an ordinary bloke who produces small disposable and unmemorable offerings that may secure throw-away laughs at a poetry reading. The new-way verse is invariably humanist (i.e., concerned with human rather than metaphysical matters) and is unaware of the One behind the many. I am reminded of the Ship of Fools. It is as if the new-way versifiers have no sails on their ship because they do not believe in the breath of God. Chaucer's *Prologue*, Shakespeare's Platonist sonnets, Dryden's 'Absalom and Achitophel', Shelley's 'Adonais' and Eliot's *Four Quartets* have set an exalted standard for the poem and the role of the poet in his culture which the new-way verses and versifiers ignore or reject.

*

My work continues the traditional poetic method; sometimes I think I am the only poet continuing it in contemporary Britain. I have retained metre/rhyme and blank verse for ready communication and I have made the quest for Reality my subject matter. Many of my poems are rooted in the English countryside, and are reflective approaches to the One behind the many (to put it in the terms of the Presocratic philosophers Parmenides and Heracleitus and of my own philosophical work, *The One and the Many*). They are Universalist poems. Universalism is a restatement of the metaphysical vision which sees the universe as a Whole and assimilates every known experience and all possible concepts, including infinity. Universalist philosophers see the universe as fundamentally One, a whole; Universalist historians see history as a whole; and Universalist poets and men of letters look at the whole of life, in both its physical and metaphysical layers, rather than from a purely humanist, social perspective. Many of my poems therefore interlock. They are about connections between the world of Nature and the metaphysical Reality hidden within it and behind it; between tradition and the individual.

This idea is expressed in my re-creation of an Elizabethan knot garden at Otley Hall in Suffolk (later reproduced in my garden in Essex), where a single white point in the centre of the garden can be seen as sending energy that becomes the events of physics and history. The 25 beds of herbs represent the civilizations of history, the forms of physics and the isms of philosophy. My poetic output is a kind of knot garden in verse that also makes a statement about the events of physics, history and philosophy.

My subject matter aims to be both universal and local. I have poems about the universe, about Europe, about English places that evoke the tradition of English culture and Englishness (for example, Warwick Castle); and I have written many pastoral poems set in Essex, Suffolk and Cornwall in which the One is never far away. Epic poetry has been regarded in all countries and at all times as the highest form of poetic achievement because it narrates heroic events on a grand scale. My [first] epic poem *Overlord*, written in 41,000 lines of blank verse, is about Eisenhower's conflict with Hitler in the last year of the Second World War but at another level it is also about the rival New World Orders of Christ and Satan.

I have tried to ensure that the range of my verse is wide. I have written sonnets; lyrics in trimeters and tetrameters that are rhymed or alternately rhymed; elegies; odes in 8, 10 or 12 stanzas, each of 8, 10 or 12 lines that are rhymed or alternately rhymed; blank verse; stress metre (my own exploration and eventual abandonment of 4-stress lines); narrative poems; epic; and dramatic verse (my verse plays, *The Warlords* Parts 1 and 2, *The Tragedy of Prince Tudor, Ovid Banished* and *The Rise of Oliver Cromwell*).

In traditional poetry there are perennial tensions between Romantic image and neo-Augustan Movement statement; between solitary-mystic-spiritual Romantic and rational-social Augustan outlooks. I have tried to combine the Romantic and classical approaches in a style I have called the Neo-Baroque, which unites sense and spirit, the social and the individual, feeling and thinking. It is important for a traditional poet to reflect a sense of what has traditionally been thought of as the metaphysical in creation. No great poetry can be written by atheists who have an exclusively social view of the world because it fails to reflect the beauty of the cosmos. An image of the true poet can be found in the Middle English poem, 'Pearl'. In a late 14th-century illustration, the 'Pearl' poet stands on one side of a river and sees his dead daughter (the pearl without price) on the far bank clothed in light. He communicates with her across the barrier between the mundane and spiritual realms. The swirling water that separates him from the beyond is full of fish, the images of his poems. The true poet is in constant touch with the "eternal truth" (Shelley) behind everyday life.

Traditional poetry is the product of Imagination. In his *Biographia Literaria* (1814-17) Coleridge refers to the "esemplastic power of the imagination", "esemplastic" meaning "shaping into One". Imagination – Coleridge's "esemplastic" power – is the intuitive, unitive faculty that sees the Whole behind the parts, the One behind the many. Where reason analyzes and reduces into parts, Imagination puts the parts back together into a Whole and takes us to the hidden metaphysical unity behind multiplicity. Fancy, by contrast, is rational and decorative. A simile within a secular humanist poem in which one "part" of the Whole is compared to another "part" of the Whole is an example of such decorative fancy. Imagination is the capacity to image in a creative, Whole-seeking way, and in doing so to perceive the Oneness of the universe. Shelley, in his *A Defence of Poetry* (1821), defines poetry as "the expression of the imagination" in vitally metaphorical language whose harmony excites. Poetry therefore "lifts the veil from the hidden beauty of the world".

Modern irregular new-way verse has lost the intuitive, unitive vision that can soar to the Whole and has settled for existing in confusion among the parts in the world of the self. The new way is lost among the many phenomena of multiplicity and ugliness and is unable to relate them to the One. And the loss of this esemplastic faculty is accompanied by a loss of feeling in poetry. The highest feeling is where the One is glimpsed, the "unknown modes of being" of Wordsworth's *Prelude*. Feeling of a high order can be found in Keats' odes, Shelley's 'Adonais' about the death of Keats and Tennyson's *In Memoriam* but not in the impersonality of Modernist work, except very obliquely – when emotion is invested exclusively in images as in Eliot's hyacinth girl – and not in the cool, rational statements that are Movement poems. Modernism and the Movement both hold emotions and feelings at a distance. The new-way verse is even more pallid in its emotion. I have tried to restore emotions and feelings in my poetry (for example in *The Gates of Hell*, 1969-72).

Since Tennyson poets have sought for a modern colloquial idiom. My fusion of Romanticism and classicism through esemplastic imagination and its focus on history and tradition has attempted to blend image and statement, feeling and reason within the same poem. Poetic diction and dead form do not make for vibrant language, but Wordsworth's concern to find a language of the common man, of "a man speaking to men" (*Poetry and Poetic Diction*, 1800), and Eliot's concern to "purify the language of the tribe" (*Four Quartets*) can be fused in a voice speaking through metre and rhyme and moving in and out of images to create a new approach to the Oneness behind the many phenomena in the universe, to approach (as Wordsworth did) the "Wisdom and Spirit of the universe". The colloquialness of the new-way verse does not justify the banality of much of its language, which is not purified by the constraints of metre and rhyme.

I am a poet who seeks to reflect Truth in all its layers in my poetry. I am open to insights into the metaphysical Whole as well as social truths; and to a mystical awareness of the way the universe has been created and of the way human beings relate to it. Human beings' consciousness has always been held to be superior to that of the animals – the animalistic, shamanic Hughes reversed this when he gave equivalence to a thrush, Mozart and a shark in one of his poems – and Nature poems should be about the place man occupies in the metaphysical universe. Artists are of two kinds: Apollonians, who are makers of art and follow Apollo, god of art and the divine Light; and Dionysians, who are possessed by a dark raw energy, like van Gogh; Lawrence; and Hughes, who wrote Dionysian, neo-Blakeian works about tiger-like jaguars and lambs. I am an Apollonian in my poetic approach, and see the consciousness of man aspiring to visionary heights and the mystical perception of the One. The tradition of the Whole, which metaphysics passed on in philosophy and which poets absorbed when our civilization was healthier and its branches were filled with metaphysical sap, is an important subject in the poetry of any Universalist. As Eliot pointed out in 'Tradition and the Individual Talent', tradition cannot be inherited, it has to be obtained "by great labour" and it involves the historical sense, a perception not only of "the pastness of the past, but of its presence" and "a feeling for the whole of the literature of Europe and Homer".

I am a poet who writes in verse partly to reflect on life, to make statements (which draw on all disciplines), of images of the One, of Truth, in specific places and situations and therefore to instruct – there is a semi-didactic purpose in Universalism; and partly to delight and please. (Horace in his *Ars Poetica* wrote that a poet should instruct or please or both: "Poets aim at giving profit or delight, or at combining the giving of pleasure with some useful precepts for life.") I am a poet who uses the esemplastic power of the Imagination to reach – and teach – my perception of the One and of its embodiment in historical and traditional scenes, and I use traditional versification – metre, rhyme and blank verse – to make this vision readily accessible.

Contrary to the disparaging views of new-way critics, it is the vision of the One that needs to be defended in our secular-humanist, declining time in which most poems are like brittle leaves which are not nourished by the metaphysical sap of the One that once unified our culture. The defence of traditional poetic method has to be fought partly at the philosophical, mystical level. The One still presses into some poets, and I certainly aim to keep it alive in my writing – and I sometimes think that I am doing so on my own. The new-way versifiers of sapless, rhymeless, metreless doodle-cartoons want a reformation of the public taste so that their sapless works will be better appreciated. In other words saplessness, metrelessness and rhymelessness are to become the norm along with multiplicity, ugliness and Onelessness. I say there has already been a huge decline in taste – and in our culture – which has allowed the debased forms of the new-way verse to be elevated to a position of superiority over traditional poetry and to enter newspapers, poetry magazines and journals as the superior successor to traditional versification. What a con. The tree has dried up, the branches of our culture are desiccated, the leaves are sere and lifeless – and are now being promoted as superior to green, tender leaves. To say it is to poke a hornets' nest (or puff smoke into it) but new-way verse is accelerating the decay in our culture.

The secularization of the 600-year-old metaphysical poetic tradition by critics, universities, Arts Council bureaucrats and recent poets has resulted in Shakespeare, Donne, Milton, Wordsworth, Keats and other poets of the tradition losing their metaphysical meaning and becoming literary tourist sites or a literary theme-park – a counterpart in literature to the recent secularization of sacred stones (pyramids, cathedrals, temples and mosques) that once embodied and housed the metaphysical Fire but which are now tourist attractions as I described in *The Fire and the Stones*. By writing secular humanist poems the new-way poets have played a part in the further desecration of this tradition. English poetry already looks like being in terminal decline.

Traditional poetry must be defended against this decline. What is needed is not a reformation of taste but a relearning of the traditional taste by which for 600 years poets from Chaucer to Eliot were appreciated, to arrest the decline and the advance of debased work whose apologists would like to see off works with residual signs of health. In a time when a blank canvas with a hole in it is perceived as being better than a Constable or a Gainsborough and a cacophonous symphony is felt to be better than Mozart or Beethoven, it is vital that the techniques and attitudes behind the unhistorical doodle-verse should not be allowed to dismiss epics, lyrics, sonnets and verse plays rooted in the tradition of the last 600 years as "old-way" and not worthy of consideration by the public.

I have drawn a distinction between verse and poetry. Not all verse (i.e. metrical patterns of sound and language with rhyme heightening their effectiveness) is poetry. Poetry has an indefinable something that transcends verse – a pressure of intensity, a soaring into the One, a glint of Truth. The new-way is struggling to be verse. It lacks a vision of the universe, a sense of the metaphysical, and seeks to redefine verse as patterns of loose cadences of free verse. It is not poetry. The continuation of poetry in the 21st century requires a rejection of debased taste and a return to the traditional poetic method defended by Sir Philip Sidney, Wordsworth and Shelley and to the taste by which it is relished.

3-4 June 1999; revised 27 October 2005

NOTES AND REFERENCES

EB refers to entries in *The Encyclopaedia Britannica* (15th edition).

Acknowledgments
1. *Letters of Ted Hughes*, sel. and ed. by Christopher Reid, pp. 663-8, letter to Nicholas Hagger dated 19 March 1994.

Prologue: The Fundamental Theme of World Literature
1. Kathleen Raine, *Defending Ancient Springs*, pp.121-2.
2. Christopher New, *Philosophy of Literature*, pp. 18, 36.
3. *Philosophy of Literature*, ed. by Eileen John and Dominic McIver Lopes, p.xii.

PART ONE
The Light and the Shadow: The Fundamental Theme's
Metaphysical and Secular Traditions
1. The Early Literature of the Ancient World
1. Ward Rutherford, *Shamanism*, p.11. Samuel Noah Kramer, *The Sumerians, Their History, Culture and Character*: "It is reasonably certain that the first settlers in Sumer were not Sumerians. The pertinent evidence derives not from archaeological or anthropological sources, which are rather ambiguous and inconclusive on this matter, but from linguistics." Quoted in Christian O'Brien, *The Megalithic Odyssey*, p.134.
2. *EB*, 11.1009; E.O. James, *The Ancient Gods*, p.79; S.H. Hooke, *Middle Eastern Mythology*, pp.39-41. The Akkadian version of this poem, 'The Descent of Ishtar to the Nether World', can be found in Mircea Eliade's *From Primitives to Zen*, pp.321-5.
3. James, *op. cit.*, p.69; O'Brien, *The Megalithic Odyssey*, p.142.
4. O'Brien, *The Megalithic Odyssey*, p.117.
5. Translated by O'Brien in *The Megalithic Odyssey*, p.115 and in *The Genius of the Few*, pp.52-3.
6. O'Brien, *The Genius of the Few*, pp.168-9.
7. Leon Stover and Bruce Kraig, *Stonehenge, the Indo-European Heritage*, p.68.

8. *Myths from Mesopotamia*, ed. and trans. by Stephanie Dalley, p.41.
9. *The Epic of Gilgamesh*, trans. by Andrew George, p.xxxi.
10. *The Epic of Gilgamesh*, trans. by Andrew George, p.xxxvii.
11. *The Epic of Gilgamesh*, trans. by Andrew George, p.xvi.
12. *Gilgamesh, Old Babylonian Version*, tablet X. Translated differently in *Myths from Mesopotamia*, ed. and trans. by Dalley, p.150.
13. *The Epic of Gilgamesh*, trans. by Andrew George, p.100.
14. *The Epic of Gilgamesh*, trans. by Andrew George, p.123.
15. *The Epic of Gilgamesh*, trans. by Andrew George, p.li.
16. This poem is translated by Kramer in *The Sumerians,* and in Eliade, *op. cit.*, p.24.
17. Hooke, *op. cit.*, p.38.
18. *The Great Hymn to Shamash*, sections 149-50, 174-7, trans. by W.G. Lambert in *Babylonian Wisdom Literature*, p.127ff, quoted in Eliade, *op. cit.*, p.276. See also G. Contenau, *Everyday Life in Babylon and Assyria*, pp.116-118, 263 and 286.
19. In G. Widengren, *The King and the Tree of Life*, p.45.
20. *The Book of the Dead*, trans. by R.O. Faulkner (who refers to Ra as Re), chapter/spell 17, p.44.
21. The whole burial ritual, including mummification, was expected to last 70 days, and sometimes took a year to complete. See Miroslav Verner, *The Pyramids, The Mystery, Culture and Science of Egypt's Great Monuments*, p.36.
22. Sir E.A. Wallis Budge, *The Book of the Dead (Theban Recension),* pp.3-17: hymn to Ra in papyri of Ani, Qenna, Hu-Nefer and Nekht.
23. Mark Lehner, *The Complete Pyramids*, pp.108, 29.
24. 'Hymn to Aton', line 53, in Eliade, *op. cit.*, pp.28-33.
25. 'Hymn to Aton', lines 94-8, in Eliade, *op. cit.*, pp.28-33.
26. For *rta* as cosmic order, see Jeanine Miller, *The Vision of Cosmic Order in the Vedas*, pp.13-28, 231, 241.
27. Jan Gonda, *The Vision of the Vedic Poets*, p.272.
28. Quoted in Champion and Short, *Readings from World Religions*, p.27.
29. See Eliade, *op. cit.*, pp.248-51.
30. *EB*, 8.910-11.
31. Quoted in Champion and Short, *op. cit.*, p.183, and in Raymond

van Over, *Eastern Mysticism*, pp.245-6.

32. See the *Buddhacarita*, ("Acts of the Buddha") by the 1st-century-AD Indian poet Asvaghosa; from Tibetan MS translated in *The Buddhist Scriptures*, trans. by Edward Conze, p.50.
33. Champion and Short, *op. cit.*, pp.156-7.
34. Quoted in *The Wisdom of China and India*, ed. by Lin Yutang, p.353.
35. *The Wisdom of China and India*, ed. by Yutang, pp.525-8.
36. Van Over, *op. cit.*, p.300.
37. In Champion and Short, *op. cit.*, pp.149-52.
38. For Wen Wang, see *EB*, V.281. See also James Legge in his introduction to the *I Ching*, p.6.
39. Quotations from the *Tao Te Ching* are taken from Wing-Tsit Chan's translation, *The Way of Lao-Tzu*. Variant readings are from Robert B. Blakney's translation.
40. See W.T. De Bary, *Sources of Chinese Tradition*, pp.70-5. In Eliade, *op. cit.*, p.604.
41. *EB*, 1.12.
42. On the stele of Hammurabi in the Louvre the king is represented as receiving a collection of laws known as the Code of Hammurabi from Shamash. Bas-relief from Sousa, 18th century BC. See *EB*, 11.1002.
43. *EB*, X.786. See also E.O. James, *op. cit.*, p.217.
44. Leo Schaya, *The Universal Meaning of the Kabbalah,* pp.362-4.
45. *EB*, 19.1176.

2. The Literature of the Classical World

1. Marija Gimbutas, *The Civilization of the Goddess, The World of Old Europe*, pp.372-3.
2. John Ferguson, *An Illustrated Encyclopaedia of Mysticism and the Mystery Religions*, p.53. For the *telesterion* as Underworld, see Walter Burkert, *Greek Religion*, p.287.
3. Ferguson, *op. cit.*, p.53.
4. The bull with the "rosette" is in the National Museum, Athens. For an illustration, See Sinclair Hood, *The Arts in Prehistoric Greece*, p.163.
5. Ferguson, *op. cit.*, p.137.

6. According to the scholar Wilamowitz (Emmo Friedrich Richard Ulrich Von Wilamowitz-Möllendorff) in *Die Ilias und Homer*, Berlin, 1916. Eratosthenes, in his lost *Chronographiai* (c.220 BC), dated the Fall of Troy to 1183BC, as we know from surviving fragments of ancient chronography.
7. *EB*, see IX.8 for Achaeans/*Ahhiyawa* as Sea Peoples and *EB*, I.56 for identification of the Achaeans with the Mycenaeans. See also *EB*, I.819.
8. T.A. Sinclair, *A History of Classical Greek Literature*, p.19.
9. Xenophanes of Colophon, Fragment. 23-5 (170-2), in G.S. Kirk, J.E. Raven and M. Schofield (eds.), *The Presocratic Philosophers*, pp.169-70.
10. C.M. Bowra, *Tradition and Design in the Iliad*, pp.17-21.
11. Peter, Levi, *The Pelican History of Greek Literature*, p.38.
12. *The Odes of Pindar*, trans. by C.M. Bowra, p.xvi.
13. *The Odes of Pindar*, trans. by Geoffrey S. Conway, p.144.
14. Clement, *Stromateis*, v109, 1 and Simplicius, *Commentary on Aristotle's Physics*, 23.11, 23.20; quoted in Kirk, Raven and Schofield, *op. cit.*, p.169; and in Robin Waterfield, *The First Philosophers: The Presocratics and Sophists*, p.28.
15. Simplicius, *op. cit.*, 22.26-23.20; quoted in Jonathan Barnes, *Early Greek Philosophy*, pp.43-4.
16. Heracleitus, *On the Universe*, in Hypocrates, trans. by W.H.S. Jones, Loeb Classical Library, vol. IV, p.47; Kirk, Raven and Schofield, *op. cit.*, p.198; Long, ed. *The Cambridge Companion to Early Greek Philosophy*, p.99.
17. Charles H. Khan, *The Art and Thought of Heraclitus*, pp.128, 28-43 and 248ff.
18. Plato, *Cratylus*, 401d, 411b, 436e, 440. Also *Philebus*, 43a; *Symposium*, 207d; *Theaetetus*, 160d, 177c, 179d, 181d, 183a. Quoted by Kirk, Raven and Schofield, *op. cit.*, p.186.
19. Heracleitus, *op. cit.*, p483.
20. Waterfield, *op. cit.*, p.53-5. For space as a plenum, see David Bohm, *Wholeness and the Implicate Order*, p.191.
21. Long, *op. cit.*, p.119.
22. Long, *op. cit.*, pp.125-7. Also, Kirk, Raven and Schofield, *op. cit.*, pp.268, 277.

23. Long, *op. cit.*, pp.126-7.

24. Kirk, Raven and Schofield, *op. cit.*, p.191.

25. Quoted in Walter Blair, *The History of World Literature*, p.45.

26. Plato, *Sophist*, 242d.

27. Plato, *Republic*, VII, 540.

28. Plato, *Republic*, VII, 515a, 532b.

29. Plutarch, *On the Soul*, quoted in Stobaues IV, translated by George Mylonas in *Eleusis and the Eleusinian Mysteries*; Edwin Hatch, *Greek Influence*, pp.295-8, quoted in Goblet D'Alviella, *The Mysteries of Eleusis*, p.122, note 30.

30. Plato, *Selected Myths*, ed. by Catalin Partenie, p.76

31. Plato, *Selected Myths*, *op. cit.*, p.143, note on 250c.

32. Plato, *Republic*, VII, 514-5. A "subterranean cavern" is mentioned in the first three lines of Book VII.

33. Raphael, *Initiation into the Philosophy of Plato*, p.71.

34. Plato, *The Collected Dialogues*, ed. by Edith Hamilton and Huntington Cairns, p.51.

35. Plato, *Selected Myths*, ed. Partenie, *op. cit.*, pp.8ff, 40ff, 57ff and 69ff.

36. Quoted in Peter Levi, *The Pelican History of Greek Literature*, p.384.

37. *EB*, 15.1085.

38. *EB*, III.984.

39. *EB*, 15.1061.

40. *The Oxford Classical Dictionary*, p.123.

41. *EB*, 15.1065-6. *The Oxford Classical Dictionary*, p.1311.

42. *EB*, 15.1063.

43. *The Oxford Companion to Classical Literature*, p.178.

44. J. Wight Duff, *A Literary History of Rome*, p.39.

45. *EB*, 15.1061; Jocelyn Godwin, *Mystery Religions in the Ancient World*, p.38.

46. Denis Feeney, *Literature and Religion at Rome*, p.100.

47. J.W. Mackail, *Latin Literature*, p.30.

48. Feeney, *op. cit.*, p.16.

49. Apuleius, *Apologia* ("Defence"), 10. H. E. Butler and A. S. Owen, *Apulei Apologia*, Oxford, 1914 http://www.amazon.co.uk/s/ref=nb_sb_noss?url=search-alias%3Daps&field-

keywords=Apulei+Apologia%2C+Oxford%2C+1914&x=0&y=0

50. Quoted in Feeney, *op. cit.*, p.20.

51. *EB*, 15.1121.

52. Virgil, *The Eclogues*, trans. by Guy Lee, pp.56-7.

53. Feeney, *op. cit.*, pp.111-2.

54. Feeney, *op. cit.*, pp.133-4.

55. For the translation 'Song of the Age', see Peter Levi, *Horace: A Life*, p.4.

56. M. Cary, *A History of Rome*, p.491; *The Oxford Classical Dictionary*, p.1378.

57. Quoted in Feeney, *op. cit.*, p.32.

58. Feeney, *op. cit.*, p.31.

59. Feeney, *op. cit.*, p.36.

60. Feeney, *op. cit.*, pp.113-4.

61. H.A. Rose, *A Handbook of Latin Literature*, p.291.

62. Quoted in Duff, *op. cit.*, p.441.

63. Ovid, *Metamorphoses*, trans. with an introduction by Mary M. Innes, pp.11-12.

64. For a full account, see Hagger, *The Light of Civilization*, pp.116-7.

65. See Hagger, *The Light of Civilization*, pp.393-8 for full details.

66. Apuleius, *The Golden Ass*, p.286.

67. For a full treatment of their sayings, see *The Sayings of the Desert Fathers*, trans. by Sister Benedicta Ward.

68. For a full account of Pope Gregory the Great's writings on the Light, see Hagger, *The Light of Civilization*, pp.133-6.

69. Plato's *Selected Myths*, ed. Partenie, p.xix.

3. The Literature of the Middle Ages

1. The term "middle times" (*media tempestas*) appeared in Latin in 1469: see Martin Albrow, *The Global Age: State and Society Beyond Modernity*, p.205. *Medium aevum* is first recorded in the 16th century: see Lester K. Little and Barbara H. Rosenwein (eds.), *Debating the Middle Ages: Issues and Readings*, p.396.

2. Caesar Baronius, *Annales Ecclesiastici*, vol. X, Roma, 1602, p.647; and John D. Dwyer, *Church History: Twenty Centuries of Catholic Christianity*, p.155.

3. Theodor Mommsen, *Petrarch's Conception of the "Dark Ages"*,

http://jstor.org/stable/2856364.

4. R.K. Gordon, *Anglo-Saxon Poetry*, p.1.
5. Sam Newton, *The Origins of Beowulf and the Pre-Viking Kingdom of East Anglia*, ch.6, 'East Anglia and the Making of Beowulf'.
6. Referred to as "Matière de Bretagne" by Jehan Bodel, in *La Chanson Des Saisnes*, c.1210.
7. See Hagger, *The Light of Civilization*, pp.139-142 and Notes for the sources of all these passages. The "eyewitness" account of Hildegard is quoted in Ferguson, *op. cit.*, p.77.
8. *The Letters of Abelard and Heloise*, trans. by Betty Radice, p.89.
9. *Everyman With Other Interludes, Including Eight Miracle Plays*, p.xv: "The earliest miracle-plays that we can trace in the town cycles date back to the early years of Edward III."
10. For quotations and further details see Hagger, *The Light of Civilization*, pp.156-60.
11. Chaucer, *The Canterbury Tales*, trans. Nevill Coghill, pp.507-8.
12. The *Koran*, trans. by N.J. Dawood, pp.221-2.
13. Quoted in Walter T. Stace, *The Teachings of the Mystics*, pp.206-7.
14. For further details and sources of the Islamic and Sufi approach to the metaphysical aspect of the fundamental theme, see Hagger, *The Light of Civilization*, pp.256-73.
15. For further details and sources of Indian Buddhist literature, see Hagger, *The Light of Civilization*, pp.311-6 and 292-3.
16. One of the seven treatises in *Tibetan Yoga and Secret Doctrines*, ed. by W.Y. Evans-Wentz.
17. For further details and sources of Tibetan Buddhist Tantric texts, see Hagger, *The Light of Civilization*, pp.343-50.
18. For further details and sources of the later Taoist texts, see Hagger, *The Light of Civilization*, pp.336-41.
19. For further details and sources for Japanese Zen and Shinto texts, see Hagger, *The Light of Civilization*, pp.319-324.

4. The Literature of the Renaissance

1. Hagger, *The Fire and the Stones*, revised and updated as *The Light of Civilization* and *The Rise and Fall of Civilizations*.
2. *The Letters of Marsilio Ficino*, vol.1, pp.37-8.
3. *The Letters of Marsilio Ficino*, vol.1, pp.80-1.

4. *The Letters of Marsilio Ficino*, vol.5, p.37.

5. *The Letters of Marsilio Ficino*, vol.7, p.63.

6. Arthur Farndell, *When Philosophers Rule*, p.33.

7. 'Lecture on Machiavelli's *The Prince*', http://records.viu.ca/~ johnstoi/introser/machiavelli.htm. Also 'Machiavelli's Prince: Political Science or Political Satire?' in *Problems in European Civilization* series, *Machiavelli: Cynic, Patriot, or Political Scientist?* ed. De Lamar Jensen.

8. 'Machiavelli: the Republican Citizen and Author of *The Prince*' in *The English Historical Review* 76:218ff. See http://www.unt.edu /honors/eaglefeather/2007_Issue/kniatt8.shtml.

9. Rousseau, *Social Contract*, bk 3, n.23. See http://www.consti-tution.org/jjr/socon_03.htm#23.

10. *EB*, 12.395.

11. Desiderius Erasmus, *Praise of Folly*, p.133.

12. Sir Thomas More, *Utopia*, ed. by Harold Osborne, pp.xxv, xxvi.

13. Legouis and Cazamian, *A History of English Literature*, p.281.

14. The probable chronological order in which Shakespeare's plays were performed is: *Two Gentlemen of Verona; Taming of the Shrew; Henry VI, part 1; Henry VI, part 3; Titus Andronicus; Henry VI, part 2; Richard III; The Comedy of Errors; Love's Labours Lost; A Midsummer Night's Dream; Romeo and Juliet; Richard II; King John; The Merchant of Venice; Henry IV, part 1; The Merry Wives of Windsor; Henry IV, part 2; Much Ado About Nothing; Henry V; Julius Caesar; As You Like It; Hamlet; Twelfth Night; Troilus and Cressida; Measure for Measure; Othello; All's Well That Ends Well; Timon of Athens; The Tragedy of King Lear; Macbeth; Anthony and Cleopatra; Pericles, Prince of Tyre; Coriolanus; Winter's Tale; Cymbeline; The Tempest;* and *Henry VIII*.

15. Castello Orsini-Odelscalsci, a five-towered fortress built in the 15th century. The Dramatis Personae for *The White Devil* list the Duke of Brachiano as "otherwise Paulo Giordano Ursini". Ursini is now spelt Orsini. Hagger visited the castle in 2000.

5. The Literature of the Baroque

1. Samuel Johnson, *Lives of the English Poets*, vol.1, p.11.

2. Johnson, *op. cit.*, p.11.
3. *Essays of John Dryden,* ed. W.P. Ker, vol.2, p.19.
4. Undated letter to Dr. Arthur Johnston. See http://www.poetryfoundation.org/bio/william-drummond-of-hawthornden.
5. The quotations from Donne, George Herbert, Lord Herbert of Cherbury, Vaughan, Crashaw, Quarles, Traherne and Marvell can be found in *The Metaphysical Poets*, ed. by Gardner. See also *John Donne*, ed. by John Hayward, *The Poems of George Herbert*, ed. by Arthur Waugh and Vaughan, *Sacred Poems*. The quotations from *Centuries of Meditation* are in F.C. Happold, *Mysticism, a Study and an Anthology*.
6. *Donne's Sermons, Selected Passages with an Essay*, ed. by L.P. Smith, no. 58.
7. Smith, *op. cit.,* nos. 71, 111, 134, 140.
8. Donne, *Devotions upon Emergent Occasions*, Meditation XVII, ed. by John Sparrow, pp.97-8.
9. Frank J. Warnke, *European Metaphysical Poetry*, pp.1, 3-4.
10. Gilbert Highet, *The Classical Tradition*, p.289.
11. John Dryden, *A Selection*, ed. by John Conaghan, p.93.
12. See http://www.poemhunter.com/poem/veni-creator-spiritus/
13. John Dryden, *Dramatic Poesy and Other Essays*, p.197.
14. T.S. Eliot, 'The Metaphysical Poets', in T.S. Eliot *Selected Prose*, ed. by John Hayward, p.120.

6. Neoclassical Literature
1. T.S. Eliot, *Selected Essays*, ed. by John Hayward, p.117.
2. See http://www.bartleby.com/220/0912.html.
3. Johnson, 'Life of Swift' in *Lives of the Poets*, vol.2, p.248.
4. For confirmation of this view, see P.N. Furbank, 'Misreading Gulliver' in the *Times Literary Supplement* of 12 November 2010.
5. Letter to Alexander Pope, September 29, 1725 from *The Correspondence of Jonathan Swift*, ed. by Harold Williams; see http://www.ourcivilisation.com/smartboard/shop/swift/letters/chap2.htm .
6. See Paul Nettl, *Mozart and Masonry*, p.10 for Goethe as Abaris.

7. Romantic Literature

1. Samuel Taylor Coleridge, Letter to Thomas Poole, 23 March 1801. In *The Collected Letters of Samuel Taylor Coleridge* ed. by Earl Leslie Griggs, Vol. 2, p.709.
2. *Letters of Samuel Taylor Coleridge*, ed. by Ernest Hartley Coleridge, I, 352.
3. William Blake, 'A Vision of the Last Judgment'.
4. Samuel Taylor Coleridge, *Biographia Literaria*, ch.XIII, ed. by J. Shawcross, I, 202.
5. William Shakespeare, *A Midsummer Night's Dream*, Act V, scene 1, 12-17 and 23-27.
6. Blake, 'A Vision of the Last Judgment'.
7. Blake, 'Marginalia to Sir Joshua Reynolds' Discourses'.
8. Blake, 'Annotations to "Poems" by William Wordsworth'.
9. Wordsworth, *The Prelude or Growth of a Poet's Mind*, II, 255-60.
10. Wordsworth, *The Prelude*, XIV, 190-2.
11. Coleridge, *Biographia Literaria*, ch.13, p.356, published 1854, original from the University of Michigan, digitized 23 November 2005. http://books.google.co.uk/books?id=5xg5G-4ai3oC&pg=PA356&dq=esemplastic+power+of+the+imagination
12. See http://www.english.uga.edu/~nhilton/Blake/blaketxt1/Letters/51.htm.
13. *The Letters of Lord Byron*, sel. and ed. by R.G. Howarth, p.viii.
14. *Byron, A Selection* by A.S.B. Glover, p.15.
15. *Letters of William and Dorothy Wordsworth: The Later Years*, ed. by E de Selincourt, II, 640; Coleridge, *Biographia Epistolaris*, ed. by A. Turnbull, p.169; and *The Letters of John Keats*, ed. by N. Buxton Forman, p.405.

8. Victorian Literature

1. Harold Nicholson, *Tennyson*, p.27.
2. See http://www.authorama.com/varieties-of-religious-experience-ii-3.html.
3. See http://www.buckingham.ac.uk/english/schools/poetry-bank/ulysses.html; http://www.rlf.org.uk/fellowshipscheme/writing/quotationsandreferences/setquotes.cfm; and http://ficml.org/jemimap/voy/colony/Ulysses.html.

4. See http://famouspoetsandpoems.com/poets/robert_browning/poems/4925.
5. Matthew Arnold, *Culture & Anarchy*, ed. by J. Dover Wilson, p.45.
6. Arnold, *op. cit.*, p.71.
7. See Yukio Irie, *Emerson and Quakerism*, for Emerson's knowledge of the Light.
8. See http://books.google.co.uk/books?id=lXjF7JnHQoIC&pg=PR8&lpg=PR8&dq=van+gogh++i+am+painting+the+infinite&source=bl&ots=-0tDuTBAq2&sig=2DokfHg-R1pMFeNru61ajdmDf2A&hl=en&ei=BtAhTYrsHtOxhQeimaC3Dg&sa=X&oi=book_result&ct=result&resnum=3&ved=0CCYQ6AEwAg#v=onepage&q=van%20gogh%20%20i%20am%20painting%20the%20infinite&f=false.
9. *The Letters of Vincent van Gogh*, ed. and introduced by Mark Roskill.

9. Modernist Literature

1. Humphrey Carpenter, *A Serious Character, The Life of Ezra Pound*, p.221.
2. Carpenter, *op. cit.*, p.221.
3. Ezra Pound, 'The Later Yeats', reprinted from *Poetry*, IV, 11 (May 1914); in *Literary Essays of Ezra Pound*, ed. by T.S. Eliot, p.378.
4. *EB*, 6.724.
5. See http://members.chello.nl/~a.vanarum8/EliotProject/Eliot_life.htm.
6. *The Waste Land: A Facsimile and Transcript of the Original Drafts, Including the Annotations of Ezra Pound,* ed. by Valerie Eliot
7. I first heard this possibility in a Professor-of-Poetry lecture by Christopher Ricks in Oxford on 15 May 2006.
8. T.S. Eliot, *Selected Prose*, ed. by John Hayward, p.111.
9. Reprinted in Ezra Pound, *Selected Prose*, 1909-1965.
10. See http://www.poetryfoundation.org/bio/ezra-pound.
11. 'A Retrospect', in *Literary Essays of Ezra Pound*, ed. by T.S. Eliot, p.4.
12. T.S. Eliot, *The Varieties of Metaphysical Poetry*, p.82.
13. T.S. Eliot, *Selected Prose*, ed. John Hayward, pp.107-8. Also see http://www.britannica.com/nobelprize/article-2088.

14. James Joyce, *Stephen Hero*, p.186.
15. James Joyce, *A Portrait of the Artist as a Young Man*, p.213.
16. James Joyce, *Stephen Hero*, pp.188.
17. James Joyce, *A Portrait of the Artist as a Young Man*, p.172.
18. James Joyce, *A Portrait of the Artist as a Young Man*, p.213.
19. Carpenter, *op. cit.,* p.192.

10. Literature in the 20th-Century Anarchy
1. W.H. Auden, 'The Quest Hero', *Texas Quarterly* 4 (1961), pp.81-93.
2. John Haffenden, *William Empson, Vol.1: Among the Mandarins,* pp.287-355.
3. Martin Esslin, *The Theatre of the Absurd*, p.5.
4. See Hagger, *The Fire and the Stones*, which was updated as *The Light of Civilization* and *The Rise and Fall of Civilizations.*
5. See http://www.nytimes.com/2005/06/26/books/chapters/0626-1st-lowell.html.

PART TWO
Chiaroscuro: Universalism's Reconciliation and Synthesis of the Metaphysical and Secular Traditions and Revival of the Fundamental Theme
1. Universalism's Reconciliation of the Two Traditions and Sensibilities
1. Ezra Pound, 'A Retrospect' (1918), in *Literary Essays of Ezra Pound*, ed. by T.S. Eliot, pp.3-4, 9.
2. T.S. Eliot, 'Hamlet' (1919), in *Selected Prose*, ed. by John Hayward, pp.107-8.
3. T.S. Eliot, *Selected Prose*, ed. by John Hayward, p.29.
4. T.S. Eliot, *The Use of Poetry and the Use of Criticism*, p.85.
5. T.S. Eliot, *The Varieties of Metaphysical Poetry*, p.55.
6. T.S. Eliot, *The Varieties of Metaphysical Poetry*, p.252.
7. T.S. Eliot, *Notes Towards the Definition of Culture*, p.26.

2. A Defence of Universalist Poetry
1. *Classical Literary Criticism*, trans. by T.S. Dorsch, p.31.
2. *Classical Literary Criticism*, *op. cit.*, p.80.

3. *Classical Literary Criticism, op. cit.*, p.90.
4. *Classical Literary Criticism, op. cit.*, p.90.
5. *Classical Literary Criticism, op. cit.*, p.101.
6. T.S. Eliot, *The Use of Poetry and the Use of Criticism*, p.51.
7. R.S. Peterson, *Imitation and Praise in Ben Jonson's Poems*.
8. John Dryden, *Dramatic Poesy and Other Essays*, p.54.
9. Yvor Winters, *In Defense of Reason*, p.11.
10. Plato, *Ion*, 533e-534b, Jowett's translation, quoted in Herbert Read, *Selected Writings*, pp.252-3.
11. T.S. Eliot, *The Use of Poetry and the Use of Criticism*, pp.68-9.
12. Nicholas Hagger, *The New Philosophy of Universalism*.
13. *The Letters of Percy Bysshe Shelley*, ed. by F.L. Jones, vol. 2, no. 606, p.263.
14. Reproduced in Appendix I of W.A. Camps, *An Introduction to Virgil's Aeneid*, pp.115-120.
15. Shelley, *A Defence of Poetry*, in *English Critical Essays of the XIX Century*, sel. and ed. by Edmund D. Jones, p.157.
16. Keats, letter to his brothers, 22 December 1871; in Lord Houghton, *Life and Letters of John Keats*, p.62.
17. Carlyle, *The Hero as Poet*, in *English Critical Essays of the XIX Century*, sel. and ed. by Edmund D. Jones, pp.286-7.
18. Allen Tate, Foreword to Herbert Read, *Selected Writings* (1958), p.8.
19. Herbert Read, *Selected Writings*, 'Surrealism and the Romantic Principle', p.262.
20. Herbert Read, *Reason and Romanticism* (1926), 'Poetic Diction'.
21. Herbert Read, 'Form in Modern Poetry' (1932); quoted in T.S. Eliot, *The Use of Poetry and the Use of Criticism*, p.82.
22. T.S. Eliot, *The Use of Poetry and the Use of Criticism*, p.83.
23. T.S. Eliot, *Selected Prose*, ed. by John Hayward, '"Romantic" and "Classic"', pp.31-2.
24. Kathleen Raine, *Defending Ancient Springs*, pp.107-8.
25. Kathleen Raine, *Defending Ancient Springs*, p.117.
26. W. Jackson Bate, *From Classic to Romantic*, p.vii.
27. Nicholas Hagger, *Collected Poems*, Appendix, pp.866-7.
28. See Evelyn Underhill, *Mysticism*.
29. Nicholas Hagger, *Collected Poems*, Appendix, pp.853-9.

30. For the intensity of the inspiration, see *Overlord*, Appendix, pp.938-9.
31. See *Overlord*, Appendix, pp.935-6 for my visit to Ezra Pound.
32. Coleridge, letter to Joseph Cottle, early April 1797 in *The Collected Letters of Samuel Taylor Coleridge*, ed. Earl Leslie Griggs, vol. 1, pp.320-1, 1956. See http://www.todayinsci.com /C/Coleridge_Samuel/ColeridgeSamuel-Quotations.htm.
33. Kathleen Raine, *Defending Ancient Springs*, pp.121-2.
34. Coleridge, *Biographia Literaria*, ch.13, p.356, published 1854, original from the University of Michigan, digitized 23 November 2005. http://books.google.co.uk/books?id=5xg5G-4ai3oC&pg=P A356&dq=esemplastic+power+of+the+imagination
35. T.S. Eliot, 'Reflections on *Vers libre*' (1917), in T.S. Eliot, *Selected Prose*, ed. by John Hayward, p.86.
36. Shelley, *A Defence of Poetry*, in *English Critical Essays of the XIX Century*, sel. and ed. by Edmund D. Jones, p.155.
37. Wordsworth, *The Prelude*, books 1 and 2.

Epilogue: A New Direction for World Literature
1. Kathleen Raine, *Defending Ancient Springs*, pp.121-2.
2. Hagger, *The World Government*, pp.4-5, 16, 39, 42-3; and *The Secret American Dream*, pp.161-200.
3. I am indebted to Christopher Ricks for sending me a first edition of this scarce work.
4. T.S. Eliot, *The Man of Letters and the Future of Europe*, Horizon, 1944.
5. Hagger, *The Fire and the* Stones, reissued as *The Light of Civilization* and *The Rise and Fall of Civilizations*.
6. Hagger, *The Fire and the* Stones, reissued as *The Light of Civilization* and *The Rise and Fall of Civilizations*.
7. Hagger, *The World Government*, pp.169-70; and *The Secret American Dream*, pp.215-8.
8. Hagger, *The Light of Civilization* and *The Rise and Fall of Civilizations*.

Chart on p.353
1. For Hagger's 'Form from Movement Theory: The Origin and

Creation of the Universe', see Hagger, *The New Philosophy of Universalism*, pp.269-273.

Appendix
Close Readings: The Emergence of a Secular Tradition alongside the Quest for Reality in English Literature

1. For the development from the rational, social ego to the universal being, see Nicholas Hagger, 'Preface on the New Baroque Consciousness and the Redefinition of Poetry as Classical Baroque' in *Collected Poems, 1958-2005*, pp.xlv-lxxvi. An earlier version appeared in *Selected Poems, A Metaphysical's Way of Fire*, and a still earlier draft predated this study.
2. This abbreviated version of the original essay was titled *Extracts from 'A Defence of Traditional Poetic Method or: Poking the Hornets' Nest'* in Nicholas Hagger, *Collected Poems, 1959-2005*, p.882.

BIBLIOGRAPHY

Abelard and Heloise, The Letters of, trans. by Betty Radice, Penguin Books, 1974.

Albrow, Martin, *The Global Age: State and Society Beyond Modernity*, Stanford University Press, 1997.

Ancient Egyptian Book of the Dead, The, trans. by R.O. Faulkner, ed. by Carol Andrews, The British Museum Press, 1985.

Apuleius, *The Golden Ass*, trans. by Robert Graves, Penguin, London 1950.

Arnold, Matthew, *Culture and Anarchy*, ed. J. Dover Wilson, Cambridge University Press, 1932/1979.

Barnes, Jonathan, *Early Greek Philosophy*, Penguin Books, London, 2001.

Bate, Walter Jackson, *From Classic to Romantic,* Harper & Row, 1946.

Blair, Walter, *The History of World Literature*, University of Knowledge, 1941.

Bodel, Jean, *La Chanson Des Saisnes*, 2 vols, tome I, text; tome II, notes, glossary and tables, Textes Litteraires Francais, Librarie Droz,1989.

Bohm, David, *Wholeness and the Implicate Order*, Routledge & Kegan Paul, 1980.

Bowra, C.M., *Tradition and Design in the Iliad*, Oxford University Press, 1930/1950.

Buddhist Scriptures, The, trans. by Edward Conze, Penguin, London, 1959.

Budge, Sir E.A. Wallis, *The Book of the Dead (Theban Recension),* Routledge, London, 1899 and 1974.

Burkert, Walter, *Greek Religion*, Wiley-Blackwell, 1987.

Byron, A Selection by A.S.B. Glover, Penguin Books, 1954.

Byron, The Letters of Lord, sel. and ed. by R.G. Howarth, J.M. Dent, 1936.

Camps, W.A., *An Introduction to Virgil's Aeneid*, Oxford University Press, 1969.

Carpenter, Humphrey, *A Serious Character, The Life of Ezra Pound*, Delta, 1988.

Cary, M., *A History of Rome*, Macmillan, 1951.

Champion, S.G., and Short, G., *Readings from World Religions*, Premier Fawcett, USA, 1959.

Chaucer, *The Canterbury Tales*, ed. Nevill Coghill, Penguin Books, 1982.

Classical Literary Criticism, trans. by T.S. Dorsch, Penguin Books, 1965.

Coleridge, Letters of Samuel Taylor, ed. by Ernest Hartley Coleridge, 2 vols., London, 1895/BiblioBazaar, 2009.

Coleridge, Samuel Taylor, *Biographia Epistolaris*, ed. by A. Turnbull, London, 1911.

Coleridge, Samuel Taylor, *Biographia Literaria*, ed. by J. Shawcross, 2 vols., Oxford, 1907.

Coleridge, Samuel Taylor, *The Collected Letters of,* ed. by Earl Leslie Griggs, 2 vols., Oxford University Press, 1956.

Contenau, G., *Everyday Life in Babylon and Assyria*, E. Arnold, UK, 1964.

Correspondence of Jonathan Swift, The, ed. by Harold Williams, 5 vols., Clarendon Press, Oxford, 1963-5.

D'Alviella, Goblet, *The Mysteries of Eleusis*, Aquarian, London, 1981.

De Bary, W.T., *Sources of Chinese Tradition*, Columbia, USA, 1960.

De Lamar Jensen, *Machiavelli: Cynic, Patriot, or Political Scientist? (Problems in European civilization series)*, D.C. Heath and Company, 1960.

De Mourgues, Odette, *Metaphysical, Baroque and Précieux Poetry*, Oxford, 1953.

Donne, John, *Devotions upon Emergent Occasions*, ed. by John Sparrow, Cambridge University Press, 1923.

Donne, John, ed. by John Hayward, Penguin Books, 1978.

Donne's Sermons, selected passages with an essay by Logan Peasall Smith, Oxford, UK, 1919 and 1932.

Dryden, John, *A Selection*, ed. by John Conaghan, Methuen, 1978.

Dryden, John, *Dramatic Poesy and Other Essays*, J.M. Dent, 1950.

Dryden, John, *Essays of John Dryden,* ed. W.P. Ker, 2 vols., Oxford Clarendon Press, 1900.

Duff, J. Wight, *A Literary History of Rome*, London, Ernest Benn, 1963.

Dwyer, John D., *Church History: Twenty Centuries of Catholic*

Christianity, Paulist Press, 1998.

Eliade, Mircea, *From Primitives to Zen*, Collins, London, 1967.

Eliot, T.S., *Notes Towards the Definition of Culture*, Faber and Faber, 1948.

Eliot, T.S., *Selected Essays*, ed. by John Hayward, Penguin Books, 1958.

Eliot, T.S., *Selected Prose*, ed. by John Hayward, Penguin Books, 1953.

Eliot, T.S., *The Man of Letters and the Future of Europe*, Horizon, 1944.

Eliot, T.S., *The Use of Poetry and the Use of Criticism*, Faber and Faber, 1933.

Eliot, T.S., *The Varieties of Metaphysical Poetry*, ed. by Ronald Schuchard, Faber and Faber, 1993.

Empson, William, *The Structure of Complex Words*, Chatto & Windus, 1951.

Empson, William, *Seven Types of Ambiguity*, Chatto & Windus, revised edition, 1953.

English Critical Essays of the XIX Century, sel. and ed. by Edmund D. Jones, Oxford University Press, 1922.

Epic of Gilgamesh, The, trans. by Andrew George, Penguin Classics, 1999.

Erasmus, Desiderius, *Praise of Folly*, trans. by Betty Radice, Penguin Classics, 1971.

Esslin, Martin, *The Theatre of the Absurd*, Anchor Books, 1961.

European Metaphysical Poetry, ed. by Frank J. Warnke, Yale University Press, 1961.

Evans-Wentz, W.Y., ed. by, *Tibetan Yoga and Secret Doctrines*, OUP, London 1958 and 1977.

Everyman With Other Interludes, Including Eight Miracle Plays, J.M. Dent/E.P. Dutton, reprint edition, 1930.

Farndell, Arthur, *When Philosophers Rule*, Shepherd-Walwyn (Publishers) Limited, 2009.

Feeney, Denis, *Literature and Religion at Rome*, Cambridge University Press, 1998.

Ferguson, John, *An Illustrated Encyclopaedia of Mysticism and the Mystery Religions*, Thames & Hudson, London, 1976.

Ficino, The Letters of Marsilio, vols.1-7, Shepherd-Walwyn, 1975-2003.

Gimbutas, Marija, *The Civilization of the Goddess, The World of Old Europe*, HarperSanFrancisco, 1991.

Godwin, Jocelyn, *Mystery Religions in the Ancient World*, Thames and Hudson, London, 1981.

Gonda, Jan, *The Vision of the Vedic Poets*, Mouton, The Hague, 1963.

Gordon, R.K., *Anglo-Saxon Poetry*, J.M. Dent, 1957.

Haffenden, John, *William Empson, Vol.1: Among the Mandarins*, Oxford University Press, 2005.

Hagger, Nicholas, *Collected Poems*, O Books, 2006.

Hagger, Nicholas, *Overlord*, O Books, O Books, 2006.

Hagger, Nicholas, *The Fire and the Stones*, Element, 1991.

Hagger, Nicholas, *The Light of Civilization*, O Books, 2006.

Hagger, Nicholas, *The New Philosophy of Universalism*, 2009.

Hagger, Nicholas, *The Rise and Fall of Civilizations*, O Books, 2008.

Hagger, Nicholas, *The Secret American Dream*, Watkins, 2011.

Hagger, Nicholas, *The Syndicate*, O Books, 2004.

Hagger, Nicholas, *The World Government*, O Books, 2010.

Herbert, The Poems of George, introd. by Arthur Waugh, Oxford University Press, 1907, 1947.

Highet, Gilbert, *The Classical Tradition, Greek and Roman Influences on Western Literature*, Oxford University Press, 1949, 1985.

Hood, Sinclair, *The Arts in Prehistoric Greece*, Penguin, UK, 1978.

Hooke, S.H., *Middle Eastern Mythology*, Pelican, London, 1963.

Hough, Graham, *Image and Experience*, Gerald Duckworth, 1960.

Houghton, Lord, *Life and Letters of John Keats*, J.M. Dent, 1954.

Hughes, Letters of Ted, sel. and ed. by Christopher Reid, Faber and Faber, 2007.

Irie, Yukio, *Emerson and Quakerism*, Kenkyusha, Japan, 1967.

I Ching, trans. by James Legge, Dover Publications, New York, 1963.

James, E.O., *The Ancient Gods*, Weidenfeld and Nicholson, London, 1962.

Johnson, Samuel, *Lives of the English Poets*, 2 vols., London: J.M. Dent, 1950.

Joyce, James, *A Portrait of the Artist as a Young Man*, Penguin Books, 1960.

Joyce, James, *Stephen Hero*, Ace Books, 1961.

Keats, The Letters of John, ed. by M. Buxton Forman, Oxford

University Press, 1935.

Khan, Charles H., *The Art and Thought of Heraclitus*, Cambridge University Press, 1995.

Koran, The, trans. by N.J. Dawood, Penguin, London, 1956.

Kramer, Samuel Noah, *The Sumerians, Their History, Culture and Character*, Chicago, USA, 1963.

Lambert, W.G., *Babylonian Wisdom Literature*, Oxford, UK, 1960.

Lao Tzu, *The Way of Life*, A New Translation of the *Tao Te Ching*, trans. by Robert B. Blakney, New American Library, 1983.

Legouis, Émile and Cazamian, Louis, *A History of English Literature*, J.M. Dent & Sons, 1964.

Lehner, Mark, *The Complete Pyramids*, The American University in Cairo Press/Thames & Hudson, 1997.

Levi, Peter, *Horace: A Life*, Duckworth, 1997.

Levi, Peter, *The Pelican History of Greek Literature*, Penguin Books, 1985.

Little, Lester K. and Rosenwein, Barbara H. (eds.), *Debating the Middle Ages: Issues and Readings*, Wiley-Blackwell, 1998.

Long, A.A., *The Cambridge Companion to Early Greek Philosophy*, Cambridge University Press, 1999.

Mackail, J.W., *Latin Literature*, Collier Books, New York, 1962.

Metaphysical Poets, The, ed. by Helen Gardner, Penguin Books, 1972.

Miller, Jeanine, *The Vision of Cosmic Order in the Vedas*, Routledge & Kegan Paul, London, 1985.

Mommsen, Theodor E., *Petrarch's Conception of the "Dark Ages"*, reprinted from *Speculum*, Vol.17, no 2, 1942, Bobbs Merrill Reprints.

More, Sir Thomas, *Utopia*, ed. Harold Osborne, London University Tutorial Press, n/d, republished by Wordsworth Editions Ltd, 1997.

Myths from Mesopotamia, ed. and trans. by Stephanie Dalley, Oxford University Press, 1989.

Nettl, Paul, *Mozart and Masonry*, Welcome Rain Publishers, 2010.

New, Christopher, *Philosophy of Literature*, Routledge, 1999.

Newton, Sam, *The Origins of Beowulf and the Pre-Viking Kingdom of East Anglia*, D.S. Brewer, 1992.

Nicholson, Harold, *Tennyson*, Anchor Books, Doubleday, 1962.

O'Brien, Christian, *The Genius of the Few, The Story of Those Who

Founded the Garden in Eden, Dianthus Publishing Ltd., 1985.

O'Brien, Christian, *The Megalithic Odyssey*, Turnstone, UK, 1983.

Ovid, *Metamorphoses*, trans. and with an introduction by Mary M. Innes, Penguin Books, 1955.

Oxford Book of English Verse, The, ed. by Christopher Ricks, Oxford University Press, 1999.

Oxford Book of Modern Verse, The, ed. by W.B. Yeats, Oxford University Press, 1936.

Oxford Classical Dictionary, The, 3rd edition, ed. by Simon Hornblower and Antony Spawforth, Oxford University Press, 1996.

Oxford Companion to Classical Literature, The, compiled and ed. by Sir Paul Harvey, Oxford University Press, 1937.

Oxford Guide to Classical Mythology in the Arts, 1300-1990s, The, ed. by Jane Davidson Reid, Oxford University Press, 1993.

Penguin Book of Contemporary British Poetry, The, ed. by Blake Morrison and Andrew Motion, Penguin Books, 1982.

Penguin Book of Contemporary Verse, The, ed. by Kenneth Allott, Penguin Books, 1962.

Peterson, R.S., *Imitation and Praise in Ben Jonson's Poems*, Yale University Press, 1981.

Philosophy of Literature, Contemporary and Classic Readings, An Anthology, ed. by Eileen John and Dominic McIver Lopes, Blackwell Publishing, 2004.

Pindar, The Odes of, trans. by C.M. Bowra, Penguin Classics, 1969.

Pindar, The Odes of, trans. by Geoffrey S. Conway, Everyman's University Library, 1972.

Plato, *Selected Myths*, ed. by Catalin Partenie, Oxford University Press, 2004.

Plato, *The Collected Dialogues*, ed. Edith Hamilton and Huntington Cairns, Princeton University Press, 1961.

Poets of the 1950s, ed. by D.J. Enright, Kenkyusha, Tokyo, 1955.

Pound, Literary Essays of Ezra, ed. by T.S. Eliot, Faber and Faber, 1954.

Pound, Ezra, *Selected Prose*, New Directions, 1973.

Presocratic Philosophers, The, G.S. Kirk, J.E. Raven and M. Schofield (eds.), Cambridge: Cambridge University Press, 1957.

Raphael, *Initiation into the Philosophy of Plato*, Shepheard-Walwyn,

1999.

Read, Herbert, *Form in Modern Poetry*, Sheed and Ward, 1932, new edition Vision Press, 1948, 1986.

Read, Herbert, *Reason and Romanticism*, Faber and Gwyer, 1926.

Read, Herbert, *Selected Writings, Poetry and Criticism*, Faber and Faber, 1958, 1963.

Rose, H.A., *A Handbook of Latin Literature*, Methuen, 1936.

Rutherford, Ward, *Shamanism*, Aquarian, London, 1986.

Sayings of the Desert Fathers, The, trans. by Sister Benedicta Ward, Mowbrays, London, 1975.

Schaya, Leo, *The Universal Meaning of the Kabbalah*, Fons Vitae, USA, 2004.

Sethe, Kurt, *Urkunden des aegyptischen Altertums*, Leipzig, 1903.

Shelley, The Letters of Percy Bysshe, ed. by F.L. Jones, 2 vols., Oxford University Press, 1964.

Sinclair, T.A., *A History of Classical Greek Literature*, Collier Books, New York, 1962.

Stace, Walter T., *The Teachings of the Mystics*, Mentor, USA, 1960.

Stover, Leon and Kraig, Bruce, *Stonehenge, the Indo-European Heritage*, Nelson-Hall, Chicago, 1978.

Traherne, Thomas, *Centuries of Meditation*, Mowbray, 1975.

Underhill, Evelyn, *Mysticism*, Methuen, 1911 and 1960.

Understanding the Lord of the Rings: The Best of Tolkien Criticism, ed. by Neil Isaacs and Rose Zimbardo, Houghton Mifflin Harcourt, 2004.

Upanisads, The, trans. by Swami Prabhavananda and Frederick Manchester, Mentor, USA, 1957.

Van Gogh, The Letters of Vincent, ed. and introduced by Mark Roskill, Collins Fontana, 1927/1963.

Van Over, Raymond, *Eastern Mysticism*, Mentor, USA, 1977.

Vaughan, Henry, *Sacred Poems*, with a memoir by the Rev. H.F. Lyte, London, G. Bell & Sons, 1914.

Verner, Miroslav, *The Pyramids, The Mystery, Culture and Science of Egypt's Great Monuments*, The American University in Cairo Press, 2002.

Virgil, *The Eclogues*, trans. by Guy Lee, Penguin Books, 1980.

Waste Land, The: A Facsimile and Transcript of the Original Drafts,

Including the Annotations of Ezra Pound, ed. by Valerie Eliot, Harcourt, 1971, Faber and Faber, 2011.

Waterfield, Robin, *The First Philosopher: The Presocratics and Sophists*, Oxford University Press, 2000.

Way of Lao-Tzu, The, trans. by Wing-Tsit Chan, Bobbs-Merrill, USA, 1963.

Weston, Jesse L., *From Ritual to Romance*, Dover Publications, 1997.

Widengren, G., *The King and the Tree of Life*, Universitets Arsekrift No. 14, Uppsala, 1951.

Winters, Yvor, *In Defense of Reason*, Routledge & Kegan Paul, 1960.

Wisdom of China and India, The, ed. by Lin Yutang, Random House, New York, 1942.

Wordsworth, Letters of William and Dorothy: The Later Years, ed. by Ernest de Selincourt, 3 vols., Oxford University Press, 1939.

Index

in the classical world 70–6

crusades 111

Churchill, Winston 268, 278–9, 291, 313

  History of the English-Speaking

    Peoples 279, 291

  History of the Second World War 268,

    278–9

Cicero 60, 77, 312

Ciceronian Age 61

circumpolar stars 20

civil wars

  American 280

  English 162, 238

  Roman 336

  Spanish 259, 264

civilizations *see* cultures and civilizations

Clare, John 192, 418

classic, definition of 295

classical literature, literary forms and

  stylistic devices 294

Classical Man 162

Clement of Alexandria 73, 78

  Gnosticism and Christianity reconciled

    73

  Miscellanies 73

Cloud of Unknowing 90

Cocteau, Jean

  Antigone 283

  The Infernal Machine 283

  Orpheus 283

Coleridge, Samuel Taylor 191, 194, 195,

  215, 267, 325, 330, 339, 449, 453

  Biographia Literaria 3, 179, 186, 321,

    455

  'Dejection: An Ode' 180, 186, 188,

    190, 194, 322, 398

  epic poems take twenty years 337

esemplastic power of the imagination 3,

  330, 342, 455

  'Kubla Khan' 182, 186, 336, 397–8,

    415

  life and imagination 302, 322, 376,

    397–8, 416

  The Lyrical Ballads 179, 186, 187, 321

  and metaphysical quest for Reality 187,

    189, 343

  One as "from within out" 187

  and Oneness of Nature 187, 266

  'Religious Musings' 186

  'The Rime of the Ancient Mariner'

    186–7, 194, 331, 452

  1798 visit to Germany 179

  as a Universalist 300

Colet, John 113

Collins, William, 'Ode to Evening' 168

Columbus, Christopher 107

Communism 348, 404

  Soviet 336

Confucius 30

Congreve, William 156, 163, 446

Conquest, Robert, *New Lines* 269

Conrad, Joseph 247–8, 362

  Heart of Darkness 248

  Lord Jim 247

  The Nigger of the Narcissus 247

  Nostromo 248

  The Secret Agent 248

  Typhoon 247–8

consciousness 26

Constable, John 310, 458

Constant, Benjamin, *Adolphe* 192–3

Constantine, Roman Emperor 74, 79–80,

  364

Constantinople 80

B O O K S

O is a symbol of the world, of oneness and unity. In different cultures it also means the "eye," symbolizing knowledge and insight. We aim to publish books that are accessible, constructive and that challenge accepted opinion, both that of academia and the "moral majority."

Our books are available in all good English language bookstores worldwide. If you don't see the book on the shelves ask the bookstore to order it for you, quoting the ISBN number and title. Alternatively you can order online (all major online retail sites carry our titles) or contact the distributor in the relevant country, listed on the copyright page.

See our website **www.o-books.net** for a full list of over 500 titles, growing by 100 a year.

And tune in to myspiritradio.com for our book review radio show, hosted by June-Elleni Laine, where you can listen to the authors discussing their books.